# Techniques
## of
# Population   Analysis

**George W. Barclay**

*Visiting Fellow*
*Office of Population Research*
*Princeton University*

# Techniques
## of
# Population Analysis

New York
John Wiley & Sons, Inc.
London

# FOREWORD

Since the Second World War there has been a great improvement
in the inventories of human populations obtained in national censuses and vital statistics. Throughout the world new censuses have
been taken, in important parts of the world for the first time. Even in
countries where census-taking is a long tradition, as it is in the
United States, there has been a rapid proliferation of information relating to the numbers, composition, and measurable characteristics
of the people.

The analysis and use of such materials has not kept pace with
their compilation. As a result of this defect much of the potential
value of the additional information has been lost both for purposes of
scientific inquiry and for more immediate purposes of national and
local planning. There is need for wider knowledge of the methods for
translating the exhaustive compilations of figures into more meaning-
ful measures of population growth and migration, of manpower available for economic production, and of social trends reflected in changing composition and characteristics of the population.

In recognition of this need the Population Council in 1955
made a research grant to Dr. Barclay to enable him to assemble
materials and prepare the text for this volume.

Dr. Barclay's book differs in purpose, in scope, and in approach
from other books in this field. The accepted texts in demographic
methods now available are designed for the specific purpose of training actuaries in the United States or in the United Kingdom. They
were prepared for use with reference to the national data of these
countries. In their approach they appropriately assume the training
and interests of actuarial students.

The present volume is intended for more general purposes of
population analysis, and attempts to provide methodology applicable
to population data of greatly varying quality and content. In particular Dr. Barclay has gone out of his way to draw illustrations from the
problems and statistics of the underdeveloped areas. He has emphasized the logic of the procedure rather than the specific technique.

At the same time he takes nothing for granted in the previous training of his readers. As Dr. Barclay points out, the methods of population analysis are less formidable than they often seem to the uninitiated once the underlying logic of the procedures is understood. With the exception of the chapter on the life table the book is written to be understandable to readers without training in mathematics or statistics.

                                        Dudley Kirk
                                        The Population Council, New York

August 1958

# PREFACE

Rarely does an extended undertaking turn out exactly as originally planned. This book is no exception. It was first proposed to the author for a rather special purpose. For years population studies have been confined chiefly to countries of Western Europe and North America, and many people have felt the need for an introductory book, applicable to a wider range of census and registration data. This volume began as a text that would be suited to the growing body of data outside the common statistical tradition of this region.

It soon became evident, however, that the deficiency did not lie in the special problems of any particular country or region. The real need was for a general introduction to research procedures and their purposes. Eventually the following chapters were designed to meet this need.

Most works on this subject emphasize the facts of some particular example. Although the basis of inquiry into these facts is virtually the same in any instance, the facts themselves may vary, sometimes to a considerable extent. For this reason, illustrations here have been gathered from diverse sources. They are selected so as to convey a sense of perspective, to represent a manner of viewing population aggregates under a variety of different conditions. Such perspective is the quality most important in examining data outside the habitual path of population studies. It is also a quality needed to gain proper understanding of the nature of these studies in the more familiar locale of Western countries.

This book is intended as a guide for persons without previous experience in analyzing census or vital registration statistics. It is designed to be as far as possible self-sufficient and appropriate for self-study. Some non-essential niceties are omitted. No definite training in mathematics is presupposed, since the procedures do not have an advanced mathematical basis. The historical development of population studies, though interesting for its own sake, is not discussed. Care has been taken to limit the vocabulary of special terms: where they refer to something that is really quite ordinary, an ordinary term is used.

Besides procedures of research, the book also gives an introduction to the major published writings. Many references are provided,
suggesting further reading on specific topics. Some general avenues
of further study are proposed in the concluding chapter. The Sections
of each chapter are numbered consecutively, permitting a detailed
system of cross-references; a reference to (3:1) means "Chapter 3,
Section 1."

It is a pleasure to acknowledge certain forms of indebtedness
during the work on this volume. First, the Population Council originated the project and provided a grant of funds that made possible the
allocation of time. Beyond this financial support, it benefited from
the personal interest of Dudley Kirk, Demographic Director of the
Population Council, whose cooperation was extremely helpful from
the beginning. In addition, Vincent H. Whitney and W. Parker Mauldin,
also of the Population Council, generously read and commented on
the manuscript.

At Princeton University, the Office of Population Research furnished a working atmosphere which has become rare in the world of
modern scholarship. Besides this cooperation, Frank W. Notestein,
the Director, contributed many valued comments from a thorough reading of the manuscript. Other members of the Office of Population Research offered suggestions on specific points, and the staff gave a
needed check of the computations for illustrative material. George F.
Mair made some especially useful comments on portions of the manuscript.

The Population Branch of the Department of Social Affairs of
the United Nations was very helpful on several specific points.
Thanks are also due to Octavio Cabello, C. H. Tuan, the American
Journal of Hygiene, Oxford University Press, Cambridge University
Press, and the Statistical Office of the United Nations, for permission
to quote brief excerpts from published works. Finally, Audrey N.
Barclay not only gave freely of assistance and criticism, but also
contributed the charts which illustrate the text.

Of course, responsibility for statements and opinions in the
book rests wholly with the author.

# TABLE OF CONTENTS

Page

# LIST OF TABLES

# LIST OF TABLES (Continued)

# LIST OF TABLES (Continued)

# LIST OF CHARTS

CHAPTER 1

# THE NATURE OF DEMOGRAPHY

Inventories of human population are a relatively young area of research. The field is not wholly new, for history records many experiments in the counting of people. The development of uses for such statistics, however, has come in recent years.

Much of this development has been merged with social and economic studies, and with some branches of medical research. As a result, there is no very sharp boundary separating population research from neighboring fields, nor a well defined body of principles setting forth what it is.

In treating the available data, population analysis follows certain customary procedures. To some extent these comprise standard techniques, but often they must be improvised to fit the situation at hand. The procedures themselves are not difficult. A great deal, however, depends on asking the sorts of questions that lead to useful answers. Hence, besides the steps of numerical calculation, we must be concerned with the basis or grounds of such inquiry.

It is the purpose here to describe, briefly but as thoroughly as possible, a few of the most useful techniques of research. Some may be too condensed, others too detailed. (These are questions of opinion, and different people never agree completely about the relative emphasis due each topic.) Though several examples are provided to illustrate computations or their meaning, the book is not intended to be either a discourse on world conditions or a manual of computation. Fortunately, such material is already available.[1]

---

[1] The reader is referred especially to United Nations, Population Division, *Determinants and Consequences of Population Trends* ... (New York, 1953), xii, 404 pp.; Political and Economic Planning, *World Population and Resources* (London, 1955), xxxviii, 340 pp.; A. Landry, *Traite de Demographie* (Paris, 1945), 651 pp.; J. J. Spengler and O. D. Duncan (eds.), *Population Theory and Policy: Selected Readings* (Glencoe, Illinois, 1956), 528 pp..

## 1:1  The Demographic View of a Population

The numerical portrayal of a human population is sometimes known as "demography." The population is viewed as an aggregate of persons, represented by certain types of statistics. Demography is concerned with the behavior of the aggregate (or some of its parts), and not with the behavior of individuals.

We are concerned especially with the process of *replacement*. A population outlives its individual members. This means that the membership is constantly changing. Some people die each year, and others are born. In addition, there may be some net gain or loss by migration. These factors are sometimes called the "vital" processes, since they are the means by which the population replenishes itself and remains in existence. Growth, decline, or maintenance of the same numbers — a very delicate balance — are all the outcome of these three factors.[2] This simple relation is one of the most important facts of demography.

There are two main aspects of the behavior of populations: the *composition* of the aggregate, and *changes* that occur during some period of observation. The composition of a population is described by the distribution of people among certain more or less standard categories. Changes, on the other hand, are the result of "events," which add or take away members of the population. For this reason births and deaths are called "vital events." Migration, marriages, divorces, and other events sometimes are also called "vital" events, though they may do no more than transfer people from one category to another in the same population.

Since a population is subject to constant change, its composition must be reckoned with reference to some particular time. Ideally this should be the *same* moment in all parts of the population.[3] The vital events that produce these changes do not happen all at once;

---

[2] To a large extent the *structure* of a population is also dependent on the kind of balance of these vital processes (see Chapter 7).

[3] For example, the population present at the middle of the year is not quite the same as the population that was present at the beginning of the year. There have been births and deaths, and perhaps some movement of people among the subdivisions of the country. Hence figures for the different sections of a population would not be quite comparable if they were not gathered at the same time. Likewise, the *total* of these figures would not be the proper total for the entire population; some people would be counted twice, and some would be overlooked. Fortunately, the size of this defect is ordinarily not large.

they are spread throughout a *period* of time, and the length of the period must be specified.

Correspondingly, there are also two main kinds of data. One is an "enumeration," counting all the persons present. This is usually provided by a *census*, which is an enumeration taken for an entire population on or about the same date.[4] The other form of statistics is a record of vital events, generally the events occurring in a calendar year. This is provided by some scheme of *registration*, designed to record all of certain events (births, deaths, migrations, marriages, and divorces) as they occur.

The same person may be recorded by a registration system several times during the year, or not at all, depending on the events which he has experienced. In a well-executed census he should be counted only once. But the distinction between these two forms of statistics is not really based on the method of getting the facts. It lies in the nature of the facts themselves — one is a record of *persons*, and the other is a record of *events*. A total population figure can be derived from a universal register,[5] by compiling a record for everyone at the same time. Some countries (notably Sweden and the Netherlands) rely on this method to get a total enumeration of their people. A census can ascertain the numbers of vital events indirectly, by asking each person or household to report the events of the past year or so.[6] Usually, however, the two systems of records are separate, and these are the data ordinarily available for analysis. These sources are described more fully in 1:3.

---

[4] Census takers sometimes go to great trouble to secure the information at an exact time. Census reports may state that the population was enumerated as it was at some instant (like 12:01 a.m. on July 1) or within some very short period. This does not mean that they really strove for such an impossible degree of precision, but that they hoped to reduce the errors of negligence in this regard.

[5] For this purpose, the register must have a permanent entry for each person, to which events are added as they occur. Such a system is very expensive and easily biased by small defects, and hence is rare. See T. Van den Brink, "Population Registers and Their Significance for Demographic Statistics," *Proceedings of the World Population Conference*, 1954 (New York, 1955), pp. 907-922.

[6] This has become a common way of finding out the past numbers of births, by asking parents the "number of children ever born." (See 6:6.) It has not been very successful in getting statistics of deaths.

## 1:2  The Techniques of Population Study

How are such data analyzed?  The statistical operations of demography can be summed up very briefly:  the calculation of conventional measurements (for a population or a group within a population), comparison of these measurements (judging which one is higher, which one lower), and estimation of certain figures that are not fully available.  Nearly all research activity in this field is made up of these tasks.

The basic techniques are not formidable, and are easily learned (see Chapter 2).  Why, then, should it be necessary to write a book to explain them?  The difficult problems are met in the *application* of these procedures — in the framing of useful questions to be answered, and in drawing reasonable conclusions from this material.  These problems are not so easily explained, for they cannot be solved everywhere in the same manner.

Is there a common strategy for treating the statistical material of demography?  Broadly speaking, yes.  We generally ask three sorts of questions:

a.  What is the level of performance in some form of behavior in the population — for example, the birth or death rates, the percentage who have some regular work, or the proportions married?

b.  Has the level of performance changed during some period of observation?  This question is answered by comparing observations at the beginning and at the end of the period.

c.  Are there patterns of variation within the population?  The answer to this question is found by comparing observations calculated for different groups — age, sex, ethnic, occupation, education groups and the like, or combinations of these.

These inquiries can be covered by broad rules of procedure, some of which are discussed in the following chapters.  Deciding what conclusions are to be drawn, however, is more than just a matter of procedure.  It depends on circumstances that vary from case to case — partly on the nature of the evidence, and partly on the focus of curiosity in the research.  A few possibilities will be suggested; but primarily this is something that the investigator must bring to his research.

## 1:3  Sources of Data

Traditionally, as we have seen, there are two types of population statistics — a census, and a registration of events.  Their general nature should be understood at the outset, for in the public mind the two are often confused.  As already mentioned (1:2), the two types of *information* are quite distinct. However, the two main types of *record-keeping* are no longer so distinct. Vital statistics can be obtained from a census, and the composition of a population can be determined from a registration system.

In addition, it is possible to secure both kinds of information by means of special surveys (rather than total inventories on a national scale). The techniques of the sample survey have made the work of data-gathering far more flexible.

For the most part these materials are found in official government reports. Though some countries keep such reports in a systematic fashion, they are not always easily available. Sometimes there are gaps which hinder any orderly analysis of the data. The reports may be widely scattered. One must become familiar with nearly all the statistical sources for a country in order to make efficient use of any part of them.

International collections of tables have been compiled. When corresponding tables for a large number of countries are published together, the collection is extremely convenient. Certain publications of the United Nations are especially noteworthy, being the widest in scope and the most comprehensive.[7] Some bibliographies have already been prepared, contributing to the knowledge of the resources in existence.[8] However, the total list of statistical publications is too large to be summarized in one place. Yearbooks and special collections are limited to selected groups of tables. They cannot give adequate attention to the peculiar features of each country's data, which must be learned by study of each statistical system.

---

[7]See especially the Demographic Yearbook, published annually beginning with 1948; individual issues emphasize specific topics (census data, mortality statistics, the economically active population) in addition to the standard tables in the series. Certain topics have been discussed separately in the United Nations series of "Population Studies," published since 1948. For earlier years, see Institut International de Statistique, *Aperçu de la Démographie, 1929-1936* (The Hague, 1939). More detailed data are often found in the statistical yearbooks of individual countries. Often, though not always, these agencies help the user of the statistics by means of introductory discussion and footnotes to the tables.

[8]Lists of related publications are frequently provided in official statistical sources, particularly those of the United Nations. A selected bibliography of training materials in this field was prepared by H. T. Eldridge, *The Materials of Demography. A Selected and Annotated Bibliography* (forthcoming). A current bibliography of publications is provided by the Office of Population Research, Princeton University, *Population Index*, appearing quarterly.

Analysis of the data may be worthless if too much is taken for granted. We must question the meaning of any given population figure, which depends largely on the manner in which the figure was obtained. Was the census or registration well organized? Did it get accurate information? Were the categories to which it assigned people clear and consistent? In particular, these categories have many arbitrary elements (see 1:5 and 3:4). Their definitions also vary from place to place, and so do the social circumstances to which they are applied. One should not assume that the categories of data are comparable in different sets of statistics, merely because they follow the same format (see also Chapter 3).

## 1:4 Census Data

In modern usage, the term "census" refers to a nation-wide counting of population. It is obtained by a direct canvass of each person or household, which is a large and complicated undertaking. Figures obtained from registration records are sometimes mistaken for census data. It is easy, however, to distinguish one from the other: a census implies a direct canvass, and registration does not. Registration goes on continuously, but a census has a definite date. Many countries take censuses at regular intervals of five or ten years.

A census is usually the best source for the total number of people present at a particular time. This total figure itself is partly a matter of arbitrary decision, for there are certain categories of people who are often not included in the scope of a census . Also, there are some groups which cannot be enumerated by ordinary procedures, without special provisions.[9]

Furthermore, there are different schemes for enumerating a population: the people actually present at some moment ("de facto population"), or the people "usually" present ("de jure population"). These two standards yield a different size of population for the same subdivision of a country. (For example, "people temporarily away from home" would be counted in one place by the first standard, and in another place by the second.) They also give slightly different *total* population figures for a country. Hence we cannot say there is any perfect or "correct" scheme for counting the population. The selection of either one of these standards — or, more commonly, some mixture of the two — has an effect which is present in every figure of the census. Obviously, the more people in the questionable categories, the greater the effect of choosing one standard or the other.

---

[9]See 3:4.

A census nearly always records some personal facts. These are sometimes referred to as "characteristics" of the people enumerated. A characteristic serves to classify each person in a statistical table. It may be any piece of personal information that can be ascertained in a consistent manner for everyone. A few have been found to be generally satisfactory. Age, sex, marital status, source of livelihood, place of birth, and perhaps number of children ever born, are frequently included in census inquiries.

Each of these "characteristics" presents certain problems, because some people do not fit into definite categories. An item like economic activity (see Chapter 9) seems to be the most difficult to classify. Even the report of a person's age (a relatively simple fact) is often ambiguous. It should refer to the number of full years elapsed since birth. In every population, however, many people give inconsistent answers regarding their ages. A few countries go to the trouble of asking the "year of birth," instead of the age that a person feels he has reached.[10] But even a direct question about age can be asked in different ways. Some censuses ask what was the person's last birthday; some ask what is the person's *nearest* birthday, and these two criteria give somewhat different answers. Certain customs also affect the age that people report. In some countries age is not reckoned in equal yearly intervals, with the result that the intervals of a table like Table 1:1 are not of equal length (see 3:9 and 4:3).

There are ambiguities in all facts collected by a census. Generally they are greater than in the case of age reports.[11] Because the distribution of most characteristics in a population is related to age, it is always helpful to have statistical tables classified by age in addition to other characteristics. Indeed, sometimes this is indispensable (see, for example, 9:5). For this reason, population tables tend to follow a typical format resembling Table 1:1. In this instance, "marital status" obviously depends on a person's age and sex, and so it would be meaningless to know the numbers of single,

---

[10] After the year of birth is reported, the census office must calculate the age of each person. This indirect manner of reporting, however, generally contains fewer errors and inconsistencies than direct reporting of age. The year of birth is only one fact to be remembered, whereas the achieved year of age changes each year and is less likely to be reported accurately. See 3:8.

[11] See the detailed criteria that have been adopted to minimize the ambiguity, in United Nations, Population Division and Statistical Office, *Population Census Methods* (New York, 1949), and Statistical Office of the United Nations, *Handbook of Population Census Methods* (New York, 1950).

## TABLE 1:1

## POPULATION OF MAURITIUS, 1944,
## BY AGE, SEX, AND MARITAL STATUS

| Ages | Total | Unmarried[a] | Married[b] | Widowed | Divorced |
|---|---|---|---|---|---|
| | | Males | | | |
| 0-4 | 25,405 | 25,405 | – | – | – |
| 5-9 | 25,023 | 25,023 | – | – | – |
| 10-14 | 23,336 | 23,305 | 28 | 1 | 2 |
| 15-19 | 23,722 | 22,854 | 839 | 12 | 17 |
| 20-24 | 20,420 | 13,474 | 6,756 | 120 | 70 |
| 25-29 | 16,396 | 5,831 | 10,249 | 219 | 97 |
| 30-34 | 15,416 | 3,242 | 11,768 | 301 | 105 |
| 35-39 | 13,567 | 2,174 | 10,853 | 428 | 112 |
| 40-44 | 12,340 | 1,610 | 9,968 | 674 | 88 |
| 45-49 | 9,882 | 1,219 | 7,884 | 701 | 78 |
| 50-54 | 8,885 | 1,071 | 6,875 | 869 | 70 |
| 55-59 | 5,803 | 693 | 4,310 | 742 | 58 |
| 60-64 | 4,352 | 489 | 3,066 | 768 | 29 |
| 65 and over | 5,028 | 590 | 3,108 | 1,295 | 35 |
| Age not stated | 751 | 455 | 269 | 22 | 5 |
| All ages | 210,326 | 127,435 | 75,973 | 6,152 | 766 |
| | | Females | | | |
| 0-4 | 25,405 | 25,405 | – | – | – |
| 5-9 | 24,657 | 24,657 | – | – | – |
| 10-14 | 22,805 | 22,222 | 574 | 4 | 5 |
| 15-19 | 23,998 | 15,054 | 8,616 | 187 | 141 |
| 20-24 | 20,687 | 6,539 | 13,539 | 434 | 175 |
| 25-29 | 16,660 | 3,429 | 12,393 | 693 | 145 |
| 30-34 | 14,300 | 2,296 | 10,885 | 993 | 126 |
| 35-39 | 12,160 | 1,754 | 8,996 | 1,290 | 120 |
| 40-44 | 11,022 | 1,479 | 7,486 | 1,962 | 95 |
| 45-49 | 8,731 | 1,095 | 5,378 | 2,183 | 75 |
| 50-54 | 8,530 | 994 | 4,268 | 3,206 | 62 |
| 55-59 | 5,855 | 775 | 2,475 | 2,563 | 42 |
| 60-64 | 5,397 | 671 | 1,689 | 3,002 | 35 |
| 65 and over | 7,793 | 1,120 | 1,503 | 5,138 | 32 |
| Age not stated | 859 | 471 | 286 | 91 | 11 |
| All ages | 208,859 | 107,961 | 78,088 | 21,746 | 1,064 |

[a]The category "unmarried" includes all persons not reported in any other marital status; presumably it also includes some persons for whom no marital status was reported.

[b]The category "married" includes those persons legally married, those married only according to religious rites, and those living together as man and wife without legal or religious marriage.

Source: Mauritius, Census Office. *Final Report on the Census Enumeration Made in the Colony of Mauritius and Its Dependencies on 11th June, 1944* (Mauritius, 1945), Tables 8 and 9.

married, widowed and divorced without also separating men and
women and knowing their ages.

How much detail should be shown in such a table? If each
single year of age were cross-classified with the other categories in
Table 1:1, the table would be too cumbersome for most purposes. If
overly condensed, the data would cease to be useful. Customarily
we compromise at a conventional set of 5-year age intervals in most
cross-tabulations; the format of Table 1:1 has become almost a
standard feature of census tables. A great deal of population analysis is adapted to these standard 5-year intervals.[12] For some purposes, however, it is expedient to condense the age intervals by consolidating some of them in broader classes (see Table 2:1)..

## 1:5 Vital Registration

As already explained, registration is best adapted to recording
events as they occur. Normally registration is compulsory. It is a
smaller task than a national census, since the clerical work is spread
throughout the year and is more easily reduced to routine.. But in
some respects the classification of personal characteristics presents
a greater problem in a registration system. There are several kinds
of events; each kind must be defined, and so there is not a "total"
record of persons to serve as a framework for the other figures. The
definitions are very difficult to follow. A registrar, who is responsible for maintaining uniform standards of classification, must get a
large part of his information from people who were not immediately
concerned with the events. A death, for example, is reported by
someone other than the deceased, and there may be little incentive
to give an accurate report..

The notion of a "live birth" is especially difficult to treat as
a statistical record. Life is very uncertain in the first few moments
and days of infancy. A great many cases cannot be classified con--
sistently without detailed criteria and rules. The definition recommended by international agencies in 1950, for example, goes to considerable length to be specific:

"Live birth is the complete expulsion or extraction
from its mother of a product of conception, irrespective
of the duration of pregnancy, which, after such separation, breathes or shows any other evidence of life, such
as beating of the heart, pulsation of the umbilical cord,

---

[12]This format also has certain disadvantages (see 3:12). But it is so
common that often no other type is available.

or definite movement of voluntary muscles, whether or
not the umbilical cord has been cut or the placenta is
attached; each product of such a birth is considered live-
born.

"All live-born infants should be registered and
counted as such irrespective of the period of gestation
or whether alive or dead at time of registration...."[13]

When a child dies soon after birth, it may be confused with a stillbirth.[14] Even when the facts are clear, people are fallible. Slipshod
reporting introduces some ambiguity into all statistics of "live"
births. There are outright errors, and there is a tendency to delay in
registration, sometimes until the following year (distorting the statistics of both years). Consequently, birth rates and infant death rates
should never be accepted without some prior study of the country's
registration system and its operation (see 2:9 and 3:10).

Besides births and deaths, vital registration may include such
events as migration, marriage, divorce, adoptions, fetal deaths, and
others. Any or all of these may be recorded together with characteristics of the persons involved — age, sex, marital status, and the
like. These characteristics form the basis of classification in statistical tables similar in appearance to Table 1:1. In Chapter 2 we
shall discuss some of the difficulties of reconciling these two sets
of records.

## 1:6 Data from Surveys

Either registration or census-type statistics can be secured by
means of a special survey. A survey may resemble a census, by asking respondents to report their characteristics. Sometimes a survey
uses this same approach to record vital events — asking people to
report the events of the past month or year in their own family or

---

[13] United Nations, Statistical Office, *Principles for a Vital Statistics
System* (New York, 1953), Statistical Papers, Series M, No. 19, p. 6. Obviously, the definition is so specific that few places in the world give it
faithful observance.

[14] The birth may be incorrectly registered as a stillbirth, or as a birth
with no record of death; or as an infant death with no record of birth; or simply not recorded at all, if the child did not survive long enough to become of
much consequence in the community. With such pitfalls, it is sometimes surprising that comparable data are obtained for vital events at different times
and places. Probably many of these statistics are *not* comparable in very
great detail.

neighborhood. Or a survey may set up a system for registering the events as they occur.

Thus a survey may be nearly the same as the conventional systems of record-keeping already discussed. It differs in having a more specific purpose. Most surveys are designed to provide some definite statistical information, as opposed to the wider scope and larger scale of a census or vital register. Not only is a survey normally smaller, but it is very often limited to a *sample* of the population. The principles of sampling open up new and more flexible possibilities in the gathering of statistical information. By reducing the number of individuals to be surveyed, sampling permits a lower total cost and a greater emphasis on the accuracy of the information about each individual.

⁰ A sample is designed to provide statistics that are applicable to the population. For this purpose, it must be drawn according to definite rules. The selection of individuals should be planned so that each individual has an equal chance of being included in the sample (that is, so as to avoid favoring some kinds of individuals over others). Usually it is also necessary to know what fraction of the total population has been selected in the sample. If the rules of sampling are followed, and only if they are followed faithfully, the sample is said to "represent" the total population.[15]

The data of a sample survey are liable to some *fluctuation,* owing to the incomplete coverage of the population. This adds another problem in reaching conclusions from sample data, for the observed figures may deviate from the "true" figures.[16] But this element is not entirely absent from conventional census and vital statistics, for they are never one hundred per cent complete; with a well-designed sample, we have a better notion of the possible extent of such fluctuation, and can make certain allowances for it. (Of

---

[15]There are many types of sample design. These form a separate subject, with a well-developed and specialized literature. Excellent summaries can be found in P. J. McCarthy, *Introduction to Statistical Reasoning* (New York, 1957), xiii, 402 pp.; L. H. C. Tippett, *Statistics* (London, 1943), 264 pp.; M. J. Slonim, "Sampling in a Nutshell," in *Journal of the American Statistical Association* 52(278): 143-161, June 1957; and, of course, in several other sources. At a more advanced level there is a larger range of appropriate texts. See, especially, F. Yates, *Sampling Methods for Censuses and Surveys* (London, 1953), xvi, 401 pp.

[16]The expected amounts of deviation can be estimated on the basis of the design of the sample. This is one of the chief reasons for taking pains to observe strictly the rules of sampling procedure.

course, many samples yield erroneous figures because they are improperly drawn — they are "biased." This defect, too, is present in the conventional sorts of data, and is not peculiar to sampling.) The economies of sample surveys allow greater attention to be given to the procedures of sample selection. Sample data are sometimes more useful than conventional registration or census figures. Sometimes they are less useful. But their usefulness is very small unless some attention is given to the errors expected in view of the design of the sample.

### 1:7 Supplementary Materials: Logarithm Tables, Interpolation

Though a mathematical training is not essential to use this book, some experience in handling numerical data is very helpful. This is true specifically of a few simple techniques that are common property of many fields, not peculiar to demography.

One of these is the use of tables of logarithms. Logarithms are sets of numbers prepared to simplify certain arithmetical calculations that would otherwise be very complex. Fortunately, a casual acquaintance with the principle of logarithms can suffice for most purposes. [17] A formula which calls for the logarithm of a number can be satisfied by merely looking up the number in the appropriate table of logarithms, and reading off the corresponding value, which is then entered in the formula. For example, $865^4$ (an awkward computation) is equivalent to "log $865 \times 4$," or $2.93702 \times 4$ (a very easy computation).[18] The result is 11.74808. Converted back to ordinary numbers by means of the table, this is 559,840,650,625. Most tables of logarithms do not show quite this amount of detail. But for most purposes 559,840,700,000, or even 559,800,000,000, is just as satisfactory.

---

[17] However, logarithms are so valuable that the time needed to learn their properties is very well spent. For example, a set of logarithm tables can partially offset the lack of a calculating machine. Explanations of their principles and applications are to be found in any elementary calculus textbook. In addition, shorter instructions generally accompany the published tables themselves.

[18] The use of logarithms follows a few simple but definite rules. The logarithm of 865 is 2.93702. The first digit or digits of a logarithm (before the decimal point) show the location of the decimal point in the original number; the remainder shows where the original number belongs in the system of logarithms. The logarithm of 8.65 is 0.93702; the logarithm of 86.5 is 1.93702. The decimal point of 865 is one place farther to the right, and so the logarithm of 865 is 2.93702. By this device, one set of logarithms is adequate for any number, regardless of the location of the decimal point.

At the end of a problem, if the term "log $r$" or "log $n$" remains, it is necessary to reverse the first step, and look up the ordinary number corresponding to this logarithm. For example, if the formula finally indicates that log $n$ = 11.74808, look up the logarithm 74808 in the table and read off the number which corresponds to it, which is 55984. Moving the decimal point eleven places to the right of the first digit, this becomes 559,840,000,000. This number is known as the "anti-logarithm." Many tables have special sections of anti-logarithms which make this reverse procedure more convenient.

There are two systems of logarithms in ordinary use — "common" and "natural" logarithms. When a formula calls for "log ___," it normally refers to a table of common logarithms, the type described above. A formula which states "log$_e$ ___" refers to a table of "natural" logarithms. For many problems of demography (see 2:8 and 7:4) tables of the "exponential function, $e^x$," are also used; this is a special form of natural logarithms.[19] In this case, log$_e$ 865 is 6.76273. Expressed in the exponential notation, $865 = e^{6.76273}$. Either form of natural logarithms may be used to solve some problems, and the result will be exactly the same.

The logarithms of numbers may themselves be treated as ordinary numbers after they have been properly substituted in a formula. Definite rules also govern the arithmetical operations required when a logarithm is used. (In the example above, $865^4$ became 4 log 865, or $4 \times 2.93702$.) These rules are normally summarized in the table of logarithms. The applications described in this book are not complicated enough to demand a detailed discussion of these procedures.

*Interpolation* is another operation that is used very frequently. It is a means of finding an approximate value between two known points. For example, if the registered total population on January 1 was 6,725,000, and the registered population on December 31 was 6,938,000, we may wish to have a figure for the middle of the year, July 1. This must be calculated by means of an assumption, since in this case the intermediate points (between the beginning and the end of the year) are not known. Standard interpolation procedures offer many possible assumptions. For most purposes, where the known points are not too far apart, we may assume that the intermediate

---

[19] In the exponential notation $e^x$, "$x$" is the exponent of e. For a given value of $e^x$, the corresponding value of x can be read from the table. For a given value of x, the corresponding value of $e^x$ can be read from the other column of the table. When the exponent is positive $(e^x)$, the table of the "ascending exponential" is used. When the exponent is negative $(e^{-x})$, the table of the "descending exponential" is used.

points fall along a straight line between them. This is as reasonable as any other assumption, and far more convenient.

Along a straight line, the value at July 1 would be just half-way between the first population figure and the second population figure, or $P_1 + \frac{1}{2}(P_2 - P_1)$. In this example, the interpolated value

would be $6,725,000 + \frac{1}{2}(213,000)$, or $6,831,500$. By the same assumption we can also estimate the population on February 1, which would

be $P_1 + \frac{1}{12}(P_2 - P_1)$, or the population at any time of the year.[20]

The same method is also followed in using a table of prepared values (such as a logarithm table) when we want to look up a figure more detailed than the values that are tabulated. For example, log 865 is given as 2.93702; if we want log 865.7 in a table that has only three-digit numbers, it is necessary to interpolate between log 865 ($= 2.93702$) and log 866 ($= 2.93752$). This is done by assuming that the logarithm of 865.7 lies 7/10 of the way between 2.93702 and

2.93752, or $2.93702 + \frac{7}{10}(.00050)$, which is 2.93737.

This is the method of interpolating along an imaginary straight line, or "linear" interpolation. It is the simplest method, and the one to be preferred in most instances. Further comments are to be found in later chapters, where specific applications are discussed.

### 1:8 Topics of Population Study

There are several recognized branches of inquiry, which pre-sent different topics for study. In the following chapters certain of these are taken up as thoroughly as the scope of this volume will per-mit. It is out of the question to survey the entire field of population study at this same level; some work falls into a more advanced category. In selecting some topics, we have unavoidably omitted others. It is hoped, however, that these chapters provide a useful introduction to the techniques of analyzing population data, which are all fundamentally very similar.

---

[20] With slight modifications to fit the circumstances, this procedure is the usual way of estimating the mid-year population, as described in 2:11.

These techniques were first developed in the study of mortality, which offers the most favorable opportunities for precise statistical measurement. An entire chapter, therefore, is devoted to the life table (Chapter 4), which illustrates the basic model of most analysis. The structure of the life table must be well understood in order to make the best use of the existing literature on any of these topics.

A chapter is devoted to other ways of measuring the incidence of mortality, when an actual life table is not available or not appropriate (Chapter 5). Another chapter discusses fertility, or the frequency of births in a population (Chapter 6). These two processes provide the replacement of population, and occupy the central part of demography. Their net effect, the growth or decline in the number of people, is discussed in Chapter 7.

The migration of people from one place to another affects the population in both places. Since it is associated with very large and rapid changes of population and population structure, it generally receives a prominent share of attention. Here, Chapter 8 summarizes the ways of measuring the currents of migration. A chapter about the study of manpower (Chapter 9) completes the topics that are treated in this book.

Beforehand, there is a summary of common notions of statistical measurement (Chapter 2). Its purpose is to cover in advance as much of this ground as possible, describing conventional rates and ratios and how to compute them, so as to avoid the usual distraction by these details later on. This provides a vocabulary of common terms and concepts and a source of reference material for later chapters.

The problem of *accuracy* is treated in a separate chapter. It is never safe to assume that population data are correct. Before looking very far into the facts, we must make some inquiry about the nature of the statistics — the methods of collection, standards of classification, errors and biases. These questions are outlined at some length in Chapter 3.

# CHAPTER 2

# RATES AND RATIOS

Statistical data are the raw materials of demography. They show
how many people or events were found at a certain date or period. This
is an actual, or "absolute," number. For some purposes it is sufficient;
if we want to know how many births occurred last year, or how many
children of ages 5-14 were counted in the last census, the answer is
given by an absolute number. For planning of school facilities or maternal welfare services, for example, this is the information that is
needed.

More often, however, we wish to measure these facts in relation
to some other number, such as the total population at that time. This
brings us to rates and ratios, which are "relative" numbers. They
provide the measurements of demography, by which behavior in one
population (or section of a population) can be compared with that of
another.

This chapter describes the uses that are made of relative numbers, and explains some of the reasons why certain data are combined
with certain others. It also describes how to compute a few conventional kinds of measurement, preparatory to later discussion of what
it is that they measure. A brief formula is provided in each instance.
This is a guide to computation, showing exactly how to calculate each
one. The few formulas actually simplify the description, and should
not make it more difficult.

## 2:1  Relative Numbers

In general, these measurements contribute in two ways to the
analysis of data—they summarize an aspect of a set of data, and they
express some relation between two or more numbers in the original
data.

Take, for example, the table (Table 1:1) in Chapter 1 showing
the population of Mauritius by age. The original data were already
reduced in detail by compilation into a statistical table (grouped by

16

5-year age intervals, separated by sex). But only an experienced reader can perceive the nature of the age composition of the population, and then only after close inspection.

When these data are put into the form of percentages (using still broader age intervals), the table is changed to a short and clear picture of the age structure itself, apart from the particular numbers of people in each group:

### TABLE 2:1

### TOTAL POPULATION OF MAURITIUS (BOTH SEXES), DISTRIBUTED BY AGE

| Age | Per Cent of Total Population |
|---|---|
| 0-14 | 35.1 |
| 15-29 | 29.2 |
| 30-44 | 18.9 |
| 45-59 | 11.4 |
| 60 and over | 5.4 |
| Total | 100.0 |

This column represents the total of both sexes together. The figures, called a percentage distribution, are no longer absolute numbers, but relative numbers. They summarize the age structure of the population by measuring the size of each age group against the size of the total. Converted to this standard distribution of 100, the age structure of Mauritius can be easily compared with that of any other country, or with that of local or regional subdivisions of the total population, wherever there is interest in the comparison (see also 2:7).

The emphasis on one aspect, however, is always achieved at the expense of something else. The age structure is shown so clearly because nothing else about the population is included. Most of the information in the original table (Table 1:1) has been left out. The age intervals are not only less detailed, but are arbitrary in their selection; for many purposes they might have to be revised, left unchanged as 5-year groupings, or even abandoned in favor of single-year intervals. Furthermore, these percentage figures would not be very useful unless they were accompanied by the absolute numbers, or by a precise reference to a source where the absolute numbers can be found.

To put the matter the other way around, having only the percentage-distribution, and nothing else, affords information of limited value about the population. It is always desirable to show the data together with calculations derived from them; when this cannot be done, because it would be too costly or too cumbersome, it is essential to explain very clearly where the data originate and what procedures were used in calculating the derived figures.[1]

## 2:2 The Use of Ratios in Demography

These percentage figures are ratios. A ratio is a single term indicating the relative size of two numbers. If $a$ is one number, and $b$ another, a ratio between the two is $\frac{a}{b}$, or $a$ divided by $b$. It measures the size of the first number in terms of the other: "$a$ divided by $b$" also means "so many $a$ per unit of $b$." Hence a ratio does not depend on the particular size of either number, but on the relation in size between them. The ratios of 3 to 2, of 75 to 50, of 10,929 to 7,286 are all equal to 1.5.

Ratios are very easy to calculate. They also provide quick and concise comparisons between many corresponding sets of numbers. Most forms of measurement in demography are ratios of some kind, based on the question "how much per unit of ___ ?"

Percentage figures, like those of Table 2:1, are called "ratios based on 100"; they are ratios of two numbers, multiplied by 100, or $\frac{a}{b} \cdot 100$, and indicate "so many $a$ per 100 units of $b$." This slight modification does not really change the meaning of a ratio, but only the form in which it is written. The purpose is to make the ratio easier to read and compare with others, by giving it a relationship to some familiar number like 100 or 1,000. Later, when describing the computation of certain ratios, we shall refer to an arbitrary number of this kind as $k$.

## 2:3 Vital Statistics Rates

The frequency of vital events in a population is measured by a vital-statistics rate, often called simply a "vital rate." The most familiar examples are birth rates and death rates, which are discussed later in this chapter and in subsequent chapters.

---

[1]This point becomes still more important when the numbers are small, as in the reports of sample surveys, because relationships based on a small number of cases may be less stable and more liable to fluctuation. Sometimes this problem is met by publishing percentages, and showing *total* numbers along one margin of the table.

It was mentioned that vital events introduce some change into the population (see 1:2). Change must be measured in relation to some period of time. Nearly *any* period might be satisfactory; but it is customary to calculate vital rates for standard periods of one year. Even where the data refer to a longer period (see 2:9) or a shorter period (see 2:12), vital rates are always computed on a yearly basis.

Thus, vital rates answer the question, "how much per unit of ___ , per year?" Given the required numbers, they are computed just like any other ratios; but they are distinguished by the kind of source material used (see 2:9). In this sense vital rates constitute a special type of ratio.

Unfortunately, the term "rate" is applied to several different things in demography, and this sometimes leads to confusion. Certain more complex indices (see 2:18) are termed "rates" according to long-standing convention. Some ordinary percentage figures are called "rates" occasionally in the literature, though they have nothing to do with changes or with vital events.[2] Hence the term itself has no exact meaning; in each case one must ask what numbers it represents. Here we have tried to avoid some of this confusion by reserving the term "vital rate" for measurements based on annual vital statistics.

## 2:4 Types of Ratios

Ratios in demography differ in some important respects, and this sometimes restricts the manner in which they may be interpreted. Ratios are computed in basically the same way, regardless of type; therefore the differences must be due to the kinds of numbers from which they are computed. Before considering some specific examples, it is necessary to distinguish the following types:

a. Ratio involving only one universe (or, a ratio of $\frac{a}{b}$, where $a$ and $b$ are numbers from the same universe). "Universe" means simply the aggregate of individuals that is under discussion. Since we discuss such an aggregate by reference to some set of statistics, by implication the term means that aggregate of individuals which is entered in a set of statistical records.[3]

---

[2] For example, a percentage of the population found to be literate is sometimes called a "literacy rate," and a percentage engaged in economic activity a "labor-force participation rate." In languages other than English, the confusion is often still greater.

[3] In this book the term "universe" is used in a special sense, referring to a set of statistical records. Elsewhere it often has a different meaning, especially in books about sampling procedure.

Statisticians often use the term "population" for this purpose. But in demography the word "population" has still another meaning: the number of people located in a given area, without reference to the operations involved

We speak of the universe of people enumerated in a census (often called the "census population"); or the universe of registered births, the universe of registered deaths, or of marriages, or of divorces. School records may provide a universe of school children, public health records a universe of persons vaccinated during a year, industrial statistics a universe of man-hours of work in some period, railroad statistics a universe of length of track, land or tax authorities a universe of square kilometers of land area. A ratio computed between numbers that lie within any one of these universes is a ratio of this first type.

b. Proportion. This is also a ratio of two numbers from the same universe, but it is a distinct category within the type above. A proportion has the form of $\dfrac{a}{a+b}$ : the numerator is included in the denominator. A true proportion, therefore, is a relation of some total number of things and one of its parts. We speak, for example, of the proportion of the total population that is 15 years of age or over, the proportion of all people age 15 or over who are married, the proportion of total married people who are childless, or the proportion of all people who have some regular employment. Because the numerator is always a *part* of the denominator, the value for the proportion will always be some decimal number between 0 and 1. This fact permits the proportion to have some important applications, as we shall see in later chapters. It is most familiar in the form of percentages, like those of Table 2:1, where the proportions are multiplied by the constant factor of 100. It is always essential to make clear just what total number is the denominator, or the "base," of the proportion.

c. Ratio of two numbers from different universes (or, a ratio of $\dfrac{a}{b}$ where a is from one universe, b from another). This type is involved if two numbers come from different sources or different sets of records. Excepting proportions, there are rather few conventional measurements in demography that draw their data, numerator and denominator, from the same source or set of records. A ratio that does not, is one that combines numbers from two universes. For example, the number of children enrolled in school records represents one universe, and the census population of school-age children another universe (even though they both refer to the same population). A ratio of these two numbers would be of this type; strictly speaking, it would not be the

---

in getting the information about them. Statistics of births, factory workers, school children or marriages all may belong to the same population, but they constitute different universes if they were collected by different means.

proportion of children attending school. In most countries the census population of school age is the larger of the two, but in some localities it may be smaller, owing to uneven administration of the two sets of records. A great many ratios combine numbers from universes more remote than these—the number of people per unit of land area, the yield of crops per unit of cultivated land, the number of known cases of illness per 100,000 in the population, the amount of income or wealth per person. If one of the two universes has a broader coverage in the total population than the other, then a ratio between the two numbers will be incorrect. Such a discrepancy is likely to be more difficult to detect when the universes are more remote.

d. More complex indices. There is finally a small but diverse group of measurements that are more complex than a ratio of two absolute numbers. Such measurements are continually being sought, tested and revised, though they do not always have immediate practical applications. These indices are often combined from simpler ratios, where one of the types above would not be adequate for more refined analysis. As a group there is not much that they have in common except a somewhat greater degree of complexity; hence they can be taken up to more advantage in later chapters, in connection with specific topics (see, for example, 6:4 and Chapter 4).

## 2:5  Sex Ratio

There are many occasions that require a brief summary of the sex composition in a population—perhaps for the total population, or for some portion, or for some type of registered event (births, especially). This is not difficult, because classification by sex usually places everyone unequivocally into one of the two categories, male or female. The ratio between the two numbers is called a *sex ratio*, and is calculated:

$$\frac{M}{F}k$$

where:

$M$ is the number of males recorded in some statistical universe of persons

$F$ is the number of females in the same universe

$k$ is an arbitrary factor of 100 (see text).

A sex ratio for some portion of the population is indicated as follows:

$$\frac{m_i}{f_i} k$$

Small letters designate a portion instead of the total, and the letter $i$ designates "the $i$th category" in the population (that is, "any category we may specify").[4]

To illustrate, in the data of Table 1:1 above, the 1944 census of Mauritius enumerated 419,185 persons, of whom 210,326 were males and 208,859 were females. A sex ratio, or ratio of males to females,[5] is obtained from these figures by dividing $\frac{210,326}{208,859}$, or 1.007. This ratio signifies that in the census population of Mauritius, the total number of males was 1.007 times the number of females.

The factor $k$ had no effect on this sex ratio of 1.007; that is to say, $k$ was equal to 1. For the sake of convenience, the ratio of 1.007 is usually multiplied by 100 (in other words, usually $k = 100$). This does not really change the ratio, but just gives us a number of 100.7, or 101, instead of 1.007, moving the decimal point out of the way. In this form, which has become the normal way to report a sex ratio, it represents the number of "males per 100 females." When males and females are equal in numbers, the ratio is 100; a higher ratio signifies more men than women, and a ratio of less than 100 means that there are more women than men.

The sex ratio is an example of the first type of ratio mentioned above. It is calculated from two numbers from the same universe. (When data are tabulated separately for one sex, they are almost always accompanied by corresponding information about the other.) There are many such tabulations, and so the sex ratio has a wide variety of uses.

What does it tell us, however, that was not already apparent? A glance at the absolute numbers of Table 1:1 would have shown that there were approximately the same numbers of men and of women in Mauritius, with a slight excess of men over women. But, how great an

---

[4] Any system of notation is arbitrary. Subscripts, like $i$, appear fairly often, and are merely a convenient way of saying "one of a series of items or classes to be distinguished from others." With one or two exceptions, we shall use capital letters for numbers which represent the total population in some area, and lower-case letters for numbers which represent some *portion* of the total population.

[5] This form, a ratio of males to females, is the conventional one. Occasionally it is found the other way around, as a ratio of females to males. Because the form may vary, in order to avoid confusion, it is necessary to specify that this is a ratio of males to females, or a ratio of "Males per 100 Females," as the case may be.

excess? How does this compare with the balance between the two sexes in other countries? How does the sex balance vary, for example, at different ages? Sex ratios permit the reader to make these comparisons by eye quickly and easily.

Sex ratios at different ages follow a rather typical pattern. Normally young boys are more numerous than girls, because male births are slightly more frequent than female births. Males suffer higher death rates, with the result that they generally fall short of the numbers of females at higher ages.[6] Fluctuations, however, are not unusual. Sex ratios by age for Mauritius, given in Table 2:2, show an unusual preponderance of adult men between ages 30 and 60, owing to the presence of some migrant groups in the population. Since these sex ratios vary only slightly, it is better to calculate them to one extra figure (101.2 instead of 101), as in this table. This is helpful in comparing numbers when their differences are small. (Occasionally, $k$ is set at 1,000 in order to keep four figures and still eliminate the decimal point; then the ratios must be titled "males per 1000 females"

TABLE 2:2

POPULATION OF MAURITIUS BY AGE AND SEX,
AND SEX RATIOS, 1944

| Ages | Males | Females | Sex Ratios (Males per 100 females) |
|---|---|---|---|
| 0-14 | 73,764 | 72,867 | 101.2 |
| 15-29 | 60,538 | 61,345 | 98.7 |
| 30-44 | 41,323 | 37,482 | 110.2 |
| 45-59 | 24,570 | 23,116 | 106.3 |
| 60 and over | 9,380 | 13,190 | 71.1 |
| Age not stated | (751) | (859) | (87.4) |
| Total population | 210,326 | 208,859 | 100.7 |

Source: Table 1:1.

---

[6] This pattern is so typical that contrary evidence may cast doubt on the adequacy of the statistics (see 3:7, and Table 3:1). Of course, a different pattern is to be expected if migrants (who are typically distinct in age and sex composition) have entered or left the population in recent years.

to indicate the change.) If there is a rule to follow, it is probably to use enough figures in the ratio to make the comparison clear, but no more. It is rare that population data are accurate enough to justify carrying out any computation beyond a few figures.

The sex composition of a population group can also be shown by *proportions*. Using the same data, it is just as easy to compute the proportion female (of the total of both sexes), or the proportion that is male. In Mauritius, the proportion female of the total population was $\frac{208,859}{419,185}$, or .4983. (The proportion male plus the proportion female equals 1; when either one of them is known, subtracting it from 1 is the quickest way to calculate the other.) In this case the proportion and the sex ratio have basically the same meaning, expressed in different forms. Sometimes it is more convenient to have one, sometimes to have the other; the proportion is preferable when such a figure is needed for some further computation. Otherwise a sex ratio as described above is the more customary form.

## 2:6 Child-Woman Ratio

The expression $\frac{a}{b}$ is called the "ratio of $a$ to $b$"; a sex ratio, for example, is referred to as a "ratio of males to females." In the same way we speak of the ratio of children to women in a census population, called the Child-Woman Ratio. It is used to measure the incidence of childbearing in the population of adult women. Specifically, it is the number of children under 5 years of age per 1,000 women of "childbearing age" (i.e., between ages 15 and 44, sometimes 15 and 49). It is computed as follows:

$$\frac{P_{0-4}}{f_{15-44}} k$$

where:

$P_{0-4}$ is the number of children, both sexes, under 5 years of age

$f_{15-44}$ is the number of females between ages 15-44. (Sometimes $f_{15-49}$ is used instead, signifying the number of females between ages 15-49.)

$k$ is 1,000.

This index also draws both of its terms from the same universe —the population by age and sex as determined by a census (or, occasionally, by a registration system). It can be computed in many situations where some data needed for ordinary birth rates are lacking. For this reason, the Child-Woman Ratio is especially useful where there is no adequate registration of births. Even where there is a registration of births, the data are not published separately for *all* groups in the population whose fertility we may wish to study; Child-Woman Ratios sometimes can be used to make up for such lack of detail in the birth statistics.

How does this index measure the incidence of childbearing? The Child-Woman Ratio does not directly refer to any actual number of births, but rather to the census population of children between ages 0-4. If these children were enumerated correctly by age (and this may be questionable), they must be the survivors of births during exactly the five-year period preceding the census. Therefore, though useful, the Child-Woman Ratio is not very precise as an index of fertility. Its evidence is indirect, derived from this group of survivors rather than from the number of actual births; and thus it is affected by several other factors besides fertility alone (see 6:4).

## 2:7 Territorial Distribution and Density of Population: Two Types of Ratios

These represent two very familiar procedures. Though not peculiar to demography, they have numerous and varied applications. We shall illustrate them as two ways of describing the distribution of people over the territory which they occupy. The first is a proportional distribution of a country's total population among the major political subdivisions; this is usually presented as a *percentage distribution* (multiplying by a factor of 100), as follows:

$$\frac{P_i}{P} k$$

where:

$P_i$ is the number of persons in the $i$th part or political division
of the country

$P$ is the total number of persons in all parts

$k$ is 100, making the whole series a set of percentage figures.

Whenever a population is subdivided into a series of parts, the proportion of the total that is found in any part is computed according to the formula above. If we calculate such a figure for each of the series of parts ($P_1$, $P_2$, $P_3$, etc.), the result is a percentage distribution of population. Of all the methods of statistical description in common use, this one is the most common and the most useful. It summarizes the distribution of any total among its parts, in terms that are readily understood and communicated. All of the necessary data come from the same universe, and so there are none of the problems of matching different sets of records.

Costa Rica, for example, is divided into seven principal political units, or provinces. The total number of persons enumerated in each province provides a value for $P_1$, $P_2$, $P_3$, etc.: these data (from the census of 1950) are listed in Table 2:3. The percentage of the population in each province is computed by entering each figure in the formula above and dividing by the total census population.[7]

The share of each province in the total population is shown by the percentage distribution in Table 2:3-a. But this is not the whole pattern of population distribution, for the provinces are not of the same size. The area of each province is also shown in Table 2:3, and can be expressed as another percentage distribution of the total land area among the provinces, as in Table 2:3-a. The procedure is exactly the same. If we let $a_1$, $a_2$, $a_3$, etc., represent the number of square kilometers of land area in each province, and $A$ the number of square kilometers in the entire country, then $\dfrac{a_i}{A}$ is the proportion of the total area in each province. The proportions become percentage figures when multiplied by 100. These numbers also come from one universe, though it is a different one—the universe of total recorded land area in Costa Rica.

On comparison, the distribution of area and the distribution of population are not the same. More than one third of the population is

---

[7] When a percentage distribution is computed with the aid of a calculating machine or slide rule, it is helpful to keep in mind that multiplying is easier than dividing. There is a saving of labor in avoiding the seven divisions $\left(\dfrac{P_1}{P}, \dfrac{P_2}{P}, \dfrac{P_3}{P}, \dots\right)$; instead, one division $\left(\dfrac{1}{P}\right)$ may be made first, and this quotient multiplied by $P_1$, $P_2$, $P_3$, $\dots$ . If a person expecting to do many such computations is not already familiar with this short cut, it will repay some time spent in learning it.

These calculations are easily checked for errors of computation, because the sum of the items in a complete set of percentage figures equals 100. Although the sum (when added) may be 0.1% or even 0.2% over or under 100.0% because of rounding of the individual items, there is a presumption that any deviation of more than 0.2% may be due to some error of computation.

## TABLE 2:3

### POPULATION AND AREA OF COSTA RICA
By Province, 1950

| Province | Total Population | Land Area (square kilometers) |
|---|---|---|
| San José | 281,822 | 4,900 |
| Alajuela | 148,850 | 9,500 |
| Cartago | 100,725 | 2,600 |
| Heredia | 51,760 | 2,900 |
| Guanacaste | 88,190 | 10,400 |
| Puntarenas | 88,168 | 11,311 |
| Limón | 41,360 | 9,400 |
| Entire Country | 800,875 | 51,011 |

Source: Dirección General de Estadística y Censos, *Censo de Poblacíon de Costa Rica, 1950; Atlas Estadístico de Costa Rica* (1953).

## TABLE 2:3a

### DISTRIBUTION OF TOTAL POPULATION AND AREA OF COSTA RICA
By Province, 1950

| Province | Per Cent of Total Population | Per Cent of Total Area | "Density" of Population (persons per sq. km.) |
|---|---|---|---|
| San José | 35.2 | 9.6 | 57 |
| Alajuela | 18.6 | 18.6 | 16 |
| Cartago | 12.6 | 5.1 | 39 |
| Heredia | 6.5 | 5.7 | 18 |
| Guanacaste | 11.0 | 20.4 | 8 |
| Puntarenas | 11.0 | 22.2 | 8 |
| Limón | 5.2 | 18.4 | 4 |
| Entire Country | 100.1 | 100.0 | 16 |

Source: Table 2:3.

concentrated in the rather small province of San José; the larger areas
of other provinces have relatively few people.[8]

It is sometimes clearer to calculate a ratio between people and
land area directly—a ratio of the number of people to the area of land
that they occupy. This is known as the "density" of population, or
the average number of persons per square kilometer (or square mile,
or any other unit) of area. For any province, the ratio is calculated:

$$\frac{P_i}{a_i}$$

where:

$P_i$ is the number of persons in the subdivision $i$ of the country

$a_i$ is the number of square kilometers of land area in the same
subdivision.

In the final column of Table 2:3-a are ratios of $\frac{P_1}{a_1}$, $\frac{P_2}{a_2}$, $\frac{P_3}{a_3}$, etc., one

for each of the provinces. For the entire country, the ratio is $\frac{P}{A}$, cal-

culated from the total figures of population and land area. Since these
ratios combine the figures for population and land area, they are *not*
ratios of numbers from one universe (like the percentages in the first
two columns), but ratios of numbers from two different universes.
Density ratios compare directly the relative degrees of concentration
of people by provinces, which was not readily apparent before. Of
course, a clearer picture emerges if detailed figures, based on
smaller subdivisions, are used.

## 2:8 The Rate of Population Growth

A great deal of study is devoted to changes of total population
size. This seems to be one of the first facts about a country's population to gain public attention. Moreover, this type of change is easy
to measure. It can be approached in two ways. One is to find the difference between the numbers of people present at two different dates
(an absolute number), and from this to calculate the annual rate of
change during the intervening period (a relative number); the other is
to reckon the rate of change from the records of individual changes as
they occurred—births, deaths, and migration—based on vital statistics.

---

[8] The explanation is found by consulting a map and a geography of the
country. The province of San José contains the principal urban area, which
is also the capital city; the sparsely settled area contains a tropical and
mountainous region that is still relatively inaccessible from outside.

Here we are concerned with the first approach. Only two numbers are needed: the total population as determined at each of two dates, either by censuses or registration. These two figures come from different universes, but they may be universes very similar in character, like the totals given in two census enumerations. (Indeed, the two universes *must* be very similar, or else much of the "growth" may be merely a difference in the kinds of records used and not a real change in the size of the population.) If two censuses cover the same territory, and follow similar rules of enumeration, the change in size of the population may be measured as the total determined in the second census $(P_2)$ minus the total in the first census $(P_1)$. In Malaya, the total population according to the census of 1931 was 4,347,704 and 5,848,910 according to the census of 1947, implying increase by 1,501,206 persons.[9]

Of course, the change may be an increase or a decrease, depending on which population figure is larger, $P_2$ or $P_1$. The

*relative* change is measured by the ratio $\left(\dfrac{P_2 - P_1}{P_1}\right)$, or the observed

change in numbers divided by the number of people at the beginning of the period. Usually it is more convenient to compute this ratio in

the form $\left(\dfrac{P_2}{P_1} - 1\right)$, which means the same thing. Sometimes it is

multiplied by 100 and called "per cent change," though one should remember that it is not a proportion, but a ratio of the third type mentioned above (2:4).

This ratio indicates a degree of growth, but it is not yet a "rate of growth." Like a vital-statistics rate, a rate of growth should express growth as a relative change in population size *per year*. The two figures for total population, $P_1$ and $P_2$, are hardly ever dated exactly one year apart, and disparities in the lengths of the intervening periods must be taken into account.[10] Before proceeding to do this, however, one should appreciate that it is not always necessary; in a great many situations the simple *ratio* of change is fully adequate as an index and no further steps are needed. Particularly,

---

[9] Federation of Malaya and Singapore combined.

[10] Even when the figures are exactly one year apart, the ratio is the same as a "rate" of growth in only the first of the two senses to be used below.

when percentages of change are being compared among several sub-divisions of the same population, and they are all computed from the results of the same two censuses, the ratios are already comparable in this form, and nothing is gained by transforming them as described below.

Otherwise, the next step is to convert the ratio of change into an annual rate. This begins with the ratio $\dfrac{P_2}{P_1}$, which measures the later population in terms of its earlier size. This ratio for Malaya (between 1931 and 1947) is $\dfrac{5,848,910}{4,347,704}$, or 1.34529.

The problem then is to find what rate of growth would produce a change in the initial population of this degree, $\dfrac{P_2}{P_1}$ or 1.34529, if continued or repeated annually for $n$ years (when $n$ is the exact number of years between the two census dates, or 16.67 years in this case).[11] The ratio is apportioned among the years that fall between $P_1$ and $P_2$. This is done by computing an average—dividing $\left(\dfrac{P_2}{P_1} - 1\right)$ into $n$ parts—and allotting each year an equal share.

However, this average cannot be found directly. Equal degrees of growth do not produce equal successive absolute increments; they follow the principle of compound interest. A constant rate of growth, repeated or maintained year after year, produces larger and larger absolute increments, simply because the base or total population steadily becomes larger.[12] When a quantity such as $P_1$ is subject to regular annual increases at a constant rate, the relation between the ratio $\dfrac{P_2}{P_1}$ and the annual rate, $r$, is as follows:

---

[11] The first census was dated April 1, 1931; the second, November 23, 1947. The intervening period was $16\dfrac{8}{12}$ years (to the nearest month), or 16.67 years.

[12] After the first year's increment has been added, the rate in the second year is applied to the original amount *plus* the first increment, and so on. Each year the base to which the rate is applied is slightly larger, because of the growth that has just occurred.

$$\frac{P_2}{P_1} = (1 + r)^n$$

where:

$P_1$ is the number of people in the population at the initial date

$P_2$ is the number of people at the later date

$r$  is the annual rate of growth

$n$  is the exact number of years between $P_1$ and $P_2$.

To find the value for $r$, even when the other values are known, would be exceedingly difficult and tedious from the equation above. It is greatly simplified through the use of logarithms.[13] By the rules of calculating with logarithms, $(1 + r)^n$ becomes $n \log (1 + r)$. In this form, it is possible to divide by $n$, instead of treating it as an exponent:

$$\log \frac{P_2}{P_1} = n \log (1 + r)$$

$$\log (1 + r) = \frac{\log \dfrac{P_2}{P_1}}{n} \ .$$

With the data given above for Malaya, the value of $r$ works out as follows:

$$\log (1 + r) = \frac{\log 1.34529}{16.67} = \frac{0.12882}{16.67} = .0077276$$

$$(1 + r) = 1.01795$$

$$r = 0.0180, \text{ or } 1.80 \text{ per cent per year.}$$

This form of equation represents a growth by regular increases, each one equal to $r$, or .0180, computed one year apart. There is another way of translating the ratio of growth $\left( \dfrac{P_2}{P_1} \right)$ into a rate of growth —by treating the growth as a continuous process rather than a set of periodic changes. For this purpose we use another system of logarithms, the "natural logarithms," (written $\log_e$), starting with the same ratio $\dfrac{P_2}{P_1}$ , as follows:

_____

[13] See 1:7.

$$\frac{P_2}{P_1} = e^{rn}.$$

When tables of $e^x$ are available, there the value of $rn$ can be found directly (where it corresponds to the value for the exponent $x$ in the table). To look up the growth ratio for Malaya between 1931-1947, or 1.34529, only one reference to this table is required:

$$1.34529 = e^{rn}$$

$$rn = .29661$$

$$r = \frac{.29661}{n} = \frac{.29661}{16.67} = .01779.$$

The meaning of $r$ is slightly different in these two formulas. Both, of course, start from the same ratio, $\frac{P_2}{P_1}$. The difference is in the manner in which the rate, $r$, is assumed to operate—successively (year by year), or continuously. On the basis of a given ratio for some definite period, the second or continuous method will indicate a slightly lower rate of growth than the first, because, operating continuously, not such a high rate is needed to produce the same amount of growth.[14]

Which formula, then, should be used? There are arguments in favor of both; both are found in the literature of demography. On the one hand, the second formula more accurately describes the nature of growth, as a continuous process going on all the time. On the other hand, it is true that vital statistics do not record growth continuously, but in distinct steps, year by year. The method may conform to the nature of these observations or to the nature of the process, but not to both. In most population growth problems the rate is low, and in such cases the two formulas give almost the same answers. Hence, in practical terms, either one is probably as good as the other. The important thing to remember is that both methods are rather crude (see 7:4).

After the value of $r$ is found, these two formulas can be used to estimate the population *between* the dates of actual observation.

---

[14] Or, if the rate and the time period are the same, the continuous method would yield a somewhat larger final population $(P_2)$; or, with $P_2/P_1$ and $r$ given, a shorter time period would be required. Because of this slight discrepancy, it is often advisable to state which formula has been used.

Suppose we wish to estimate the population of Malaya at July 1, 1940, assuming growth at the rate of 0.0180 (or 0.0178) since the census of 1931. Knowing the values of $r$, $P_1$, $P_2$, and $n$ $(n = 9\frac{3}{12}$, or 9.25 years), we simply substitute the numbers for these terms. The estimated population, $\bar{P}$, is found either as

$$\bar{P} = P_1 \, (1 + r)^n, \quad \text{or as} \quad \bar{P} = P_1 \, e^{rn}$$

where $n$ is the exact number of years between April 1, 1931 and July 1, 1940. This is recognizable as a kind of interpolation (see 1:7, also 2:11), using an assumption more complex than that of growth along an imaginary straight line. The same formulas can also be used to *extrapolate* (to estimate the population *after* the date of $P_2$), by setting $n$ equal to the desired number of years.[15] These estimates are, of course, hypothetical figures, since they are arrived at by means of a very arbitrary assumption.

To summarize, these formulas will answer three sorts of questions:

a. What is the rate of growth in some known period, when $P_1$ and $P_2$, and the length of the period, $n$, are known? (Solve the equation for $r$.)

b. How large would the population become if it increased at some given rate, $r$, for a definite period of years, $n$, beginning with some known size, $P$? (Solve the equation for $\bar{P}$.)

c. How many years would be required for the population to increase (or decrease) by some definite amount — let us say, to double — if it changed steadily at the rate $r$? (Solve the equation for $n$.)

## 2:9 Crude Birth and Death Rate

Most forms of measurement in demography are based on numbers from more than one universe. The reason is fairly obvious. In order to keep within one universe, we are limited to one set of records representing one date. But most of the questions to be answered pertain to some change or process, involving observations at different

---

[15] For example, the mid-year population estimate for 1950 would be $5,848,910 \times e^{(2.58)(.0178)}$ or $5,848,910 \times 1.04697 = 6,124,000$. The final digits of the estimate are rounded, since it is merely an approximate figure. For further cautions and comments about this procedure, see 7:4.

dates. One way of securing these observations is to use the results of two censuses, like the example in 2:8.

Another way is to analyze factors which are the source of change. These are the so-called vital events. As they happen, they alter the size of the population and its composition (see 1:1). We generally find records of this type among the vital statistics of a country, and statistics of people present at some particular time in census reports. A ratio of numbers from two such dissimilar universes is difficult to interpret. Of course, it is not difficult to compute — any two numbers can be combined, regardless of source. But it is important to be able to regard it as more than simply the ratio of two numbers; and so some considerations about the nature and relations of the two universes must be taken into account.

Vital rates come from the registration of certain events, and measure the *frequency* of occurrence of the events. There are two aspects to be measured: frequency during some definite period of time, and frequency among the number of people who are present. Thus, these rates represent *"births per person per year,"* or *"deaths per person per year."* Actually, they are expressed as births or deaths "per 1000 persons" per year, but this is merely a matter of convenience and does not change their meaning.

Some of these are called "crude" rates because they show the frequency of a class of events throughout the entire population, without regard to any of the various smaller groupings that are sometimes used for better observation (some of which will be illustrated shortly).

The Crude Death Rate is a ratio of the total registered deaths of some specified year to the total population, multiplied by 1,000. It is computed as follows:

$$\frac{D}{P}k$$

where:

$D$   is the total number of deaths registered during the calendar year (January 1 to December 31)

$P$   is the total population at the middle of the year (July 1)[16]

$k$   is 1,000.

The Crude Birth Rate is a ratio of total registered live births to the total population, also in some specified year, also multiplied by 1,000, or:

---

[16]The reason for the particular date, "the middle of the year," is explained in the following section.

$$\frac{B}{P}\,k$$

where:

B  is the total number of births registered during the calendar year

P  is the total population at the middle of the year (July 1)

k  is 1,000.

The crude birth rate carries a burden of some vagueness and confusion over what a "live birth" actually is.  This is defined by different standards and births are registered with differing degrees of efficiency from country to country, whereas there is less ambiguity in the registration of deaths (see 1:5 and 3:11).

The Crude Rate of Natural Increase is the *gap* between the crude birth rate and the crude death rate:

$$\frac{B}{P}\,k \; - \; \frac{D}{P}\,k \; ,$$

or else $\dfrac{B-D}{P}\,k$, whichever form is easier to compute with the data

at hand.  It is the change in population size, per 1,000 persons, due to the difference in the numbers of births and of deaths, in a given year.  The change may be either gain or loss.  This rate represents only the change due to the balance of births and deaths, and does not include the effect of migration.

Vital rates are most often computed for the year of a census, because the census provides a convenient figure for the total population.  The period represented by the rate is called a "base period." A rate for just one year is affected by fluctuations in the numbers of births or deaths.  This may be a distortion, especially if a trend over a period of many years is being measured.  (On the other hand, it is sometimes the fluctuation itself that we want to measure.)  Such distortion can be reduced by using the *average* of births or deaths over a three-year or longer period, centered on the census year, as the numerator of the ratio.

There are two common ways of computing this average.  A

crude death rate may be calculated as $\dfrac{1}{3}\left(\dfrac{D_1}{P_1} + \dfrac{D_2}{P_2} + \dfrac{D_3}{P_3}\right)k$, where the subscripts 1, 2 and 3 designate each of three consecutive years. But reliable figures for the total population are not often available for each individual year; and so it is customary to use the number of deaths for three consecutive years and the population figure of the middle year (usually a census figure), as follows:

$$\frac{\frac{1}{3}(D_1 + D_2 + D_3) k}{P_2}$$

where $P_2$ is the census figure. This second type of average is some-what less precise, but its results are approximately the same. These same remarks, of course, apply to birth rates and rates of natural in-crease as well as to death rates. It is desirable to state which of these two averaging procedures has been followed.[17]

Crude, or "general," rates can also be computed for any other kind of event that is regularly registered among the entire population — marriage, divorce, or migration. The procedure is exactly the same.

Each of these rates is based on numbers from two different uni-verses. The numerator is taken from registration of events as they occur through the year, and the denominator represents the total num-ber of people determined with reference to some particular date in the year. Certain defects of crude rates in measuring the frequency of occurrence of these events can be traced to the relations between the two universes:[18]

a. Each event in the numerator of a crude birth or death rate (or rate of natural increase or of migration) changes the number of persons in the population — in other words, changes the size of the denominator. A birth is one person added to the total population, and a death is one person removed. Therefore crude rates do not indicate merely the rates of occurrence of events, but mix them up together with changes in population size.

b. The two universes do not refer to quite the same popula-tion. The size of the enumerated population is fixed at the time of a

---

[17] The first type is called an "unweighted" average, because the data of each year have equal weight. The second type is called a "weighted" average, because a large (or small) number of deaths in one year will have a large (or small) influence on the value of the rate.

[18] There are also other defects, associated with the nature of the events themselves and of statistical procedures in counting them. These are taken up in later chapters, especially the chapters devoted to mortality and fertility.

census,[19] while the population included in vital registration fluctuates in size during the course of a year (as new people are added and some people are removed by death or migration). Furthermore, the two universes have different limits, because they are not administered in the same way: they are not coextensive. Only by extreme coincidence could they be of the same size. Hence all vital rates are distorted in some degree, though fortunately this is normally not large. Sometimes this is a slight discrepancy in the boundaries of the two universes, trivial in its effect. Sometimes entire large categories of people are omitted from one universe but included in the other. If the coverage of registration of births and deaths is the smaller of the two, then the birth or death rate becomes too low; if the total population as determined for the denominator is smaller, this makes the rate too high.[20] Usually a census is able to cover a larger part of the entire population, and so vital rates tend to be too low.

c. The two universes are different in their units of counting. The events of the numerator are distributed throughout the year. The population figure is not; it refers to only one part of the year. A ratio of these two numbers is really not a measurement of the frequency of occurrence (of births, deaths, or other events). Strictly speaking, the denominator should likewise have some reference to the year, rather than just to some particular moment. That is, it should represent the number of persons who were present throughout the year. It is rigorous to speak of "deaths per person per year" only in the sense of deaths per person-year lived by the population.

## 2:10 Person-Years Lived in a Population during a Calendar Year

Suppose that a person, alive on January 1, died on January 15. Would his individual "death rate" during the year be the same as it

---

[19] Even if the population figure (for the total population) is taken from the same registration lists that record births and deaths, it represents that universe (or each person in that universe) at one particular moment, while the figures for births and deaths reflect all the changes in the size of that universe during the year.

[20] It is possible to get an accurate vital rate even if *both* universes are deficient, provided that the same groups are omitted in both cases. For example, the excluded people may belong to groups that can be clearly defined (like military personnel, transient population, or nomads). In this instance, the correct rate would pertain to the reduced universe; it may not be the same as the correct rate for the entire population. But probably such a rate would not be correct even for the reduced universe. Population groups are usually excluded more effectively from one set of records than from the other.

would be if he died on the following December 31? He actually lived
for two weeks during the year before dying. He might have lived
through one entire year[21]; his lifetime during the year if he died on
December 31 would have been 26 times as long.

With a complete set of individual records for a hypothetical
population, we can determine the length of each person's life during
the year, and afterwards count the total number of years lived. A person who survives through the entire year contributes one year of life
to the aggregate of person-years lived; a person who survives only
two weeks (after January 1) contributes only 1/26 of a year. Let us
assume that the population consists of exactly 500 persons on January
1. This population gains and loses members by births and deaths, as
follows:

The person who died on January 15 contributed only 15 person-
days, or 0.04 person-years, to the total person-years lived by the entire population. A child born on January 11, dying on November 9,
contributed the duration of his life, or 0.83 person-years. Others contributed the amount of time they spent as members of the population,
during the year. The total population at the end of the year was 508.
The total number of person-years lived by everyone can be computed
by summing the entries in the last column of Table 2:4. It is 504.26.

This is the same as the average number of persons present per
day throughout the year; the reader may make this latter calculation
if he wishes, though it would be rather laborious. Vital rates computed with this figure as denominator represent deaths per person-
year lived, or births per person-year lived. (By convention, they are
expressed as rates per thousand person-years.) The crude birth rate

in this hypothetical population was $\dfrac{14}{504.26} \times 1,000$, or 28. The

death rate was $\dfrac{11}{504.26} \times 1.000$, or 22.

## 2:11 Estimating the Mid-Year Population

Obviously, it is not practical to count person-years exactly.
Vital statistics are not compiled in such detail (except in some types
of sample survey); and if they were, the calculations of person-years
would be too laborious to be worth while on a large scale.

How do we estimate the number of person-years? As an approximation, the only practical alternative is to take the number of

---

[21]In practice it is not worth while to take account of very small time
intervals. Only a few records are tabulated in intervals smaller than one
year. In this example, all time intervals are based on units of one full day.

## TABLE 2:4

## BIRTHS, DEATHS, AND PERSON-YEARS LIVED DURING ONE YEAR IN A HYPOTHETICAL POPULATION

| Number of Persons | Events and Dates | | Number of Days Lived | Person-Years Lived |
|---|---|---|---|---|
| 1 | | Died Jan. 15 (1/15) | 15 | .04 |
| 1 | Born 1/11 | Died 11/9 | 302 | .83 |
| 1 | | Died 4/8 | 98 | .27 |
| 1 | Born 6/24 | | 190 | .52 |
| 1 | Born 10/7 | | 85 | .23 |
| 1 | | Died 6/22 | 173 | .47 |
| 1 | Born 9/13 | Died 11/13 | 61 | .17 |
| 1 | | Died 6/1 | 152 | .42 |
| 1 | Born 3/6 | Died 3/31 | 25 | .07 |
| 2 | Born 10/19 | | 146 | .40 |
| 1 | Born 10/7 | | 85 | .23 |
| 1 | | Died 8/16 | 228 | .62 |
| 1 | | Died 6/30 | 181 | .50 |
| 1 | | Died 6/5 | 156 | .43 |
| 4 | Arrived from abroad 4/18 | | 1032 | 2.83 |
| 1 | Born 8/26 | | 127 | .35 |
| 1 | Born 1/11 | | 354 | .97 |
| 1 | Born 10/1 | | 91 | .25 |
| 1 | Born 2/21 | Died 4/27 | 65 | .18 |
| 1 | Arrived from abroad 10/25 | | 67 | .18 |
| 1 | Born 6/7 | | 207 | .57 |
| 1 | Born 4/10 | | 265 | .73 |
| 493 | Lived uneventfully, 1/1 to 12/31 | | | 493.00 |

Total Person-Years    504.26

Total Births    14
Total Deaths    11
Immigrants    5

persons present at some moment. This is the reason why the term "mid-year population" was used in first explaining the computation of vital rates (2:9). But why the middle of the year? This is the point at which roughly half of the year's changes in the size of the population will have occurred. If the events that change the size of the population were distributed evenly through the year, the population at mid-year would be exactly the same as the average number of persons present during the year, and thus the same as the number of person-years lived. Actually these events are *not* distributed evenly, but vary by season, sometimes in very marked degree. Nevertheless, the mid-year population gives a reasonable approximation of the number of person-years lived, and it is very convenient to compute.

But this estimated figure must be based on census or registration data, which probably do not represent the exact middle of the year. There are several ways of dealing with this problem:

a. Ignore the discrepancy. If a census has been taken during the same year, the easiest course is to use it as if it were taken on July 1. The changes of population size within one year are normally small; this cannot lead to serious error, provided the census date is reasonably close to the middle of the year — say, some time within one quarter of July (between April 1 and October 1). Beyond these limits, it may be advisable to adopt one of the alternatives described below. This course is the most common, not because it gives the "best" estimate (though it is often as good as any other), but primarily because it is simple. When computing rates by age or sex, or for other groups within the population, we often cannot make separate estimations of the population in each group at the exact middle of the year. (Moreover, different groups may be affected differently by the factors of change during the year, and using the same method of estimation might distort some of the data.) This is the principal reason why rates are computed where possible for the census year, or for a period centered around a census year.

b. A continuous population register may provide a figure for the population of January 1 (or December 31) of each year. Here the most reasonable estimate of the mid-year population is $P_1 + \frac{1}{2}(P_2 - P_1)$ (where $P_1$ is the number of people recorded at the beginning of the year, and $P_2$ the number at the end, or the beginning of the next year). This is a simple case of interpolation (see 1:7), showing exactly what the mid-year population would be if all vital events were distributed evenly through the year.

c. If the date of the estimate lies between two censuses more than one year apart, it is still possible to interpolate between them. Assuming that yearly changes in the size of the population are equal, we can make estimates along a straight line for any intercensal date. This is done by dividing the change in the size of the total population (between $P_1$ and $P_2$) according to the point where the date of the estimate falls between the two censuses.[22] The estimate $(\overline{P})$ is as follows:

$$\overline{P} = P_1 + \frac{n}{N}(P_2 - P_1)$$

where:

$\overline{P}$ is the population estimate at some date between two censuses

$P_1$ is the size of the population, as determined in the first census

$P_2$ is the size of the population, as determined in the second census

$N$ is the number of months between censuses

$n$ is the number of months between the date of $P_1$ and the date of the estimate. (Any other unit of time may be used. A month is convenient, and accurate enough for nearly all purposes.)

Between the censuses of 1931 and 1947 in Malaya, for example, are 200 months (in 1931 the census was taken on April 1, in 1947 on November 23). To estimate the mid-year population of 1940, we first determine the number of months from the census of 1931 to July 1, 1940 (111 months). According to the formula above, the solution is

$$\overline{P} = 4,347,704 + \frac{111}{200} (1,501,206) = 5,180,873, \text{ or simply } 5,181,000.$$

d. If a long period has elapsed between the two census or registration dates, or if the rate of growth during this period has been rather high, it may be preferable to interpolate according to a compound-interest formula (see 2:8). After having found a value for $r$, we need merely substitute another value for $n$ (i.e., the amount of time

---

[22]This procedure is known as "linear" interpolation, because it follows the path of a straight line between two points (see 1:7 and Chart 3:2). It has many applications, owing to its simplicity and convenience, wherever there is no need to assume a more complex pattern of change. It is merely an extension of the procedure "b," in a more general form.

between the first census and the date of the estimate), and re-calculate. This method calls for one warning: $n$ and $r$ must refer to the same units of time — if the rate has already been determined on an annual basis, then the period $n$ must also be stated in years, and the months represented as fractional or decimal values.

In this case the value of $r$ has already been found (in 2:8). The same data for Malaya can be substituted in the formula $\overline{P} = P_1\, e^{rn}$, where $n$ here is equal to 9.25, the number of years between the census of 1931 and July 1, 1940:

$$\overline{P} = 4,347,704 \ e^{(.01779)\,(9.25)}$$

$$= 4,347,704 \times 1.17887 = 5,125,378.$$

This estimate is smaller than the estimate by linear interpolation, because it apportions the growth between censuses according to the compound interest law. However, in this instance it would be inappropriate to use either method of interpolation. The total period between censuses is long, and the history of Malaya during this period suggests a considerable fluctuation in population growth, particularly in migration. It would be unrealistic to assume a steady pattern of growth.

e. Estimating the mid-year population *after* the date of the last census. Often these ("extrapolated") estimates are needed in order to compute vital rates for very recent years, or even months. For a short time after the census, they can be made with either of the interpolation formulas "c" or "d" described above. No special steps are required. The procedures are exactly the same; it is necessary only to vary the value of $n$ in the formulas. However, these estimates go beyond the range of observation, and should be made very cautiously. Estimates by interpolation are themselves crude enough and subject to error; but their only real safeguard—the likelihood that the true values probably lie between two known figures, $P_1$ and $P_2$ — is lacking as soon as the same method is pushed beyond the date of one of these figures. Extrapolated estimates become suspect if extended for more than a few years or if applied to small areas where patterns of migration may have changed. More elaborate methods are then required.[23]

## 2:12 Vital Rates by Month

Birth or death rates are also computed by month of the year or by quarter. This may be done to show monthly or seasonal patterns

---

[23] See also 7:13.

of variation, because an annual rate hides any variation from month to month within the year. Monthly rates also show something about the current trend of rates before the entire year's data have become available.

First, of course, it is necessary that the numbers of events be tabulated month by month. The procedure of computation is then almost the same as that for annual rates, except for one fact. Monthly rates represent what the annual rate *would be* if conditions of one month persisted for an entire year. This is because people are accustomed to discussing annual rates, and monthly figures are always implicitly compared against this customary standard. Therefore an adjustment is necessary in order to convert the monthly rate to an "annual" basis. The calculation is done as follows (in the cáse of a monthly crude birth rate):

$$\frac{365}{n}\left(\frac{B_i}{P}\right)k$$

where $B_i$ is the number of births in the month represented by the rate, $n$ is the number of days in that month, and 365 is the number of days in a year (366 in a leap year). The value of $k$ is 1,000. (Taking account of the number of days in the year and month is merely a convenient way of allowing for the different lengths of various months — it does not imply any exceptional degree of exactitude.)

The figure for population $(P)$ represents "person-months" lived rather than person-years. This number might be estimated by determining the "mid-month population," but it is not worth while. A population changes very little in size during a one-month period. A mid-year population estimate (for July 1) is fully adequate to represent the population on July 15. In fact, the figure for the mid-year population is sometimes used as the mid-month population estimate for every month. If the rate of growth is slow, this procedure may be close enough, and it may often be justifiable as a short cut. However, separate population estimates for each month according to the linear interpolation formula described above are not much trouble, and these are usually preferable (see 2:11).

### 2:13 Diversity and the Averaging Effect on Crude Vital Rates

Though the question of matching of statistics presents obstacles in the interpretation of crude vital rates, these are chiefly obstacles of a rather formal character. They interfere with clear formulation of concepts, but not with the practical side of the everyday work. Normally the defects that we have been discussing (2:9) do not lead to errors of large size.

There are other shortcomings of crude rates that are just as
serious, arising from the manner in which the events are distributed
in the population.  A crude rate, as mentioned earlier, is a single
number measuring the frequency of some type of event in the entire
population.  It summarizes the incidence of the event among a great
many individuals.  This, of course, is arbitrary.  People differ.  If
the rate is to be an accurate description of a large proportion of the
people to whom it refers, they must be fairly homogeneous; not necessarily alike in all respects, but at least homogeneous with respect to
the event measured by the rate.  If such homogeneity is lacking, then
the rate is merely a balance struck by the combination of diverse elements.  It is an *average* of all of these elements, and may not accurately represent the rate of any section of the population.

## 2:14  Age-Specific Death Rate

It is not possible to reduce the diversity hidden in crude vital
rates, since by definition they apply to everyone in the population.
But if the population is separated into groups whose members are
relatively homogeneous, rates computed for each group will be less
affected by diversity among individuals.  These are called "specific
rates," or rates for some specified group within a population.

There are many kinds of specific rates, and it is not enough to
say that a rate is "specific."  We must state what kind of specific
rate it is.  In order to compute specific rates, it is necessary only to
have the data divided into classes.  A sex-specific death rate, for
females, consists of female deaths per 1,000 females at mid-year (or
per 1,000 person-years lived by females in the population); correspondingly for males.  It is essential that the categories be defined
comparably for the numerator and the denominator – the universes
should match exactly in this respect.  Thus, although deaths and
population are often both tabulated according to occupation, it is rare
to be able to calculate occupation-specific death rates without distortion, because the two universes are not well matched.[24]  Therefore a
few types predominate among specific rates.  Of these the most important are age-specific rates, and age-sex-specific rates.

Age-specific Death Rates are computed as follows:

$$\frac{d_i}{P_i}k$$

[24]See 5:14.

where:

$d_i$ is the number of deaths during the year in the $i$th age group

$P_i$ is the mid-year population in the same age group

$k$ is 1,000.

Various intervals of age are used, according to the needs of the moment and the degree of detail in the data. Five-year groupings are most common. These are fine enough to show a great deal about the age pattern of mortality, but not so fine as to clutter and confuse with unnecessary detail. One-year groupings are rarely seen except in the construction of life tables (see Chapter 4) and in studying infant mortality (which is treated somewhat differently). In order to remove the effect of infant mortality, it is preferable to begin a table of age-specific death rates with the age interval 1-4; but the interval 0-4 is frequently found instead. Groupings of ten years are too broad for most purposes, though they are sometimes used to save space in presentation or to offset certain inaccuracies of age reporting. Occasionally 5-year and 10-year groupings are combined in the same table, as in Table 2:5.

The death rates of Ceylon are typical of the pattern of death rates by age. The highest rate in this table is 96 per thousand, which is more than thirty times the lowest rates for children. In a detailed study of mortality the rates should also be computed separately by sex (see 5:7).

Even these age-specific rates are average figures, representing the averages of age groups 1-4, 5-9, 25-34, and so on. However, it is apparent that they have the effect of removing a large amount of the variation present in crude death rates. Therefore the various age-specific death rates must represent universes more homogeneous (in their mortality) than did the death rates for the total population.

A greater degree of comparability between the two universes is required when so-called "specific" rates are computed. The universes must correspond, not only in their totals, but also in their classifications (in this case, each age group). Each class should refer to the same group of people in both universes. Age-specific rates demand accuracy and consistency of a high level in both sets of records, and open up many additional possibilities of error.

Like crude rates, age-specific death rates are based on the notion of "deaths, during a year, per 1,000 person-years lived," at the specified age. As before, the number of person-years is approximated by the number of persons present at the middle of the year or base period. This figure is usually estimated on the basis of census data.

It is much more difficult to estimate the population at precisely the middle of the year when it is divided into age groups, for each age group must be dealt with separately. This can be done by means of a special estimating ratio. After a ratio of the estimated *total* mid-year population to the nearest census population is computed (as in

2:11), this same ratio $\left(\dfrac{\bar{P}}{P}\right)$ is applied to the census population in

## TABLE 2:5

## AGE-SPECIFIC DEATH RATES FOR THE POPULATION OF CEYLON

### Both Sexes, 1945-1947

| (1) | (2) | (3) | (4) |
|---|---|---|---|
| Ages | Population (Census of 1946)[a] | Average Yearly Deaths, 1945-47[b] | Death Rates (Deaths per 1,000 Population)[c] |
| 1-4 | 700,762 | 20,683 | 29.5 |
| 5-9 | 811,363 | 5,451 | 6.7 |
| 10-14 | 805,642 | 2,589 | 3.2 |
| 15-19 | 680,614 | 3,345 | 4.9 |
| 20-24 | 641,571 | 5,104 | 8.0 |
| 25-34 | 1,027,405 | 9,305 | 9.1 |
| 35-44 | 790,514 | 8,775 | 11.1 |
| 45-54 | 515,695 | 8,209 | 15.9 |
| 55-64 | 293,598 | 8,075 | 27.5 |
| 65 and over | 229,498 | 21,958 | 95.7 |
| All ages | 6,657,339 | 125,803 | 18.9 |

[a]The census, taken on March 19, 1946, was assumed to represent the population at the middle of the base period 1945-1947.

[b]The sum of registered deaths in 1945, 1946 and 1947, divided by three. An average of 45 yearly deaths ("age not stated") have been omitted.

[c]Column (3), divided by Column (2), times 1,000.

Sources:  Department of Census and Statistics, *Census of Ceylon, 1946*, Vol. 2, Table 6; Registrar-General, *Report on Vital Statistics* (1945, 1946, and 1947), Table 23.

each age group. That is, the census population by age is multiplied by the estimating ratio calculated for the total population.

But it is sometimes doubtful whether this further estimation is really a gain in precision. The purpose of applying an estimating ratio to the census population by age is to take account of change in the numbers of people present, between the date of the census and the middle of the proper year. In doing this, one assumes that the population changes at the same rate at each age, which may not be true. Therefore it may be just as accurate to use the census figures without modification (as in Table 2:5), provided the census was taken during the same year for which the rates are to be computed.

## 2:15 Infant Death Rate

Infants are defined in demography as an exact age group, namely age "zero," or those children in the first year of life, who have not yet reached age one. As mentioned earlier, death rates for infants receive special treatment, different from death rates at other ages. Owing to the unique pattern of mortality during infancy, it is impractical to estimate the number of person-years lived in the first year of life from the kinds of statistics that are usually available. Therefore a different denominator is used.

The Infant Death Rate is a ratio of registered deaths of infants during a year to the live births registered during the same year:

$$\frac{d_0}{B} k$$

where:

$d_0$ is the number of deaths below age one registered during the year

$B$ is the number of live births registered during the same year

$k$ is 1,000.

For example, the Report on Vital Statistics in Ceylon showed a total of 238,494 live births during 1945, and 33,309 deaths among infants. The Infant Death Rate is 33,309/238,494 times 1,000, or 139.7 per thousand births. An Infant Death Rate computed for both sexes together is often used for a brief and superficial view of conditions or trends. A more detailed study of infant mortality requires separate rates for males and females, since infant mortality differs markedly by sex.

The Infant Death Rate is a ratio of rather mixed type. It is not a ratio of deaths per thousand person-years lived in infancy during the year; because the denominator is not an estimate of person-years, but the number of live births that were registered. Nor does it represent the proportion of a year's babies that died before age one, because the numerator and denominator do not belong to the same universe.[25]

Statistics of registered births and registered infant deaths are often found together, as products of the same registration system. For this reason, Infant Death Rates can be computed in many instances where death rates at other ages cannot for lack of census data. It is only fair warning, however, to point out that infant deaths are extremely difficult to register, especially under conditions of high infant mortality. Even a country that keeps an adequate registration of births may not have an equally adequate record of infant deaths. Consequently it is to be expected that infant death rates are too low for the actual facts. The higher the level of infant mortality the greater the likelihood of this deficiency.

Because the Infant Death Rate is a peculiar kind of rate, further discussion will be postponed until the subject of infant mortality can be taken up in more detail (see 5:8). There is a considerable amount of confusion about various ways of measuring mortality in infancy. It is therefore necessary to emphasize that *this* rate, which is rather crude, will be referred to in this book as the "Infant Death Rate," in order to distinguish it from another measurement, which we shall call the "Infant Mortality Rate."

## 2:16  Age Specific Birth Rates

Age-specific birth rates are computed for the same reason as age-specific death rates: the frequency of childbirth varies markedly with age. In this case, the "age" which is to be specified is not that of the child being born, but the age of each *parent* at the time of birth. But the two parents very likely are not of the same age, and so a choice must be made between birth rates of fathers and birth rates of mothers (sometimes called paternal birth rates or maternal birth rates, or paternal or maternal fertility rates).[26] Age-specific birth

---

[25] Some of the infants who died during 1945 had been born in the previous year, but had not yet reached their first birthday; some of the infants born during 1945 would die before reaching their first birthday, but not until 1946. For further discussion of this point, see 5:8.

[26] The terms "paternity rate" and "maternity rate" have been suggested for the purpose of distinguishing between birth rates among potential

rates nearly always are calculated for women rather than men. For this reason, the explanation below will be carried on in terms of birth rates for women, though the procedure is exactly the same with birth rates for men. They are computed as follows:

$$\frac{b_i}{P_i} k$$

where:

$b_i$ is the number of births registered during the year to women in the age interval $i$ (usually an interval of 5 years)

$P_i$ is the mid-year population of women in the same age group

$k$ is 1,000.

The raw materials are registered births classified by age of mother, and the population of women 15-49, in the same age groups. These data for Japan are shown in Table 2:6.

Some preliminary adjustments are necessary in this instance. First, the few registered births of women under age 15 and over age 49 were transferred to the categories 15-19 and 45-49, respectively. This is an arbitrary step, but necessary to avoid omitting some of the registered births. Second, some births were registered without information about age of mother. Altogether there were 7,171,834 registered births, 1945 to 1947; there were 7,170,077 registered with age of mother stated. The total figure is larger by 7,171,834/7,170,077, or 1.000245. We multiply the average figures (Column 2 of Table 2:6, births with age of mother known) by this ratio, thereby raising them to the correct total (Column 3). The result is an estimate of all registered births according to age of mother. (This has the effect of allocating the unknown cases according to the distribution of the known cases.) Finally, since birth registration in Japan applies to Japanese nationals only, Column 4 includes women of Japanese nationality only, instead of all women counted in the census. With these figures, the birth rates are computed simply by dividing the numbers of Column 3 by those of Column 4.

Age-specific birth rates have certain other peculiarities which set them off from death rates, but most of these will have to be deferred until a later chapter on fertility (see 6:2). An age-specific birth rate is like a death rate in its method of computation. It is less definite as a statistical record. There are some fundamental ambiguities in the registration of births, which do not affect the registration

---

fathers or potential mothers. "Birth rate" and "fertility rate" have remained the standard terms, and are used throughout this book.

of deaths. Moreover, the estimate of person-years lived is less adequate for the purpose of computing a birth rate. In the case of death
rates, it is the number of person-years lived by persons who *might die.*
It is not true that everyone in an age group is exposed to some "risk"
of childbirth, not even women of "childbearing ages." Though anyone in an age group can die, some women are not capable, in a given
year's time, of giving birth. (On the other hand, the notion of person-
years lived is more rigorous in the case of age-specific birth rates,
in the sense that births — the event being measured — do not alter
the size of the denominator.)


### TABLE 2:6

### AGE-SPECIFIC BIRTH RATES FOR JAPANESE WOMEN
### 1949-1951

| (1) Ages | (2) Average Yearly Births, 1949-1951 | (3) Adjusted Average (2) x 1.000245[a] | (4) Female Population, Census of 1950[b] | (5) Birth Rates (3)/(4) x 1,000 |
|---|---|---|---|---|
| Under 15 }<br>15-19 } | 56,545 | 56,558 | 4,229,005 | 13.4 |
| 20-24 | 626,087 | 626,240 | 3,870,468 | 161.8 |
| 25-29 | 809,529 | 809,727 | 3,341,590 | 242.3 |
| 30-34 | 515,142 | 515,268 | 2,825,769 | 182.3 |
| 35-39 | 291,657 | 291,728 | 2,657,741 | 109.8 |
| 40-44 | 86,217 | 86,238 | 2,273,441 | 37.9 |
| 45-49 }<br>50 and over } | 4,847 | 4,848 | 1,978,362 | 2.5 |
| Total | 2,390,024 | 2,390,609 | | |

[a]The total of registered births, 1949-1951, was 7,171,834. Age of mother was
stated for only 7,170,077. The ratio of 7,171,834/7,170,077, or 1.000245, in-
flates the incomplete figures of Column 2.

[b]Japanese nationals only.

Sources: *Population Census of 1950*, Vol. 7, Table 38;
         *Vital Statistics for 1949, 1950, 1951.*

## 2:17  General Fertility Ratio

This is another ratio of just two numbers, each from a different universe. It is also called General Fertility Rate. It is a single ratio of all births to the number of women of "childbearing age" (15 to 44 or 15 to 49):

$$\frac{B}{P_i}\, k$$

where:

$B$ is the number of live births registered during the year

$P_i$ is the mid-year population of women between ages 15-44; or the mid-year population of women between ages 15-49

$k$ is 1,000.

It is referred to as a ratio of "births per 1,000 women of childbearing age," being a "general" ratio in the sense that it attributes all births to all women within these age limits, without further distinctions among them. This places it somewhere between a crude birth rate and an age-specific birth rate. Births are not attributed to these women on the basis of direct information about them, but rather because we know, indirectly, from comparison of detailed data of many countries, that all but a negligible portion of each year's births can be traced to mothers between the ages of 15 and 49.

As in the case of other vital statistics, the mid-year population is used as an estimate of the number of person-years lived by the women in the age group. The General Fertility Ratio is thus the number of births per 1,000 person-years lived by the population of adult women, those who form the universe of potential mothers. Compared with the age-specific birth rates of the preceding section, it conceals a large amount of variation according to age. For this reason it is not adequate for a very detailed examination of fertility patterns. The chief advantage of the General Fertility Ratio is that it can be computed in situations in which the registration of births and the enumeration of population are satisfactory, but where direct evidence of births by age of parents is lacking.

## 2:18  Total Fertility Rate, Gross Reproduction Rate

The chief obstacle to computing age-specific birth rates is not that they are too detailed, but that until recent years the essential data have not been available for many countries. Age-specific birth rates have advantages even when it is not the pattern of fertility at each age that is being investigated:  their values are not noticeably affected by changes or differences of age composition within the population of women of reproductive age.  The General Fertility Ratio *is* so affected, independently of actual changes or differences in birth rates at each age.  (It should be added that such differences in age composition are often of very minor significance.)

But a whole series of seven birth rates (as in Table 2:6) is sometimes too long and cumbersome to be useful.  When necessary, they can be condensed by combining them into a single figure.  There are two conventional ways of doing this.  The more straightforward one of these is the Total Fertility Rate:

$$\overset{i=49}{\underset{i=15}{S}} \left(\frac{b_i}{P_i}\right) k$$

where:

$b_i$   is the number of live births registered during the year to mothers of age $i$, where $i$ is an interval of one year

$P_i$   is the mid-year population of women of the same age

$k$   is sometimes 1,000, sometimes 1.

Contained in this formula is the same ratio $\left(\frac{b_i}{P_i}\right)$ that appeared previously for age-specific birth rates, *except that in this formula the birth rates are rates by single year of age,* and not rates for 5-year groups as before.  Otherwise, all that is new in computing the Total Fertility Rate is to *sum* the birth rates secured for each age.  And this is the special meaning of the symbol "S."

The symbol "S" gives an instruction to do something with the terms that follow: "sum a series of numbers."  In order to be fully explicit, it says, "Sum the series from___ to___," showing (by means of the subscript and superscript) where to start adding and where to stop.  In the formula above, it means:  "Sum the birth rates for each year of age $\left(\frac{b_i}{P_i}\right)$ from age 15 to 49, inclusive" (i.e., "from the rate at which $i=15$ to the rate at which $i=49$ years").  As before, the Total Fertility Rate can be calculated either for men or for women. This explanation concerns a Rate for women only.

In practice the Total Fertility Rate is calculated somewhat differently. As we have already pointed out, birth rates are scarcely ever calculated in single-year intervals of age. The subscript *i* nearly always represents some 5-year interval, like 15-19, 20-24 ... 45-49, and the birth rate for each 5-year age group is an average for the group. This is not quite the same as the sum of the rates for all five single years. (For the *exact* sum, one must calculate these rates separately and then add the five of them together.) It is a close approximation, however, to multiply the birth rates for each group of women by 5. There are only seven of these birth rates between ages 15-49, and so they are summed from 1 to 7, as follows:

$$5 \sum_{i=1}^{7} \left( \frac{b_i}{P_i} \right) k$$

where:

$b_i$ is the number of live births registered during the year, to mothers of age *i*, where *i* is an interval of 5 years

$P_i$ is the mid-year population of women of the same age

$k$ is sometimes 1,000, sometimes 1.

The procedure is illustrated in Table 2:7. Starting with the age-specific rates for 5-year age groups (calculated in Table 2:6), one can multiply the rates by five, and sum. It is still easier to sum the rates first, and then multiply by five. The result is the Total Fertility Rate. The rates may be expressed either as "births per thousand women" (Column 2) or as "births per woman" (Column 3). Since *k* in the formula is arbitrary in either case, it makes no real difference whether we fix it at 1 or 1,000. The meaning of the Total Fertility Rate is discussed in Chapter 6.

The Gross Reproduction Rate is a slight modification of the Total Fertility Rate. It is computed as follows:

$$5 \sum_{i=1}^{7} \left( \frac{b_i^f}{P_i} \right) k$$

where:

$b_i^f$ is the number of live *female* births registered during the year, to mothers of age *i*, where *i* is an interval of five years

$P_i$ is the mid-year population of women of the same age

$k$ is sometimes 1,000, sometimes 1.

## TABLE 2:7

## TOTAL FERTILITY RATE FOR JAPANESE WOMEN
## 1949-1951

| (1) | (2) | (3) |
|-----|-----|-----|
| | Age-Specific Birth Rates | |
| Ages | Births per 1,000 women | Births per woman |
| 15-19 | 13.4 | .0134 |
| 20-24 | 161.8 | .1618 |
| 25-29 | 242.3 | .2423 |
| 30-34 | 182.3 | .1823 |
| 35-39 | 109.8 | .1098 |
| 40-44 | 37.9 | .0379 |
| 45-49 | 2.5 | .0025 |
| Sum of Column | 750.0 | .7500 |
| Total Fertility Rate | × 5 = 3750 | × 5 = 3.75 |

Source: Table 2:6.

*Note:* The Total Fertility Rate is also the same as the total number of
children that would ever be born to a (hypothetical) group of women,
if the group passed through its reproductive span of life with these
birth rates at each year of age. For a discussion of this point, see 6:5.

The only distinction is that the numerator of the Gross Reproduction
Rate is based on *female* births instead of total births.  Birth rates for
female births can be computed for women of each age group in the
same manner as for total births, if the data show female births separately by age of mothers; but often such detail is not available, and
so it is more common to proceed with the computation of the Total
Fertility Rate (using births of both sexes).  Afterwards the Total
Fertility Rate is multiplied by the proportion of all births (during the
corresponding base period) that were female, as follows:

    (a)  Total Fertility Rate (from Table 2:7),  3.750

    (b)  Proportion of births that were female, 1949-1951, .48719

    (c)  Gross Reproduction Rate:  (a) × (b) = 1.82

The interpretation of the Gross Reproduction Rate is basically the same: "Daughters per woman." Like the Total Fertility Rate, the Gross Reproduction Rate is also calculated giving $k$ a value of 1,000 instead of 1; the result is then the number of "daughters per 1,000 women," under the same conditions. Either the Total Fertility Rate or the Gross Reproduction Rate may be computed using birth rates by age of men instead of women, though these rates are rather rare. A Male Gross Reproduction Rate, however, would be constructed on the basis of male births rather than female births.

## 2:19 Applications of Rates and Ratios

The material of this chapter provides an indispensable background of common terms and procedures in demography. This is essential in approaching the later chapters, and in using the existing literature of research. It would be desirable to treat a larger part of population study in the same way. Unfortunately, this is not possible. When coping with the actual problems of research, we increasingly face questions of interpretation and the defects of data rather than matters of procedure. These are the questions which must receive primary consideration in the succeeding chapters.

# CHAPTER 3

# ACCURACY AND ERROR

The rates and ratios discussed in Chapter 2 can be no more accurate than the original data. Although the standard research procedures are very simple, they are subject to constant limitation by defective statistics. The question of accuracy (and of error) should be considered before investing any substantial amount of work in the analysis of population statistics.

Unfortunately there is no very extensive literature on the subject.[1] It has received separate attention only recently, and most authors have treated it only in relation to their particular problems. Most of the appraisal of population data must still be treated in this way. Here we shall discuss criteria of accuracy, suggest ways of putting them to test, and illustrate some of the more useful procedures. There are no general solutions to these problems. A large exercise of judgment is required, and in order to make expert judgments one must become thoroughly familiar with the peculiarities of the data.

But first we must have the data. Without certain fairly detailed tabulations there is little that can be said about the adequacy of population statistics; usually the more detail the better. Official agencies occasionally withhold the original figures, divulging merely

---

[1] For very helpful summaries see A. J. Jaffe, *Handbook of Statistical Methods for Demographers* (Washington, D.C., 1951), Chapters 4 and 5; United Nations, Population Branch, *Methods of Appraisal of Quality of Basic Data for Population Estimates* (New York, 1955); United Nations, Population Division, *Methods of Estimating Total Population for Current Dates* (New York, 1952); United Nations, Statistical Office, *Demographic Yearbook*, particularly the First and Second Issues, 1948 and 1950. For a painstaking and exhaustive survey and appraisal of fragmentary data — no longer applicable to all of the areas covered — see R. Kuczynski, *Demographic Survey of the British Colonial Empire* (London and New York, 1948-1953), 3 volumes.

a ratio, a percentage, or a vital rate. Whatever the motive, this practice withholds the basis for accepting or rejecting the findings. Without such evidence, there is no reason for their acceptance.

### 3:1 What is Meant by "Accuracy"?

The term can be used in different ways, with somewhat different meanings. With respect to the results of research, it suggests
that the figures are what they purport to be. An "accurate" figure
for the male population of a country would be the exact number of
males (as they should have been counted according to the rules of
enumeration); and likewise for the female population. An "accurate"
sex ratio for the entire population would be the correct ratio between
these two figures.

A general standard of accuracy would be so strict and so detailed as to be inapplicable to real data. There are deviations from
such a standard at every stage in the handling of data — planning, or-
ganizing, recording, compiling, tabulating, publishing and analyzing.
In most instances we have control only over the last of these stages,
and so the matter of accuracy must be considered in a more limited
and specific context.

Accuracy is not just a property of the data. It also depends on
the purposes for which the figures are used. A small defect may have
serious consequences for the particular purpose involved, and a large
defect in the data may be of little importance. A sex ratio for the
population may be more accurate in spite of large defects of the two
population figures — for example, if 10 per cent of both men and
women had been missed by the census — than it would be with a
small defect in only one of them (or perhaps two small defects in opposite directions). This is the chief fact to be recognized in weighing the results of any of the tests to be described later.

### 3:2 Some Sources of Error

In the analysis of population data, there are three principal
sources of numerical errors: defects of the data, chance fluctuations,
and errors due to computation.

Any computation in which a number (other than zero) is rounded
off introduces some error into the result. But this error is usually
very small, and it can be held under control by some simple precautions.[2] Chance fluctuations likewise may be present in any data.

---

[2] Errors of rounding are dealt with conventionally, by rules to be
found in nearly any elementary textbook on applied statistics. These rules

This is due to an inherent variability of things. For example (supposing, for the sake of the argument, that all the relevant conditions could be exactly duplicated), there is no way to be certain that any given sex ratio would be exactly the same as another sex ratio representing the identical conditions. The results of such experiments always tend to vary. This variability tends to be greater in small populations or small population groups, merely by reason of the smallness of their numbers. Such fluctuations are usually not large in demographic data. They are not given special attention unless tables representing small numbers of cases are involved.[3]

*Defects of the original data* demand and receive the most attention. This emphasis is warranted, for these defects are often large, hidden, and irremediable. They fall into two groups — the failure to include all the intended people in the statistics, and errors in the information recorded about the people who *were* included. Either of these may lead to distorted results, because the statistics do not have quite the information that they purport to have. Whether or not this shortcoming is serious, of course, depends on the type of use made of the data as well as on the nature of the defect. Inconsistent reporting of economic activities in a census, for example, does not interfere with the computation of a crude birth rate.

## 3:3 Finding Defects in Population Data

The analyst ordinarily has access only to published statistics, gathered by someone else, and beyond his control. He must utilize these materials as they are, and search for their defects as best he can, often by very indirect means. Principally this appraisal consists of searching for a few familiar defects, items which give something definite to look for, and provide fairly good results. We try to devise specific tests for flaws that are shown by experience to be major pitfalls or obstacles.

---

have the effect of distributing the errors at random over a large number of computations. In order to benefit from such a rule, one should first decide how many figures are significant in the final result, and carry at least one extra figure in the calculations up to the final result. (As a practical expedient, it is usually fair to assume that no more than the first four figures of population data are dependable. Hence, five significant figures are sufficient for most purposes in calculating rates and ratios.)

[3] This problem is also explained in most textbooks on statistical method. It cannot be dealt with within the scope of this book.

No such test is conclusive. Failing a satisfactory result, it is advisable to look further. If no discrepancies are revealed, this by no means demonstrates that the material is without fault; by their nature, many tests are subject to some of the same defects as the data being examined. A critical or even skeptical attitude is well justified throughout the analysis of population data.

The method of appraising population data is always the same: to compare two or more statistics which have a definite relation (known or assumed), and to consider whether or not they agree. In other words, it is simply a test of consistency between two or more sources. There is no fixed set of procedures for this purpose; it is necessary to improvise a great deal with the particular forms of data that are available. Any conceivable test may be helpful in some instance. All of them rely on one or more of the following comparisons.

a. Reference to the original records, or the original respondents. Reviewing each case is an excellent check on incorrect responses, and provides the only opportunity to revise the individual records. It is less effective in finding cases that were omitted from the original records, since these cases are likely to be missed again.

b. Special surveys. The same sorts of information may be collected again with greater care, on a sample basis. Such a survey can check on the original figures, provide more accurate data, and collect additional information. It affords no access to the individual records for their revision.

c. Comparison with some other existing statistics. This likewise is not a check of individual records, but a comparison with another aggregate figure. Various other statistics are sometimes available — data gathered in connection with rationing of commodities, tax or voting lists or the like. An independent source may refer to a particular category of the census population, instead of the total figure — children in school, persons eligible to receive old-age pensions, those subject to military service, registered physicians, or other groups. The chief limitation is that population data (census or vital statistics) are generally more comprehensive than these other sources, and are not very adequately tested by them. Moreover, the categories being compared cannot exactly correspond, and such a test gives at best only a rough comparison between the two sets of figures.[4]

---

[4] Sometimes, however, this is the only possible check on the population data. For examples of some useful external comparisons with other material, see United Nations, Population Branch, *Methods of Appraisal of Quality of Basic Data for Population Estimates* (New York, 1955), p. 7.

d. Internal comparisons of figures, within the same body of data. Certain relations of size are expected among categories, in the absence of specific disturbing factors. The age and sex composition of census data, and distributions of vital rates, are the most common examples. Departure from obvious expected patterns is a sign suggesting defective data, without indicating the nature of the defects.

e. Tests of consistency between the records of some particular group (or "cohort") of persons at different dates. The same people can be identified at different times according to their ages. The group of children 5-9 years of age in 1955 all came from the 0-4 group in 1950; the question is, were they reported consistently in two successive censuses? (They were all born between 1945 and 1950, and can also be checked against the registered births of that period.) This is the basis of the most sensitive tests that are available. The real difference in a cohort's ages between two dates is known exactly, and the change in its numbers can often be estimated very closely (see 3:9). Therefore census data by age, which are important in all branches of population study, can be appraised for accuracy as well as for the thoroughness of enumeration.

f. Examination of the rules of procedure in gathering and compiling the statistics. A census or vital registration requires very detailed preparation, and these rules (together with the standards of classification employed) may reveal various inadequacies. Moreover, these provisions are effective only as far as they are followed, and so the administrative arrangements for carrying them out are also important. Such evidence can be assessed before the data themselves. It yields results that are less definite; even if it appears that ample or insufficient attention was given to gathering of the statistics, further appraisal is needed before we can judge whether the data are defective.

## 3:4 The Extent of the Universe of Data

Any system of statistical records refers to some *universe* of cases, as explained in Chapter 2. The universe is the realm encompassed by the statistics, and is determined by the manner of performance of the statistical system as well as by the facts being observed (see 2:4).

First, it is specified by a definition. It may be "children born during the year" (the universe of registered births); people dying during the year, persons married for the first time during the year, persons married for the second time (or more), holders of official identity cards, people subject to military conscription, persons admitted to a hospital during the year. Nominally this definition may be any stated category in the population, the entire population, or the entire population *excepting* some stated category.

Though the definition may include everybody, the actual universe is never complete. In practice, some people are always missing. It is impracticable to include all cases which belong to the universe by definition: no statistical system functions perfectly. Some cases which ought to be covered according to the rules are always omitted. On the other hand, some cases may be recorded more than once.[5]

In addition, other groups of people may be omitted because they were not specially provided for. Some evade registration. Special plans are needed to enumerate infants, people who are traveling at the time of a census, transients who are staying at no permanent address, inmates of hospitals, prisons or other institutions, civilians living in military reservations, residents in isolated districts. Many are likely to be missed if these problems are overlooked. Thus the administrative organization of a census or registration system, and its budget, become an implicit part of the definition of the universe.

Owing to these factors, population records are always incomplete. This is the principal defect, and the target of most common testing procedures. The discrepancy is not subject to exact measurement. Most of the time it is necessary to be satisfied with a rather crude idea of its size. We can only ascertain the intended scope of the statistics and the procedures for their collection, and judge the degree to which these intentions were successfully carried out.

The next question about a set of data is to ask how nearly it represents its counterpart in the entire population. For some purposes the omission of cases may be immaterial; in studying the *composition* of a population, it is not in itself a disadvantage. What matters is that the cases omitted are not "typical." They do not represent all portions of the population equally, but tend to be concentrated in the "difficult" categories just mentioned. If these are the categories being studied, then the composition of the universe of data will not be the same as the composition of the actual population.

### 3:5 Practical Testing Procedures

Here we cannot be concerned with tests which depend on refer-

---

[5] Some biases are obvious from the nature of the records. People who travel or are away from home may be counted twice in a census, especially if no effort is made to prevent this. Records of rationing or family allowances are liable to double-counting. Tax records or military conscription rolls, on the other hand, tend to be less than complete.

ence to individual records or on a re-survey. They are beyond the resources of the ordinary researcher. The usual situation calls for examination of the data already available. As already mentioned (3:3), there is fundamentally just one way to do this — to devise comparisons of different statistics, when we believe that we know in advance what the result should be.

When the actual and the expected results disagree, we must decide where to attribute the discrepancy. Does it indicate a defect of the figure tested, or some fault of the standard of comparison? Or mistaken assumptions in the test? The answer depends to a large degree on the particular circumstances. Hence it is necessary to learn as much as possible about the peculiarities of the data and of the conditions they represent. This is the reason why there are so few general rules to guide the testing of population statistics. Thus a rather arbitrary element enters these tests, larger in some than in others.

For the sake of illustration, a few examples of concrete testing procedures are described in the following sections.

### 3:6 Testing the Adequacy of Total Numbers

A total figure, one for the entire population together, is very difficult to judge. It is accessible to only the cruder sorts of test. Obviously, if this one figure were the sole information, then nothing could be said about its accuracy. But this usually not the case. There are administrative reports and the detailed instructions to enumerators and registrars. These often reveal the amount of care and preparation devoted to the statistics, and may call attention to neglected aspects. Where special problems are known to exist, it is helpful to find out how they have been treated. Even a failure to recognize them is a clue to the quality of the data.[6]

Sometimes the total figures of a census can be checked by more specific means:

a. Comparison with the total population in an earlier or later census, showing the growth or decline during the interval (see also Chapter 7). Is the amount of growth "reasonable," in view of known circumstances? Is the annual rate of growth similar to the rate in earlier periods? If not, is there an apparent reason for the dif-

---

[6] For discussion of many of these problems on an international scale, see United Nations, Statistical Office and Population Division, *Population Census Methods* (New York, 1949) and United Nations, Statistical Office, *Principles for a Vital Statistics System* (New York, 1953).

ference (changing economic or health conditions, migrations of people
in or out, or changes of birth rates)? Is the observed change consistent with the net gains and losses by birth, death and migration between the two censuses?

     b. Examination of the population totals of subdivisions or
districts of a country. Are they distributed in accord with known
facts about the country? Comparing their growth between censuses,
does the pattern of gains or losses seem inconsistent with their probable vital rates or with the recent history of migration within the
country? Do birth rates and death rates computed with these figures
seem reasonable, or are some suspiciously high or low?

     c. Comparison with other data or estimates for the country's
subdivisions. The census population should be more comprehensive
than other statistical sources; for this reason it comes under some
doubt when it yields a *smaller* figure. Other sources also contain
biases, of course, and a rough degree of correspondence is usually
the best to be expected. Where a census and register of population
are kept side by side, fairly independent of each other, they provide
an excellent mutual test of consistency which may reveal defects in
both.

     Some total figures of registered events can be given similar
scrutiny:

     a. There are many specific incentives or deterrents to
registering vital events, to be found in the ordinary circumstances
of life in a country. Would registration of births help to prove children's eligibility to attend school? (Note that this would be little or
no encouragement to register babies who died soon after birth.) Are
these records a basis for military conscription, or for family assistance allowances, or taxation? Are there health regulations which
discourage the reporting of a death from an infectious disease?

     b. Do crude birth and death rates appear plausible for
smaller subdivisions of a country? Wide variations may signify uneven registration in different places. (Note that they may also indicate uneven quality of census data from place to place; there must
be some independent basis for judging these two sources.) Is any
trend of rates apparent; and if so, does it accord with expectation
(see 3:11)?

     Even total figures depend to some extent on standards of defi-
nition. As explained in Chapter 1, a census may enumerate people
in the place of usual or "permanent" residence ("de jure population"), or at the place where they are at the time of enumeration
("de facto population"). The two standards yield slightly different
figures. Obviously the discrepancy is greater in the subdivisions of

a country than in the country as a whole.  By the first standard, people who have moved to another district may be included in the census population where they lived before (and sometimes in *both* places, being counted twice).  Births or deaths among these people are sometimes attributed to one place, and sometimes to the other. In such cases, the registration does not apply to quite the same universe of people as the census in each district.  Vital rates computed from these data will be distorted; not seriously, however, unless a large part of the population in a particular district or city is affected.[7]

Total numbers do not permit a very thorough testing of statistics.  But analysis of the data faces the same limitation — the less the information, the less that can be said, and the handicap is therefore not very great.  Nevertheless it is worth while to find out as much as possible at this stage.  Even if the results later appear trivial, they may help to avoid costly mistakes.

The only way to get a more adequate appraisal is to utilize the statistics of distribution of characteristics in the population.  Some examples are shown in the following sections.

### 3:7  Expected Distribution by Sex

It is generally safe to assume that people are reported correctly by sex, even if the same data contain errors in the reporting of other characteristics.  Most vital processes have typical distributions by sex.  Birth, marriage and death occur in predictable proportions between men and women, and certain typical patterns by sex are observed in the composition of a population.  Failure to find these expected patterns is a signal to give further scrutiny to the data.

A population has nearly equal numbers of men and women (unless this balance has been changed by migration), and this should be reflected in census data.  At birth, boys are more numerous than girls. The initial excess of male births is offset in later life by higher rates of mortality among men than women (leading to an expected sex composition at different ages, shown in 3:9).  The sex ratio of a coun-

---

[7]Some countries attempt to remedy this defect by making two separate tabulations of registered events, one by the place of "residence" and one by the place where the birth or death occurred.  Birth and death rates can then be computed on either basis, whichever seems better matched to the census population.  See 5:15 and 6:13.  For a more detailed account of the possible tests of this nature, see United Nations, Population Branch, *Methods of Appraisal of Quality of Basic Data for Population Estimates* (New York, 1955), Chapters 1 and 2.

try's total population should normally be close to 100. *Within* the country, the sex ratios may vary considerably from place to place, owing to migration. For example, where men migrate more frequently than women, the in-migrant sections should have higher sex ratios, and the places with net loss of migrants should have rather low ratios. Because the predominant flow of migration is from country to city, sex ratios in urban areas normally resemble the sex ratios of the migrants, and sex ratios in rural areas do not.

The registration of births may be judged on similar grounds. As just mentioned, there are normally more male births than female births in a particular year. This holds true for subdivisions as well as for an entire country, unless the births are so few as to accentuate chance fluctuations. Extreme values of sex ratios of births are a warning that there may be defects of registration — possibly some births omitted, mis-reporting of stillbirths or early infant deaths. Just what defects are involved cannot be learned without further information.

Registered deaths should be approximately balanced between men and women, but the actual relation depends on the age and sex structure of the population besides the levels of age- and sex-specific mortality. Hence there is no definite advance expectation of what the pattern should be. (Age-specific death *rates*, however, show a very regular pattern of distribution by sex and age. See 5:7.)

The distribution of people or events by sex is often an insufficient criterion by itself. It is most valuable as an extra item permitting far more specific appraisal of other categories. Almost any other test becomes more sensitive if it is conducted separately for men and for women.[8]

### 3:8 Defects of Statistics by Age

Probably all defects are somehow linked to age. This makes age statistics especially important, for most analyses must also be performed according to age. In both instances the information is needed for essentially the same reasons. Many activities (and the characteristics associated with them) are unevenly distributed by age. Hence, age becomes an excellent means of separating the groups of people to be studied. Also, age groups are the only means of identifying a particular cohort of people in the statistics of different years; and this is often necessary in both appraisal and analysis of data (see 3:9 and 8:7).

---

[8] For example, see C. L. Pan, "The Population of Libya," *Population Studies,* Vol. 3, pp. 100-106, June, 1949.

Fortunately many of the defects are evident immediately on inspection of detailed data. The main features of these data are illustrated in Chart 3:1, where the male population of Venezuela in the census of 1950 is plotted by single year of age. Viewed differently, the figures represent the survivors of each year's batch of male births during the last several decades.[9] The census was dated November 26; the actual population under age one therefore must have been born between December 1949 and November 1950 (or, nearly all during 1950), the group age one nearly all in 1949, age two in 1948, and so on. In the upper part of Chart 3:1 are shown the corresponding yearly numbers of registered births, for comparison.[10]

The flow of births into a population fluctuates from year to year, and this should be reflected in some unevenness of the population data by age. But some of the fluctuation shown in Chart 3:1 is inconsistent with the history of annual registered births in the preceding period. Obviously, too many people were reported as "age 5," "age 10," and "age 12." Even before the period represented by registered births in the chart, the ages ending in "0" and "5" seem to have an excess of population, and several even-numbered ages too.

These concentrations of people at regular intervals — sometimes called "heaping" — are a very common result of inaccurate declaration of age. They are conspicuous by the strong preference or avoidance that is shown for certain numbers. Preference is sometimes noticed for certain ages of special legal or ceremonial significance — the lowest legal working age, the minimum voting age, age of legal majority, the age of eligibility to receive retirement pensions. The fluctuations are naturally greater in countries (or population groups within countries) where precise determination of age is not important in everyday affairs.[11]

---

[9]There are different standards for reckoning age, and this is one of the difficulties of using the statistics of various countries. As explained in Chapter 1, the recommended international standard defines age as the number of full years elapsed since birth, which corresponds to the simple criterion of "age at last birthday." This is being adopted in increasing numbers of countries. It encounters obvious difficulties when applied where calendar systems do not establish years of equal length.

[10]Each year's registration of births, in this case, covers approximately the 12-month period before the census date. Otherwise the data of births would have to be separated by month (or by quarter of the year) in order to match the 12-month period preceding the census date.

[11]Many factors probably contribute to defects of age data — including false reports of age (given unintentionally or deliberately), mere careless-

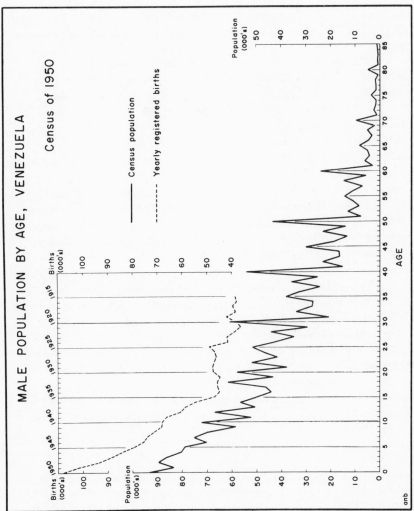

Chart 3:1  Male population by age, Venezuela (1950).  Compared with past history of registered male births.

## 3:9  Tests of Census Age Statistics

Census data by single year of age provide the most sensitive test, for they are detailed enough to put a strain on the accuracy of data. However, this material is too cumbersome for use in most problems of analysis, which are conducted on the basis of 5-year age groups. (The chief exception is the construction of life tables, where the detailed data are often used with special modifications to smooth over irregularities of distribution.)

Without access to the original records, there are only a few ways of looking for defects. Variations of procedure are possible (or even necessary) according to the peculiarities of a set of data.

a. Inspection of the age distribution. Its correct shape, of course, cannot be fully predicted. We expect the groups to be generally larger at younger ages, slightly irregular from one age to the next but without pronounced peaks and troughs at regular intervals. Chart 3:1 locates at a glance some of the worst errors of age reporting in Venezuela. But with such detailed examination, or indeed with any type of test, we cannot be sure to find *all* the important defects, nor do more than guess at their size.[12] In particular, single-year age statistics give clear signs of incorrect reporting of ages, but a rather poor indication of people omitted from enumeration (unless they were very numerous and very much concentrated by age).

These defects are disturbing when we think of using the data in the conventional 5-year groups. The "heaping" of people in Chart 3:1 is most pronounced at ages ending in "5" and "0." Some of these people probably have reported their ages too high, and some too low. This means that age distributions are faultiest in the neighborhood of the *boundaries* of the 5-year age groupings. Some of these errors are avoided by using larger age intervals. But some are not: part of the group enumerated at ages 30-34 (for example) actually belongs in the lower group 25-29, and part belongs to the next higher group 35-39.

---

ness by census enumerators, and systematic omitting or double-counting of people of certain ages. So many different motives are involved, and the information about them is so speculative, that little could be gained here by further general discussion. For a very interesting study of census statistics, where special attention has been given to this subject, see G. Mortara, *Les erreurs dans les déclarations de l'âge dans les recensements brésiliens de 1940 et 1950* (Rio de Janeiro, 1953).

[12] Special measures have been developed to summarize the extent of incorrectly reporting ages ending in some preferred number ("0", "2", "5",

In order to look further, it is necessary to make some assumptions about the nature of the errors. The data for Chart 3:1 include the following figures:

| Age | Men Counted by Census | Average, Ages 29-31 | Ratio: (Age 30/Average) |
|---|---|---|---|
| 29 | 29,203 ⎫ | | |
| 30 | 60,817 ⎬ | 37,005 | 1.643 |
| 31 | 20,994 ⎭ | | |
| Total, 29-31 | 111,014 | | |

If we assume that the "heaping" at age 30 came entirely from people who were really age 29 or 31, then the actual number of people age 30 might be estimated (subject to possible error) by the average of the three adjoining groups, as shown in this example (1/3 × 111,014 = 37,005). A rough measurement of the degree of "heaping" at age 30 is the ratio of the observed size of this group to the estimated size (60,817/37,005 = 1.643). In the absence of "heaping," we might expect a ratio of about 1.0. This ratio can be calculated for any age, though it is not advisable under age 10 (where omissions are probably greater). It is too specific, however, neglecting any other type of error[13], and taking no account of people who were omitted altogether.

---

or other digit) throughout the range of ages in a population. See R. J. Myers, "Errors and Bias in the Reporting of Ages in Census Data," *Transactions of the Actuarial Society of America*, Vol. 41, p. 395, October 1940; also described in United Nations, Population Branch, *Methods of Appraisal of Quality of Basic Data for Population Estimates* (New York, 1955). Though ingenious, these devices are of rather limited and special interest. They summarize a large amount of information in one index, which facilitates comparisons among different populations. But they show practically nothing about the particular pattern of these defects in one population. For most purposes we are not interested in an index of "heaping" through the *entire* age distribution, for we do not analyze it as a whole, but in parts.

[13] Some people who reported age 30 may have been really age 28 or age 32, or farther away. Furthermore, a few people of age 30 may have reported themselves at some other age. This very limited approach to the

A slightly different scheme is more useful, when applied to broader intervals of age. The "true" size of a 5-year age group is first estimated by the average of the two adjoining groups. The ratio of an enumerated age group (for example, ages 30-34) to the average of the two adjoining groups (ages 25-29 and 35-39) roughly measures the deviation from this "expected" number. Being less detailed, it reveals only rather gross defects. Such defects are often the most important, especially in preparing to study other characteristics of 5-year age groups. A few of these ratios enable us to examine the entire set of age statistics. The "age ratios" for the population of Japan (see Table 3:1) fluctuate very slightly from a value of 1.0, confirming the known excellent quality of age statistics in Japanese censuses. This test probably is more sensitive to the *omission* of cases from one age group than to errors in the reporting of age; the test gives little weight to the errors, and some of them (as just mentioned above) do not extend beyond the 5-year intervals. Older people appear to make larger mistakes in reporting their ages, and there the test is sensitive to defects of both kinds. However, deviations may be attributable not only to faulty data, but also to the impact of actual events on some age group (chiefly losses due to war, or gains or losses by migration).[14]

Sex ratios usually follow a typical pattern by age. Owing to the excess of males at birth and their higher mortality in later years, males generally are more numerous among children, and are outnumbered by females at older ages. In 5-year age groups, sex ratios normally should progress gradually from high to low with increasing age, as in Table 3:1. An erratic pattern of sex ratios or "age ratios" is often a sign of defects located in certain sex or age groups, or affecting some groups more than others. An exceptional sex ratio does not

---

problem of defects is the basis of the smoothing procedures employed in actuarial calculations. They spread the peaks and troughs of the age distribution among neighboring ages, achieving a regular and "smooth" progression of numbers from age to age. These modified data are convenient to work with, but there is no assurance that the distribution is more accurate than it was before (see 4:13).

[14] There are a great many factors to be considered in interpreting these "age ratios." See United Nations, Population Division, "Accuracy Tests for Census Age Distributions Tabulated in Five-Year and Ten-Year Groups," [United Nations] *Population Bulletin* No. 2, pp. 59-79, October 1952; and an attempt to refine their use in a particular situation, in A. J. Coale, "The Population of the United States in 1950 Classified by Age, Sex, and Color — a Revision of Census Figures," *Journal of the American Statistical Association*, Vol. 50, pp. 16-54, March 1955.

## TABLE 3:1

## "AGE RATIOS" AND SEX RATIOS BY AGE
### Computed from Census Population of Japan, 1935

| (1) | (2) | (3) | (4) | (5) | (6) | (7) |
|---|---|---|---|---|---|---|
| | Population | | Age Ratios[a] | | Sex | Sex Ratios, |
| Age | Males | Females | Males | Females | Ratios | Tokyo City |
| 0-4 | 4,714,001 | 4,614,500 | | | 102 | 103 |
| 5-9 | 4,303,263 | 4,228,156 | 1.002 | 1.004 | 102 | 102 |
| 10-14 | 3,876,774 | 3,808,473 | 1.013 | 1.013 | 102 | 108 |
| 15-19 | 3,350,713 | 3,290,204 | .969 | .962 | 102 | 122 |
| 20-24 | 3,036,783 | 3,034,288 | 1.009 | 1.036 | 100 | 114 |
| 25-29 | 2,670,248 | 2,569,835 | .986 | .972 | 104 | 112 |
| 30-34 | 2,379,492 | 2,253,145 | .995 | .996 | 106 | 115 |
| 35-39 | 2,093,446 | 1,952,400 | 1.010 | 1.003 | 107 | 120 |
| 40-44 | 1,767,627 | 1,638,384 | .959 | .943 | 108 | 121 |
| 45-49 | 1,591,179 | 1,521,655 | 1.003 | .992 | 105 | 116 |
| 50-54 | 1,404,376 | 1,428,499 | .987 | 1.007 | 98 | 107 |
| 55-59 | 1,255,092 | 1,316,045 | 1.081 | 1.078 | 95 | 99 |
| 60-64 | 916,820 | 1,013,791 | .973 | .978 | 90 | 90 |
| 65-69 | 630,008 | 757,084 | .961 | .988 | 83 | 76 |
| 70-74 | 394,223 | 519,200 | .922 | .949 | 76 | 67 |
| 75-79 | 224,829 | 336,975 | | | 67 | 55 |
| 80 and over | 125,259 | 237,381 | | | 53 | 41 |
| Total, all ages | 34,734,133 | 34,520,015 | | | 101 | 110 |

[a] An "age ratio" is a ratio of an enumerated age group to the average of its two adjoining age groups (see text).

Source: Japan, Census of 1935.

indicate whether to look for the cause in the numbers of males or females. The regularity of sex ratios by age (Column 6 of Table 3:1) is also disturbed by war or migration, even when the data are not defective. Sex ratios of Japanese in Tokyo City, for example, are different from those of the entire country, because a great many of the young adults were migrants from other sections of the country, and predominantly male (Column 7 of Table 3:1).

      b. Comparison of the same cohort of people, enumerated in two censuses. The people of ages 20-24 in 1940 belonged to the same group, or "cohort,"[15] of births as the people aged 30-34 in 1950. The cohort was smaller at the later date, because some had died.[16] (Note that this information can be taken from ordinary census age distributions, but the use of 5-year age groups means that the censuses must be separated by five years or some multiple of five years.) The data showing change in the size of cohorts may be examined directly, or by means of an estimate of the expected loss of persons in the intervening period. These two alternatives ("A" and "B") are illustrated in Table 3:2. In both cases, the censuses are 10 years apart, and so the people are 10 years older at the later date. As usual, it is preferable to treat men and women separately.

      With census data for Egypt, the ratio of each cohort's size in 1947 to its size in 1937 is computed directly in Column 4 of Table 3:2. These ratios represent the change from all causes; insofar as they represent survival of the risks of mortality, they should fit a more or less standard pattern (described in 4:1): *high* in the younger ages (except in the first few years, not even shown in Table 3:2), gradually decreasing in later life (as fewer people succeed in surviving the 10-year period between censuses). Any pronounced fluctuation − especially a value greater than 1.0 − is inconsistent with the expected pattern of mortality. The pattern itself can be predicted only in its general form, and is only a rough criterion.

      Alternatively, if an appropriate life table is available,[17] the comparison can be more convenient and precise. Survival ratios for

---

[15] A *cohort* is the group of people who were born during some specified period. The term "cohort" is just a convenient way of referring to this group later in life. For example, see 4:1.

[16] But if some members have emigrated, or if immigrants of these ages have arrived between the censuses, the relative size of the cohort will be affected. At most ages, the influence of mortality is more important.

[17] A life table is a conventional device for representing mortality, and is explained at some length in Chapter 4. An "appropriate" life table, in

## TABLE 3:2
## COMPARISON OF THE SIZE OF MALE COHORTS
## AT TWO CENSUS DATES
## EGYPT, 1937 and 1947

(A cohort is the group of people born during a given period, identified in a census as an age group.)

| (1) | A. Ratios of Cohort Size | | | B. Earlier Size of Cohorts (1937) estimated from later size (1947) | | |
|---|---|---|---|---|---|---|
| (1) | (2) | (3) | (4) | (5) | (6) | (7) |
| Age | Census Population 1937 | Census Population 1947[a] (By ages in 1937) | Ratios of Cohort Size (3)/(2) | Survival Ratios[b] ($\frac{L_{x+10}}{L_x}$) | Estimated Size of Age Groups 1937 (3)/(5) | Ratio:[c] (2)/(6) |
| 0-4 | 1,021,900 | 1,142,332 | 1.118 | | | |
| 5-9 | 1,107,879 | 984,033 | .888 | .88036 | 1,117,762 | .991 |
| 10-14 | 1,030,949 | 677,765 | .657 | .88945 | 762,437 | 1.352 |
| 15-19 | 713,185 | 685,730 | .962 | .90487 | 757,821 | .941 |
| 20-24 | 539,659 | 620,074 | 1.149 | .90530 | 684,938 | .788 |
| 25-29 | 616,659 | 659,225 | 1.069 | .88327 | 746,346 | .826 |
| 30-34 | 557,875 | 569,069 | 1.020 | .84004 | 677,431 | .824 |
| 35-39 | 600,423 | 428,502 | .714 | .78160 | 548,237 | 1.095 |
| 40-44 | 474,768 | 421,222 | .887 | .73330 | 574,420 | .827 |
| 45-49 | 345,106 | 171,105 | .496 | .70092 | 244,115 | 1.414 |
| 50-54 | 330,313 | 252,020 | .763 | .66571 | 378,573 | .888 |
| 55-59 | 144,706 | 83,788 | .579 | .61922 | 135,312 | 1.069 |
| 60-64 | 201,702 | 107,787 | .534 | .55424 | 194,477 | 1.037 |
| 65-69 | 72,281 | 23,443 | .324 | .46682 | 50,218 | 1.439 |
| 70-74[d] | 100,850 | 34,834 | .345 | .38753 | 89,887 | 1.122 |

[a]The 1947 census population has been advanced 10 years of age, in order to match the 1937 population in Column 2. Persons of undeclared age have not been distributed by age. No allowance is made here for the apparent over-enumeration of Egypt's population in 1947.

[b]Survival ratios are computed from the life table by M.A. El-Badry, in *Milbank Memorial Fund Quarterly*, July 1955. Here the ratios $(L_{x+10}/L_x$, which normally go forward with time) are *divided* into the 1947 population, in order to give them a *backward* effect.

[c]The ratios of Column 7 measure the size of the 1937 census population in relation to the "expected" population (Column 6). A ratio of 1.0 indicates "perfect" correspondence. A higher ratio indicates an "excess" in 1937; a lower ratio indicates a "deficit" in 1937 (as compared with 1947, by means of this life table).

[d]This is the last cohort shown separately (ages 80-84) for 1947. Above this age the available data were published as "age 85 and over."

any cohort are easily computed from a life table; they express the relative change in each cohort's size attributable to mortality while it is passing from one age to the other. Going forward 10 years, the population aged 10-14 in 1937, multiplied by the survival ratio (10-14 to 20-24) yields an estimate of the number expected to survive (aged 20-24) at the same date in 1947; this estimate is then compared with the number actually enumerated in 1947. We may also go backward in time: the census population aged 20-24 in 1947, *divided* by the survival ratio (10-14 to 20-24) gives an estimate of the number who were alive at the same date in 1937. Survival ratios apply equally well either forward or backward; the example in Table 3:2 goes backward from 1947 to 1937.[18]

A set of survival ratios, one for each age group, between 1937 and 1947 is shown in Column 5, Table 3:2. They are computed from a life table prepared for Egypt by a special procedure.[19] By a reversal of their normal application (dividing instead of multiplying), they are used to estimate the former size of each group or cohort, as just described, in order to test the census data in 1937. Let us make the usual assumption — not always justified — that the more recent census is more reliable. For each age group, a ratio of this 1937 census population to the estimated figure (Column 7) expresses the relative agreement or disagreement of this 1937 census population with the population "expected" on the basis of the 1947 census. Perfect agreement would be indicated by a ratio of unity, 1.0.

The result of this test is to show some marked inconsistencies

---

this instance, is one that is believed to represent reasonably well the age-specific mortality rates of the period between censuses. Obviously this belief is largely a matter of subjective judgment. Since a life table must sometimes be borrowed from another population for this purpose, there may be little evidence to aid in deciding how appropriate it is. See 5:4.

[18]"Survival ratios" are computed from the $L_x$ values of a life table (values of "$L$" for each age "$x$"). For an explanation of these terms and their meanings, see 5:4. A ratio to estimate 1947's survivors from the size of a cohort in 1937 is computed $L_{x+10}/L_x$, going forward with time. A ratio to estimate the size of a cohort in 1937 from its size in 1947 is computed $L_x/L_{x+10}$, going backward. Here, "$x$" refers to the middle year of an age group in 1947 (the date of the later census) — age 12 for the group 10-14, age 22 for the group 20-24, and so on; "$x+10$" means simply "12+10" or 22, and so on. See the discussion of the life table in Chapter 4.

[19]See M. A. El-Badry, "Some Demographic Measurements for Egypt Based on the Stability of Census Age Distributions," *Milbank Memorial Fund Quarterly*, Vol. 33, pp. 268-305, July 1955.

in these two censuses of Egypt. In Column 4, the ratios of change in
cohort size fluctuate to some considerable degree, and especially for
the groups aged 10-14, 20-24 and 45-49 in 1937. A few groups in
1937 were actually found to be *larger* in 1947, an impossibility if
both censuses were correct. Note that one exceptional ratio in Column 4 is usually accompanied by opposite fluctuation in adjoining
ratios. These ratios may be compared with the corresponding survival ratios from the life table, in Column 5; they should be approximately the same, age for age, but there are many discrepancies.
(More pronounced inconsistencies appear in the data for women.) The
fluctuations are more noticeable in Column 7; *these* ratios should
tend toward a presumed norm of unity (see Table 3:2). It is noteworthy that the majority are below 1.0, suggesting that the enumeration of the cohorts was smaller in 1937, larger in 1947.[20]

For a more detailed and sensitive test, cohorts can be identified by single year of age instead of by 5-year groups, and compared
in the same manner. Men of age 22 in 1947 were age 12 at the census date of 1937; those age 21 were formerly age 11, and so on.
This is too detailed for many purposes. However, it is often the only
basis for checking the census enumeration in the younger ages. The
census population 0-4 is nearly always more deficient than the
people counted at ages 10-14. The census population of ages, 10,
11, 12, 13 and 14 (and an appropriate life table) may provide a very
satisfactory estimate of the former numbers of small children, at each
age, following the procedure shown in Table 3:2; where the earlier
census fails to agree, it is usually wrong. This procedure can give a
good indication of the nature of the defect, as shown in Table 3:4 below. (The enumeration between ages 0-4 may also be tested by
means of registered births, as described below.)

Though these tests provide the most exact form of comparison,
unfortunately their meaning is never wholly clear. We expect both
censuses to enumerate a particular cohort consistently at two dates;
the ratios of Column 7 in Table 3:2 should usually be close to 1.0.
When there are inconsistencies — as indicated by some of the ratios
of Table 3:2 — they do not identify the fault or its source. They may

---

[20]It appears that the census of 1947 was an over-enumeration — a
rare occurrence — as a result of a rationing survey which preceded it. Thus
each cohort was probably inflated beyond its correct size in the age data of
this census. This conclusion is supported by a remarkable similarity of the
biases of age reporting in Egypt's five past censuses, suggesting that the
1947 census was not an exception to the rule. For a critique of these data
on the basis of the meager information available, see M. A. El-Badry, *op. cit.*

be due to discrepancies between the censuses (people omitted in one who were counted in the other, or inconsistent declarations of age at the two dates).[21] The estimated effect of mortality may be inaccurate, perhaps through an unwise choice of life table; but such an error is likely to be spread among many age groups, not concentrated in a few.[22]

The chief disadvantage of this test is that it also measures *migration.*[23] Migration is typically age- and sex-selective, most frequent among young adult men. A net movement of migrants entering or leaving the population will alter the size of a few cohorts and bring the two censuses into sharp disagreement, irrespective of the quality of data. It is always necessary to ask whether an unexpected result reflects a gain or loss of migrants. (Of course it is possible that migration and inconsistent reporting may coincide; in this case, migration may offset or accentuate defects of the data, and be indistinguishable.) However, most migrants are concentrated in a few age groups, and thus do not confuse the results of the test for the rest of the population.

c. Comparing the enumeration of children with the registration of their births. In a crude manner this was already done in Chart 3:1, where the two sources evidently do not quite agree: the erratic age distribution of population figures is not matched by fluctuations in the yearly numbers of registered births. This comparison can be improved by means of an appropriate life table,[24] provided that the census data are available by single year of age.

---

[21] An inconsistency does not reveal *which* census is in fault. Usually the census which produces a larger enumeration is assumed to be more nearly "complete." But this assumption may be wrong, for undoubtedly some people have been reported at the wrong age, or counted more than once. Even if the test shows the two censuses to be perfectly consistent, it does not prove that they are correct, because both censuses may contain identical or similar errors. Some errors of age declaration (e.g., favoring "0" or "5" digits) tend to repeat themselves in censuses that are 10 years apart.

[22] There are exceptions. War or epidemic between the censuses may have a greater effect on certain cohorts, overlooked by the estimates of mortality.

[23] Indeed it is one of the principal ways of estimating the flow of migrants. See 8:7.

[24] Here, an "appropriate" life table is one which approximates the actual level of mortality of infants and young children; it may not be the same life table that is appropriate at other ages. A life table constructed

The procedure is fundamentally the same as before: with the life table we estimate how many of the children in a cohort died between the time of birth and the time of the census. Again males and females should be treated separately. Here it is generally safe to ignore gains or losses of migrants, for children of these ages seldom migrate in large numbers. With strict adherence to the recommended standard for reckoning age, each age group in the census should correspond to a cohort of births. The change of each cohort's size between the time of birth and the time of the census can be estimated by a survival ratio, computed from the life table.[25]

Table 3:3 illustrates the latter kind of calculation. The registered male births in Venezuela from 1937 to 1941, times the survival ratios from the life table of 1941-42, yield an "expected" population at each year of age between 0 and 4. These are not realistic estimates of the population in 1941, though such estimates are sometimes possible. This is a test of consistency between registered births and census population, which are brought into closer correspondence by means of the life table.[26] Hence it is at the same time a test of both. In the first place, it reveals that the registration of births was far from complete before 1941. Their survivors (Column 4) were exceeded by the people actually enumerated at the end of 1941 (Column 5); the census population ages 2-4 was 167,737, or 10 per cent more than the number 152,958 expected from the registered births. In the second place, it suggests that the census population is deficient at ages 0-1, for in these instances the "expected" numbers (Column 4) were larger. Undoubtedly the registration of births was being improved during these years, but there is no indication that the gain was so rapid as to reverse the results of the test at these youngest ages. In other words, the test discloses defects in both sets of data.

---

from the data of the same country is often deficient in representing mortality at these ages, even though it may be adequate at other ages.

[25] To estimate the number of births from the census population, age $x$, compute the ratio $l_0/L_x$. To estimate the expected census population at age $x$ from the registered births, compute the ratio $L_x/l_0$. In most life tables, $l_0$ is a standard 100,000; $L_x$ is the value of "$L$" for each age, "$x$," corresponding to the census figures. For an explanation of these terms and the principle of these estimates, see 5:4.

[26] This life table itself prevents the test from being very exact, for it is known to be deficient in representing Venezuela's infant mortality. With better mortality data this comparison can become the basis for revising either the birth registration or the census statistics.

As a test of consistency, this procedure serves equally well to appraise either birth statistics or census data. Obviously it does not indicate all defects. Nor can it distinguish very clearly among defects, for the survival ratios also may contribute some inexactitude to the comparison. Again the factor of personal judgment tends to prevail in interpreting the results. As shown in this example, one need not attribute the entire discrepancy to one set of data.

### TABLE 3:3

### COMPARISON OF CENSUS DATA WITH REGISTERED BIRTHS
### VENEZUELA, 1937-1941
(Males only)

| (1) | (2) | (3) | (4) | (5) | (6) | (7) |
|---|---|---|---|---|---|---|
| (Year of Birth) | Registered Male Births | Survival Ratio | "Expected" Population December, 1941 (2) x (3) | Census Population December, 1941 | Ratio (5)/(4) | (Age in 1941) |
| 1941 | 69,208 | $L_0/l_0 = .91076$ | 63,032 | 64,957 | 1.031 | 0 |
| 1940 | 68,738 | $L_1/l_0 = .85582$ | 58,827 | 56,269 | .957 | 1 |
| 1939 | 66,680 | $L_2/l_0 = .83158$ | 55,450 | 59,006 | 1.064 | 2 |
| 1938 | 61,009[a] | $L_3/l_0 = .81617$ | 49,794 | 55,942 | 1.123 | 3 |
| 1937 | 59,209[a] | $L_4/l_0 = .80585$ | 47,714 | 52,789 | 1.106 | 4 |
| | | | 152,958 | 167,737 | 1.097 | 2-4 |

[a]Male births are estimated from total births, using the proportion .51496 male in 1939-1941.

Note: The births represent approximately 12-month periods preceding the census date, which was December 7, 1941. If the census were farther removed from the beginning or end of the year, these birth data would have to be rearranged in order to correspond to the groups of children enumerated by age.

Sources: Venezuela, Seventh Census of Population (1941), Volume VIII, Table 2. E. Michalup, "The Construction of the First Venezuelan Life Tables, 1941-1942," Estadística, No. 30, 1951.

The age group 0-4 is notoriously difficult to enumerate. Among them the most difficult of all are infants, some of whom are likely to be missed altogether. Some infants are reported as age 1; a census population may have more children age 1 than the number expected from registered births. In addition, some children age 1 may be reported as age 2. It is safer to compare the population ages 2, 3, and 4 (or the total of these) and the respective annual numbers of births, as in Table 3:3.

Since there are undoubtedly deficiencies in both census and registration, a separate standard is desirable. Another census was taken in Venezuela in November of 1950. Of course it too has defects; but they are not likely to be the same defects in the same cohorts, nine years after the earlier census of 1941. With the 1950 census figures for boys of the ages 9, 10, 11, 12 and 13, and survival ratios from the life table of 1941-42,[27] we can calculate the approximate size of these cohorts nine years before. This is done in Table 3:4. The "expected" population between ages 0-4 may be unduly large, because the life table (based on the heavy mortality at the beginning of the period) exaggerates the numbers who had died, and restores too many (in Column 5). This test corroborates fairly well the numbers of children enumerated between ages 2-4 in 1941 (they are very close to the "expected" population). It also confirms the finding that the enumeration of children was deficient at ages 0-1 (compare the last two lines of Column 5 and Column 6, in Table 3:4).

The latest census, however, is often the one that is in question. In such a case, this corroboration is impossible. A rough guess can be made on the basis of the age distribution of the column of $"L_x"$ values in an appropriate life table (see 5:5). In countries of at least moderately high fertility, if the proportion of children 0-4 in the population fails to exceed the proportion of the corresponding $L_x$ values $(_5L_0)$ to the total of the $L_x$ column (or $T_0$), the census is almost certainly deficient at these ages.

---

[27]Here again survival ratios are calculated from the $L_x$ values of the life table. In this case, to carry the children forward from 1941 to 1950, the ratios would be $L_{x+9}/L_x$; to carry the children backward from 1950 to a given age "x" in 1941, the survival ratios are $L_x/L_{x+9}$. This latter form is used in Table 3:4. It should be noted that the life table is slightly out of date by 1950, when the level of mortality had fallen. Consequently the survival ratios represent too high a level of mortality; the "expected" size of these cohorts in 1941 (Column 5) is probably too large. Nevertheless the pattern of omissions in 1941 is fairly clear from this test.

## 3:10   Defects of Vital Registration

Vital registration also refers to some universe. This may include virtually the entire population. But it may exclude substantial portions — either fairly definite categories not provided for in the plans of registration (see 3:4 above), or an indefinite portion omitted through laxity of enforcement. The excluded portions sometimes differ for different kinds of events. Births may be more thoroughly registered than deaths; this is the main flaw of infant death rates, as explained in 5:8. Both may surpass the registration of marriages or migration, even though all these records are kept by the same system.

### TABLE 3:4

### COMPARISON OF COHORTS ENUMERATED IN 1941 (AGES 0-4) AND IN 1950 (AGES 9-13) IN VENEZUELA

(Males only)

| (1) | (2) | (3) | (4) | (5) | (6) |
|---|---|---|---|---|---|
| (Age in 1950) | Census Population December, 1950 | Survival Ratio[a] | (Age in 1941) | "Expected" Population December, 1941 (2) x (3) | Census Population December, 1941 |
| 9 | 58,435 | $L_0/L_9$ = 1.16419 | 0 | 68,029 | 64,957 |
| 10 | 71,992 | $L_1/L_{10}$ = 1.09794 | 1 | 79,043 | 56,269 |
| 11 | 52,434 | $L_2/L_{11}$ = 1.07040 | 2 | 56,123 | 56,290 |
| 12 | 66,842 | $L_3/L_{12}$ = 1.05394 | 3 | 70,447 | 59,006 |
| 13 | 50,864 | $L_4/L_{13}$ = 1.04397 | 4 | 53,100 | 55,942 |
| | | | 0-1 | 147,072 | 121,226 |
| | | | 2-4 | 179,670 | 171,238 |

[a]Survival ratios are computed from the life table of 1941-42 (see Source for Table 3:3).

Sources:   Same as Table 3:3.

It is likely that some districts of a country have better registration than others.

Most vital statistics are analyzed in relation to census data, not alone. Hence they should generally be appraised in relation to census data, for no vital-statistics rate can be accurate unless these two universes are well matched.

Vital registration is subject to many of the same errors as a census enumeration. Any of the information about personal characteristics may be incorrect — the age, sex, occupation, marital status, nationality or ethnic background, or other items.[28]  The events seem *more* susceptible to certain kinds of errors. They may be incorrectly classified — some "live" births as stillbirths, some second marriages as first marriages, some deaths as emigrants. Registration is carried on as a by-product of an administrative routine, not primarily for the sake of the information. The accuracy of the information assumes a secondary importance.

Vital events also may be registered at the wrong place or time. If births are registered at a former residence of the parents (perhaps an ancestral home) and the parents are enumerated in some other place (perhaps a city or town where they live at the time of the census), the birth rates of both places will obviously be distorted — too high in one, and too low in the other.[29]  The *time* of occurrence is also subject to error. Many events are recorded late. When births are registered a year or more after they happened, they no longer match the original census data of parents; age-specific birth rates become distorted, for the universe of women, aged 20-24, for example, is no longer quite the same.[30]  A delay of registration also invites a distortion of rates by *place* of occurrence, as just mentioned above. These errors are often not large enough to be serious, at least not

---

[28] If the information were *consistent* in vital statistics and in a census (the same people making the same errors in both sets of records), the errors would have practically no effect on vital rates, and the problem could be ignored. To some extent this is the case, but the errors are not consistent enough to eliminate the problem.

[29] On the other hand, the opposite distortion is found if births are registered where they occur and parents are enumerated at some other place (see 6:13). Statistics of marriage and divorce are subject to the same defect in relation to the census population.

[30] See R. Jiménez Jiménez, *Exactitud del Registro de Nacimientos y Algunos Análisis Demográficos de Costa Rica* (San José, 1957).

large enough to be very serious in comparison with other defects; and
it is almost impossible to gauge the magnitude of their effect.[31]

### 3:11  Ways of Testing Vital Statistics

It is difficult to devise tests of vital registration. There are
fewer possible internal comparisons, for vital statistics are not collected at one time and do not all refer to the same universe. An independent standard is necessary, and this is usually a census (which
has its own defects). The two sets of data do not correspond closely
enough to permit many definite tests. And so in practice most items
of vital statistics are used with very little scrutiny. The mainstay of
common testing procedures is the distribution of registered events by
age and sex — compared either with some standard derived from a
census, or with some expected pattern of the events themselves.

The first step is to find out how the facts were registered — the
definitions, regulations, and reporting procedures. Vital registration
has little chance to succeed unless it is compulsory, and compulsion
is ineffectual (in securing good statistics) without a well-organized
control over the quality of the records. With regard to omissions, it
is reassuring to know whether childbirths receive medical attention
and whether permits are required before burials. Similar factors determine the accuracy of the registered information. It is more likely
to be consistent (for example, in the troublesome records of "live"
births) if the reporting is done by licensed physicians or midwives;
the information about "cause of death" is practically meaningless
without some medical diagnosis before burial. These are preliminary
inquiries, but they suggest what degree of skepticism is appropriate
in further examination of the data.

There are some fairly specific tests which may be applied to
the data themselves. Because most of them are aimed solely at omissions, they give only a limited appraisal of the data.

a. By inspecting the distributions of registered events, we
can sometimes judge whether they fit a "reasonable" pattern. Unfor-

---

[31] There are no positive tests that will reveal errors of this sort. Of
course, if birth rates or death rates by district follow a pattern contrary to
expectation (for example, low rural birth rates, high urban rates), this is a
warning that the data may be biased. But this is a poor criterion, for our
expectations in this realm are not very reliable. The statistical and administrative procedures of the country sometimes indicate what standards were
followed in compiling the data. Some countries publish special tables showing late registrations, by year of occurrence. It would be negligent not to
investigate this material before drawing conclusions from the figures.

tunately there is no very satisfactory criterion of what is a "reasonable" expectation; less so than with respect to census data. We rely chiefly on distributions by sex and age.

(1) With remarkable regularity, yearly numbers of births seem to be almost evenly divided by sex, boys being slightly more frequent than girls (subject to some fluctuation when the numbers are small, below a few thousand yearly births). Wide experience leads us to expect about 105 male to 100 female births. Otherwise the sex ratios hardly ever vary beyond a range of 102-108, and data which produce more extreme ratios are probably suspect. Registered deaths should be nearly balanced by sex, though this cannot be predicted with such assurance. If there are more women than men in the population, female deaths may be slightly in excess. Male deaths should exceed female deaths during infancy; more women than men die at advanced ages (because there are more women than men surviving at these ages). Since men and women must be married in equal numbers, this is not a real test of marriage statistics, which are more affected by failure to register some marriages altogether and perhaps by errors in the information recorded.[32] Men very often preponderate among migrants; but men and women are found in various proportions, depending on the circumstances.

(2) Registration statistics are also of uneven quality at different ages. Failure to register is more common at some ages than at others, and age itself is not accurately reported, especially among the very old and the very young. Here too there is a marked tendency to state ages in certain preferred numbers, producing uneven distributions of cases, with peaks and troughs at regular intervals. Such figures are not often available by single year of age. Even if they were, there is no definite expected pattern of distribution to serve as a standard. Often data for elderly people are so erratic that they cannot be used at all, even in 5-year age intervals.

There are gaps in the registration of infant deaths in every country. Undoubtedly these are larger where infant mortality is heavy; the same *percentage* of under-registration would forfeit up to 10 times as many death records under conditions of high mortality as under conditions of low mortality. There is no systematic way of

---

[32] The registration of these events may be checked against census data, but such checking is laborious and not very exact. See, for example, B. Benjamin and N. H. Carrier, "An Evaluation of the Quality of Demographic Statistics in England and Wales," *Proceedings of the World Population Conference, 1954* (Papers: Volume 4), New York, 1955.

measuring these deficiencies. Infants whose deaths go unregistered were probably not recorded as births. Hence infant death rates are usually too low, and neither figure can be tested by the other. Even the procedures of estimating the numbers of births from census data (see 3:9) become questionable.

Marriages, divorces and migration are rather concentrated in a small range of young adult ages. But this furnishes no standard for discriminating between good and poor data. In most instances the distribution is typical in general form, but highly variable in its details.

b. "Expected" patterns of vital rates. Since the objective is to find out what the vital rates are, it would be unsound to test the data by a preconception of what they ought to be. Nevertheless, vital rates sometimes display patterns that are self-evident anomalies, raising doubts about the accuracy of some of the data.

(1) Age-sex distribution. The distributions of births and deaths by age vary with the age and sex composition of the population as well as with the levels of birth and death rates by age and sex. Vital rates are more predictable. Despite some variation, birth rates have typical distributions by age (see Chart 6:1) and death rates by age and sex (2:14). It is better to compute birth rates and death rates by age (in 5-year intervals). Any sharp fluctuations in these rates are suspicious signs, especially at higher ages.

(2) Territorial distribution of vital rates. One should question this evidence when it seems inconsistent with known characteristics of the subdivisions of a country. A perverse distribution of death rates — high in prosperous and healthy districts, and low in backward or neglected areas — may reflect merely better statistics is the better places. If birth rates are high in cities and low in rural areas, the reason may be the same. The main currents of migration within a country are probably known to everyone, and the statistical evidence should not be wholly contradictory. In any country the registration is not everywhere equally thorough; the distribution of vital rates by subdivisions reflects to some extent the distribution of effort in keeping the records.

(3) Trends. The rates may be inconsistent with the trend of events (though it may be difficult to ascertain the true nature of the trend by any other means). If birth rates have risen when fertility has not greatly changed, the evidence is highly suspect. This is a very common result of improvements in the registration of births; however, it may also occur because census enumeration (which supplies the denominator of the birth rate) has deteriorated. The same progress in registration may cause death rates to rise, or

to obscure the extent of their actual decline. The quality of all population records is likely to shift with the passage of time, introducing
a multitude of distortions into the changes of vital rates. Contradic-
tions are sometimes apparent when trends are compared in different
portions of the population — districts or special groups. Changes of
age-specific death rates should show some consistency with the
known progress in public health (a program to control diseases of infancy, for example, having its principal effect on infant mortality).

  c. Testing vital statistics against census data. Such a
test contributes very little if we also intend to test the census by
comparison with the vital statistics. (Both, however, gain some corroboration if they are consistent.) In order to adopt the census as the
standard of accuracy, there should be some independent reason for be-
lieving it to be more dependable. It is worth repeating that these two
sets of data can provide the most exact comparisons that are available in any test.

  (1) The growth or decrease of population between two
censuses, as already explained, is entirely the result of intervening
vital events — births, deaths, and migration.[33] It provides a simple
and quick test of consistency of all four sets of data. The chief limitation is that it fails to indicate which one is the source of a possible discrepancy. If there has been little net migration in or out, the
comparison applies principally to the censuses and the registration of
births and deaths. In many countries the test can be reduced to these
terms, ignoring a small amount of migration. Births normally are not
over-registered; assuming that there is reason for confidence in the
census data, if the registered natural increase exceeds the amount of
growth between censuses, it probably signifies incomplete registration of deaths. If natural increase is less than the intercensal
growth, it probably indicates deficient registration of births. However, if the registration has missed about the same numbers of births
and of deaths, this test will fail to show any discrepancy; in this
respect its results are quite untrustworthy. This flaw is overcome
in the next test.

  (2) Change in the size of separate cohorts. Except by
net immigration at the same ages, a particular group or cohort of
people can only decrease in size from one census to the next. As
explained above (3:9), this change can be measured by comparing the

---

[33] It is of course confined to the period between the two censuses.
The registration data must be matched exactly to this period. The test is
procedurally identical with the example in 3:9, but its interpretation is different.

data of two censuses, identifying the members of the same cohort by
their ages at both times. Males and females are considered separately. The census data, if acceptable, indicate how many people were
lost from the cohort, independently of the registration of births. The
loss is composed of deaths and migrants; if the net flow of migrants
was slight, then this loss represents (approximately) the number of
deaths in the cohort, the standard f )r testing the registration of
deaths.[34]

It is hard to meet the requirements of data for this test.[35] Because people of the age group 30-34 in 1950 all became one year older
each year, most of their deaths in 1951 were between ages 31-35, and
32-36 in 1952, and so on.[36] Therefore, in order to make the comparison with census data, even by 5-year age groups, it is necessary to
have the death statistics classified by single year of age (or to estimate this distribution by interpolation). The test is then performed,
putting the burden of a discrepancy on the death statistics rather than
on the census data. Registered births can be tested in the same way
(preferably with a life table, or with adjustments of the registered
deaths below age 5).

It may be possible to avoid these problems. If comparisons of
two censuses have been conducted with satisfactory results by means
of a life table (as described in 3:9), the age-specific death rates
computed from vital statistics should be in rough agreement with the
corresponding death rates of the life table (see 4:10). (For purposes
of this test it would be reasonable to take an average of the age-

---

[34] Migrants can sometimes be incorporated into the test by means of
separate figures. Aside from their unreliability, migration data are seldom
available in sufficient detail. They must be tabulated by single year of age,
in exact correspondence with the registered deaths. Though this detail can
be achieved by interpolating in broader age groups, the usefulness of such
material soon becomes questionable; migration is usually tolerated as a disturbing factor, confined to a few age groups.

[35] See A. J. Jaffe, Handbook of Statistical Methods for Demographers
(Washington, D.C., 1951), Chapter 5.

[36] This is not quite correct, but a close enough approximation. Because the events are recorded throughout the year, some of them actually
refer to the adjoining cohort, not the exactly corresponding age group in the
census (which was taken at one time in the year). (See 4:10.) This discrepancy is a common problem in dealing with age statistics by single-year
intervals, but is negligible in 5-year groupings. The discrepancy grows to
significant size below age 5, where an adjustment must be made. See M.
Spiegelman, Introduction to Demography (Chicago, 1955), Chapter 5.

specific death rates at each age, at the beginning and the end of the period, in order to take account of change of mortality between the censuses.)

Following the same procedure, registered births in the period before a census can be tested against the census population by age. It is done exactly as illustrated in Table 3:3, though with a different interpretation of the results. It is advisable to have some independent reason for confidence in the census data as a standard of comparison.[37]

### 3:12 Revising Defective Data

It is sometimes possible to revise data that are known to be defective. We first need some standard of adjustment. This may be obvious from the nature of the data. Frequently, for example, a table contains some people of unknown or unreported age. The total figure (the "correct" one) is then larger than the number whose ages are stated. If the gap is not very large, the ratio of the total figure to the sum of persons of stated ages may be used to inflate the incomplete figures in all age groups (as shown in 2:16 and Table 2:6). This adjustment provides the correct total of persons, on the assumption that all cases were distributed just as were those of stated ages.

Any test that indicates the size of a defect can also furnish the basis for a revised figure. The revision is implicit in the test. For example, if the registration of births of a given year is found to be only 92 per cent complete, then the registered figure can be revised in one step: simply multiply it by $\dfrac{1}{.92}$. This yields the "correct" figure, by adding back the 8 per cent of the year's births that were presumably omitted. With a 95 per cent complete enumeration of infants, the census figure is multiplied by $\dfrac{1}{.95}$, thereby increasing it to the assumed 100 per cent. In general, if the degree of "completeness" (the proportion of actual cases that has been recorded) is measured by $R$, then the correct figure must be the observed figure times $\dfrac{1}{R}$.

There are certain objections to this course. In the first place, it presupposes a very simple source of all error, recognizing only the

[37] For an example employing registered deaths instead of a life table, see O. Cabello, "Integralidad del Registro de Nacimientos y Oportunidad de la Inscripción en Chile, 1920-1953," *Estadística* 14(51):302-308, June-July 1956.

omission of cases from the statistics. A brief acquaintance with the vagaries of population statistics shows that this is inexact. The revision may be ill-advised, owing to some flaw in the test. The preceding sections give ample illustration of this possibility. The adjustment may be useless, because it is confined to one table of data and cannot be applied to others, except by arbitrary assumption about the distribution of characteristics in the population. An adjusted table by age, for example, is of little or no help in revising the data of population by marital status or occupation. Raising the number of births does not answer the question of their distribution by age of parents. It is a considerable exaggeration to regard these crude and arbitrary revisions as "corrections."

But if the figures are used at all, the problem is not solved by leaving them unadjusted. If they are kept in their original form, this is tantamount to assuming that the facts are as indicated by the data. In any case we should recognize what assumption we are making, and convey this as clearly as possible in reporting the results. This is more essential than searching for the "correct" figure in every instance.

Moreover, a defective statistic may be preferable. With a registration of births that is 99 per cent complete and a census enumeration only 90 per cent complete, the birth rate would be 1.10 times its "correct" level, or 10 per cent too high. The crude birth rate would be more accurate if birth registration were more defective (that is, if it were comparable to the census data). In this case, a *revision* of the figure for registered births, making it 100 per cent complete, would only increase the error of the birth rate. The operations involved in adjusting data are so easily carried out that they can be applied without comprehension of their meaning. In this process they seem to nourish a sense of confidence that is generally unwarranted.

When there is doubt about the meaning of a contemplated revision, it is better not to adopt it. One solution is to make alternative calculations, showing the result of adopting or rejecting the revision. When the amount of adjustment rests on a subjective judgment, it is often helpful to calculate separate results based on extreme high and low assumptions about the defect. For example, the most extreme assumptions about the actual sex ratio of yearly births may have so little effect that the original figure remains as satisfactory as the revision.

The defects of statistics by age present a more serious problem. They involve an entire distribution over many categories. Short of drastic smoothing devices which produce a fictitious distribution,

there is little that can be done.  However, with access to detailed
tabulations (by single year of age) there is often an advantage in re-
constituting the 5-year groups so as to move the points of greatest
error (ages ending with "5" or "0") to the *center* of each group.
Thus, by re-grouping the data in categories of 8-12, 13-17, 18-22,
and so on, the major effect of poor age reporting is probably kept
within the respective 5-year groups.

This was done in a recent sample survey of fertility among
Indian women.  For Kolaba District (in the State of Bombay), the
following age-specific birth rates were reported for 1952:

| Age Group | Births per Person-Year |
|-----------|:---------------------:|
| 13-17 | .037 |
| 18-22 | .251 |
| 23-27 | .224 |
| 28-32 | .168 |
| 33-37 | .092 |
| 38-42 | .050 |
| 43-47 | .009 |

Birth rates, death rates and virtually any ratios or proportions by age
groups can be treated in this way.  In order to compare the results
with other data, it is necessary to return to the conventional groupings.

This is easily accomplished by interpolation, finding approximate values that lie between these numbers.  Interpolating between
age-specific birth rates is facilitated if we first *cumulate* these rates,
in the manner of computing a total fertility rate (see 2:18).  This is
done for these survey data in Table 3:5, where the birth rates (births
per person-year in each age group) are added from young to old (Column 3).[38]  With the cumulative values of Column 3, it is easy to interpolate values between them.  The simplest expedient is to assume
that the value for the age group 15-19 is mid-way between the recorded values for the groups 13-17 and 18-22, or 1/2 (.037 + .288) = .162.
For the age group 20-24, we may take 1/2 (.288 + .512), or .400, and
so on (Column 4).  Each age-specific birth rate is then computed
from the cumulative rate at that age, minus the cumulative rate at the
next lower age (Column 5), in reverse of the cumulation in Column 3.

---

[38] This is not quite the same as the computation of a total fertility
rate, where the age-specific rates are multiplied by 5, the number of person-
years in each age interval.  That step is unnecessary here.

## TABLE 3:5

## AGE-SPECIFIC BIRTH RATES OF INDIAN WOMEN, AND INTERPOLATED VALUES

(Data for "Rural" Women in Kolaba District, Bombay State, 1952)

| (1) | (2) | (3) | (4) | (5) | (6) |
|---|---|---|---|---|---|
| Age Group (Original data) | Birth Rates (births per person-year) | Cumulation of Rates by Age | Mid-point between Cumulative Rates | Interpolated Birth Rates (see text) | Age Group (Interpolated data) |
| 13-17 | .037 | .037 | | | |
| | | | .162 | .162 | 15-19 |
| 18-22 | .251 | .288 | | | |
| | | | .400 | .238 | 20-24 |
| 23-27 | .224 | .512 | | | |
| | | | .596 | .196 | 25-29 |
| 28-32 | .168 | .680 | | | |
| | | | .726 | .130 | 30-34 |
| 33-37 | .092 | .772 | | | |
| | | | .797 | .071 | 35-39 |
| 38-42 | .050 | .822 | | | |
| | | | .826 | .029 | 40-44 |
| 43-47 | .009 | .831 | | | |
| | | | (.831) | .005 | 45-49 |
| 48-52 | . . . | (.831) | | | |

*Note:* This procedure is a "linear" interpolation between each pair of adjoining rates, by finding a mid-point between them along a straight line (see the illustration in Chart 3:2). We have chosen to ignore births to women under 15 years of age.

Source: N. V. Sovani and K. Dandekar, *Fertility Survey of Nasic, Kolaba and Satara (North) Districts.* Gokhale Institute of Politics and Economics, Poona [India], 1955, Table 4:4.

The procedure is illustrated by Chart 3:2.[39] Because the cumulative distribution is used in place of the original rates, the error involved is very small. (Many of the age-specific proportions or rates encountered in population study are already of a cumulative nature, and do not require prior modification.) It is sometimes preferable to interpolate directly from a chart, by drawing a freehand curve connecting the points of the original data, instead of taking the midpoints (which is equivalent to drawing straight lines between points,

[39] In drawing a graph an age-specific rate is attributed to the *mid-point* of an interval.

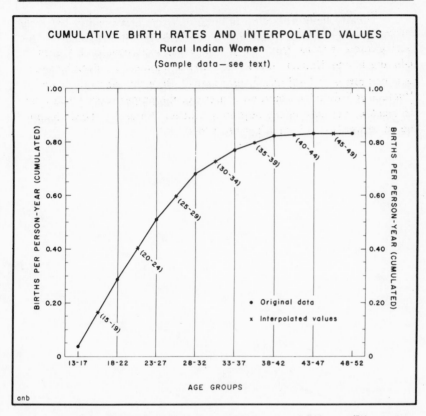

CUMULATIVE BIRTH RATES AND INTERPOLATED VALUES
Rural Indian Women
(Sample data—see text)

Chart 3:2  Birth rates of Indian women, and interpolated values. (Illustrating the process of interpolating between age intervals in original data. See Table 3:5.)

as illustrated here). Though crude, these results are probably no less accurate than the original data, and may be an improvement over using the original data in the conventional groupings.[40]

---

[40]There are a great many methods of interpolation, both simple and complex. They constitute a special field of procedures that cannot even be summarized here. (See, for example, A. J. Jaffe, *Handbook of Statistical Methods for Demographers* [Washington, D.C., 1951], pp. 92-101, 127-134.) Fitting a free-hand curve in a graph, however, is satisfactory for a great many purposes, with the use of some imagination to describe the shape of the curve between the points of observation. The approximate values at the desired points are quickly read from the graph itself. It is safer to apply this device to data (like age-specific birth or death rates) in which the typical shape of the distribution is well known. Any curve hand-fitted to data involves some arbitrary judgment, and may not give the same results when repeated on different occasions.

Finally, defective data in some districts of a country may sometimes be dealt with by removing the questionable districts before computing rates or ratios (see 4:14). However, some people or events missing in one district may be recorded in another, as often happens between cities and adjoining rural areas. Here the removal of the "defective" district would be a mistake; the proper course would be to *combine* the data of the adjoining places. Naturally there should be an explanation of what has been done.

# CHAPTER 4

# THE LIFE TABLE

The most successful efforts of demographic measurement have been made in the study of mortality. This was the first subject brought under rigorous analysis, and has found commercial applications in the field of insurance.

Mortality is traditionally represented by the life table. Owing to its precision and clarity, this is one of the simplest measuring devices for vital processes, though at first glance it appears rather intricate. It is also important as the model of several forms of analysis of topics other than mortality.

The life table is a life history of a hypothetical group, or *cohort*, of people, as it is diminished gradually by deaths. The record begins at the birth of each member,[1] and continues until all have died. The cohort loses a predetermined proportion at each age, and thus represents a situation that is artificially contrived. This is done by means of a few simplifying assumptions, which may be described as follows:

a. The cohort is "closed" against migration in or out. Hence there are no changes in membership except the losses due to death.

b. People die at each age according to a schedule that is fixed in advance and does not change.

c. The cohort originates from some standard number of births (always set at a round figure like 1,000, 10,000, or 100,000) called the "radix" of the life table. This standardized aspect facilitates comparisons between different life

---

[1] It is possible to construct a life table beginning at any age, and not just at birth. Most life tables, however, follow the cohort from birth to the death of all its members.

tables.  Also, the *proportion* surviving from birth to any given
age is apparent from a glance at the table itself — for example,
if 5420 members of a starting cohort of 10,000 survived at age
35, it means that exactly 54.2 per cent reached that age.

d.  At each age (excepting the first few years of life),
deaths are evenly distributed between one birthday and the
next.  That is to say, half the deaths expected between age
9 and age 10 occur by the time everyone reached age 9-1/2.
(The significance of this assumption will be seen somewhat
later.)

e.  The cohort normally contains members of only one sex.
It is possible to construct a life table for both sexes together,
but the differences between male and female mortality at most
ages are sufficient to justify treating them separately.

## 4:1  Survivors at Each Age in the Life-Table Cohort

The life table represents very clearly the effects of mortality
by age on the size of a cohort, without interference by the complicat-
ing factors of the actual world.  By isolating the implications of a
given schedule of mortality, it offers the view shown in the upper
portion of Chart 4:1.  The cumulative effect of mortality, of course,
is to reduce the original cohort; Chart 4:1-A represents the survivors
by age.  Of the group of 100,000 people at time of birth (age "zero"),
a large number are removed by death immediately after birth, and
others die at each age until eventually the last person has dis-
appeared.

The pattern of depletion is determined by the schedule of proportions dying.  At the ages where these proportions are high, they
take away a large share of the cohort's survivors; where they are
low, the cohort is diminished less rapidly, and the curve of survivors
in Chart 4:1-A becomes almost level.

A life-table cohort loses a great many of its original members
at a very early period of life, when deaths are relatively frequent.
The loss of life is least during the years of later childhood and young
adulthood, but increases again at advanced age.  This is the typical
pattern.  It is emphasized if we devise a simpler one to compare with
it.  If the same cohort lost an equal number of its members at each
age, the "curve" of survivors would be simply a straight line (represented by the broken line in Chart 4:1-A).  (Or, if equal *proportions*
were removed at each age, still another pattern would be produced —
not shown in Chart 4:1-A, but very different from both of these.)

The schedule of proportions dying in this cohort is illustrated in Chart 4:1-B, the lower portion of the graph. The ages of most rapid loss among the cohort's survivors (Chart 4:1-A) are also the ages of relatively large proportions dying (see Chart 4:1-B). At older ages, though the *numbers* of people dying are rather small, the proportions reach their highest point; the cohort is again being reduced rapidly, but very few remain to die. This peculiarity of the relation between numerical losses and proportional losses is a rather obvious one; but it needs to be singled out for special attention, for it is sometimes overlooked.

### 4:2 The Special Meaning of "Age" and Some Conventions of Notation

Every value in the life table refers to some particular age. Although age is reckoned casually and inexactly in everyday discourse, here it is defined very strictly. For each individual it is the exact number of complete years that have elapsed since birth.

A special notation is followed in order to be entirely explicit. Life-table terms are written with subscripts to indicate age — 0, 1, 2, 10, and so on, or with the general subscript, $x$ (meaning *any* age). When the phrase "exact age 20" is used in a life table, it means the moment when a person has lived exactly twenty full years. A person reaches exact age $x$ when he reaches his xth birthday. For a year afterwards, he remains in the interval $x$ to $x+1$ until he reaches the next birthday, when $x+1$ becomes his exact age. During this interval, $x$ is not his exact age; he is $x$ plus some fraction of a year of age.

Some life-table terms refer to *exact age* ($l_x$, $e_x$, $T_x$); others refer to the *interval* $x$ to $x+1$ ($q_x$, $p_x$, $L_x$, $d_x$). In the example of Table 4:1, each horizontal line of figures refers to some age or age interval. The first column in a life table states the age (or interval of age) of all members on the same line. "Age 5" means "exact age 5" in those columns where exact age is applicable, and it elsewhere means the interval "5 to 6." The term, $q_x$, for example, means "the probability of dying between exact age $x$ and exact age $x+1$." Another subscript, placed *before* the term, states the length of the interval if it is more than one year: $_5q_x$ means "the probability of dying between exact age $x$ and exact age $x+5$." In general, when the length of the interval has not yet been specified, $_nq_x$ means "the probability of dying between exact age $x$ and exact age $x+n$."

### 4:3 The Entire Life Table

The record of a cohort's diminishing numbers (Chart 4:1-A) is only a portion of a life table. It is represented by just one column

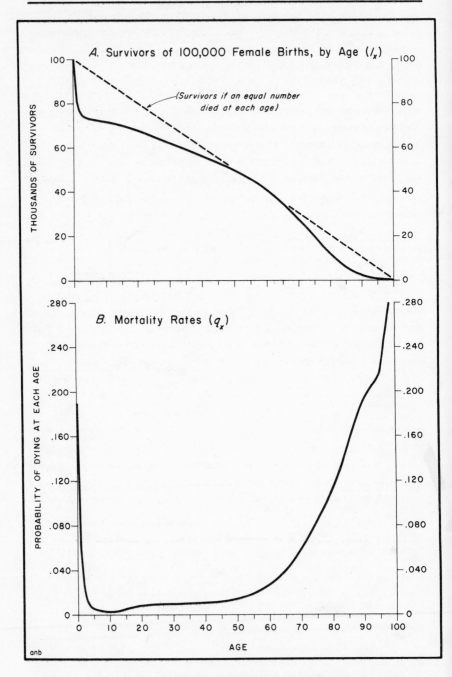

Chart 4:1 Life table for females in Chile (1940). Survivors by age ($l_x$), and proportions dying ($q_x$), of an initial cohort of 100,000 births.

($l_x$, or Column 5 in Table 4:1). Other columns are also implied by
the structure of the life table. Table 4:1 presents an entire life
table, females only, for Chile in 1940. The symbols at the heads of
the columns are traditional:  $q_x$, $p_x$, $d_x$, $l_x$, $L_x$, $T_x$, $e_x$.[2]

Column 5, or $l_x$, contains the data of Chart 4:1, being the numbers that survive from an initial cohort of 100,000 births, according
to mortality rates at each age in Chile, 1940.

Of these survivors at each exact age, the proportion failing to
survive until the next birthday is shown in Column 2, $q_x$, on the same
line. Thus, of 100,000 "survivors" at age 0, or 100,000 births, 18.8
per cent (the proportion .18848) die before reaching age one. The
proportion who *do* survive through a given interval of age, $p_x$, is
merely the other side of the proportion who do not:  if $q_x$ is .25, then
$p_x$ is .75;  if $q_x$ is .400, then $p_x$ is .600.

Since 100,000 persons begin life, and since the proportion
.81152, or $p_0$, survive beyond infancy, the number of survivors at
age one is the product of these two numbers, or 81,152; this is one
way of finding the number of survivors at each age in Column 4. The
number of deaths $(d_x)$ between one (exact) age and the next age is,
naturally, the number of survivors at that age minus the number at the
next. These calculations are the same through all ages in the life
table.

The number of years lived by the persons who have reached
each age, before they (or, more accurately, their survivors) reach the
next higher age, is shown in Column 6, $L_x$. Column 7, $T_x$, assembles
these values into the total number of person-years lived by the cohort
at all ages from exact age x onwards until all have died. This is an
intermediate step in calculating the last column, $e_x$, which is the
*average* number of years lived by the cohort's survivors from (exact)
age x onwards; or, as it is more often called, the average "life-
expectancy" of members of the cohort. This last column, $e_x$, is the
most familiar part of the life table. In popular usage, a reference to
it nearly always means the life expectancy *at birth* (or $e_0$); but, like

---

[2]Other columns are used in the process of making a life table, and still
others are added for use in calculating insurance risks. Table 4:1 contains,
however, the columns needed for most demographic analysis. Even some of
these may be omitted on occasion.

# TABLE 4:1
## LIFE TABLE FOR FEMALES IN CHILE, 1940

| Age | Probability of dying between age x and age x + 1 | Probability of surviving between age x and age x + 1 | Number of deaths between age x and age x + 1 | Survivors at exact age x | Years lived between age x and age x + 1 | Total years lived after exact age x | Expectation of life. Average number of years lived after exact age |
|---|---|---|---|---|---|---|---|
| (1) | (2) | (3) | (4) | (5) | (6) | (7) | (8) |
| x | $1000\,q_x$ | $p_x$ | $d_x$ | $l_x$ | $L_x$ | $T_x$ | $e_x$ |
| 0 | 188.48 | .81152 | 18,848 | 100,000 | 86,505 | 4,306,463 | 43.06 |
| 1 | 60.50 | .93950 | 4,910 | 81,152 | 78,451 | 4,219,958 | 52.00 |
| 2 | 25.75 | .97425 | 1,963 | 76,242 | 75,172 | 4,141,507 | 54.32 |
| 3 | 12.35 | .98765 | 918 | 74,279 | 73,791 | 4,066,335 | 54.74 |
| 4 | 7.47 | .99253 | 548 | 73,361 | 73,087 | 3,992,544 | 54.42 |
| 5 | 5.05 | .99495 | 368 | 72,813 | 72,629 | 3,919,457 | 53.83 |
| 6 | 4.08 | .99592 | 296 | 72,445 | 72,297 | 3,846,828 | 53.10 |
| 7 | 3.53 | .99647 | 255 | 72,149 | 72,022 | 3,774,531 | 52.32 |
| 8 | 2.37 | .99763 | 171 | 71,894 | 71,809 | 3,702,509 | 51.50 |
| 9 | 1.93 | .99807 | 139 | 71,723 | 71,654 | 3,630,700 | 50.61 |
| 10 | 2.04 | .99796 | 146 | 71,584 | 71,511 | 3,559,046 | 49.72 |
| 11 | 2.52 | .99748 | 180 | 71,438 | 71,348 | 3,487,531 | 48.82 |
| 12 | 3.20 | .99680 | 228 | 71,258 | 71,144 | 3,416,187 | 47.94 |
| 13 | 3.93 | .99607 | 279 | 71,030 | 70,891 | 3,345,043 | 47.09 |
| 14 | 4.68 | .99532 | 331 | 70,751 | 70,586 | 3,274,152 | 46.28 |
| 15 | 5.41 | .99459 | 381 | 70,420 | 70,230 | 3,203,566 | 45.49 |
| 16 | 6.12 | .99388 | 428 | 70,039 | 69,825 | 3,133,336 | 44.74 |
| 17 | 6.77 | .99423 | 471 | 69,611 | 69,376 | 3,063,511 | 44.01 |
| 18 | 7.36 | .99264 | 509 | 69,140 | 68,886 | 2,994,135 | 43.31 |
| 19 | 7.88 | .99212 | 541 | 68,631 | 68,361 | 2,925,249 | 42.62 |
| 20 | 8.32 | .99168 | 566 | 68,090 | 67,807 | 2,856,888 | 41.95 |
| 21 | 8.68 | .99132 | 586 | 67,524 | 67,231 | 2,789,081 | 41.31 |
| 22 | 8.94 | .99106 | 594 | 66,938 | 66,639 | 2,721,850 | 40.65 |
| 23 | 9.12 | .99088 | 605 | 66,339 | 66,037 | 2,655,211 | 40.02 |
| 24 | 9.23 | .99077 | 607 | 65,734 | 65,431 | 2,589,174 | 39.39 |
| 25 | 9.28 | .99072 | 605 | 65,127 | 64,825 | 2,523,743 | 38.75 |
| 26 | 9.31 | .99069 | 601 | 64,522 | 64,222 | 2,458,918 | 38.11 |
| 27 | 9.32 | .99068 | 596 | 63,921 | 63,623 | 2,394,696 | 37.46 |
| 28 | 9.35 | .99065 | 592 | 63,325 | 63,029 | 2,331,073 | 36.81 |
| 29 | 9.39 | .99061 | 589 | 62,733 | 62,439 | 2,268,044 | 36.15 |
| 30 | 9.45 | .99055 | 587 | 62,144 | 61,851 | 2,205,605 | 35.49 |
| 31 | 9.52 | .99048 | 586 | 61,557 | 61,264 | 2,143,754 | 34.83 |
| 32 | 9.61 | .99039 | 586 | 60,971 | 60,678 | 2,082,490 | 34.16 |
| 33 | 9.72 | .99028 | 587 | 60,385 | 60,092 | 2,021,812 | 33.48 |
| 34 | 9.84 | .99016 | 588 | 59,798 | 59,504 | 1,961,720 | 32.81 |
| 35 | 9.98 | .99002 | 591 | 59,210 | 58,915 | 1,902,216 | 32.13 |
| 36 | 10.14 | .98986 | 594 | 58,619 | 58,322 | 1,843,301 | 31.77 |
| 37 | 10.32 | .98968 | 599 | 58,025 | 57,726 | 1,784,979 | 30.76 |
| 38 | 10.52 | .98948 | 604 | 57,426 | 57,124 | 1,727,253 | 30.08 |
| 39 | 10.73 | .98927 | 610 | 56,822 | 56,517 | 1,670,129 | 29.39 |
| 40 | 10.94 | .98906 | 615 | 56,212 | 55,905 | 1,613,612 | 28.71 |
| 41 | 11.16 | .98884 | 621 | 55,597 | 55,287 | 1,557,707 | 28.02 |
| 42 | 11.38 | .98862 | 625 | 54,976 | 54,664 | 1,502,420 | 27.33 |
| 43 | 11.58 | .98842 | 629 | 54,351 | 54,037 | 1,447,756 | 26.64 |
| 44 | 11.79 | .98821 | 634 | 53,722 | 53,405 | 1,393,719 | 25.94 |
| 45 | 12.03 | .98797 | 639 | 53,088 | 52,769 | 1,340,314 | 25.25 |
| 46 | 12.32 | .98768 | 646 | 52,449 | 52,126 | 1,287,545 | 24.55 |
| 47 | 12.68 | .98732 | 657 | 51,803 | 51,475 | 1,235,419 | 23.85 |
| 48 | 13.12 | .98688 | 671 | 51,146 | 50,811 | 1,183,944 | 23.15 |
| 49 | 13.67 | .98633 | 690 | 50,475 | 50,130 | 1,133,133 | 22.45 |
| 50 | 14.32 | .98568 | 713 | 49,785 | 49,429 | 1,083,003 | 21.75 |
| 51 | 15.10 | .98490 | 741 | 49,072 | 48,702 | 1,033,574 | 21.06 |
| 52 | 16.02 | .98398 | 774 | 48,331 | 47,944 | 984,872 | 20.38 |
| 53 | 17.07 | .98293 | 812 | 47,557 | 57,151 | 936,928 | 19.70 |
| 54 | 18.23 | .98177 | 852 | 46,745 | 46,319 | 889,777 | 19.03 |
| 55 | 19.46 | .98054 | 893 | 45,893 | 45,447 | 843,458 | 18.38 |

98

# TABLE 4:1 (Continued)
## LIFE TABLE FOR FEMALES IN CHILE, 1940

| Age | Probability of dying between age x and age x + 1 | Probability of surviving between age x and age x + 1 | Number of deaths between age x and age x + 1 | Survivors at exact age x | Years lived between age x and age x + 1 | Total years lived after exact age x | Expectation of life. Average number of years lived after exact age x |
|---|---|---|---|---|---|---|---|
| (1) | (2) | (3) | (4) | (5) | (6) | (7) | (8) |
| $x$ | $1000\,q_x$ | $p_x$ | $d_x$ | $l_x$ | $L_x$ | $T_x$ | $e_x$ |
| 56 | 20.71 | .97929 | 932 | 45,000 | 44,534 | 798,011 | 17.73 |
| 57 | 21.95 | .97805 | 967 | 44,068 | 43,585 | 753,477 | 17.10 |
| 58 | 23.16 | .97684 | 998 | 43,101 | 42,602 | 709,892 | 16.47 |
| 59 | 24.43 | .97557 | 1,028 | 42,103 | 41,589 | 667,290 | 15.85 |
| 60 | 25.86 | .97414 | 1,062 | 41,075 | 40,544 | 625,701 | 15.23 |
| 61 | 27.57 | .97243 | 1,103 | 40,013 | 39,462 | 585,157 | 14.62 |
| 62 | 29.68 | .97032 | 1,155 | 38,910 | 38,333 | 545,695 | 14.02 |
| 63 | 32.25 | .96775 | 1,218 | 37,755 | 37,146 | 507,362 | 13.44 |
| 64 | 35.20 | .96480 | 1,286 | 36,537 | 35,894 | 470,216 | 12.87 |
| 65 | 38.40 | .96160 | 1,353 | 35,251 | 34,575 | 434,322 | 12.32 |
| 66 | 41.71 | .95829 | 1,414 | 33,898 | 33,191 | 399,747 | 11.79 |
| 67 | 45.01 | .95499 | 1,462 | 32,484 | 31,753 | 366,556 | 11.28 |
| 68 | 48.23 | .95177 | 1,496 | 31,022 | 30,274 | 334,803 | 10.79 |
| 69 | 51.54 | .90023 | 1,522 | 29,526 | 28,765 | 304,529 | 10.31 |
| 70 | 55.17 | .94483 | 1,545 | 28,004 | 27,232 | 275,764 | 9.85 |
| 71 | 59.35 | .94065 | 1,570 | 26,459 | 25,674 | 248,532 | 9.39 |
| 72 | 64.30 | .93570 | 1,600 | 24,889 | 24,089 | 222,858 | 8.95 |
| 73 | 70.14 | .92986 | 1,634 | 23,289 | 22,472 | 198,769 | 8.53 |
| 74 | 76.60 | .92341 | 1,659 | 21,655 | 20,826 | 176,297 | 8.14 |
| 75 | 83.24 | .91676 | 1,665 | 19,996 | 19,164 | 155,471 | 7.78 |
| 76 | 89.70 | .91030 | 1,644 | 18,331 | 17,509 | 136,307 | 7.44 |
| 77 | 95.56 | .90444 | 1,595 | 16,687 | 15,890 | 118,798 | 7.12 |
| 78 | 100.60 | .89940 | 1,518 | 15,092 | 14,333 | 102,908 | 6.82 |
| 79 | 105.27 | .89473 | 1,429 | 13,574 | 12,860 | 88,575 | 6.53 |
| 80 | 110.18 | .88982 | 1,338 | 12,145 | 11,476 | 75,715 | 6.23 |
| 81 | 115.96 | .88404 | 1,253 | 10,807 | 10,181 | 64,239 | 5.94 |
| 82 | 123.23 | .87677 | 1,177 | 9,554 | 8,966 | 54,058 | 5.66 |
| 83 | 132.37 | .86763 | 1,109 | 8,377 | 7,823 | 45,092 | 5.38 |
| 84 | 142.87 | .85713 | 1,038 | 7,268 | 6,749 | 37,269 | 5.13 |
| 85 | 153.97 | .84603 | 959 | 6,230 | 5,751 | 30,520 | 4.90 |
| 86 | 164.91 | .83509 | 869 | 5,271 | 4,837 | 24,769 | 4.70 |
| 87 | 174.94 | .82506 | 770 | 4,402 | 4,017 | 19,932 | 4.53 |
| 88 | 183.47 | .81653 | 666 | 3,632 | 3,299 | 15,915 | 4.38 |
| 89 | 190.50 | .80950 | 565 | 2,966 | 2,684 | 12,616 | 4.25 |
| 90 | 196.17 | .80383 | 471 | 2,401 | 2,166 | 9,932 | 4.14 |
| 91 | 200.66 | .79933 | 387 | 1,930 | 1,737 | 7,766 | 4.02 |
| 92 | 204.12 | .79588 | 315 | 1,543 | 1,386 | 6,029 | 3.91 |
| 93 | 206.85 | .79315 | 254 | 1,228 | 1,101 | 4,643 | 3.78 |
| 94 | 209.67 | .79033 | 204 | 974 | 872 | 3,542 | 3.64 |
| 95 | 213.59 | .78642 | 164 | 770 | 688 | 2,670 | 3.47 |
| 96 | 219.56 | .78044 | 133 | 606 | 540 | 1,982 | 3.27 |
| 97 | 228.57 | .77143 | 108 | 473 | 419 | 1,442 | 3.05 |
| 98 | 241.88 | .75812 | 88 | 365 | 321 | 1,023 | 2.80 |
| 99 | 261.84 | .73816 | 73 | 277 | 241 | 702 | 2.53 |
| 100 | 291.08 | .70892 | 59 | 204 | 175 | 461 | 2.25 |
| 101 | 332.25 | .66775 | 48 | 145 | 121 | 286 | 1.97 |
| 102 | 349.63 | .65037 | 38 | 97 | 78 | 165 | 1.70 |
| 103 | 401.87 | .59813 | 27 | 59 | 46 | 87 | 1.47 |
| 104 | 454.86 | .54514 | 17 | 32 | 24 | 41 | 1.28 |
| 105 | 496.49 | .50351 | 9 | 15 | 11 | 17 | 1.13 |
| 106 | 514.72 | .48528 | 4 | 6 | 4 | 6 | 1.00 |
| 107 | – | – | – | 2 | – | – | – |

Source: From O. Cabello, J. Vildósola and M. Latorre,, *Tablas de Vida para Chile, 1920-1930-1940* (Santiago, 1953), Table 3. The table is based on deaths registered between 1939 and 1942, and the census population by age (adjusted for under-enumeration).

all other terms of the life table, there is a value of $e_x$ for each age shown in a life table.

## 4:4 The Actuarial Notion of "Risk"

The various columns of the life table, though all related, originate from the set of proportions dying $(q_x)$ in Column 2, Table 4:1. This same term, $q_x$, is also called, in Table 4:1 and throughout most technical writings, the "probability of dying" at age x. Does this suggest a discrepancy in usage?

Both expressions refer to the notion of the "risk" of death, which is a way of saying that people live continually exposed to some chance of dying, a chance that is precisely measurable. Everyone of course dies some time, but the prospect is uncertain at any given moment. The *risk* is the *degree* of uncertainty. The "proportion dying" and the "probability of death" both indicate how great the risk of dying is. The numerical value measuring this degree is also called a "mortality rate."

For most purposes all of these names may be used interchangeably; they all range in value between impossibility (0.0) and absolute certainty (1.0). The risk of dying is always measured from one exact age to another. It is also measured in relation to a definite universe: the total number of people *who could possibly die* during that interval. This universe defines the maximum number of possible deaths — the number of survivors who *reached* the age interval. It is the *universe of opportunities* to die during that interval. (The cohort of Table 4:1, at time of birth, can muster a maximum of 100,000 possible deaths — there are this many people "exposed to the risk" of dying. Only 81,152, however, succeed in reaching age one, and make up a universe of only 81,152 people exposed to the risk of dying at age one. And so on, at higher ages.)

In both the definition of the interval and the definition of the universe, the notion of risk is more precise than a death rate. The distinction between the two kinds of rate is important, though not very carefully preserved in the literature. In this book a "death rate" refers to a ratio of deaths to person-years lived; a "mortality rate" is a rate based on the notion of risk, expressed as a probability or a proportion.

According to Table 4:1, of the 100,000 live female births in the cohort, 18,848 die before reaching age one. (This figure can be read from Column 4, $d_x$.) If we choose an individual at random from the original cohort, it is customary to say that the probability that he will be one of those who fail to survive is 18,848/100,000, or .18848, which is the same as the proportion that die according to the $q_x$ column.[3] Among those members of this cohort who are exposed to the risk of dying at age x, therefore, $q_x$ is said to be the probability of dying before age $x+1$; and $_5q_x$ is the probability of dying before age $x+5$.

The term *risk* has many other applications; we speak of the "risk" of marriage, the "risk" of childbearing, the "risk" of entering some economic activity, the "risk" of incurring some kind of illness. In each instance it is a probability that confronts a group of people, the universe exposed to the risk of occurrence of a specific type of event. Wherever used in demography, the notion has the same meaning; but the universe is not always the same. The people exposed to the risk of dying at age 20, for example, are all those who succeed in surviving until age 20 — this many people can die, but no more. Those exposed to the risk of marriage at age 20 are the ones who reach age 20 *and* also remain unmarried. Persons exposed to the risk of widowhood at age 20 are those who have both reached age 20 and already been married but not yet widowed (either before age 20 or during the interval between age 20 and 21). People exposed to the risk of getting a job are those who reach some specified age and have no regular employment. A person may be exposed to the risk of certain events more than once, and the measurement of risk is then made far more difficult. (This is one reason why mortality can be measured more easily than fertility; death is an unambiguous change in a person's status, while childbearing is not.)

### 4:5 Some Relations between Columns of the Life Table

The mortality rates, $q_x$, of a life table are normally the first portion to be computed from original data. The remainder of the life table is all related, by its structure, to this column. Certain of these relations between the various terms of the life table can be expressed exactly, since this indeed is the purpose of the life table. They summarize the structure of the entire life table, and provide a guide for

---

[3] Strictly speaking, the probability would not pertain to *any* member of the 100,000 members of the cohort unless they were all equally "exposed" to the risk of dying. Actually the members of a cohort are *not* all exposed to the same degree of risk. A real population, even at some particular age, is diverse in its composition, and a vital rate represents an average of dissimilar experience. Where possible, separate life tables are prepared for distinct groups in a population, in order that a fairly homogeneous distribution of risk may be represented in a mortality rate.

computing one column from another; the actual constructing of a life table is a separate problem, and is taken up separately in an *Appendix*.

*Mortality rates and survival rates.* Surviving and failing to survive are alternatives (they are "mutually exclusive"), and they leave no middle course. Therefore, $p_x + q_x = 1$; during any age interval, it is a certainty that a person must do one or the other. If the value of $q_x$ is known, then $p_x = 1 - q_x$ (which is the way in which values of $p_x$ are usually found). Both terms refer to the interval from (exact) age x to age $x+1$.[4]

*Deaths at each age in the life-table cohort.* The number of deaths at each age $(d_x)$ is equal to the number of people who reach that age multiplied by the probability of dying before reaching the next higher age: $d_x = l_x \times q_x$. In Table 4:1, the number of infant deaths is $(l_0 \times q_0) = 100,000 \times (.18848) = 18,848$. The number of deaths at age 39 is $56,822 \times (.01073) = 610$. Of course, the number of deaths is also equal to the number of people lost from the cohort between ages x and $x+1$: $d_x = l_x - l_{x+1}$. For different intervals of age, $_n d_x = l_x - l_{x+n}$; for example, the total number of deaths between ages 5 and 10 $(_5 d_5)$ is $(l_5 - l_{10})$, or $72,813 - 71,584$, or $1,229$.

*Age-specific death rates.* An age-specific death rate for the life table, designated $m_x$, is the number of deaths per person-year at any age: 
$$m_x = \frac{d_x}{L_x}.$$

*Number of survivors by age.* The value of $l_x$ represents the cumulative effect of deaths from birth to some (exact) age, x, in the hypothetical cohort. The radix, or initial cohort, of Table 4:1 has suffered no losses: $l_0 = 100,000$. To find how many reach age one, multiply 100,000 times the probability of surviving through infancy, $p_0$. At any age, $l_{x+1} = l_x \times p_x$. If the column, $l_x$, is given, any value of $p_x$ can be found in this way: 
$$p_x = \frac{l_{x+1}}{l_x}.[5]$$
(The corresponding value of

---

[4] As mentioned in 4:4, a longer interval is indicated by another subscript before the term itself, leaving the relation unchanged: $_n p_x + _n q_x = 1$.

[5] In general, $_n p_x = \dfrac{l_{x+n}}{l_x}$.

$q_x$ is, as before, $1 - p_x$.) In this way, values of $p_x$ or $q_x$ can be easily computed for broader intervals of age; the probability of surviving from age 15 to (exact) age 65, or $(_{50}p_{15})$, is equal to $\dfrac{l_{65}}{l_{15}}$. In Table 4:1, this is $\dfrac{35,251}{70,420}$, or .50058.

*Person-years lived at each age.* Values of $L_x$ (the number of years lived by the life-table cohort between ages x and x+1) are not calculated exactly. It is necessary to rely on some method of approximation instead, because exact calculation is not practical or even possible. Fortunately this is not difficult.

The curve of survivors $(l_x)$ moves in a regular and fairly smooth course from each age to the next. Therefore it is safe to make the assumption that deaths are distributed evenly throughout a year of age (see 2:10); above age five, mortality rates change so slowly from one age to the next that the assumption cannot be in serious error. We can thus plot the hypothetical path of survivors in the cohort between ages x and x+1 as a straight line, representing a very short segment of the curve of survivors in Chart 4:1-A. Such a segment is shown below, in an expanded diagram, between exact ages 27 and 28.

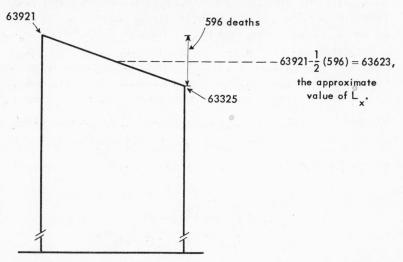

63921

596 deaths

$-\,63921 - \dfrac{1}{2}\,(596) = 63623,$

the approximate value of $L_x$.

63325

There were 63,921 survivors at age 27; 63,325 survived until age 28 or longer. The remainder, 596, died between age 27 and age 28. Thus, 63,325 women lived one year each, or 63,325 person-years; the 596 who died, lived on the average one-half year each (according to the assumption above). Hence, the years lived by the cohort during

the age interval 27-28 must have been $63{,}325 + \dfrac{1}{2}(596)$. This is the

same as $l_{27} - \dfrac{1}{2}d_{27}$, or $63{,}921 - \dfrac{1}{2}(596) = 63{,}623$. Being the mid-point

between $l_{27}$ and $l_{28}$, it is equal to $\dfrac{1}{2}(l_{27} + l_{28})$. (This is the same

as $l_{26\frac{1}{2}}$, or the survivors at the middle of the year of age; it is

analogous to the mid-year size of an actual population, which may be
estimated by a very similar procedure, as in Chapter 2.)

In general, this estimate, which is the most useful approxima-

tion of $L_x$, is calculated as $\dfrac{1}{2}(l_x + l_{x+1})$. Its chief advantage is

simplicity, for it is adapted to quick and easy computation. It also
gives very reasonable values of $L_x$, *except* (a) values of $L_x$ under
five years of age, and (b) values of $L_x$ for intervals greater than one
year ($_nL_x$). These two situations require special attention.

(a) During infancy and very young childhood, mortality
changes rapidly with age, even within the interval of a single year.
Then it is no longer reasonable to use this approximation. Deaths
are not distributed evenly over the age interval, but are concentrated
at the earlier portion. Because the deaths occur earlier, the cohort
loses more person-years, and therefore lives fewer person-years, than
it would if the deaths were distributed uniformly. The mid-point between $l_x$ and $l_{x+1}$ would be too high an estimate for $L_x$; the true figure must be closer to $l_{x+1}$. In a few countries, the relative weighting
of $l_x$ and $l_{x+1}$ may be determined directly; but such data are rare,
and the following is often a good approximation:

$$L_0 = .3\, l_0 + .7\, l_1$$
$$L_1 = .4\, l_1 + .6\, l_2$$
$$L_2 = .5\, l_2 + .5\, l_3, \text{ or } \dfrac{1}{2}(l_2 + l_3),[6]$$

---

[6] These proportional weights for $l_x$ and $l_{x+1}$ will fit a wide variety of
cases. They are less accurate where infant mortality is very low, but a considerable degree of inaccuracy can be tolerated here without serious distortion.

and the same for higher ages. A somewhat more detailed scheme of weighting is presented below, in 4:7, and may be used in calculating $L_0$ when the necessary data are available.

(b) When the age interval is greater than one year, the number of person-years sometimes cannot be estimated by the procedure described above. The person-years lived during a 5-year interval $(_5L_x)$ are the sum of $L_x$ for each year included in the interval. In many life tables, however, the values of $l_x$ are not given for each year of age, but only for the beginning and end of 5-year or 10-year intervals (see 4:8 and Table 4:1-a). A cruder estimate must then be made. Several ways have been devised (see, for example, 4:15). In reality they do not differ greatly. One should remember that all methods give only estimated values of $L_x$ or $_5L_x$.

*Total number of years lived after each age (the Column, $T_x$).* The *total* number of years lived by a cohort is simply the sum of the years lived at every age. This is the value of $T_0$. Corresponding values exist for other ages. The number of years lived *after* exact age 6 is the sum of the person-years lived in the age interval 6 to 7

(or $L_6$) and at all higher ages. In other words, $T_6 = \overset{\infty}{\underset{6}{S}} L_x$.[7] There is a series of such sums, one for each exact age shown in the life table. They are generally calculated by starting with the small number of years lived $(L_x)$ at the highest age interval,[8] and adding the value of $L_x$ for each younger age (though in Table 4:1 this first value of $T_x$ was calculated by a different formula). In general, $T_x = T_{x+1} + L_x$. At age 6, the value of $T$ is $T_7 + L_6$, or $(3,774,531 + 72,297)$ $= 3,846,828$.

*The mean expectation of life, $(e_x)$.* After the column, $T_x$, has

---

[7]Like the previous use of this notation (2:18), this gives an instruction: "Sum the values of $L_x$, beginning with age x, up to infinity ($\infty$), or the end of life in the cohort."

[8]Mortality rates at advanced ages are not reliable. Actually, these values of $L_x$ and $T_x$ do not originate with mortality rates at these ages, but with an extension of the rates at lower ages by mathematical formula. They do not really give any information about the last years of life in the cohort, but merely serve to complete the life table. It is also possible to group the last few years of age together in one large interval, which is the practice we shall follow in the making of life tables later in this chapter.

been completed, it is very simple to compute the *average* number of years lived by the cohort after each age $(e_x)$. This is equal to the *total* number of years lived after age $x$, divided by the number of persons who survived at that age: $e_x = \dfrac{T_x}{l_x}$. Part of the cumbersome procedure for assembling a life table has been designed to promote convenience at this stage. In order to find the value of $e_x$, it is necessary only to divide any value of $T_x$ by the value of $l_x$ on the same line. The result is the average number of years lived by members of the cohort after age $x$. This is sometimes called the "average future lifetime" of the cohort; one should remember, however, that it pertains, strictly speaking, to this hypothetical cohort only, and not to any other group of people. The value of $e_0$ (the "expectation of life at birth"), is the total number of years lived at all ages divided by the initial number of members in the cohort, or, in Table 4:1, $4,306,463/100,000 = 43.06$ years.[9]

### 4:6 Intervals Other than One Year of Age

One year is not the only interval of age found in life tables. This has been more or less standard in published life tables, but other intervals are often useful and convenient. When the size of the interval is altered, the relations of the various columns must be stated more explicitly. The relations themselves are not changed, except in the case of $L_x$ (which has only an approximate value in any case).

In measuring infant mortality, it is common (where possible) to subdivide the first year of life into monthly or quarterly intervals; this is discussed in 4:7. In constructing original life tables from population data, a broader interval of age is frequently used — five years, or even ten, with one or two odd-sized intervals where five or ten years would be inappropriate; this is discussed in 4:8.

### 4:7 Mortality by Month of Age during Infancy

The age-specific risk of dying, if reckoned in very short inter-

---

[9] It has sometimes been customary to distinguish two forms of the mean expectation of life: one, the average number of years lived by members of the cohort after age $x$, or $(\overset{\circ}{e}_x)$; and the other, the average number of years *completed* after age $x$, disregarding any incompleted portion of a year in any person's life $(e_x)$. We shall pay no attention to the second form, and use the symbol $(e_x)$ to represent the full expectation of life, described above.

vals, varies most widely during infancy. It is greatest at about the
time of birth, and falls quickly as an infant advances into the first
year of life (disregarding, of course, trends or seasonal fluctuations
in mortality not directly associated with age). By the time the survivors have reached age one, the risk begins to approach the level of
the later years of childhood, and fall more slowly. This peculiar pattern makes it especially difficult to estimate accurately the number
of person-years lived by the cohort during infancy.

Because of this marked change, life tables sometimes separate
the first year of life into months, as in Table 4:2 (or into quarters, or
sometimes also into days and weeks within the first month). The
first column refers to "month of age." The number of survivors at
each month of age $(l_x)$ is determined in the ordinary manner from the
mortality rates $(q_x)$, which in this case are the proportions dying
from one month of age to the next.

Likewise, $L_x$ may be estimated, as usual, at the point where
one-half the deaths of each interval have occurred, since mortality
has not changed much within each month of age. But this alone
would be an estimate of the number of *months* lived, whereas $L_x$ conventionally represents the number of *years* lived. Therefore, within
the first year of age, it is computed in units of years, as follows:

$$L_x = \frac{1}{2}(l_x + l_{x+1}) \times \frac{1}{12} .$$ Where the interval includes more than one

month, the calculation must be altered accordingly. For example, in
Table 4:2, the years lived in the interval 3-5 (altogether three months)

are $_3L_3 = \frac{1}{2}(l_3 + l_6) \times \frac{3}{12}$ . Afterwards, these monthly figures (Col-

umn 5 of Table 4:2) may be summed, to find the number of years lived
by the cohort during the entire first year of age.

Mortality in the first year of life cannot always be dealt with
in such detail. The data are often not available in such small intervals; or, if available, they are patently inadequate, owing chiefly to
omissions in the first month of age. Indeed, figures for any country
like those of Table 4:2 should not be taken literally as measurements
of infant mortality, however useful they may be as approximations.

### 4:8 Age Intervals Greater Than One Year: The "Abridged" Life Table

Except for special purposes, single-year intervals of age in a

life table are unnecessarily detailed. Indeed, from the standpoint of
the accuracy of data, single-year tables (or, "complete" life tables,
as they are called) often are hardly warranted. In many cases it is
advantageous to construct a life table omitting some of this detail.

Such a table is called an "abridged" life table. It covers the
complete range of age but is based on larger intervals of age. Mortality rates for the first year or so of life are calculated separately
(because it is important to know their pattern in more detail). Thereafter the customary five-year intervals of age are followed (see Table
4:3). Such a table is almost as accurate as a "complete" life table,
requires far less work in construction, and provides all the information ordinarily needed. Values for smaller intervals must be estimated from an abridged table by interpolation.

As mentioned earlier, a slight change in notation accompanies
the change of interval. Another subscript, placed before a term, indicates the number of years in the interval. For example, $_5q_{10}$ means
the "probability of dying (or mortality rate) within 5 years after reaching age 10" — that is, in the age interval 10-14 (between age 10 and
age 15). In general, $_nq_x$ means the probability of dying between age
x and age $x+n$. The additional subscript is used with those terms
which refer to an interval of age $(_nq_x, \ _np_x, \ _nd_x, \ _nL_x)$; it does not
apply to those which refer to an exact age $(l_x, \ T_x, \ e_x)$. The extra
subscript does not add anything new to the meaning of these terms.
It merely indicates the size of an age interval when we cannot take
for granted that it is a single year. If the interval varies, some of the
relations of life-table terms must be stated more explicitly:

$$_nq_x = \frac{l_{x+n}}{l_x}$$

$$_np_x = 1 - {}_nq_x$$

$$l_{x+n} = l_x \times p_x$$

$$_nd_x = l_x \times {}_nq_x = l_x - l_{x+n}$$

The shift to larger intervals of age does not change any of
these relations. However, calculating the person-years lived in a
larger interval is more troublesome. We should remember that the relation of $L_x$ to $l_x$ (see 4:5) is not exact, but approximate. In view of

this, the simplest course is to adapt the formula $_1L_x = \frac{1}{2}(l_x + l_{x+1})$

to a five-year interval, by substituting "5" for "1," or $_5L_x$
$=\dfrac{5}{2}(l_x + l_{x+5})$. For any interval of $n$ years, $_nL_x = \dfrac{n}{2}(l_x + l_{x+n})$.
However, this calculation is slightly biased. At most ages it yields
values for $_nL_x$ that are too large. If the values of $_nL_x$ are to be used
in survival ratios (as illustrated in 3:9, 5:4, and 7:13), the effect is
inconsequential, and this is by far the most practical formula.

On the other hand, if the column $_nL_x$ is computed in order to derive the final column of the life table, $e_x$, then the bias of this formula is somewhat more serious. It may be advisable to find $_nL_x$ by
other means. One possibility is a slight modification of this formula,
adjusting for the effect of a broader age interval.[10]

Another expedient is to estimate the number of person-years
from an ordinary age-specific death rate. Such a death rate in the life
table is $_nm_x = \dfrac{_nd_x}{_nL_x}$, the number of deaths per person-year lived in a
given age interval. If the values of $_nm_x$ and $_nd_x$ were known, then
number of person-years must be $_nL_x = \dfrac{_nd_x}{_nm_x}$. But $_nm_x$ cannot be calculated until $_nL_x$ is found. However, it *is* possible to compute the
corresponding death rate for the actual population, which may be
called $_nM_x$. By assuming that the death rate in the life table is the
same as the death rate in the population, we can calculate $_nL_x$

$=\dfrac{_nd_x}{_nM_x}$.[11] Though these estimates of $_nL_x$ do not have a consistent

---

[10] The following modification has been suggested: $_nL_x = \dfrac{n}{2}(l_x + l_{x+n})$
$+ \dfrac{n}{24}(_nd_{x+n} - _nd_{x-n})$. This formula, as the additional portion indicates,
makes an approximate correction according to the numbers of deaths in the
two adjoining age intervals. It is applicable, however, only when the three
neighboring intervals $(x-n$ to $x$, $x$ to $x+n$, $x+n$ to $x+2n)$ all contain the same
number of years, and therefore often may not be used. See T. N. E. Greville,
"Short Methods of Constructing Abridged Life Tables," *The Record of the
American Institute of Actuaries*, Vol. 32, Part 1, June, 1943, p. 40.

[11] The source of $_nM_x$ is outside the life table. It comes from the population on which the life table is based. Its connection with the life table is
explained in 4:10.

tendency to be too high or too low, they do tend to be rather erratic, especially with data that have not previously been smoothed. The errors do not have a very large effect on values of $e_x$ at younger ages, but are concentrated at values of $e_x$ for the highest ages, which become very unreliable. Unfortunately it is at the highest age interval that this procedure is most convenient (see Table 4:1-A).

The remaining two columns of an abridged life table are related just as they are in a "complete" table. The notation is slightly different, because the intervals are larger. $T_x$, the total number of years lived by members of the cohort after reaching age $x$, is equal to $\overset{\infty}{\underset{x}{S}} L_x$, or $T_{x+n} + {}_n L_x$. As before, $e_x = \dfrac{T_x}{l_x}$. Both columns are calculated in the manner explained in 4:5.

For example, if the life table for Chile (Table 4:1) were an abridged table, it would look like Table 4:1-a. The values of ${}_n L_x$ in

## TABLE 4:2

## LIFE TABLE FOR MALE INFANTS, BY MONTH OF AGE, JAPAN, 1935–1936

| Age in months | Probability of dying between age x and age x + n | Number of deaths between age x and age x + 1 | Survivors at exact age x | Years lived between age x and age x + 1 |
|---|---|---|---|---|
| (1) | (2) | (3) | (4) | (5) |
| $x$ | ${}_n q_x$ | ${}_n d_x$ | $l_x$ | ${}_n L_x$ |
| 0 | .04702 | 4,702 | 100,000 | 8,137 |
| 1 | .01390 | 1,325 | 95,298 | 7,886 |
| 2 | .00967 | 909 | 93,973 | 7,793 |
| 3-5 | .01829 | 1,702 | 93,064 | 23,053 |
| 6-11 | .02917 | 2,665 | 91,362 | 45,015 |
| (12) | | | (88,697) | |

Source:  Japan, Welfare Minister's Secretariat, *The 8th Life Table* (1947) Appendix II.

Column 4 have been computed according to the first formula shown above, as if the single-year values of $L_x$ were not known. The final value of $_nL_x$ at "age 75 and above" $(_\infty L_{75})$ is computed from the ratio of $\dfrac{_\infty d_x}{_\infty M_x}$ , using the source data of the original life table.[12] Hence it cannot be considered reliable; nor can the value of $e_{75}$, which is derived from it.

The values of $_5L_x$ taken from Table 4:1 are shown in Column 5 for the sake of comparison. They confirm that most of the abridged values of Column 4 (calculated by the first method explained above) are too high; the final estimate for age 75 is too low. The effect of the abridged procedure on selected values of $e_x$ can be seen as follows:

|  | Complete life table (Table 4:1) | Abridged life table (Table 4:1-a) |
|---|---|---|
| $e_0$ | 43.1 | 42.9 |
| $e_{10}$ | 49.7 | 49.4 |
| $e_{30}$ | 35.5 | 35.2 |
| $e_{50}$ | 21.8 | 21.4 |
| $e_{75}$ | 7.8 | 6.9 |

## 4:9 Construction of Life Tables: Two Additional Assumptions

Life-table structure, without other considerations, presents no very serious problems. A life table has a factual basis, however. It is constructed from the data of an actual population. Because the facts do not fit the assumptions of 4:2 very well, new difficulties arise at this stage. First, how can the values of the life table be related to actual recorded experience? Second, how can we represent the history of a complete lifetime, when the available data, and most interest in the subject, pertain to only short periods?

On account of these questions, two added assumptions are required before a life table can be constructed. Usually these questions are settled (a) by assuming that the mortality rate $(q_x)$ is re-

---

[12] The sum of $d_x$ from age 75 on must be exactly the number of people remaining in the life table at age 75. Hence it is equal to $l_{75}$. The ratio $_\infty M_{75}$ is the death rate for all women age 75 and above, computed from the data given in the original source of Table 4:1.

## "ABRIDGED" LIFE TABLE FOR FEMALES IN CHILE, 1940
(Based on Table 4:1)

Illustrating the Calculation of $_nL_x$ and Subsequent Columns

| (1) | (2) | (3) | (4) | (5) | (6) | (7) |
|---|---|---|---|---|---|---|
| | | | | $_nL_x$ | | $e_x$ |
| Ages | $_nq_x^{(a)}$ | $l_x^{(b)}$ | $_nL_x^{(c)}$ | (Copied from Table 4:1)$^d$ | $T_x^{(e)}$ | in years (6) + (3) |
| 0 | .18848 | 100,000 | 86,806$^f$ | ( 86,505) | 4,294,554 | 42.9 |
| 1 | .10276 | 81,152 | 307,930 | (300,501) | 4,207,748 | 51.9 |
| 5 | .01688 | 72,813 | 360,992 | (360,411) | 3,899,818 | 53.6 |
| 10 | .01626 | 71,584 | 355,010 | (355,480) | 3,538,826 | 49.4 |
| 15 | .03309 | 70,420 | 346,275 | (346,678) | 3,183,816 | 45.2 |
| 20 | .04352 | 68,090 | 333,042 | (333,145) | 2,837,541 | 41.7 |
| 25 | .04580 | 65,127 | 318,178 | (318,138) | 2,564,499 | 38.5 |
| 30 | .04721 | 62,144 | 303,385 | (303,389) | 2,186,321 | 35.2 |
| 35 | .05063 | 59,210 | 288,555 | (288,604) | 1,882,936 | 31.8 |
| 40 | .05558 | 56,212 | 273,250 | (273,298) | 1,594,381 | 28.4 |
| 45 | .06222 | 53,088 | 257,182 | (257,311) | 1,321,131 | 24.9 |
| 50 | .07818 | 49,785 | 239,195 | (239,545) | 1,063,949 | 21.4 |
| 55 | .10498 | 45,893 | 217,420 | (217,757) | 824,754 | 18.0 |
| 60 | .14179 | 41,075 | 190,815 | (191,379) | 607,334 | 14.8 |
| 65 | .20558 | 35,251 | 158,138 | (158,558) | 416,519 | 11.8 |
| 70 | .28596 | 28,004 | 120,000 | (120,293) | 258,381 | 9.2 |
| 75 | 1.0$^g$ | 19,996 | 138,381$^h$ | (155,471) | 138,381 | 6.9 |

$^a$Computed from $l_x$ in Column 3, by the formula $\dfrac{l_{x+n}}{l_x} = {}_nq_x$ .

$^b$Copied from Table 4:1.

$^c$Computed from abridged values of $l_x$ (Column 3) by the formula

$$_nL_x = \frac{n}{2}(l_x + l_{x+n}).$$

$^d$Copied from Table 4:1, summed in 4-year and 5-year groups. Included here for comparison.

$^e$Summed from Column 4, from bottom up.

$^f$Computed by arbitrarily assuming $L_0 = .3\, l_0 + .7\, l_1$ .

$^g$Assumed value.

$^h$Computed from the ratio $\dfrac{_\infty d_x}{M}$ , where $_\infty d_x$ is the sum of deaths age 75 and above (equal to $l_{75}$, or 19,996), and $_\infty M_x$ is .14450, obtained from the source of Table 4:1.

lated to the ratio, $M_x$ (discussed in 4:10), and (b) by combining the mortality rates of a given base period to form a synthetic cohort (taken up in 4:11).

## 4:10  Link between the Life Table and Actual Population Data — $M_x$

In order to construct a life table, some mortality rates (or survival rates) must be found.  As already explained, these rates are equal to the proportions of people surviving or failing to survive through given intervals of age.  The life table itself very clearly specifies the components of such a rate:  how many members of a cohort have survived to a particular age, $x$, and how many have reached (or failed to reach) age $x+n$.

Population records are rarely kept in such a way as to provide this information.  Ordinarily they do not separate people into cohorts.  In order to identify a cohort, we select an age group — that is, the people born some definite number of years ago.  There are two kinds of data commonly available for the measurement of mortality:  an enumerated population, and a registration of deaths.  But it is not consistent to identify a cohort in both types of data by means of an age classification.

An age group enumerated in a census does contain approximately the survivors of some yearly cohort or cohorts of births.  The age group 0-4 represents approximately the survivors of the people born during the past five years, enumerated at the time of the census.  But the two are not precisely the same.  For example, the infant population enumerated this year would not be the same as the survivors of this year's cohort of babies.  Some members of this cohort would be included, and some would be excluded;  some of the infants included would be members of *last* year's cohort of births.[13]  There is the same type of discrepancy at every age.

Registered deaths, by age, also are not precisely allocated to cohorts born during each year (even though these statistics are normally gathered and published for each calendar year).  A year's registered deaths of a given age represent parts of *two* yearly cohorts.  For example, this year's infant deaths are not quite the same as the infant deaths of this year's cohort of babies.  A large part will be members of *last* year's cohort (infants born some time last year

---

[13] A census taken on July 1, if it followed internationally recommended standards, would classify as infants (age zero) everyone born between July 1 of last year and June 30 of this year.  An age group in a census will correspond exactly to some yearly birth cohort only if the census is taken on December 31 or January 1.

but not yet past the first birthday when they die); part of the infant deaths of this year's cohort will not occur until next year (because many survivors of this year's babies will pass some time after December 31 before reaching their first birthday, during which they will be "exposed to some risk" of dying at age zero).[14] This discrepancy, too, is present at every age.

In most life tables, mortality is measured by the ratio of a year's registered deaths by age $(D_x)$ to the estimated person-years lived (the mid-year population by age, $P_x$). It is this ratio,

$$M_x = \frac{D_x}{P_x} k,$$

that provides the link between the life table and actual population data. This is the ordinary age-specific death rate (see 2:14), expressed in slightly different notation. If the age interval is greater than one year, the death rate includes the entire interval:

$$_n M_x = \frac{_n D_x}{_n P_x} k \text{ (where } n \text{ indicates the number of years in the interval).}[15]$$

This is not the same as the mortality rate of a life table (see 4:4). How, then, can $M_x$ be used to measure $q_x$? The answer is that it cannot. But an approximate value can be found for the mortality rate if we assume that $q_x = \dfrac{M_x}{1 + \dfrac{1}{2} M_x}$ , and this is the most common

---

[14] Some countries prepare special tables of deaths which distinguish the year of birth as well as the actual age at death. Though this greatly facilitates analysis of mortality, the enumerated age groups and the deaths registered by age still do not match. Only an extraordinary classification by age in the census (illustrated in the following Section), or a census taken at the end of the year, can bring these two records into correspondence.

[15] The value of $k$ is often set at 1,000, in order to avoid writing down long decimal figures. Before proceeding with life-table calculations, it must be changed from 1,000 to 1 (restoring the original decimal figures). The symbol "$M$" is adopted here to avoid the usual confusion with its counterpart, $m_x$, in the life table $\left( m_x = \dfrac{d_x}{L_x} \right)$.

formula for calculating mortality rates.[16] Computation is made easier

by putting the expression into this form: $q_x = \dfrac{2 M_x}{2 + M_x}$. Where the

age interval is some number of years *(n)* greater than one, this form

is used: $_n q_x = \dfrac{2n \, _n M_x}{2 + n \, _n M_x}$.

We should repeat that this link between $M_x$ and $q_x$ is merely an

approximate one. Despite its practical value (which is immense), it
is never fully satisfactory. The ratio, $M_x$, does not refer to any distinct cohort of people. Registered deaths and the mid-year population are not exactly matched at any age: they do not represent the
same universe. This approximation introduces unknown errors into

------

[16] The nature of this assumption may be explained as follows. In the

life table, $q_x = \dfrac{d_x}{l_x}$. If the structure of the population were the same as that

of the life table, then $q_x = \dfrac{D_x}{E_x}$ (where $E_x$ is the number of people in a cohort

who reach age $x$, and $D_x$ is the number of deaths in this group before their

survivors reach age $x+1$). Also, $P_x$ would be not merely the size of the mid-

year population, but the size of the cohort at the middle of the age interval,
$x$ to $x+1$. Lacking the figure for $E_x$, we could then calculate it, $E_x = P_x$

$+ \dfrac{1}{2} D_x$ (just as, in the life table, $l_x = L_x + \dfrac{1}{2} d_x$). Then we could also de-

fine the mortality rate as $q_x = \dfrac{D_x}{P_x + \dfrac{1}{2} D_x}$ (simply substituting equivalent

terms from the equations above). After dividing the numerator and the denominator by $P_x$, we could finally reach the formula given in the text:

$q_x = \dfrac{D_x}{P_x + \dfrac{1}{2} D_x} = \dfrac{D_x / P_x}{1 + \dfrac{1}{2} \dfrac{D_x}{P_x}} = \dfrac{M_x}{1 + \dfrac{1}{2} M_x}$. An understanding of this assumption

does not make it true, but does reveal what further conditions are needed in
order to make it true. The work of actuaries has also shown that other conditions may (if fulfilled) nullify a bias due to this defect.

mortality rates, and contributes to large fluctuations in the values of $q_x$ by age, especially when calculated by single year of age. The devices for treating these symptoms are described briefly in 4:13, on the smoothing of data.

### 4:11 Actual Cohorts and Synthetic Cohorts

The second assumption mentioned in 4:9 meets a need of another kind. Some members of a cohort will live as long as a full century, which is too long to wait for the information. The uses of the life table are more immediate, and they demand a summary of the mortality of a short period.

Therefore it is assumed that mortality rates at each age may be applied successively to form a hypothetical cohort, even if they pertain to the same year. Most life tables do not represent the life history of any actual cohort. Instead, a life history is *synthesized* from the mortality rates by age during some year or short base period, and thus represents short segments of the experience of many cohorts.[17] Age-specific death rates are first prepared and converted to a series of mortality rates (as described in 4:10 and illustrated in the Appendix). Then the mortality rates $(q_x)$ are treated *as if* they were the successive proportions dying in the hypothetical cohort. This basic shift in the meaning of the entire life table is accomplished merely by changing the source of one column, $q_x$. In every other way the structure of the life table remains unaffected.

What is the purpose of introducing this artificial or hypothetical element into the design of the life table? As suggested above, this device permits us to construct life tables from the data of a short period, which are often useful in comparing the mortality of different populations. The result is a summary of a year's death rates, rather than an actual life history. It shows what *would be* the implications if the synthetic schedule of mortality did apply to an actual cohort.

Synthetic-cohort life tables thus have a restricted meaning. They represent past or future mortality of the hypothetical cohort, but only the mortality of the base period in the actual population. This limitation impairs their principal use, estimating how many members of some actual cohort die from one age to another. Such an estimate

----

[17] The practices of naming these two types of life tables are not uniform. A table based on the experience of an actual cohort is sometimes called a "generation life table" or a "fluent life table"; here we shall call it an "actual-cohort life table." A synthetic-cohort life table is usually not distinguished by *any* name; encountering a reference to just a "life table," one can be sure that it means this second type.

covers a definite period of time.  Between ages 5 and 15, for example, it will cover a period of 10 years, going far beyond the normal base period of life table values.  These values could not fit the experience of the actual population unless its risks of death by age remained fixed throughout the entire period; and this is what must be assumed.

Today, conditions affecting mortality sometimes change very rapidly; it is unrealistic to suppose that they do not change at all. Yet such estimates are continually needed in practical problems of research.  A life table — sometimes even a life table borrowed from another population in similar circumstances — is extremely convenient for this purpose.  Hence a prominent part of demography is concerned with the application of the life table (representing the experience of a synthetic cohort) to show the effects of mortality on certain age groups (actual cohorts) in a population (see 5:2).  Of course, this is done with the knowledge that the answers will be wrong.  But the results are often of sufficient value, and the expected errors sufficiently small, to outweigh the objections against extending the meaning of the life table in this manner.

### 4:12  Construction of Synthetic Life Table by Direct Computation of $q_x$

The roundabout practice of converting observed death rates $(M_x)$ into mortality rates $(q_x)$ is not an essential part of constructing life tables, but a necessary step when available data provide no closer approach to the values of $q_x$.  It would be more straightforward to compute mortality rates by age directly from the statistics of a census and death registration.  With data in the required form, it is a single step to calculate the proportion of the people, reaching each age during a base year, who died before reaching the next age.  The other life-table columns are determined from this series of proportions, according to the relations of 4:5 and 4:8.[18]

The procedure is illustrated below with some early population data from Taiwan.  A census in 1915 classified the population by calendar year of birth (as an indirect method of determining age); regis-

---

[18]It should be pointed out that the mortality rate obtained by this procedure is not quite identical in its form with the mortality rate that has become rather standard in actuarial work.  This rate is based on the deaths of some cohort during a given year of age (and these deaths occur during two calendar years); the usual type of rate is based on deaths of the calendar year, whether or not they belong to any particular cohort.  Therefore, this rate does not represent exactly the mortality of the calendar year (or whatever base period), but the mortality of "persons who *reach* age x during the calendar year."

tered deaths were classified by year of birth as well as by age at
death. The statistics on the whole are remarkably complete and reliable. With these materials we can match the deaths of each cohort to
the people in the cohort, and this is what is wanted.

However, even under these favorable circumstances the data
must be adjusted slightly. The size of each cohort must be determined as it was at the beginning of the year. The census (taken on
October 1) counted the people of each cohort on October 1, and not at
the beginning of the year. By means of a simple estimate, the census data can be moved back to the beginning of 1915.[19]

Then it is easy to determine how many survivors of each cohort
passed a birthday (that is, "reached age x") during 1915. Those
counted at the time of the census, plus the estimated number who had
died between January 1 and September 30, indicate the size of the cohort on January 1. Of the cohort of boys born in 1914, this was
63,053, the total group that *might* reach age one during 1915. But
some members failed to reach age one, because they died at age zero.
Therefore, 63,053 minus 4,051 (members who died before their birthday in 1915), or 59,002, were the (estimated) universe of boys who
reached age one in 1915:

| | | |
|---|---|---|
| Counted in census, October 1 (born in 1914) | 58,162 | |
| Estimated deaths to cohort, Jan. 1 to Sept. 30 *(add)* | 4,891 | |
| Estimated number in cohort on January 1 | | 63,053 |
| Died in 1915 *before* reaching age one *(subtract)* | 4,051 | |
| Survivors who reached age one in 1915 | | 59,002 |

The same calculation is carried out for every cohort counted by the
census.

The result is the number of males who reached each age during
1915. This is the figure referred to as $E_x$ above (footnote 16). We
then determine how many died before reaching the next year of age
(by slight rearrangement of the death statistics at each age, excluding members of other cohorts who died at the same age, and including

---

[19] There were 58,298 registered male deaths at all ages in 1915; the
deaths at all ages from January 1 to September 30 in 1915 were 41,363. The
proportion $\frac{41,363}{58,298}$, or .7095, multiplied by the number of deaths in 1915

among the members of each cohort, gives an estimate of the deaths, by cohort, that occurred between January 1 and September 30. These deaths are
added to the members of each cohort counted in the census. The sum is the
estimated size of each cohort on January 1, 1915. See Table 4:3.

members of the same cohort who died at that age in 1916). Of 3,460
male deaths at age one registered in 1915, 2,843 were boys born in
1914. There were also 1,716 deaths, age one, among members of the
same cohort during 1916, before the entire cohort reached age two.
Total deaths of this cohort at age one were 2,843 + 1,716, or 4,559,
and the mortality rate is calculated as follows:

| Year of Birth | Deaths Registered in 1915 $D_1'$ (After Birthday) | Deaths Registered in 1915 $D_0''$ (Before Birthday) | Deaths Registered in 1916 $D_1''$ (Before Birthday) | Survivors January 1, 1915 (estimated) | Age at Birthday in 1915 | Survivors Reaching Age 1 in 1915 $(5) - (3)$ | Mortality Rate $q_1$ $\dfrac{(2) + (4)}{(7)}$ |
|---|---|---|---|---|---|---|---|
| (1) | (2) | (3) | (4) | (5) | (6) | (7) | (8) |
| 1914 | 2,843 | 4,051 | 1,716 | 63,053 | 1 | 59,002 | .07727 |

## TABLE 4:3

## ARRANGEMENT OF MORTALITY DATA OF TAIWAN, 1915–1916 AND CACULATION OF $q_x$

Taiwanese Males, Ages 0-9

| Year of Birth | Deaths Registered in 1915 $D_x'$ (After Birthday) | Deaths Registered in 1915 $D_{x-1}''$ (Before Birthday) | Deaths Registered in 1916 $D_x''$ (Before Birthday) | Survivors January 1, 1915 (estimated)[a] | Age at Birthday in 1915 | Survivors Reaching Age x in 1915 $(5) - (3)$ | Mortality Rate $q_x$ $\dfrac{(2) + (4)}{(7)}$ |
|---|---|---|---|---|---|---|---|
| (1) | (2) | (3) | (4) | (5) | (6) | (7) | (8) |
| 1915 | 10,502[b] | — | 3,967 | — | 0 | 71,629[c] | .20200 |
| 1914 | 2,843 | 4,051 | 1,716 | 55,886 | 1 | 59,002 | .07727 |
| 1913 | 1,333 | 1,617 | 1,013 | 54,250 | 2 | 52,269 | .04323 |
| 1912 | 977 | 1,009 | 653 | 52,294 | 3 | 53,241 | .03062 |
| 1911 | 703 | 617 | 401 | 49,548 | 4 | 51,667 | .02137 |
| 1910 | 504 | 444 | 314 | 46,729 | 5 | 49,104 | .01666 |
| 1909 | 333 | 308 | 207 | 43,777 | 6 | 46,421 | .01163 |
| 1908 | 269 | 209 | 162 | 44,555 | 7 | 43,568 | .00989 |
| 1907 | 195 | 194 | 156 | 42,904 | 8 | 44,361 | .00791 |
| 1906 | 175 | 150 | 118 | 44,196 | 9 | 42,196 | .00694 |

[a] See footnote 19 in text.

[b] Includes an allowance for under-registration, equal to the assumed number of under-registered births in Column 7.

[c] Live male births registered in 1915, plus an allowance of 1.1 per cent for under-registration.

The number who died at age one, divided by the total number who reached age one, yields the proportion who died $(q_1)$, or the mortality rate at age one.

Each cohort identified (by the census) in 1915 may be given the same treatment, assembling the complete record of its deaths between age $x$ (the age reached during 1915) and age $x + 1$. The calculations are illustrated in Table 4:3 for several cohorts. If continued through all ages, they would provide the mortality rates for a complete life table. The number of "survivors" who reached age zero is supplied by the statistics of births registered during 1915 (plus an allowance of 1.1 per cent for under-registration, based on analysis of the registration of infant deaths in Taiwan that is too extensive to describe here).

However, direct as it is, this procedure does not find frequent opportunities for application. It depends on the existence of a particular tradition of keeping population records, which is confined to a few countries. As a practical guide to methods of constructing life tables, the Appendix explains three other procedures of wider applicability, after a brief discussion of the smoothing of mortality data.

### 4:13  The Smoothing of Data

The "smoothing" of data does not enter into the forms of life-table construction demonstrated in this chapter. Yet it should not pass without mention, for smoothing is an important part of more refined methods, and something should be understood of its purpose, its effects, and the circumstances in which it is needed.

When values are computed for $M_x$ and $q_x$ by single year of age, in the making of a "complete" life table, they are found to have an erratic pattern; it appears when plotted on a graph as an unmistakable jagged outline, with marked irregularities instead of a completely smooth progression from age to age. These are more than a mere representation of the facts; they also represent accumulated inaccuracies of data, defects of method (like the use of $M_x$ to estimate $q_x$), and random fluctuations (due to no fault of either data or method).

It is generally assumed that mortality rates tend to fit a pattern like that of Chart 4:1-B, and that the irregularity is a distortion of the "true" picture. Accordingly, a formidable body of procedures has been developed to modify these distortions. Nothing can be done about the defects of method, because they stem from a fundamental lack of correspondence between the data and what they are supposed to measure. The irregularities are therefore treated as errors, and some effort is made to reduce their effect.

This is done by smoothing, or "graduation" of data. The age distribution of the enumerated population may be smoothed before calculation of the death rate $(M_x)$; the age distribution of registered deaths may likewise be smoothed. (After smoothing one of them, it is almost unavoidable to treat the other in the same way, for accurate observations are altered indiscriminately with errors.) Later, if some lingering unevenness is still apparent in the pattern of death rates or mortality rates by age, these may be independently smoothed.

The process of smoothing alters the values in a series of numbers where they deviate from neighboring values, drawing them in (from both high and low) toward a line drawn approximately through the center of the fluctuations. It is done under some rigorous restrictions, in order to retain as much as possible of the shape of the original distribution. Various smoothing procedures have somewhat different characteristics. Making these adjustments of data is a complicated operation. It is a task too specialized and too advanced for adequate treatment in this book.[20] Even when done with the greatest care, one is never certain that smoothing has brought the results closer to the exact or "true" mortality rates in the population.

This is not a very immediate problem, for these elaborate methods are designed principally for use in constructing "complete," or single-year, life tables. For most purposes, construction of abridged tables is to be recommended, where the intervals of age are larger than one year. A death rate for a larger interval is a kind of *average* of the data of several single years; most of the erratic behavior of single-year data is absorbed in this average. Hence the death rates of abridged life tables $\left( {}_{n}M_{x} \right)$ are already smoothed, informally and almost by accident. To what extent this affects their accuracy cannot be ascertained, for there is little chance to exercise control over the process.[21] Abridged life tables often differ slightly from life tables calculated (from the same data) by detailed methods, but the results of the two approaches have been found to be remarkably close.

As stated at the outset of the chapter, the life table by itself is easily understood. And so are the major assumptions that are involved. For this reason the life table has been treated separately,

---

[20] See M. Miller, et al., *Elements of Graduation* (Philadelphia, 1949), or H.W. Haycock and W. Perks, *Mortality and Other Investigations* (Cambridge, 1955), Chapters 7, 8.

[21] For example, these death rates may be distorted, in either direction, by the typical skewed pattern of internal composition of an age group in the population.

apart from other practical problems related to its use. One of these, the steps of constructing abridged tables from population data, is discussed in an Appendix to this chapter.[22] Another problem, the common applications of the life table in research, is treated in Chapter 5, and elsewhere at specific points where necessary.

[22]The Appendix is found on pages 286-305. It does not cover all methods, but just those regarded as most useful at this level. Suggestions for further reading are offered in Chapter 10.

# CHAPTER 5

# THE STUDY OF MORTALITY

As pointed out in the first chapter, the statistical operations of demography consist largely of computing conventional ratios and rates. In other words, they are primarily descriptive. This is true of the study of mortality as well. However, most conventional measurements have very little meaning except as they rank "high" or "low" according to the standards of the time. Hence it is necessary to compare death rates representing a variety of experience, and to some extent such comparisons are involved in all study of mortality.

Many purposes are served by mortality analysis. As mentioned before, there are practical applications in life insurance. It has a bearing on matters of public policy, for every country is committed to a goal of extending the longevity of its people sooner or later. But the facts are also of interest for their own sake, as a sign of processes and changes in a population. Uniformities and differences of mortality within a country reveal the distribution of other related factors. Similar conclusions can be drawn from the evidence of trends. The patterns of mortality are sometimes valuable indications of the levels of health, having considerable medical significance. Changes of mortality also are a basis for appraising the effects of a program that seeks to improve public health. Estimates of mortality are a step, usually the most reliable step, in estimating the size of the population at dates before or after a census. Finally, analysis of mortality contributes to the study of replacement and population growth, as the brief mention of the stable population will suggest.

"Mortality," however, is not a single factor to be expressed as a single number or index. We have already seen that the risk of death is something that must be measured in several aspects. In many instances these measurements might be provided by life tables, if there were enough life tables in existence. But this is not the case, and so various kinds of death rates, more or less conventional, are commonly adopted. Most of this chapter is devoted to describing these devices, and ways to arrange them for comparisons which answer worth-while questions.

Most types of death rates are *specific*, which means that they pertain to some specified portion of a population. A specific death rate refers to this part of the population, but not to the mortality of the entire population. Selection of a type of death rate therefore is tantamount to selection of some particular aspect of mortality for study. Where there are definite rules of procedure, they usually apply to the manner of computing the rates, and not to their interpretation, which is left open to a wide scope of judgment and decision.

### 5:1 Applications of the Life Table

What place does the life table have in the study of mortality? In order to justify all the trouble of learning its structure and carrying out the laborious steps of construction, it must have some distinct advantages over other measurements of mortality. First, its conventional terms, discussed in Chapter 4, are generally recognized, and are an efficient medium of communication. These measurements are also clear and unambiguous; they do not have conflicting meanings. They are in a convenient form. And finally, the life table provides the basis for a "stable population," the foremost theoretical model of population processes, and its related aspects. [1]

There are several ways of utilizing the life table in demographic analysis: (a) description and summary of age-specific risks of death in a population, (b) comparisons of these risks in different populations or population groups, (c) construction of hypothetical models, and (d) estimation. These are discussed in the following sections below.

### 5:2 Descriptive Uses of the Life Table

When available, a life table is an unexcelled fund of detail. It indicates the level of mortality at any interval of age during some base period, as in Chart 4:1-B or Table 4:1. Values can be copied directly, or computed easily according to the relations of the several columns (as explained in 4:5). They are useful for various purposes:

$q_x$ or $_nq_x$. These rates represent mortality by age, apart from other ages. Mortality rates for larger intervals of age $(_nq_x)$ can

---

[1] The principle of the life table also has important other applications not necessarily related to mortality, in the study of marriage, manpower and migration. There is not enough space to explain all these applications in this book, but the reader will be referred from time to time to some of the existing discussions. For a general and very readable treatment, see M. Spiegelman, *Introduction to Demography* (Chicago, 1955).

be computed as follows: $_nq_x = 1 - \left(\dfrac{l_{x+n}}{l_x}\right)$. Rates for smaller inter-

vals than those shown in an available table must be computed by interpolation (see 1:7, 3:12 and 4:16). The rate for the first year of
life, $q_0$, is the standard form for measuring infant mortality; rates for
other ages are sometimes used in preference to age-specific death
rates because they are presumed to reflect considerable care and critical attention in preparation.

$p_x$ or $_np_x$. These rates contain the same information, expressed in a different form. They are survival rates, and are directly
related to mortality rates: $p_x = 1 - q_x$. For some purposes, survival
rates are more useful (see, for example, 7:10).

$l_x$, the number of survivors by age in the life-table cohort,
shows the *cumulative* effect of mortality rates, from birth to some
given age, x. It is dependent on mortality rates at all younger ages,
and influenced most by the relatively high level of mortality during
infancy $(q_0)$ and early childhood. Hence, $l_x$ is best suited to representing mortality in the first few years of life, when the risk of dying
is most likely to be related to the level of infant mortality. The value
of $l_5$, for example, is sometimes a useful indication of mortality in
the first few years of age, even though it gives the largest weight to
the effect of infant mortality. Of course, $l_x$ is not a mortality rate; it
expresses the *effect* of mortality rates, based on exactly the same information. It can be restored to the form of a mortality rate (see 4:5).

A mortality rate from birth to age 5 is $_5q_0 = 1 - \left(\dfrac{l_5}{l_0}\right)$; according to

the life table for Chilean females in Chapter 4, this is $1 - \left(\dfrac{72,813}{100,000}\right)$,
or .27187.

$d_x$ is useless outside the context of the particular life table,
because it is dependent on the numbers surviving, and has no meaning apart from them.

$L_x$ has a value close to $l_x$,[2] but represents the number of
person-years lived during some interval of age. It corresponds approximately to an age group enumerated in an actual population.
Therefore the chief application of $L_x$ beyond the life table itself is

---

[2]It always lies between $l_x$ and $l_{x+1}$

to furnish estimates of the mortality in an actual population, based on the experience of the life table (see 5:3 and 3:9).

$e_x$ is the average number of remaining years of life per person in the life-table cohort after some given age, x. Compared with $l_x$, the expectation of life measures the effect of mortality in the opposite direction: $e_x$ shows the effect of mortality at later ages (from exact age x upward), whereas $l_x$ shows the effect of mortality at earlier ages (from birth to age x). The higher the life expectancy, the lower the mortality rate. The life expectancy is no less accurate than any other of these measurements; it is based on the same facts, expressed in different form. By the ratio $\dfrac{1}{e_x}$ , the life expectancy is converted into a special kind of death rate, "deaths per person-year in the life-table cohort after exact age x." If the members of the life-table cohort at each age are all assembled into a hypothetical population (the "stationary population," explained in 5:5), this death rate is interpreted as a ratio of "deaths per person age x and above." This may appear less awkward as a measurement of mortality, and may be substituted for $e_x$; it will give exactly the same results as $e_x$ in comparing the mortality of different populations.[3]

## 5:3  Using the Life Table to Compare Mortality in Different Populations

The values of a life table permit some very exact comparisons between two or more populations or population groups. This is because the risks of death are closely associated with age, and because the age structure of a population is a changeable aspect of its composition. For these two reasons, the mortality of different populations cannot be accurately compared unless age is taken into consideration. The life table is extremely well suited to analysis by age. Moreover, it provides a variety of measurements suitable for many purposes.

The life table has the advantage of being extremely flexible in summarizing different parts of mortality experience by age in a population (see 4:5). But this advantage may be of no value in comparing different populations, because each life table is limited to the mortal-

---

[3] Values of $e_x$ do not foretell the future mortality experience of anyone; they merely summarize the information already known about the life-table cohort, which is a special technique for describing the mortality of a particular year or base period (see 4:5).

ity of some particular base period. In order to be useful, it must be available for the right place and the right time. Consequently, most comparisons must be made on the basis of ordinary death rates of some type, as described in 2:9 and 2:14.

## 5:4 Use of the Life Table in Making Population Estimates

The life table is indispensable in making population estimates by age, for it shows the approximate effects of mortality in an actual group of people. Knowing the approximate losses through death, we can estimate the size of this group at various dates when there has been no census, even at dates after the most recent census. These estimates can be extended for some considerable time into the future, with certain assumptions about possible changes of mortality.[4]

For example, 572,869 girls were enumerated at age 12 in the 1940 census of Brazil. How many of this group would be alive exactly 5 years after the census date? It is not possible to assemble the exact information from a register of deaths; if possible, this would still be impracticable. But the same question is answered easily if it refers to a life-table cohort. The column of $L_x$ values shows the number of person-years lived at age 12, and at age 17, after the cohort had passed through the mortality rates of the intervening five years of age. (In both the actual population and the life-table cohort, it is assumed that the average age of the group is 12½ years at the beginning of the period, and 17½ at the end.)

Suppose that the mortality rates of the actual population were equal to the mortality rates of the life table. Then the ratios of the numbers of persons, or person-years, must also be equal:

$$\frac{L_{17}}{L_{12}} = \frac{P_{17}}{P_{12}}$$

(where $P_x$ is the number of persons enumerated in some interval of age). The use of the life table in making population estimates consists of finding a life table that is believed to represent approximately the mortality of the actual population, and proceeding on the assumption that these two ratios are equal. For the sake of illustra-

---

[4] Estimates of future population are usually called "projections," to emphasize that they rest on hypothetical assumptions. When carried into the future, of course, there must be extra assumptions about the future levels of fertility and migration, which determine the number of new members gained by the population. See 7:13.

tion, we shall use the life table for Chile in 1940.[5]  To estimate how many Brazilian girls would have been enumerated at age 17 in 1945, the ratio of $\dfrac{L_{17}}{L_{12}}$ is computed from the life table, and the population at age 12 (according to the census of 1940) is multiplied by this ratio:

$$\overline{P}_{17} = P_{12}\left(\frac{L_{17}}{L_{12}}\right), \text{ or } 572{,}869 \times .97515 = 558{,}633.$$

This is the basic element in nearly all population estimates by age. There is only one definite rule of procedure: the data of the life table should exactly match, by age, the data for the actual population.[6]  $L_{12}$ corresponds to $P_{12}$, and $L_{17}$ to $P_{17}$. If we wish to estimate how many Brazilian girls of the age group 10-14 in 1940 would be alive in 1945, the ratio $\dfrac{L_{17}}{L_{12}}$ is still appropriate, because the average age of the group is still roughly 12½ years, and 17½ years at the later date. However, the ratio $\dfrac{_{5}L_{15}}{_{5}L_{10}}$ is equally appropriate; and this ratio is more convenient if an abridged life table is employed, because the values for $L_{12}$ and $L_{17}$ would have to be calculated by interpolation. These two ratios are nearly the same — the first is equal to .97515, the second to .97524.

The same procedure can be applied in the reverse direction. Again using the enumerated population of Brazilian girls age 12 in 1940, we can estimate the size of this group in 1935 by assuming $\dfrac{P_7}{P_{12}} = \dfrac{L_7}{L_{12}}$ . The amount of the estimate would be $\overline{P}_7 = P_{12}\left(\dfrac{L_7}{L_{12}}\right)$ 572,869 × (1.01234), or 579,938. These estimates can be extended for a period of any number of years, or even fractions of years, merely by adopting the corresponding interval of years of age between $L_x$

---

[5] A life table exists for Brazil, constructed (despite the lack of adequate death registration) by special methods. The life table for Chile is used here to show the applications of the information in Table 4:1.

[6] Even this requirement is sometimes relaxed when the life table lacks a column of $L_x$ values. Above age 5, values of $l_x$ may be used instead, with virtually the same numerical results.

and $L_{x+n}$ . The longer the period, however, the greater the likelihood of error, because the mortality of the population may change, whereas the mortality of the life table remains fixed.

It is also possible to estimate the size of the population from the statistics of registered births, or to estimate the numbers of births from the enumerated population. Naturally, the two sets of figures must refer to the same cohort of people, which requires that enumerated population by year of age be matched against registered births by year of occurrence. For example, on the basis of the births registered during the preceding year, how many infants should we expect to count in a census? The answer rests on the same analogy between the actual population and the life table. In the life table, $L_0$ represents the number of person-years lived during infancy, and corresponds to the infant population at a given moment; $l_0$ represents the number of births in the life-table cohort. We assume that $\dfrac{P_0}{B} = \dfrac{L_0}{l_0}$, where $P_0$ is the number of infants at a particular moment, and $B$ is the number of births during the preceding 12 months. The estimated number of infants is $\overline{P}_0 = B\left(\dfrac{L_0}{l_0}\right)$. The estimated number of *births* in the preceding year, based on an enumeration of infants, is

$$\overline{B} = P_0\left(\frac{l_0}{L_0}\right).$$

Estimates can be made over a longer period, always provided that the births and enumerated population are properly matched so that they refer to the same cohort of people. In general, it is assumed that $\dfrac{P_x}{B} = \dfrac{L_x}{l_0}$. Some special steps are often needed in order to match the data to the proper cohorts of people.[7]

---

[7]Since births are normally registered by calendar year (January to December), the birth statistics usually must be re-arranged to match the cohorts counted by age in the census (see 3:8). This is easily done if birth statistics are tabulated by month or quarter in which they occurred. If not, the births may be re-apportioned approximately. For example, births in the period March 1949 to April 1950 are approximately 3/4 of the total births registered in 1949, plus 1/4 of the total births registered in 1950. These proportions should be varied to suit the position of the census date in the year.

Population estimates fill needs of two kinds. They provide figures required for further research or guidance of administrative decisions, and they provide a test for the consistency of different statistical sources.

There are gaps in the existing statistical records of every country. It may be necessary to know the size of the population at dates when there has been no census, or before the results of a census have been fully tabulated. Administrative planning often demands such figures. The probable numbers of children of school age, needed for the operation of public schools, and the numbers reaching the minimum school age each year, can be calculated, with the help of a life table, from the annual records of births. The future size of the working population is often estimated as a guide to economic forecasts. Most studies of future population trends by age also use this approach, applied at every 5-year age group (though additional estimates must also be made of births and migration).[8] If the registration of births is unreliable, it may be reasonable to guess the annual numbers of births during the past five or ten years, based on a life table and the enumerated population under age 5 or under age 10 (see Table 3:3).

When a discrepancy is suspected between the data of two or more independent statistical sources at different dates, a life table is the principal basis for testing their consistency. The first step is to identify the members of some cohort of births, at different dates; the data must refer to the same cohort in both sources. The life table indicates the probable losses by death during the intervening period. On this basis, the estimate from one source is checked against the observed figure from the other. If the life table fits the situation, and if there have been no gains or losses through migration, this comparison provides the test for consistency. If the sources are consistent, this obvious cause for questioning their accuracy is removed. If they disagree, the amount of the discrepancy may be a reasonable measurement of the error of one of them.[9]

The technique of making these estimates is very simple so far as mortality is concerned, and presents no special problems. Yet it is very widely abused in actual practice. This is due partly to a misinterpretation of the entire nature and purpose of the estimates. The life table makes only a limited contribution, which is to indicate the

[8] The life table is also employed to estimate the future population of potential parents, in order to determine the probable future members of births, and to estimate the amount of migration. See 7:13 and 8:7.

[9] This is the basis of the tests described in 3:9 and 3:10.

approximate effects of mortality on a group of people during a specified period; the effects of fertility or migration must be dealt with separately. When these other factors are present, this contribution may become unimportant.

Partly, too, the danger in making these estimates, where mortality is concerned, is due to unwise selection of the life table which is to represent a particular situation. Many arbitrary elements are concentrated at this point. Obviously the mortality conditions of the life table should be as similar as possible to those being estimated, but there may be very little to guide the choice. Moreover, the life table has an inherent defect in this application. The life table is based on death rates at the same time, and yet it is made to represent the mortality of several successive years. Because mortality is subject to change, this technique produces estimates that we know to be wrong. It is often more useful to have such information than none. The goal is to keep the error as small as possible. While there is no general method for accomplishing this, the user of the information can be forewarned if the assumptions of the estimate are described as fully as possible.

## 5:5 Hypothetical Models Based on the Life Table

A. *Stationary Population.* In Chapter 4, a life table was defined as the life history of a hypothetical cohort of people, born in the same period and subject to gradual losses by mortality at each age. One column $(L_x$, or $_nL_x)$ shows the number of person-years lived, or the average number of persons present, at each interval of age. It resembles a table of a population classified by age according to the results of a census in some particular year. Indeed, the $L_x$, or $_nL_x$, column of a life table may be regarded as a hypothetical population, classified by age. That is to say, it may be treated as an entire population present at one time, rather than one cohort observed successively at each age.

It is a special type of case. Like the hypothetical cohort, this hypothetical population is determined at each age by the fixed rates of mortality of the life table — by these alone, and not by the structure of any actual population. It is assumed that these rates have remained fixed for every cohort represented in the population, and not for just one cohort. Likewise, the number of births must have remained fixed at 10,000, or 100,000, each year. The population is "closed" against migration, and therefore is maintained solely by a balance of births and deaths. This balance is also fixed (the number of births each year always equals the number of deaths), and so the size of the population is stationary. Moreover, the size of each age group is also stationary: in each age group, the number of person-years lived is always the same as that of the original life-table cohort. The age composition therefore is also stationary.

This hypothetical model of a population, based on perpetually unchanging conditions of fertility, mortality and total size, is called a *stationary population*. It is completely derived from the data of one life table.[10] The annual number of people reaching each year of age is indicated by the column, $l_x$. The annual number of deaths at each age is given in the column, $d_x$. The mid-year population, by age, is shown by the column, $L_x$, or $_nL_x$. The sum of the numbers in this column is the total size of the stationary population, shown in the first entry of the column, $T_x$, at age zero $(T_0)$.

The crude death rate is, of course, the total number of annual deaths divided by this total population. The number of births each year is $l_0$, ordinarily 10,000 or 100,000. The crude birth rate is thus $\dfrac{l_0}{T_0} k$. Since the population is stationary, the number of births and the number of deaths each year must be equal, and the death rate is likewise equal to $\dfrac{l_0}{T_0} k$. (Since the expectation of life at birth is $\dfrac{T_0}{l_0}$, the death rate and birth rate are both equal to $\dfrac{1}{e_0} k$.)[11]

---

[10] The life table provides the information for a stationary population of either males or females separately. In order to construct a stationary population containing both sexes, they must be mixed in some definite ratio. This is usually the sex ratio of births in the actual population, or simply an arbitrary ratio of 1.05 to one. The male person-years at every age $(_nL_x)$ are multiplied by this ratio, and the results are added to the person-years of women at the same ages. The result is to mix males and females in the stationary population exactly as they would be if this sex ratio had always prevailed among its births.

[11] They are not necessarily the same as the birth and death rates of the actual population. The stationary population has its own age structure, and this is determined independently of the age structure of actual population on which the life table is based. If the age structures are different, then the death rates and the birth rates are also somewhat different (see 7:10).

What are the uses of this hypothetical model? It has limited descriptive value, because of its restrictive assumptions. In particular, the natural increase (balance between births and deaths) is fixed arbitrarily at zero. The number of deaths is determined by the structure of the life table. The number of births is fixed at exactly the same figure, and the crude birth rate must always be the same as the crude death rate. Thus the stationary population is not a very realistic model, for fertility and mortality in the actual world are not so closely connected. Its chief application is to represent what *would be* the structure of a population based on these fixed conditions. There is often something to be learned by comparing this structure with that of the actual population which experienced the mortality rates, and observing what differences are due to the departure from these conditions in the actual population.[12] The stationary population also can show the size of a population that would be maintained under the same risks of death by any constant stream of births (simply by constructing a life table which starts with a radix of any given size, not just 100,000).

*B. Stable Population.* Another use of the stationary population is an extension to a less restricted type of model. The hypothetical population need not be stationary. It can be constructed from independent schedules of mortality and fertility, permitting some annual increase or decrease. In English and American usage, this type of model is called the *stable population;* it has many of the characteristics of the stationary population (the assumptions still remain fixed, and the age structure is determinate), but it is derived by a more complex procedure. The structure of the stable population is described in 7:8 by means of an example.

The stable population represents the permanent structure that a hypothetical population would ultimately have, if the assumed age-specific birth rates and death rates persisted without change. It is derived completely from these birth rates and death rates, is closed against migration, and is not dependent on the composition of any concrete population. The stable population succeeds in bringing together fertility and mortality in a single self-sufficient scheme. It is the most ambitious model yet developed in demography, and the most ambitious application of the life table. Opinions are not unanimous about its practical significance in research, but there is no doubt that it has greatly aided the knowledge of relations among various population processes. One must understand clearly the nature of the stable

---

[12] For example, this comparison is the basis of the *Replacement Index,* discussed in 7:6.

population in order to follow the recent literature of population analysis.

## 5:6  Crude Death Rates

A large part of mortality analysis is carried on without the benefit of a life table.  Other measurements have at least as much practical value, and are often to be preferred for their convenience.  But there is a considerable distance separating the life table with its elaborate details and some of the other indices of mortality, and it is only with some hazard that one is able to approach the same questions by these various routes.

The commonest of these measures is the crude death rate.  It represents deaths per thousand persons, which has become a familiar basis of discussing the general level of mortality.  There is a wide range between high and low crude death rates.  A distinction of "high" and "low," however, is merely one of convenience, without absolute or permanent significance.  Before the period of modern records, death rates of 40 and above were probably normal, though now this is considered extremely high.  Today crude death rates as low as 7 to 10 per thousand have been achieved by several countries, and rates of 10-15 are within reach of most of the world.  But such low mortality is to be expected together with the most advanced and expensive medical and sanitary arrangements, and where these conditions are absent, very low recorded death rates should be viewed with some skepticism.

The crude death rate, a ratio of deaths during a year to the total mid-year population, is the crudest possible type of rate based on data of registered deaths.[13]  It expresses the frequency of death in an entire population as a single number, and its principal merits, as well as its shortcomings as a conventional rate, stem from this fact.

The crude death rate has many advantages.  As just mentioned, it shows the level of mortality in an entire population; for this reason it is the usual index of mortality found in yearbooks and general statistical publications.  Its meaning can be communicated to the general public.  It is easily and quickly computed, requiring the bare minimum of data for a vital rate.  Even where a detailed analysis is contemplated, a crude rate often gives a preliminary indication of the level or trend of mortality.  Tentative results can be found before the checks and tests of the data are completed.  At this stage these are valuable, even if later found to be wrong, in deciding what further research to pursue.

---

[13]The computation of crude rates is discussed in 2:9.

On the other hand, due to this simplicity the crude death rate
has two important limitations.  It mixes together many population
groups whose mortality varies widely; whereas the major results of
mortality study have come from examination of these components
separately by means of more detailed analysis.  Second, the crude
death rate mixes these elements indiscriminately, in the form of an
average, thereby giving greater weight to the mortality experience of
groups that are large and to all mortality experience that is extremely
high or extremely low.  Thus the level of the crude death rate is affected not only by the level of mortality, which it is supposed to
measure, but also by the distribution of people of differing mortality.

For example, suppose that a crude death rate of exactly 16 per
thousand has been observed in each of two different countries.  Does
this imply that the general level of mortality is the same in both?  In
a superficial sense this is true, for the average number of deaths per
1,000 people is 16 in both cases.  But if one population has a larger
proportion of adults, this gives its crude death rate a somewhat higher
tendency (because deaths at these ages make a large contribution to
total mortality).  Indeed, there may be definite differences in the pattern of mortality between the two populations, unrevealed by the
crude death rates.[14]

On the basis of the crude death rate, we can make broad statements about the level of mortality and reach preliminary conclusions
about trends or patterns.  It does not depend on the accuracy of age
reporting, and therefore can be used before these details are tested;
however, neither does it help in detecting inaccuracies of age reporting.  Crude death rates are excellent for observing yearly or seasonal
fluctuations, because such a period is normally too short to introduce
serious change of composition in a population.  They are poor indices
of mortality wherever such changes have occurred, especially where
there has been a shift in age groups or other groups of distinctive
mortality experience.  Sometimes it is possible to compromise between crude and detailed death rates by means of an age-adjusted or
"standardized" rate, using a single figure for a population but making some allowance for differences of age composition (see 5:16).

It is not safe to base very definite conclusions on the evidence
of crude death rates alone.  Because of their limitations, a thorough
study of mortality must go beyond this stage, proceeding to some of
the rates of the following sections.

---

[14]To illustrate, the crude death rates of Japan have been consistently
*lower* than those of France in recent years; but Japan's age-specific death
rates have actually been *higher*, in every age group.

## 5:7 Death Rates by Age

Any gain of precision requires more detailed rates, which imply the existence of more information. The largest single step in this direction is to take account of variation by age, and this is done by computing death rates separately by age group (see 2:14). It is usually advantageous to prepare these rates separately for males and females, making them age-sex-specific death rates.

What is it that age-specific death rates contribute to the study of mortality? As explained before (2:13), large differences of risks of death among members of a population are related to age. Separating the people according to age is a very efficient means of reducing the hidden effects of this diversity in a death rate. And, of course, it is the only means of calculating a death rate that is unaffected by the age composition of a population. Age-specific death rates are a valuable basis for comparison between populations or population groups. By inspecting the pattern of age-specific death rates one can sometimes form an opinion about possible deficiencies of the data. [15]

Aside from removing unwanted effects of population composition, age-specific death rates also indicate the distribution of mortality by age, which has several significant aspects. The processes of physical degeneration are linked to age; so is an early period of helplessness and high susceptibility to fatal illness among infants and very young children. Hence, death rates very early and late in the normal life span are relatively high. Many environmental conditions affecting mortality are also associated with age. Marriage, economic activity, travel, and leisure fall at rather definite periods of life, and join in creating the familiar age pattern of death rates (see Chart 4:1).

Thus, death rates by age are very often worth computing, even when the primary object is to study some other aspect of mortality. They provide virtually the same information as the mortality rates of

---

[15] Certain patterns of death rates by age are usually to be expected; if they do not appear, it may indicate that there are errors or omissions in the data. The infant death rate is always high in relation to the rates of later childhood; other death rates below age 15 are the lowest. At nearly every age, male death rates are expected to exceed those of females; the difference between the two typically becomes greatest at old age.

These regularities are useful guides, but evaluating the accuracy of data by such evidence is mere guesswork. They give no clue to what may be the correct pattern, nor to the adjustments needed to bring the records into closer approximation to the correct pattern. See 3:11.

a life table.[16] Since age-specific death rates are a means of getting detailed information, there is inevitably a question of *how much* detail to include: how small should the intervals be? This choice cannot be governed by any general rule. Nor is the scope of decision very broad, for the age intervals are limited by the form of the original data. Chiefly for this reason, five-year intervals have become the most familiar form of age-specific death rates (see Table 2:5).

The conventional 5-year intervals are satisfactory for most purposes. They reveal the major patterns of variation by age, and ordinarily the data are not accurate enough to justify the use of categories that are finer. These death rates are sometimes separated for intensive study into four periods of life: infancy, childhood, working life or reproductive life, and old age.

## 5:8 Infant Mortality

Mortality during the first year of life receives the most attention. This is unavoidable, for the basic records are vague and the mode of computation is different. Also, infant mortality takes a relatively heavy toll of life; even a fairly low death *rate* implies a substantial *number* of infant deaths, because infants are a large portion of a total population. Where death rates at infancy are high, infant deaths constitute a large share of all deaths.

All records of vital events early in life are somewhat vague, and this calls for continual reservations about their accuracy. There is, first, the problem that babies who die very soon after birth may never be registered, either as births or deaths. Moreover, it is often uncertain what constitutes a "live birth." Even expert medical opinion is troubled by the question of separating infant deaths, stillbirths and abortions.[17] The deficiencies of death registration are likely to be concentrated at infancy, and, among infants, to be concentrated at the first few hours or days of life. These errors of the data are a constant source of difficulty in analyzing infant mortality.

---

[16] It is impossible that they should not, since life tables normally originate from death rates of this kind. Of course, death rates and life-table mortality rates do not have the same values; it would be meaningless to analyze the mortality of two populations by comparing age-specific death rates in one with corresponding values of $q_x$ in the other.

[17] International authorities have cooperated in devising regulations to standardize these records. But these are hard to carry out, especially where many births occur without medical attendance. The regulations themselves are not yet entirely uniform throughout the world. See, for example, United Nations, Department of Social Affairs, Population Division, *Foetal, Infant and Early Childhood Mortality*, Vol. 1, *The Statistics*, pp. 3-9 (New York, 1954).

Assuming, however, that reasonably complete and accurate data are available, there are some special problems in the computation of rates to measure infant mortality. The basic notion is the infant mortality rate $(q_0)$ of the life table (see 4:4). But this is not a very practical basis of computation, for data are rarely found in the necessary form. Instead, it is nearly always measured as the *infant death rate*, a ratio of infant deaths to the number of registered live births during the same year (see 2:15, and also the latter portion of this section). As a vital rate, this is a hybrid, falling between the usual type of age-specific death rate and the infant mortality rate as defined in the life table.[18] Many of the difficulties of analyzing infant mortality can be traced to this fact.

There is a large range of observed infant death rates, from high to low. It appears that they are universally higher for males than for females in the same population. For both sexes, rates of 250 to 300 or more (per 1,000 births) were once typical of most populations, signifying a loss of one-fourth to one-third of each birth cohort during the first year of age. Today, infant mortality has been lowered to the neighborhood of death rates of 20 to 40 in several countries. Infant death rates above 200 are now hard to find; even though such levels of infant mortality may persist in some areas, they are not reliably documented in statistics. There is a wide awareness of the possibility of improvements, and of the necessary technical knowledge. Further reductions can therefore be expected in the countries that are now between these high and low extremes. In an environment of changing death rates, the mortality of infancy will probably continue to receive heavy emphasis, and it is advisable to explain the nature of the infant death rate in considerable detail.

The infant death rate, though adopted because of expediency, is very useful. This is better appreciated, together with its faults, if we recognize its relation to the more exact measurements of infant mortality. As explained in 2:15, the infant deaths that occur during a year represent deaths among *two* annual cohorts of births. The situation is illustrated in the following diagram (subscripts indicate the year in which the births and deaths occurred).[19] The infant deaths

---

[18] In this book, a ratio of infant deaths to births of the same year is called an "infant death rate," in order to distinguish it from the infant mortality rate, or $q_x$. The reader should be warned that this distinction is not widely observed.

[19] This particular diagram has been adapted from the example given in W. P. D. Logan, "The Measurement of Infant Mortality," *Population Bulletin*

|  | Live Births | Infant Deaths |
|---|---|---|
| Year 1 | $B_1$ | $D_1'$ $D_1''$ |
| Year 2 | $B_2$ | $D_2'$ $D_2''$ |
| Year 3 | $B_3$ | $D_3'$ $D_3''$ |

during Year 2 are $D_2'$ (infants who had been born in the same year) and $D_2''$ (infants who had been born in the previous year, Year 1). The infant deaths among babies born in Year 1 occurred partly in Year 1 $(D_1')$, but partly in Year 2 before all members of this cohort of babies reached the first birthday $(D_2'')$. Using the notation of this diagram, the infant death rate (described above) is $\dfrac{D_2'' + D_2'}{B_2} k$. Note that the births and deaths do not all represent the same cohort.

The proportion of one year's births (for example, $B_2$) dying in infancy is $\dfrac{D_2' + D_3''}{B_2}$. It is computed by rearranging parts of the infant deaths of two calendar years (which is possible only when they are tabulated according to year of birth as well as age. See 4:11). This represents the complete experience of one cohort during infancy, and corresponds exactly to the notion of infant mortality $(q_0)$ in the life table. But it represents only a part of the experience of all infants $(B_1$ and $B_2)$ who might die during Year 2. For this reason, it is usually avoided as a measurement of infant mortality, in favor of computing rates for a single calendar year.

Evidently, in order to compute an infant mortality rate that is both "correct" and based on the deaths of a given calendar year (and no other year), some special adjustment is required. There are two approaches that change the form of the infant death rate, bringing it closer to the notion of the infant mortality rate. One is to adjust the numerator so that it matches the cohorts of the denominator; the other is to adjust the denominator so that it matches the cohorts of the nu-

of the United Nations, No. 3, October 1953, p. 34 (New York). Similar examples may be found in many parts of the actuarial literature.

merator.[20] For calendar Year 2, the rate must combine those portions of the mortality experience of two cohorts $(B_1$ and $B_2)$ which occurred during Year 2.

Separating the deaths in the numerator to match the two cohorts of births in the denominator, the infant mortality rate may be computed as follows: $\dfrac{D_2''}{B_1} + \dfrac{D_2'}{B_2} k.$[21] It is very often not known exactly which portion of a year's deaths belongs to each of the two birth cohorts. The two portions may then be separated approximately according to the data of another population, or to some other data of the same population. These supplemental data are used to calculate a proportion, called a "separation factor" $f = \dfrac{D_2''}{D_2'' + D_2'}$ . The total number of infant deaths during Year 2, multiplied by $f$, is the estimate of $D_2''$; the total number of deaths, multiplied by $(1 - f)$, is the estimate of $D_2'$. The mortality rate is $\left( \dfrac{f D_2}{B_1} + \dfrac{(1-f) D_2}{B_2} \right) k.$ The estimated separation factor, $f$, may be considerably in error, and should be computed from a population of a similar level of infant mortality. A moderate error, however, has a very minor effect on the mortality rate. (In the absence of any supplemental data, $f$ may be assigned an arbitrary value of .30 without danger of very serious distortion of the mortality rate. But it is always uncertain whether a purely arbitrary adjustment such as this is an improvement over the infant death rate.)

The other approach, adjusting the denominator to include only those births related to deaths in Year 2, always requires estimation. We must estimate what portion of each cohort of births $(B_1$ and $B_2)$ contributed to the total number of infant deaths in Year 2. The exact

---

[20] In these paragraphs is presented a very abbreviated discussion of these adjustments. For a clear and comprehensive treatment, including other possible variations, see W. P. D. Logan, op. cit.

[21] Strictly speaking, it is not correct to compute the portion of two cohorts' experience by adding them in this manner. They ought to be combined by multiplication, using the proportions surviving instead of the proportions dying. The actual difference, however, is negligible, and it is more important to proceed with the explanation on this basis than to insist on complete precision in this detail.

separation factor is not known; but it is probably almost the same as the separation factor for deaths, which is sometimes known. By assuming that the two factors are equal, and that $B_1$ and $B_2$ may be separated by the same factor, this mortality rate is calculated as follows: $\dfrac{D_2}{f B_1 + (1-f) B_2} k$, (where $D_2$ is the total number of infant deaths in Year 2, or $D_2'' + D_2'$). Care is required to avoid confusing the two parts of the separation factor, applying them in the wrong order to $B_1$ and $B_2$.

The purpose of these adjustments is to rectify the defect of the common infant death rate. In actual effect, the inexactness of the infant death rate — its failure to match infant deaths to the proper cohorts of births — is not large except at times of rapid fluctuation of either the risk of death in infancy or the yearly numbers of births. In such periods, the infant death rate of a given year may be considerably distorted.[22]

However, it is laborious to calculate the composite rates by the adjustments described above, and the adjustments may rest on estimates of doubtful accuracy. Unless there is need for a sensitive series of observations, one for each year, these refinements are not worth while. A satisfactory degree of accuracy is achieved by computing an infant death rate for a combined base period of three or more years, as follows: $\dfrac{D_1 + D_2 + D_3}{B_1 + B_2 + B_3} k$. Except at the beginning and the end of this base period $(D_1''$ and $D_3')$, the deaths are matched to the proper births by combining the data of consecutive calendar years.[23]

In Table 5:1 these alternatives are illustrated by data from Japan. The data are shown for males only, though the same principle applies to female deaths, or to deaths of both sexes combined. (The value of $k$ is set at 1, and so all the rates are decimal numbers.)

---

[22] It is also possible that the two types of composite rate just described may be slightly distorted when the factor $(f)$ is used, because they make no allowance for the distribution of change within a year. For more elaborate methods of circumventing this difficulty, see Logan, *op. cit.*

[23] This infant death rate is a type of average, and may be somewhat distorted for that reason if the cohorts are of unequal size. The size of this distortion, however, is small compared with that of infant death rates by single years.

The four different types of rates, calculated from these data, are
given in the lower section of the table.  It is clear that in this example the results are all very close.  The rates of Type (A) differ by
the greatest amount; but one must remember that they represent the
complete mortality experience of yearly cohorts of births (the exact
proportion dying before age one), which is a different definition of
mortality, not confined to the events of one calendar year.  More important is the effect of the decline of the number of births in 1950,

## TABLE 5:1

## INFANT MORTALITY, JAPAN, 1948 - 1950
## MALES ONLY

DATA (arranged according to diagram above)

| Year | Live Births | Infant Deaths |
|------|-------------|---------------|
| 1947 | 1 376 986 | |
| 1948 | 1 378 564 | 66403 / 24376 |
| 1949 | 1 380 008 | 66444 / 24978 |
| 1950 | 1 203 111 | 54830 / 21417 |

RATES (computed according to the formulas indicated)

| Year | Infant Death Rate | Mortality Rates | | | |
|------|-------------------|--------------------------------|--------------------------------|------------------------------------|--------|
| | | (A) $\dfrac{D_2' + D_3''}{B_2}$ | (B) $\dfrac{D_2''}{B_1} + \dfrac{D_2'}{B_2}$ | (C) $\dfrac{D_2}{f\,B_1 + (1-f)\,B_2}$ | $(f)$[a] |
| 1948 | .0659 | .0663 | .0659 | .0659 | (.269) |
| 1949 | .0662 | .0637 | .0662 | .0663 | (.273) |
| 1950 | .0634 | b | .0611 | .0609 | (.281) |

[a]The separation factor $f_2 = \dfrac{D_2''}{D_2'' + D_2'}$

[b]Data shown here are insufficient to compute this rate.

Source:  Japan: Division of Health and Welfare Statistics, Welfare Minister's
Secretariat, *Vital Statistics for 1947, 1948, 1949, 1950*, Part 1.

after a slight rise in 1949. The infant death rate for 1950 is slightly too high, because the numerator includes some deaths (21,417) belonging to the larger birth cohort of 1949. When an adjustment is made in either the numerator (Type B) or the denominator (Type C), the rate for 1950 is stated more accurately. If the fluctuation of births were greater, or the level of infant mortality higher during this period, or its decline more rapid, the distortion of the infant death rate would probably have been larger than the size of the discrepancy here.

In choosing which alternative to use, it is sufficient to keep in mind a few points about these relations. The infant death rate is usually adequate to reveal the level of infant mortality in a population, especially when computed for a base period of three years or more. It is most subject to error in measuring year-to-year fluctuations. To describe annual fluctuations there are advantages in some form of adjusted infant mortality rate, of which two have been suggested above. When the statistics of infant deaths are not separated according to birth cohort, adjusted rates can be computed by an assumed separation factor. The first type of infant mortality rate explained above (the proportion of a cohort of births dying before the first birthday) is correct in principle, but it does not fit the popular notion of a rate based on events of just one calendar year, and therefore is not fully conventional. For the sake of clarity, one must always explain the procedure of computation, whatever it is; the mere term, "infant mortality rate," is not altogether clear in its meaning.

There are several other proposals, beyond the limited ground of this discussion, for measuring infant mortality. In various ways they seek to analyze separate aspects of mortality of the first year of age. For example, because the mortality of infancy begins directly after the time of birth, part of it is affected by the circumstances of birth. This portion is called *neonatal mortality*, and is conventionally measured by death rates for the first month of age.[24] The neonatal death rate is of special interest, for it accounts for a large share of all deaths of infancy.[25]

---

[24] The neonatal death rate, by convention, is a ratio of a year's infant deaths of the first month (more exactly, 28 days) of age to the number of births registered during that calendar year. Also of interest is the mortality of smaller portions of the first month of age, but ordinary registration data are rarely adequate for such detailed rates.

[25] For a recent survey of the international statistics of infant mortality, see United Nations, Department of Social Affairs, Population Division, *Foetal, Infant and Early Childhood Mortality* (New York, 1954).

These other proposals consist chiefly of additional refinement, to be adopted only when the data permit. In most countries, deficiencies of the statistics far outweigh deficiencies of method as sources of error in the measurement of infant mortality. Nearly everywhere there is evidence that infant deaths have been under-registered.[26] Omissions seem to be more widespread where infant mortality is high, and most frequent among the deaths in the first few hours or days of age, with the result that the data of neonatal deaths are the most unreliable of all.[27]

### 5:9 Mortality during Childhood

The principal obstacles to constructing infant death rates are absent in observing mortality at older ages. Beyond the first year or so of life, the calculation of death rates for childhood ages is simple and straightforward. They are ratios of a year's deaths to the mid-year population. The first death rate above infancy is usually for the group 1-4 years of age; beyond this point, 5-year intervals are usually adequate.

Young children who have survived infancy and the second year of age enjoy a relatively sheltered environment as they approach physical maturity. It is during this time of life, between ages 5 and 15, that the risk of dying reaches its lowest point. The low pattern of death rates among children is especially pronounced in the detailed values of a "complete" life table (see Table 4:1). Mortality at this stage has not been thoroughly investigated, perhaps because few person-years are lost; attention is more easily drawn to ages where larger numbers are involved. Hence, though it is possible that patterns of mortality in later life may originate at these childhood ages, little evidence is available about the subject.

---

[26] Sometimes the laxity in registration affects births as well as infant deaths; either one may be affected more than the other. It is of little help to assume that the omissions are equal among births and infant deaths, for this would not leave the measurement of infant mortality unbiased. It would make the infant death rate too low, because the infants who were completely overlooked would be those who died, not those who survived — in other words, a biased selection from the two groups. Deficiencies of this kind also impair the records of fertility.

[27] Indeed, one of the principal uses of the neonatal death rate is not as evidence of mortality but evidence of poor registration of infant deaths. A very unusual pattern of neonatal and post-neonatal infant death rates is one of the few dependable criteria for assuming incomplete registration of infant deaths.

## 5:10  Mortality of Working or Reproductive Ages

People's adult activities begin to show an effect on mortality somewhat later in life. This is attested by death rates between, let us say, ages 15 and 60 or 65. Together with a general rise of death rates with advancing age, there are rather consistent differences according to sex. Men typically are subject to heavier losses and exposed to a wider variety of risks. This large age interval represents the working life, from the ages when young men undertake the responsibilities of livelihood until the stage at which they begin to retire from work.[28]

Death rates of women, while also influenced by certain working activities, reflect different sorts of activities, and the added impairments of maternal health associated with childbirth and early infant care. The mortality of adult women sometimes has a distinctive pattern by age, with a heavy portion near the ages of maximum fertility (above 15 and under 40).[29] At these ages, their death rates are occasionally higher than those of men. The effects of these various factors occur within the age range 15-64; one must be prepared to observe them by means of age-specific death rates alone, since supplementary information is scarce.

## 5:11  Mortality at Advanced Ages

In later life, it is well known that death rates rise rapidly with age. Already rather high by age 65, they reach maximum levels at extreme old age, greater than the rates of infants. At these ages, there is remarkably little variation between countries of otherwise very different mortality. The high death rates do not represent great numbers of deaths, because rather few people are involved.[30]

Consequently it is not regarded as unusual to lose each year a substantial proportion of the people who have survived to these ages. Their mortality has not been thoroughly studied, except where the age structure is such as to make the affairs of elderly persons felt as a special problem of public concern. Little emphasis is placed on the records of people of advanced age — not enough to secure ac-

---

[28] Their mortality is also affected by the particular types of occupation that they pursue, as discussed in 5:14.

[29] However, there is no universal pattern of this kind. The normal familial and occupational roles of women vary widely in different countries, and likewise their general level of health.

[30] See the article of P. Vincent, "La Mortalité des viellards," *Population*, Vol. 6, pp. 181-204 (Paris, 1951).

curate classification by age, or to publish the full information that is recorded. This neglect probably encourages reporting that is inaccurate rather than incomplete, and detailed death rates for the aged may be worth very little, even where the data are provided. Often the only course is to compute a single death rate for persons "age 60 and above" or "age 70 and above" (see 4:14). A death rate for this large age interval is very crude, and has the same shortcomings as the crude death rate for the population at all ages. It is a poor basis for comparing different populations or population groups if they differ in composition. For this reason, it is advisable at least to try to determine the age-specific mortality among elderly persons; and, failing this, to draw only very cautious conclusions from a single death rate for the entire group.

### 5:12 Trends of Mortality

Death rates also provide comparisons of mortality at different dates. This is the customary manner of measuring change or trend. (A death rate, of course, represents a base period, not a definite date. Usually the discrepancy can be ignored, though it may be confusing when the base period is longer than one year. In such cases the death rate is treated as if it represented the midpoint of the base period.)

The measurement is unavoidably affected by the length of the interval between two observations. Hence, when trends are being compared — for example, in different populations — they should cover an equal interval of time. It may be awkward or impossible to judge between two changes, if one pair of observations is 10 years apart and the other is 12 years apart. Census data are involved in most death rates, and fortunately many countries take censuses 10 years apart.

Before the period of modern sanitation and medicine, there is only indirect evidence of the levels of mortality. Such as it is, it indicates considerable fluctuations but not steady change. The prevailing trend of mortality in the past two or more centuries, on the other hand, has been downward. These changes have not been uniform everywhere, nor have they been uninterrupted, despite the fact that reduction of death rates has become a goal of public policy nearly everywhere. The periods of reliable observation are short and recent. Within this limitation, a great deal is to be learned from the patterns by which the decline has spread, and the differences of speed and timing of change in various areas and population groups.

There is no special set of methods for analyzing changes of

mortality.  Any type of death rate can be used to indicate a trend.
The choice is guided by the aspect of mortality that is being investigated, though it is also limited by the types of data that are available.  It may be necessary to select a type of rate that fits the purpose poorly, because no other pertinent information is at hand.  When
statistics of "neonatal" deaths (see 5:8) are lacking, a series of infant death rates may serve to indicate whether neonatal mortality has
changed; yet these two types of death rate do not vary in exactly the
same way.  Similarly, the course of "maternal mortality" (death rates
of women due to ailments of childbirth) often cannot be determined
directly for lack of reliable data on deaths from this cause; it may
have to be observed by means of death rates for all women in the
ages of maximum childbearing.[31]  The adoption of any particular
kind of death rate in a series of observations is tantamount to selecting some aspect of mortality change for study — that aspect indicated
by the rates.

  A series of crude death rates is the most common index.  They
have, of course, the advantages explained in 5:6.  Also, crude death
rates can be computed in the form of yearly observations, since there
is little difficulty in estimating the total mid-year population.  Infant
death rates are likewise well adapted to providing yearly values,
since they do not require estimation of the mid-year population.
Other types of specific death rates are less convenient indices of
change, for they are more dependent on census data, and the mid-year
population in specific portions of a population is not easily estimated between the dates of successive censuses.

  The measurement of a trend is limited by the accuracy of the
observations on which it is based.  It may be less accurate.  In addition to the peculiarities of the death rates themselves, there are a
few sources of distortion peculiar to the measurement of a trend.
Shifts in the composition of the population and lack of continuity
in the statistical system deserve special attention.

  Over a fairly long period, a series of crude rates may reflect
not only changes in the level of mortality but also changes in the
composition of the population, particularly its age structure.  Normally these shifts are gradual and hardly noticeable in a trend for
the same area.  Even when they are rapid, perhaps due to migration,

---

[31] Evidently, these age-specific death rates are a better index of "maternal mortality" when fertility is high than when fertility is low, simply because childbearing is more frequent and affects a larger proportion of adult
women each year.  When birth rates are declining, the influence of childbearing on these age-specific death rates will also decline, whether the risks
associated with childbirth itself have declined or not.

they are more likely to escape attention than the same effects in a comparison between different populations.

The recorded trend of mortality may also be distorted if the manner of operation of a statistical system has changed. The scope or total area may become larger, bringing new groups of people into the data. Within the same area, the statistics may become more nearly complete.[32] The schemes of classifying data, and even the biases of a statistical system, are constantly subject to change. (For example, by strictly enforcing the rules for reporting stillbirths, the reporting of infant deaths may suddenly be made to rise, and this would bring about an "increase" of the infant death rates.) Though the crude death rate is susceptible to most kinds of distortion, the actual effect of a given shift in statistical practice on a series of crude death rates may be small. The effect of the same shift may be much larger on the trend shown by some other rate.

However, a series of crude rates is rather superficial evidence. The level of mortality does not change uniformly in all parts of a population. In order to find what patterns are involved, it is necessary to treat certain groups in the population separately, by adopting some sort of specific death rates. This also has the advantage of avoiding some of the distortion due to altered composition of the population. Changes of age-specific death rates, to mention the foremost example, are unaffected by changing age structure.

Table 5:2 indicates the principal changes of mortality by age in Ceylon, over a period of seven years between the census of 1946 and the census of 1953 (Column 2 and Column 3). However, it presents a view that is too thorough, too detailed to be comprehended at a glance. In order to make the pattern of the trend clearer, we may measure it apart from the values of the rates themselves, as in Columns 4 and 5 of Table 5:2. But there are two ways of viewing these changes. We must first decide whether to compare the *actual* or *absolute differences* of death rates, or the *proportional changes* of these rates. The absolute changes of death rates (Death Rate in 1946 minus Death Rate in 1953, noting the plus or minus sign) are

---

[32] As a statistical system becomes more complete, or less complete, the trend of death rates may be influenced in various ways. With more thorough registration of deaths, death rates tend to rise, giving a false appearance of "retrogression" in public health work. Ironically, in some countries, deterioration of the registration system has caused death rates to fall, giving an unwarranted impression of "progress." Improving the extent of census enumeration, on the other hand, has the opposite effect, of making the death rates smaller. Of course, the distortions themselves may be minor, and not large enough to lead to incorrect conclusions.

shown in Column 4.  The relative changes are shown by ratios

$$\frac{\text{Death Rate in 1953}}{\text{Death Rate in 1946}}$$ in Column 5.  Either type of comparison gives

a more convenient picture of the change of mortality by age.  (Mortality declined in Ceylon very rapidly between 1946 and 1953; the decline affected every interval of age.  Nevertheless there were large differences of degree, as shown by the table.)

The two types of comparison do not give the same picture. The absolute declines in Table 5:2 were greatest among young children and older people.  The relative declines were greatest among

## TABLE 5:2

## CHANGE OF AGE-SPECIFIC DEATH RATES IN CEYLON, 1946 TO 1953

## BOTH SEXES

| (1) | (2) | (3) | (4)ᵃ | (5) |
|---|---|---|---|---|
| Ages | Death Rates 1945-1947 | Death Rates 1952-1954 | Absolute Changes (Col.2) – (Col.3) | Relative Changes Ratio: (Col.3) ÷ (Col.2) |
| 0-4 | 61.5 | 34.0 | – 27.5 | .55 |
| 5-9 | 6.7 | 3.5 | – 3.2 | .52 |
| 10-14 | 3.2 | 1.4 | – 1.8 | .44 |
| 15-19 | 4.9 | 1.9 | – 3.0 | .39 |
| 20-24 | 8.0 | 2.9 | – 5.1 | .36 |
| 25-34 | 9.1 | 3.6 | – 5.5 | .40 |
| 35-44 | 11.1 | 4.8 | – 6.3 | .43 |
| 45-54 | 15.9 | 7.7 | – 8.2 | .48 |
| 55-64 | 27.5 | 16.6 | –10.9 | .60 |
| 65 and over | 95.7 | 74.5 | – 21.2 | .78 |
| All ages | 18.9 | 11.1 | – 7.8 | .59 |

ᵃ" – " indicates decline.

Source:  Rates for 1945-1947 are the same as those in Table 2:5. Rates for 1952-1954 were computed from registered deaths in *Report of the Registrar-General of Ceylon on Vital Statistics* (1952, 1953, 1954), Appendix Table 14; 1953 census population as reported in *Ceylon Year Book, 1956*, Tables 4 and 5.

young adults, and least among older people and small children. Of course, a more detailed pattern would emerge from rates calculated for smaller age groups.

The ratios of Column 5 better represent the relative degree of change at different ages. As usual, there is a wide range between the highest and lowest age-specific rates; hence we do not expect to find the same absolute changes. The rates that were already low could not decline by the same amount, for some of them would fall below zero. Possibly just as great an improvement of health or a public effort toward this goal is reflected in a decline of 10 per cent in death rates at ages 10-14 as a 10 per cent decline of death rates among younger children, or even infants. In representing the different incidence of change according to age, the relative changes seem less likely to encourage over-emphasis of declines at ages where the rates were initially high. When possible, with either approach the reader should be given some access to the original data.

A common problem is illustrated by these figures. For a general view of change in the entire population, crude.rates· give too little information, and age-specific rates give too much. A possible solution is to compute a "standardized" death rate for each year (see 5:16), which is a type of crude death rate adjusted for differences of age structure. Standardized rates counteract the distortion of crude rates due to shifts of composition, but this is only part of the problem. They also forfeit the detail shown in Table 5:2 above. The only way to study the distribution of change by age is to keep this information. Hence, it is usually worth while to compute specific death rates (by age or other characteristics) when the data are available; afterwards, if the trends of these specific rates seem to contribute little, the findings can be reported in any way that seems appropriate.

### 5:13 Causes of Death

Mortality is the outcome of circumstances involving some risk to life — specific illness, levels of general health and vigor, accidents or even violence. In most countries that keep systematic mortality statistics, some factor which appears to be immediately connected with each death is singled out and recorded as the "cause." A rise of longevity in the population, which implies some postponement of death, may be viewed as a reduction of the frequency of these factors, or lessening of their lethal effect.

From this standpoint we can discover patterns of declining mortality, by finding which kinds of deaths, classified by cause, have become less frequent.  The mortality of different populations can be compared on this basis.  This approach is also suited to appraising specific public health projects, or determining the needs for such efforts.  And it may be the only available source of statistical information about the general state of health in a population.[33]

Death rates by cause are of a peculiar form.  They are ratios of a year's deaths due to some cause to the total mid-year population $(\frac{D_i}{P} k$, where $D_i$ is the number of deaths classed according to a cause or group of causes, and $P$ is the size of the total population; $k$ is usually 10,000 or 100,000).  These rates are also referred to as "cause-specific" death rates.  Sometimes they are computed separately by age group $(\frac{D_{i,x}}{P_x}$, using this same procedure for each age group, $x$), in which case they are age-and-cause-specific death rates.  Some problems resulting from this mode of calculation are taken up somewhat later.

The effect of reducing the frequency of a specific disease is illustrated by the remarkable case of malaria control in recent years.  Techniques that can eliminate malaria-bearing mosquitoes for a sufficient period have been developed only since 1940, but they have rapidly altered the pattern of mortality where malaria was formerly one of the leading causes of death.  An example is the drop in frequency of malaria deaths, and in the crude death rates, of Ceylon.  Infant death rates have also fallen sharply in the same period, as shown in Table 5:3.[34]  But the effect of any specific type of public effort is eventually exhausted; from this approach we can see that further gains of longevity must come from another source.  In Ceylon, future reductions of mortality by malaria control (beyond the level of 1952) cannot be large.  Still lower death rates now can be achieved only by attacking other causes of death.

---

[33]Independent records of illness, or "morbidity," are rare and never very reliable.  But most people die after a period of recognizable illness.  Records of deaths, which are of a more definite nature, can supply indirect evidence of morbidity.

[34]Of course, there were other applications of modern medicine during this period, and the change was not due entirely to the conquest of malaria.  But 6 per cent of all deaths were ascribed to malaria in 1936-1940, and only 1.1 per cent in 1952.  See also H. Collumbine, "An Analysis of the Vital Statistics of Ceylon," *The Ceylon Journal of Medical Science*, Vol. VII, Parts 3 and 4, December, 1950.

## TABLE 5:3

## CHANGES OF DEATH RATES IN CEYLON
## FOLLOWING MALARIA CONTROL

| Year | Crude Death Rate | Infant Death Rate (per 1000 births) | Malaria Death Rate (per 100,000 population) |
|------|------------------|-------------------------------------|---------------------------------------------|
| 1930-1935 | 25.2 | 185 | |
| 1936-1940 | 21.4 | 160 | 123 |
| 1941 | 18.8 | 129 | 118 |
| 1942 | 18.6 | 120 | 85 |
| 1943 | 21.4 | 132 | 110 |
| 1944 | 21.3 | 135 | 89 |
| 1945 | 22.0 | 140 | 131 |
| 1946 | 20.3 | 140 | 187 |
| 1947 | 14.3 | 101 | 66 |
| 1948 | 13.2 | 92.1 | 47 |
| 1949 | 12.6 | 87.0 | 33 |
| 1950 | 12.6 | 81.6 | 25 |
| 1951 | 11.6 | 88.3 | 21 |
| 1952 | 12.0 | 78.2 | 13 |

Source:   Adapted from E. J. Pampana, "Effect of Malaria Control on Birth and Death Rates," *Proceedings of the World Population Conference,* Rome, 1954, Volume 1, p. 504.

Besides revealing patterns of mortality change, death rates by cause may be helpful in comparing the mortality of different populations. They distinguish the risks of death according to source, thus calling attention to the different conditions affecting mortality. Table 5:4 presents death rates by cause for Ceylon, Egypt, Japan and Chile.[35]  Though very much abbreviated (from the standard International List of Causes of Death), these rates indicate substantial differences.  One should observe that many deaths were classified under poorly-defined or unknown causes, implying fairly widespread

[35]The total of a population's cause-specific death rates is equal to its crude death rate—in this case, the rate per 100,000 persons. For Ceylon in 1951, the crude death rate of 1,293 per 100,000 corresponds to a rate of 12.9 per 1,000. There is a slight discrepancy in Table 5:4, due to rounding.

errors of diagnosis. This recommends some caution in comparing
these data; but it is obvious that further reductions of mortality involve different programs of action in these four countries.

This type of analysis is faced with certain problems, due to

## TABLE 5:4

## DEATH RATES BY CAUSE, SELECTED COUNTRIES[a]
(Deaths per 100,000 Total Population)

| Causes of Death | Ceylon 1951 | Egypt[b] 1951 | Japan 1952 | Chile 1951 |
|---|---|---|---|---|
| Tuberculosis | 50.2 | 44.1 | 82.5 | 148.2 |
| Syphilis | 0.8 | 2.9 | 5.0 | 5.4 |
| Typhoid fever | 8.9 | 5.9 | 0.2 | 8.0 |
| Dysentery, diarrhea, enteritis | 59.4 | 845.3 | 67.1 | 101.6 |
| Diphtheria | 1.8 | 4.8 | 0.7 | 4.1 |
| Whooping cough | 1.2 | 0.6 | 2.8 | 16.0 |
| Smallpox | 0.6 | 0.0 | – | 0.1 |
| Measles | 0.7 | 26.9 | 3.6 | 2.4 |
| Typhus | – | 0.0 | 0.0 | 0.4 |
| Malaria | 20.7 | 0.2 | 0.0 | 0.0 |
| Other infectious & parasitic diseases | 81.5 | 12.1 | 12.3 | 13.1 |
| Heart diseases | 44.7 | 65.3 | 62.7 | 164.3 |
| Cancer | 16.7 | 20.1 | 81.3 | 88.1 |
| Influenza | 12.2 | 0.6 | 0.3 | 20.1 |
| Pneumonia | 102.6 | 111.8 | 44.1 | 278.6 |
| Bronchitis | 14.6 | 203.7 | 17.2 | 6.6 |
| Other respiratory diseases | – | – | – | 9.8 |
| Accidents, suicide, homicide | 43.6 | 62.0 | 57.1 | 159.2 |
| Other known causes | 115.7 | 113.8 | 220.0 | 240.7 |
| Unknown or ill-defined causes | 717.1 | 710.6 | 238.1 | 302.0 |
| Total | 1292.6 | 2230.7 | 894.8 | 1568.5 |

[a]Deaths were classified according to the International List of Causes of
Deaths. Data for Chile represent the Fifth Revision of this list (1938);
data for Ceylon, Egypt and Japan represent the Sixth Revision (1948). In
this table, the data have been condensed by combining many categories.

[b]Rates represent Health Bureau localities, not the entire country.

Source: *Demographic Yearbook, 1954*, Table 30.

the manner of computing these death rates and due to peculiarities of statistics classified by cause of death.

Cause-specific death rates are prepared in a rather special manner (deaths attributed to some cause, per person-year lived by the entire population or population group). In this respect they are different from other specific death rates (see 2:14). This is because we do not know the number of person-years of exposure to each type of risk (that is, to each "cause" of death). Nearly *everyone* is exposed to *some* potentially fatal illness or event during a normal base period, but there is no way to determine the amount of exposure in each case. It is possible to separate the deaths according to cause, but not the population. Therefore, death rates by cause are less precisely defined than other specific death rates.[36]

Far more important are the inaccuracies of cause-of-death statistics, which stem chiefly from problems of diagnosis. The "cause" of death is not always easy to identify; a classification of these factors is ambiguous. In the first place, it is basically a matter of judgment, and individual opinions -- even expert opinions -- often disagree. A scheme of classification cannot be followed uniformly. Cause-of-death data are affected by variations of medical skill and by the geographical distribution of medical service; hence, regional comparisons within a country and often international comparisons are often biased.[37] Moreover, there may be two or more contributing causes, without any clear basis for choosing between them.[38] In

---

[36] Death rates by cause are defined as $\dfrac{D_i}{P}$, in contrast to $\dfrac{D_i}{P_i}$, the usual form of specific death rates (as explained above and in 2:16). In other words, the numerator refers to a specific category, and the denominator refers to the general population.

It is possible to improve the situation somewhat. The fatal effects of some diseases are concentrated at certain ages; there are "typical" diseases of infancy, childbirth, and old age. For this reason, some age-and-cause-specific death rates are better defined than others.

[37] Detailed rules of classification have been prepared in order to promote consistency. See World Health Organization Bulletin, *Manual of the International Statistical Classification of Diseases, Injuries, and Causes of Death* (Sixth Revision, Geneva, 1948). These guides undoubtedly help to improve the reporting of deaths by cause. But the lists are long and complicated, are revised from time to time, and have not been adopted in every country.

[38] The International Lists seek to establish uniform rules for this purpose. But these are subject to the same limitations, i n practice, as the scheme of classification itself. No set of instructions can completely offset the effects of careless or inexperienced reporting of the information.

every country there are fashions among medical practitioners, leading them to pronounce certain types of diagnosis on the basis of
superficial evidence. Finally, reports may be deliberately falsified,
perhaps in order to escape a stigma or compulsory quarantine after a
death from some infectious disease.

A few precautions are advisable in utilizing this information.
It is important to assess the completeness of death registration, for
omissions will almost certainly distort the reported distribution of
deaths by cause. One can easily ascertain whether the government
has taken steps to impose a standard list of causes and criteria for
classifying individual cases. One should be warned by a large proportion of deaths lacking medical certification of cause, or a large
proportion reported under vague or unknown causes (such as "senil-
ity," "diseases of infancy," or "other"). In order not to put the accuracy of the data to too severe a test, cause-specific death rates
should be computed only for broad categories of "causes." Certain
major categories of infectious diseases, perhaps malaria, respiratory
ailments, digestive disturbances, or accidents can be distinguished
rather clearly. Even without a high standard of accuracy, this information is so valuable that a considerable degree of error may be
tolerated.

## 5:14 Death Rates by Occupation or Social-Economic Status

A neglected aspect of mortality is its distribution among portions of a population grouped by some index of personal position, activities, or manner of participation in the society. There is good
reason for the neglect, for it is rare to find acceptable records of
mortality according to such groupings. The closest approach to this
subject in ordinary official statistics is through data classified by
occupation.[39] Hence, where possible, it is worth some effort to calculate death rates by occupation, or as they are sometimes called,
death rates by social-economic status or social "class."

The available data consist of the numbers of people in each
occupation in some particular year (census statistics) and the num-

---

[39]It is sometimes possible to analyze the mortality experience of life-
insurance records according to categories of this nature. They offer many
advantages over ordinary census and registration statistics, because the
groupings can be arranged with greater freedom, and because the numbers of
deaths exactly match the numbers of persons "exposed to risk." But insurance data cover only a portion of the population, a specially selected portion which does not have quite the same characteristics as the total population.

bers of deaths during that year, classified by occupation (registration statistics). Some of the peculiarities of such material are described in Chapter 2. A death rate can be computed for each occupation: a ratio of the deaths reported in that category to the number of
persons who were engaged in the same occupation (that is, to the estimated number of person-years spent at that occupation) during the
year. (See the general discussion of computing specific rates in 2:14.
It is convenient to adopt a value of $k = 10,000$.) In other words, the
death rate resembles an age-specific death rate, except that it is
based on categories of occupation; indeed, it is necessary to compute occupation-specific death rates separately by age group and by
sex, in order to avoid profound confusion over their meaning.

How useful are death rates by occupation? There are not many
successful analyses of this kind to indicate what their significance
may be; the most famous are the studies of "occupational mortality"
in England and Wales, from which this brief example of Table 5:5 is
drawn. To some extent, these death rates indicate the risk of dying
associated with occupations. Mining, quarrying or construction work
are more hazardous than a clerical or commercial livelihood. But the
variation by occupational groups cannot be due entirely to different
conditions of work. Many differences of environment and activities
are also associated with types of occupation — income, style of living or habits of diet, place of residence, and circle of associates —
and these undoubtedly have an influence on the mortality of a
group.[40]

The death rates in some occupations also reflect extraneous
factors. Strenuous types of work tend to attract vigorous and robust
workers, and many people of ill health are undoubtedly drawn to
sedentary tasks; some workers, having damaged their health in one
pursuit, die after having moved to another that is fundamentally
safer. In such circumstances as these, the results may be perverse
and misleading, and a death rate is not an accurate indicator even of
the conditions associated with an occupation.[41] One cannot correct-

---

[40] The death rates of wives seem to follow the same pattern by occupation as the death rates of their husbands, indicating that a category of occupation embraces many aspects of personal and family life, in addition to
the job itself.

[41] For a concise and clear discussion of this entire subject, see J.
Daric, "Mortalité, profession et situation sociale," Population, No. 4, Oct.-
Dec., 1949, pp. 671-694. (English translation is available in U.S. National
Office of Vital Statistics, Vital Statistics — Special Reports, Vol. 33, No.
10, September 21, 1951.)

ly interpret the meaning of death rates by occupation without first
being very familiar with the occupational classification of the data.

In addition to this fundamental ambiguity, there are several
other difficulties of a more practical and immediate nature.  Death
rates by occupation must be age- and sex-specific, for occupations
differ widely in their age composition; lacking a cross-classification
of the data by age and sex, it would be a waste of time to compute
the rates by occupation.  The deaths registered among employed persons probably do not represent quite the same universe as the population of employed persons enumerated in a census.  A discrepancy

## TABLE 5:5

## DEATH RATES OF EMPLOYED MALES, BY AGE AND OCCUPATION
### (Selected Occupations)
## ENGLAND AND WALES, 1931

(Rates per 10,000 population in each group)[a]

| Occupational Group[b] | Age Group | | | | |
|---|---|---|---|---|---|
| | 20-24 | 25-34 | 35-44 | 45-54 | 55-64 |
| All Occupied and Retired Males | 32 | 34 | 55 | 111 | 236 |
| 1 Farmers & their relatives | 23 | 25 | 36 | 79 | 179 |
| 3 Agricultural labourers | 26 | 27 | 40 | 75 | 164 |
| 44 Coal hewers and getters | 37 | 40 | 66 | 122 | 262 |
| 20 Metal machinists | 34 | 29 | 55 | 114 | 224 |
| 45 Bricklayers | 26 | 28 | 42 | 101 | 216 |
| 61 Retail proprietors, etc. | 45 | 36 | 66 | 130 | 283 |
| 67 Bank and insurance officials | – | 17 | 29 | 80 | 164 |
| 73 Physicians, surgeons, etc. | – | 32 | 52 | 120 | 260 |
| 74 Teachers | 29 | 24 | 31 | 68 | 177 |
| 83 Typists & other clerks | 29 | 34 | 56 | 115 | 248 |
| 87 Labourers (general) | 41 | 45 | 77 | 145 | 289 |

[a]Rates are based on the census population of 1931 and registered deaths,
1930-1932.

[b]Numbers in this column refer to the number of the occupational group in the
list given in the original source. This classification contained 88 occupational categories.

Source:  Great Britain, *Registrar-General's Decennial Supplement, 1931,*
Part IIa, Appendix Table 4a (London, 1938).

is most likely at older ages,[42] but can be avoided by excluding all
data of persons age 65 and over. Starting at age 15, the death rates
may be computed by occupation for 5-year, 10-year, or even 20-year
intervals of age. Death rates by occupation are probably more reliable for men than for women, because the classification by occupation is more definite among males.

The most serious questions of accuracy arise over inconsistency between the registration and the census, in classifying the
working population into categories of occupations. Under the best
conditions, the occupational classification of a census is a difficult
task; but the classification of deaths cannot have more than a rough
correspondence with the classification of the enumerated population.
Many people change their type of livelihood in the course of a year,
and some may be enumerated in one occupation and die while engaged
in another. It is impossible to apply exactly the same rules in collecting the two kinds of statistics; even the scheme of categories is
sometimes not identical. Some discrepancy is unavoidable, and
there is no satisfactory test to determine the extent to which the two
classifications are consistent.[43] The inconsistency of classification increases when fine categories are used; the resulting distortion
can be moderated by computing death rates only for very broad categories. Occupation-specific death rates as detailed as those of
Table 5:5 are almost never warranted.

The size and detail of Table 5:5 can be condensed. It has
been the practice in studies of mortality by occupation in England
and Wales to combine these rates by age into a single death rate for
the entire group 20-65, based on a standard age composition for all
occupational groups (see Great Britain, *Registrar-General's Decennial Supplement, 1931*, Part IIa; see also 5:16).

## 5:15  Regional Differences of Mortality

Population statistics are collected by territorial divisions within a country, and if data are tabulated separately for any sub-divisions of the population they are usually available for these administrative areas. There is some interest in knowing these death rates,
just to compare the principal sections of a country. They also serve

---

[42]Some persons enumerated as "retired" may be classified at death
as "employed" (in their previous occupation) when the deaths are registered.

[43]Though occupation-specific death rates do not fall into any very
typical expected pattern, like the distribution of age-specific death rates, an
extremely wide range between highest and lowest rates in one population
should cast heavy doubts on the entire set of rates by occupation.

to measure the effects of certain known local conditions. But, in addition, we must frequently rely on death rates by district or region to look for patterns of mortality that cannot be observed by other means.

Evidence of this kind is difficult to interpret. It may reflect local differences of prosperity or wealth; or differences of the distribution of activities, of degrees of access to medical care, of levels of education, of factors affecting the incidence of disease or the severity of disease. Death rates calculated by district or region are sometimes the only way to observe these effects. They constitute a clumsy approach, depending for its success on a fortunate location of boundaries and a wise arrangement of data.

A comparison of rural and urban death rates is a good example. The changes and dislocations of modern life are often concentrated around a few urban centers. In some countries, this has led to lower death rates in cities, and stability of health conditions in rural sections. Elsewhere urban conditions have created a less favorable environment, and urban death rates have become higher. In the rapid economic development of recent years, it is inevitable that there should be some differences of this sort; but the nature of the pattern cannot be predicted in advance. After discovering such a pattern it is a very long step to identifying its source or weighing the importance of the various contributing factors. It is not safe to take this further step without the help of additional evidence.

These death rates are of course subject to the same defects as death rates for national totals.[44] A further problem is introduced: even though the data of the numerator (deaths) and the data of the denominator (census population) may represent the same universe of people in the total population, this very likely is not true in the population of particular districts. The two sets of data will not match exactly if there has been movement of people across the boundaries of a district during the year, because deaths are registered, as they occur, throughout the year, and the enumeration of the population occurs only once during the year. Some people who were enumerated in the district will die while absent, and some people will die in the district who were enumerated elsewhere.[45]

---

[44] The defects may have more serious consequences in subdivisions of a country than in the total. Some distortion in separate district data may have been cancelled out in the data for the entire population.

[45] This same discrepancy affects death rates by occupation (see 5:14), and to some extent any death rate based on registration and census data. But the effect of migration across local boundaries is more serious, because it is often rather large. The discrepancy scarcely affects most death rates

It is possible that the one kind of error may approximately balance the other, without affecting the death rate. But this is a slender hope, for the migration and the mortality may be related. Where people with serious illness go to hospitals for treatment, many deaths each year occur in towns or cities containing hospitals, which should be attributed to some other place (to the place where the decedents were enumerated, probably the place of usual residence). Death rates computed from these data will be distorted — too high at the place these deaths of migrants occur, and too low where the decedents had previously resided. Depending on the patterns of migration, this distortion of death rates may be substantial and widespread. On the other hand, it may be large in a few places and even negligible in others; or it may be so small that it can be completely ignored. If a small proportion of all deaths occur in hospitals, the discrepancy may be negligible.[46]

In order to cope with this problem, some countries provide special tabulations of births and deaths, according to *place of residence* as well as *place of occurrence*. With such tables, deaths can often be allocated to the places where they are most likely to match the universe of population — that is, to the places where the decedents most probably had been enumerated in the most recent census.

Notwithstanding these defects, death rates by district provide information about the distribution of risks of death that might otherwise be unobtainable. For example, they throw light on a national trend of mortality. Public health and sanitation works do not suddenly become effective everywhere at the same time.[47] Even in their absence, differences in the levels of death rates are found; with the uneven effect of new health services, these differences may grow larger. On the other hand, it is also possible to reduce a national

---

on a national scale, because movement across national boundaries is more restricted by the action of governments.

[46] Various kinds of migration may distort these death rates. Where women are accustomed to return to a former family residence, or go to a hospital, to give birth, the infant death rates are affected in both places (and of course the birth rates too). If a district has such an influx of births, it probably will also have extra infant deaths during the first few days of life; but it is unpredictable where the remaining infant deaths will occur. It is apparent that no amount of adjustment of data will completely untangle these complicated patterns of error.

[47] These limitations are less rigid than they were in the past, for the newer techniques of controlling disease have a more powerful "mass" effect. But the limitations are not all of a technical nature; where they are administrative, this same uneven pattern can still be found.

death rate by narrowing this range between the highest and lowest
regional rates. Either pattern of change can be traced by the trends
of local or regional death rates, and the trends of differences between these rates.

## 5:16 Adjusted or Standardized Death Rates

Summarizing the level of mortality in the various parts of a
population (called the "general" level of mortality) presents an awkward problem. The death rates discussed so far are not well suited
to this purpose. A crude death rate, though convenient, is not a very
reliable index; more detailed measures, like age-specific rates, are
so detailed that they are clumsy indices for the entire population.
Basically this obstacle is not a fault of the rates themselves, for the
notion of "general" mortality is vague and inexact.

Occasionally, however, brevity is essential, and a single accurate figure is needed as a basis of comparison. This is secured
by condensing the detailed information for a population to a *standardized* or *adjusted* death rate. The procedure is a roundabout manipula-
tion of the data, combining some of the advantages of both crude and
specific rates, and avoiding some of their disadvantages.[48]

An age-standardized death rate fills either of two needs. One
is simply to summarize a set of age-specific rates independently of
the age composition of the population. The other is to show the
probable influence of a population's age composition on its crude
death rate when its actual age-specific death rates are not known.

Thus there are two common types of procedure for computing
standardized rates. One consists of applying different age-specific
rates to a standard population; this is called (for no very good reason)
in English and American usage, "direct standardization." The other
consists of applying a standard set of rates to different populations
by age; this is called "indirect standardization." In both types, the
object is to calculate the number of deaths to be expected in one
population, on the basis of some information from another population.
This number of "expected deaths" is used in calculating the standardized death rate.

[48]Here we shall discuss only the computing of standardized death
rates by age. The procedure has much broader applications; it is also possible to "standardize" death rates according to other categories. Indeed,
any set of rates or percentages that refer to definite categories (such as age,
sex, marital status, economic activity) can be reduced to a standardized figure for comparison with some corresponding figure. There is already a large,
though scattered, literature on the nature and uses of these adjusted rates.
The basic techniques, however, are the same as those described below.

a. Different age-specific death rates combined with a standard population (the "direct method"). Obviously, the age composition of two populations could not spoil a comparison of their crude death rates if it were the same in both cases. Hence we try to find what the crude death rates would be if the two populations *did* have the same age composition. This is done by means of age-specific death rates in 5-year intervals, which for this purpose are virtually independent of the age structure of the population.[49] These rates are multiplied by the number of people in each age group of a "standard" population, which is any population selected to be the basis of the comparison. The multiplications indicate how many deaths would be expected if the death rates had prevailed for one year in the standard population. The total of these expected deaths, divided by the total standard population, is the standardized death rate.

Take, for example, the data of Table 5:5 (age-specific death rates by occupation, England and Wales). It is easier to compare the mortality associated with an occupation by means of a general index, representing each occupation by a single figure. First we ask how many deaths would be expected in a standard population if it experienced the age-specific death rates of the groups under comparison. This procedure is illustrated in Table 5:6, which compares the death rates of agricultural labourers (Group "A") and general labourers (not otherwise classified by occupation, Group "B"), by applying them to the "standard" population of all occupied and retired males in 1931. The deaths expected according to these two sets of age-specific rates are then used to compute crude death rates for the entire standard population (Columns 5 and 6 of Table 5:6). These crude death rates, which are hypothetical, are .00610 and .01097, or 61.0 and 109.7 per 10,000. In other words, under these assumptions mortality was generally lower in Group A than in Group B, the former standardized rate being less than 60 per cent of the latter.

b. A standard set of death rates combined with different populations (the "indirect method"). Lacking age-specific rates for one population, this type of standardized rate can be computed with fewer data. It requires statistics of the actual population by age (the "mid-year population"), the total number of deaths (at all ages) in the actual population during the year, the complete schedule of age-specific death rates of a standard population, and the crude death

---

[49] These rates are affected by the composition of the population *within* the 5-year age groups, but that effect is negligible here. In the adult ages, even 10-year intervals may be used without serious harm.

rate of the standard population. The actual population figure at each age is multiplied by the corresponding standard age-specific death rate. These multiplications yield numbers of "expected" deaths for the actual population; added together, these are the total number of deaths expected if the actual population had experienced the standard death rates at each age. But it did *not* experience these death rates at each age, because the death rates originated in a standard population. The relation between the general level of mortality in the actual population and the level of mortality in the standard population is expressed (imperfectly) by the ratio of actual deaths to ex-

## TABLE 5:6

## "DIRECT" STANDARDIZATION OF DEATH RATES BY AGE FOR TWO OCCUPATION GROUPS

Using the total population of occupied and retired males as the standard. Males only.

(Based on data of Table 5:5)

| (1) | (2) | (3) | (4) | (5) | (6) |
|---|---|---|---|---|---|
| | Death Rates (Males)[a] | | Standard | "Expected" Deaths[b] | |
| Ages | Group A (Agricultural Labourers) | Group B (Labourers, general) | Population (All Occupied and Retired Males) | According to Death Rates "A" (2) × (4) | According to Death Rates "B" (3) × (4) |
| 20-24 | .00265 | .00413 | 1,651,416 | 4,376 | 6,820 |
| 25-34 | .00268 | .00446 | 3,029,176 | 8,118 | 13,510 |
| 35-44 | .00404 | .00768 | 2,489,703 | 10,058 | 19,121 |
| 45-54 | .00749 | .01450 | 2,277,821 | 17,061 | 33,028 |
| 55-64 | .01645 | .02893 | 1,736,275 | 28,562 | 50,230 |
| Total, ages 20-64 | | | 11,184,391 | 68,175 | 122,709 |
| "Age-Standardized death rate," ages 20-64[c] | | | | .00610 | .01097 |

[a] Copied from Table 5:5. For ease of computation, the decimal point has been put in its proper place.

[b] Deaths expected on the assumption that rates of Group A apply to the standard population (Column 5) and the assumption that rates of Group B apply to the standard population (Column 6).

[c] The "crude" death rate in the entire standard population of 11,184,391, ages 20-64, based on the total expected deaths "A" and total expected deaths "B".

pected deaths $\left(\dfrac{\text{Actual deaths}}{\text{Expected deaths}}\right)$. This ratio, multiplied by the crude death rate of the standard population, is the standardized death rate for the actual population.

Suppose that we wish to compare the same occupation groups of Table 5:6, knowing only their age composition and the *total* numbers of deaths between ages 20-64 (that is, lacking age-specific death rates for each group). We must first ask the question in this way: how many annual deaths would be expected in Group A and Group B if both groups had the same age-specific death rates as the standard population? The answer is given in Table 5:7 (Columns 5 and 6). It is 3,601 for Group A, 6,196 for Group B. The deaths between ages 20-64, *actually* registered were 2,574 in Group A, 7,929 in Group B (yearly average, 1930-32). The crude death rate in the standard population (Column 2), multiplied by the ratios of actual to expected deaths in Group A and Group B (Columns 5 and 6), yield age-standardized rates of .00611 and .01094 respectively, or 61.1 and 109.4 per 10,000. Note that these are almost identical with the rates computed by the "direct" procedure above.[50]

The first type of standardized death rate (by the "direct method") is useful when there are strong reasons for a single index of mortality, and yet crude rates seem likely to be affected by differences of age composition. To compare the mortality of many subdivisions of a country would be confusing on the basis of age-specific rates, but their relative standing is apparent at a glance from a set of standardized rates. Death rates by occupation (see 5:14) are far less cumbersome if they are standardized by age, especially when there are many categories of occupations.

The second type ("indirect" standardization) is designed to make an approximate allowance for the effects of differing age structure on a comparison of death rates, when some (or all) of the actual age-specific death rates are not known. This expedient is useful, for example, in comparing the mortality in districts or regions if their crude death rates might be biased by differences of age composition, but if there are no data for age-specific death rates.

These rates, in short, have a wide variety of possible applications. Their use, however, is not always advisable. In some re-

---

[50]The two procedures do not always give such close results. One should also note that the age-standardized death rates of 61 and 109 per 10,000 do *not* correspond so closely to the actual death rates for Group A and Group B, which were 62 and 114. In other words, standardization is not an adequate substitute for real data.

spects they are not fully satisfactory.  The selection of a standard
is arbitrary; different results may be obtained if a different standard
is adopted.  The choice of standard is likely to have a greater effect,
or at least a more uncertain effect, with the "indirect" method, because this method relies more heavily on the hypothetical information drawn from the standard population.

Table 5:7

"INDIRECT" STANDARDIZATION OF DEATH RATES BY AGE
FOR TWO OCCUPATION GROUPS

Using death rates of the total population of occupied and retired
males as the standard.  Males only.

(Based on data of Table 5:5)

| (1) | (2)[a] | (3)[b] | (4)[b] | (5) | (6) |
|---|---|---|---|---|---|
| Ages | Death Rates in Standard Population (Males) | Group A (Agricultural labourers, male) | Group B (Labourers, general, male) | "Expected" Deaths[c] | |
| | | | | Group A | Group B |
| 20-24 | .00315 | 77,085 | 93,665 | 243 | 295 |
| 25-34 | .00339 | 111,361 | 192,064 | 378 | 651 |
| 35-44 | .00554 | 76,904 | 147,067 | 426 | 815 |
| 45-54 | .01111 | 76,602 | 143,238 | 851 | 1,591 |
| 55-64 | .02364 | 72,058 | 120,289 | 1,703 | 2,844 |
| Total ages 20-64 | .00855[d] | 414,010 | 696,323 | 3,601 | 6,196 |
| Total deaths actually registered, ages 20-64[e] | | | | 2,574 | 7,929 |
| Ratio:  Actual deaths/Expected deaths | | | | 0.71480 | 1.27970 |
| Age-Standardized Rate for Group A and Group B: (Ratio) x (Rate in Standard Population) | | | | .00611 | .01094 |

[a] The group "All Occupied and Retired Males" is selected as the standard.
Rates are those of Table 5:5.

[b] Census data, 1931.

[c] Deaths expected on the assumption that the rates of the standard population
apply to Group A (Column 5) and Group B (Column 6).

[d] This is the "crude" death rate for the entire group 20-64.

[e] Copied from the original source of the data.  This is the yearly average of
deaths registered in the period, 1930-1932.

It is not possible to make a general appraisal of standardizing procedures, for their value varies according to the circumstances in which they are used. At best, they permit concise comparisons, removing some of the hidden effects of population structure from crude rates. At the worst, they may distort the facts and, perhaps very rarely, lead to unwarranted conclusions. Between these extremes, standardized rates are very practical devices. But they add no new information; in the forms described above, they actually sacrifice some information already available, in order either to summarize or to fill a gap where actual knowledge is lacking. They are not a substitute for analysis of the detailed data, because they give an answer to another type of question. It is more important to recognize and grasp the meaning of standardized death rates when they are encountered than to be prepared to employ them in research.

# CHAPTER 6

# MEASUREMENT OF FERTILITY

At the outset, we should recognize that fertility is a more troublesome subject than mortality. First, it may be defined in several different ways. In large part this is due to inherent peculiarities of the distribution of births in a population. It is due also to the awkwardness of statistical measurement with available data, most of which have been collected for other purposes. These factors create problems of method, of finding ways to derive measurements from these data, and this is the main concern of this chapter. However, it is also true that the greatest practical problem is caused by defects of the data. This must be the first concern in actual research work, and cannot be neglected when we are discussing methods of procedure.

The fundamental notion of *fertility* is an *actual* level of performance in a population, based on the numbers of live births[1] that occur. It must be distinguished from *fecundity*, the *potential* level of performance (or physical capacity for bearing children) of the population. Fertility can be ascertained from statistics of births. The study of fertility does not indicate the level of fecundity, for which there is no direct measurement.

Fertility is measured as the frequency of births in a population. Thus it is similar to the notion of mortality. Beyond this, however, there are the problems just mentioned, without a definite solution that is satisfactory for most purposes (as the life table is in the study of mortality). Hence, modern fertility study still places heavy stress on developing adequate forms of measurement.

## 6:1 Different Approaches to Measurement of Fertility

Though fertility is measured as a frequency of births, the defi-

---

[1] The difficulties of defining just what is a "live" birth are mentioned in 1:5.

nition remains ambiguous in two respects: a frequency during what period, and a frequency reckoned within which section of the population? These questions serve to distinguish the two major types of approach.

On the one hand, it seems most natural to view fertility as the number of births per person, or per couple, during the childbearing period of life (usually the births in a group of adults from the beginning to the end of that period). This is sometimes called the *size of completed family*, meaning the average number of children ever borne by people who will bear no more. On the other hand, fertility is also measured by a vital rate, as described in 2:3, based on the births and population data of some calendar year.

We shall follow the usual practice of measuring fertility in relation to *women* only, with one or two exceptions. The same procedures are applicable in every case to the fertility of men, but the data usually pertain to women.

The distinction between these two approaches must be clearly maintained, for they do not yield the same sort of conclusions. The first represents the complete reproductive performance of one group of women, which may last about 35 years (see 6:6). The second includes part of the performance of many different groups (age groups) of women, lasting for just one year. This will be recognized as the distinction between synthetic and actual cohorts, mentioned in relation to mortality (4:11). Both approaches are often encountered in the study of fertility.

## 6:2 Peculiarities of Birth Statistics

A birth rate is computed like a death rate — a ratio of a year's births to the estimated number of person-years lived. In one respect, it is simpler. The number of person-years lived by women "exposed to the risk" of childbirth is neither increased nor lessened by a birth. Consequently the age-specific birth rate also measures the "risk" of childbirth (or the proportion of maternities) among these women. In principle the two types of rate are the same, and the awkward translation from a death rate $(M_x)$ to a mortality rate $(q_x)$, as in (4:10), is avoided.

In other respects, however, the distribution of births in a population is more complex, creating special problems in measuring their frequency:

a. Among the people who are "exposed to the risk" of childbirth, parenthood is an event that can occur more than once. From the standpoint of statistical record, death presents a simpler problem, for it happens only once. Having a birth does not necessarily remove a parent from the ranks of future potential parents[2]; in fact, most parents have more than one child.

(1) There are several categories of parenthood, according to the order of a particular birth. After having had four births, a woman's "risk" of having one more child this year is affected by the fact that it would be her fifth. It is far less common for mothers of 14 children to bear a fifteenth than it is for mothers of two children to bear a third. Hence the distribution of births in a population depends to some extent on the distribution of women by number of children already born.

(2) The "population exposed to the risk" of childbearing, which is the standard for measuring the frequency of a group of births, becomes an extremely vague category; for it includes women exposed to many different types of risk (as well as some women exposed to no risk). Therefore it is difficult to estimate the "population exposed to the risk" of childbirth in a given year. For example, even age-specific birth rates are not very adequate in this respect, for in an age group there are women who have previously borne different numbers of children; hence they are exposed to different kinds and degrees of risk.[3]

b. A birth involves two parents, but most birth rates must be restricted to either one or the other. Because the distribution of births in relation to other characteristics is not the same for men and for women, specific rates cannot represent both sides of parentage at the same time.[4] This is the reason why specific birth rates are sometimes referred to as "maternity" rates and "paternity" rates (see 2:16).

c. Parenthood is limited to portions of a population. The

---

[2] The birth of a child sometimes does have this effect, rendering some women sterile thereafter. The birth and early care of a child generally has this effect temporarily, rendering a woman sterile for an indefinite period. The uncertainty in both instances further complicates the distribution of births among women.

[3] The methods so far developed to solve this problem go beyond the scope of this book. Indeed, they are so detailed and cumbersome as to have very limited application. Here we shall follow the more conventional procedures of fertility measurement, merely calling attention to the direction in which these problems lead.

[4] The duration of marriage, of course, is the same for husbands and wives. Hence birth rates by duration of marriage ("duration-specific" rates) do not fall within this restriction. Crude birth rates are also free of this restriction.

very young and the very old, for example, are not "exposed to the risk" of childbearing. Furthermore, at any particular moment some people avoid this risk through choice (see below), failure to marry, widowhood, divorce or sterility. Among women, there are fairly definite age limits of childbirth: virtually all births occur while the mothers are between ages 15 and 50. This is one reason why age-specific birth rates are usually computed for women instead of men.

d. A small proportion of births, perhaps between 1-2 per cent, produce more than one child. These "plural" births introduce some confusion into fertility rates — is the birth of twins one event, or two? It is not clear which should be adopted as the unit of measurement — the children born, or completed pregnancies (sometimes called "confinements").[5] The statistics of most countries indicate only "births" (that is, children born alive), without this distinction, and so this is the basis that must be used. However, the effect of choosing one standard or the other is very small, and is usually ignored.

e. Personal choice and preference have a wide and various influence on fertility, and this further complicates the distribution of births in the population. In the case of mortality, these factors are all presumed to run in the same direction — nearly everyone would rather live than die. There is not such unanimity about childbearing. People differ in their preferences regarding a birth during a given year, and in the total number of children they expect to have. Their attitudes also vary, in both of these respects, according to the number of children already born. Moreover, they may change any of these views in response to the trends of the times. The possible combinations of all these factors become so complicated that they have never yet been set into systematic order preparatory to investigation. Because preferences vary so widely, the birth rates of a population in a calendar year often do not correspond closely to the size of family finally attained. Yearly observations give poorer indication of the level and changes of fertility than of mortality (see, for example, 6:7).

## 6:3 Some Conventional Forms of Measurement

In practice there is very little that can be done to overcome these problems. More attention is usually given to detecting and lessening the effects of errors in the data — and properly so, since the

---

[5] It is probably more appropriate to measure fertility on the basis of confinements, and to measure replacement of population (see Chapter 7) on the basis of the number of children born. And yet as a matter of principle, even this solution is open to some question.

errors are often too large to be overlooked, and since they are reme-
died by commonsense means rather than by general techniques.

It is in making a plan of research and drawing conclusions from
the observed data that these problems must be taken into account.
Between these two stages, one must decide which types of rates to
adopt, for evidently no single form of fertility measurement is suitable for all purposes. The next three sections discuss the use of
several conventional forms of measurement. Some will be recognized
as rates already described in Chapter 2; here the purpose is to consider the questions that arise in their application to common tasks of
research. They are presented under the two main methods of approach, calendar-year birth rates and reproductive histories.

## 6:4 Birth Rates Based on Yearly Performance

The principal basis for measuring fertility in a population is
some index of yearly performance. Until fairly recently this was the
only approach, partly because it was considered sufficient and partly
because data were not available in any other form. It leads to the familiar kind of vital-statistics rate, as explained in Chapter 2. The
conventional birth rates are ratios of a year's births to some number
of person-years lived during the year. Births of a base period longer
than one year are sometimes used, expressed as a yearly average;
the number of person-years is assumed to be the same as the mid-
year population, and a census figure is usually an acceptable estimate. The following rates are in common use:

a. *Crude Birth Rate,* a ratio of a year's registered births to
the total mid-year population (see 2:9). This is analogous to the
crude death rate (in 5:6), and shares the same advantages and shortcomings.

b. *General Fertility Rate,* or *General Fertility Ratio,* a
ratio of total yearly registered births to the population of women of
"childbearing age" (either the age group 15-44 or the group 15-49).
The purpose is to restrict the denominator of the rate to potential
mothers, by excluding all men and large groups of women not "exposed to the risk" of childbearing by reason of age. This refinement
is a step in the direction of measuring fertility against the proper portion of the population. It is a rather crude and ineffective step, because it defines this portion by the same arbitrary standard (the age
interval 15-44 or 15-49) under all circumstances (see 2:17).

c. *Age-Specific Birth Rates,* ratios of births by age of
mother to women in each age interval, usually in 5-year age intervals.
Like age-specific death rates, these comprise a whole set of rates instead of just one average figure. Age-specific birth rates form a

relatively convenient set of *seven* rates, as illustrated in 2:16. They reveal the distribution of frequencies of births among women according to age. They represent the most useful single step in analyzing the fertility performance of a calendar year. It is a large improvement in precision, for these rates are not significantly distorted by variations of age composition, either in the total population or among the women of childbearing ages. It also identifies, approximately, a few stages in the reproductive careers of the different age groups of women. Though the information is difficult to interpret (referring to a *different* stage for each age group of women), it is extremely valuable. Finally, age-specific rates are utilized in calculating other important measurements, to be discussed below.

Sometimes age-specific birth rates are computed separately for married women, as a further refinement when the effect of variations in marriage patterns must also be excluded. No new procedures are involved. However, the birth statistics must also refer just to married women. Such material ("legitimate" births, excluding the "illegitimate") is not very reliable. The classifications used in the two universes — census and registration statistics — are likely to match rather poorly, and such rates should be treated with reservations. Naturally the pattern of distribution shown by these birth rates is not comparable with that of ordinary age-specific rates.

d. *Child-Woman Ratio*, a ratio of children under age 5 to women of "childbearing ages" (defined sometimes as 15-44, and sometimes as 15-49). This index is plainly a makeshift, designed to furnish a measurement of fertility when birth statistics are lacking (see 2:6). It is derived entirely from the data by age in one census. Though the child-woman ratio is useful chiefly because of this fact, it demands caution for the same reason. Instead of births, the ratio is based on the *survivors* of previous births; it includes the survivors of births during the five years preceding the census, and unavoidably includes the effects of infant and childhood mortality during this period. (The age group 0-4, moreover, is one of the least reliable parts of the enumerated population; sometimes another interval must be substituted, like the age group 1-4 or 5-9.) Therefore the *absolute* values of the child-woman ratio have rather little significance, being affected by other factors besides fertility. It serves best as a relative measure, to compare the fertility performance of different sections of the same population, where the disturbing effects of these other factors are presumed to be smaller.[6]

---

[6]There is another application, in the measurement of replacement, based on an analogy to the structure of the life-table population (see 7:5).

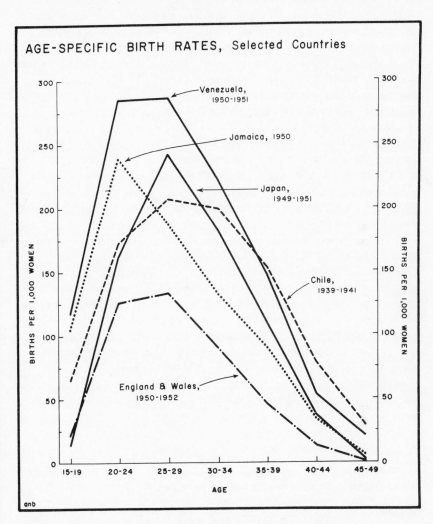

Chart 6:1  Age-specific birth rates, selected countries.

e. *Total Fertility Rate*, the sum of age-specific birth rates of women, at each age from 15 to 49 (see also 2:18). As stated above, it is sufficient to compute these birth rates by 5-year age intervals.[7] For this purpose they are usually expressed as rates "per woman" instead of rates "per 1,000 women" – that is, the factor $k = 1$.

The total fertility rate represents the same population of women as the general fertility rate, but takes account of the distribution of the year's births among women of different ages. Hence it is a far more effective means of summarizing the frequency of births of a particular year. With a moment's reflection, this procedure is recognizable as an example of standardization, corresponding to the "direct method" (see 5:16): the birth rate at each age is multiplied by a standard population of *1 person* (or, at each 5-year interval, is multiplied by 5). For this reason, the total fertility rate remains unaffected by peculiarities of the age composition of the women in the interval of ages 15-49.

f. *Gross Reproduction Rate*, the sum of age-specific birth rates of women of ages 15 to 49, restricted to female births only. Otherwise, this rate is essentially the same as the total fertility rate, yielding values that are about half as large; the computation is carried out in practically the same steps (see 2:18). The gross reproduction rate has achieved wider currency in the study of replacement (see Chapter 7), and is somewhat more familiar for this reason.

g. *Total Fertility Rate*, computed by indirect procedures.[8] Since the total fertility rate is a type of standardized rate, as just mentioned, the corresponding *indirect* procedure is useful in the absence of certain of the basic data (age-specific birth rates). This device was not described in Chapter 2, and so it is explained in the following example. An estimated total fertility rate is computed for El Salvador, postponing for a moment the question of whether the data

Strictly speaking, births preceding the census ought not to be measured against the census population of women, since these women are not quite the same group that were of "child-bearing age" when the births were occurring. This objection is valid, but insignificant compared with the defects mentioned above.

[7] These abridged rates must then be multiplied by 5, in order to approximate the actual sum of the rates at each year of age (see 2:18).

[8] An estimated gross reproduction rate is computed in almost exactly the same manner. It differs by one added step: the estimated total fertility rate is simply multiplied by the proportion (actual or estimated) of female births to total births (see 2:18). The reader may sometimes find these indirectly computed rates referred to as "substitute" rates, though this term is not quite accurate.

are adequate.

First, let us suppose that these data for El Salvador have not been tabulated by age of mother. What would be the total fertility rate if the births were distributed according to the pattern of age-specific birth rates in Puerto Rico, 1949-1951?

The necessary calculations are summarized in Table 6:1. The age-specific birth rates of Puerto Rico are multiplied by the number of women in each age group, yielding a first estimate of the number of births of women in El Salvador, by age (Column 4 of Table 6:1). The total number of these estimated births is not quite the same as the total (of 89,676) actually registered in El Salvador. The ratio of

## TABLE 6:1

## TOTAL FERTILITY RATE COMPUTED BY INDIRECT PROCEDURE

(For Women in El Salvador, Based on Birth Rates of Puerto Rico, 1949-1951 and Total Registered Births in El Salvador)

| Age | Women enumerated in Census, 1950 | Birth rates of Puerto Rican women 1949-1951 | First estimate of annual births in El Salvador (2) × (3) | Revised estimate of birth rates (3) × 1.16058 | (Actual birth rates of women in El Salvador, 1949-1951) |
|---|---|---|---|---|---|
| (1) | (2) | (3) | (4) | (5) | (6) |
| 15-19 | 101,760 | .0993 | 10,105 | .1152 | (.1264) |
| 20-24 | 93,297 | .2784 | 25,974 | .3231 | (.2944) |
| 25-29 | 73,857 | .2575 | 19,018 | .2988 | (.3152) |
| 30-34 | 57,394 | .1976 | 11,341 | .2293 | (.2504) |
| 35-39 | 57,598 | .1410 | 8,121 | .1636 | (.1457) |
| 40-44 | 45,161 | .0512 | 2,312 | .0594 | (.0580) |
| 45-49 | 34,833 | .0114 | 397 | .0132 | (.0198) |
| Total, 15-49 | | | 77,268 | 1.2026 | (1.2099 |
| Total Fertility Rate | | | | × 5 = 6.01 | × 5 = 6.05) |

Total estimated births, 77,268; 89,676 births were actually registered (yearly average, 1949-1951). 89,676/77,268 = 1.16058, the basis for revising the first estimate.

Total of Column 5, multiplied by 5, is 5(1.2026) = 6.01, the estimated Total Fertility Rate. For comparison, the rate calculated from the actual data of El Salvador (Column 6) is 6.05. (In the rates of Column 6, births with mother's age not stated and multiple births were arbitrarily allocated by age, as shown in 3:12.)

actual births to estimated births is 89,676/77,268, or 1.16058. In other words, the birth rates borrowed from Puerto Rico were too low for El Salvador in 1949-1951.

Each of the transplanted age-specific rates is then multiplied by this ratio (Column 5). (That is, we assume that each rate deviates from the "true" rate in the same degree.) These revised rates are added, and the sum is multiplied by five (the number of years in each interval of age).[9] The resulting figure of 6.01 is the estimated total fertility rate for El Salvador. It is the same kind of adjusted ratio as the standardized death rates in Table 5:7.

It would be just as easy to use the age-specific birth rates of any other country as the standard. How, then, is it possible to judge whether the standard is appropriate? Of course, we can never be certain. The information that would answer this question is normally missing. Otherwise there would be no need to make an indirect estimate. The age-specific rates taken from Puerto Rico had to be raised by 16 per cent in Table 6:1 in order to provide the total number of births actually observed; obviously they were too low.

This might have been foreseen. In El Salvador, the crude birth rate in 1949-1951 was 48 per thousand, signifying a "high" level of fertility,[10] and the crude birth rate for Puerto Rico was 39. In this instance, age-specific rates actually are available for both populations (compare Column 3 and Column 6 of Table 6:1). The greatest part of the disparities between the two schedules is reconciled by the ratio of actual births to estimated births (Column 5). The final discrepancy is very small; the estimated total fertility rate (6.01) is just slightly lower than the rate computed from the actual data (6.05). Though another schedule of rates might give a better estimate of the total fertility rate, the discrepancy is so small that the gain could not be very large.

No matter how exact, the indirect procedure is still dependent on the known data — registered births and enumerated population —

---

[9]It is not necessary to go to this much trouble, except for the sake of illustration in Table 6:1. The same result, with a small discrepancy due to rounding, is obtained by applying the ratio 1.16058 to the sum of Column 3 (times five): $5(1.0364) \times 1.16058 = 6.014$.

[10]Lacking any statistics of births in El Salvador, they might be estimated from the number of children enumerated in the census, and an appropriate life table (see 5:5, and Table 3:3). This estimation introduces further opportunity for error in the results. The estimated numbers of births would not refer to the year of the census, but to the period preceding the census.

which are the chief source of error.[11] This is a wholly different problem. Without some independent reason to trust these figures, there is little or no advantage in calculating a total fertility rate from them. These data of El Salvador are of uncertain reliability. We cannot determine whether the original data would justify calculating a total fertility rate by either method.

## 6:5 Uses of Calendar-Year Rates

In many instances, there is little question of selecting among these rates, for the data do not leave room for choice. If no more than the total numbers are known, of births and population, then only a crude birth rate is feasible. There may be an age classification of the census figures, but not the birth data; this permits the use of a general fertility rate, or the indirect calculation of a total fertility rate as just described. With only census data (by age), lacking any trustworthy statistics of births, a child-woman ratio may be satisfactory.[12]

If there is specific reason to doubt the accuracy of detailed tabulations, it is better to avoid them in favor of simpler rates. The crude birth rate is most widely applicable. Like the crude death rate, it is convenient, concise, quick to compute, and easily explained to a general audience. However, it is subject to distortion, not only on account of the age structure of the population, but also due to the typical pattern of the distribution of births.

What is gained by employing the more elaborate types of meas-

---

[11] Faulty registration of births creates a bias, usually a bias of insufficiency, which may go completely undetected. For this reason, all fertility rates based on registered births tend to yield measurements that are too low. The indirect procedure is somewhat more vulnerable, because some of the information about the distribution of births, which might furnish grounds for skepticism, is missing.

However, registration data are not the only source of error. Birth rates are also biased by inadequate census returns at any of the age groups included in their calculation.

[12] The data by age should first be inspected, especially for signs of incomplete enumeration of children ages 0-4.

Using the census data for children, it is possible to estimate the recent annual numbers of births, and thence to make an indirect calculation of total fertility rate (see 3:9, 5:3 and 6:4). These estimates of yearly births ought (preferably) to be based on the census population by single year of age, though approximations can be made with data for children 0-4, or even 5-9. Such estimates may offer only questionable advantage over the original child-woman ratio.

urement? They provide separate consideration of birth rates by age and sex groups in the population. The advantages of specific rates may be judged partly from the standpoint of accuracy, and partly from the standpoint of the additional information that is conveyed.

With regard to accuracy, the refined rates are better in most instances, in the sense that they are less affected by extraneous factors. The important question is, how much better? Age-specific birth rates, and the other measurements derived from them, remain undisturbed by peculiarities of age-sex composition of a population which affect the crude birth rate and general fertility rate. This is an important point, but not necessarily critical for the case at hand — not, for example, unless substantial differences of age and sex composition are involved, and not unless these differences affect the age and sex groups in which fertility is measured. In national total figures, these variations, though they have some disturbing effect, often are not large enough to weigh very heavily.[13] In figures for separate groups *within* a national population, age and sex composition are more likely to vary. When comparing the fertility of these groups, the more elaborate rates offer a greater improvement over the crude birth rate and general fertility rate.

Therefore a crude rate may, or may not, be as satisfactory as a total fertility rate, depending on these circumstances. It is not clear just how such relative merits should be appraised.[14] The basic data also contain unknown errors. In view of these, we are not justified in attaching importance to small differences between rates, no matter how refined the procedure of computation.

How wide must be the margin of safety, in order to guarantee against a biased comparison of birth rates? There is no valid rule. In comparing two crude rates, they should probably be scrutinized very closely before a difference of less than, say, ten per cent of their value is accepted. Perhaps this margin is unnecessarily large

---

[13] Particularly, the age composition of the female population (which is the basis for computing most specific birth rates) is less variable than that of the male population.

[14] For example, it was possible for two authors to reach divergent conclusions from rather similar evidence, by differing in their emphasis on what constitutes a "large" or a "small" effect of age-sex composition on crude birth rates. See F. Lorimer, "Relations among Measures of Fertility," (paper presented at United Nations Seminar on Population Studies, Rio de Janeiro, 1955), p. 7, and G. J. Stolnitz, "Uses of Crude Vital Rates in the Analysis of Reproductivity," *Journal of the American Statistical Association*, Vol. 50, p. 1228 ff., (December, 1955).

in some cases, perhaps insufficient in others; probably it may be somewhat reduced in comparing the more refined types of rates. The decision rests largely on subjective judgments, which tend to betray a rather unwarranted degree of trust in the original data. The advantages of age-specific rates in measuring fertility can easily be exaggerated. These advantages lose a great deal of their practical significance when questions of defective data are considered.

Do these other types of measurement contain any additional information? In reality, they provide very little more than the crude birth rate. Excepting age-specific rates, they summarize the frequency of a year's births, expressing it in a single index. The index may be arrived at by different means, but it is still based on the same total number of births. [15] Among the calendar-year indices, only the total fertility rate (and of course the gross reproduction rate) makes use of any additional facts about the distribution of these births.

The total fertility rate and gross reproduction rate, however, have a special meaning. By analogy with the life table, they have a unique place in population studies, owing to their peculiar mode of construction. Both are computed by adding the birth rates of women (the number of births per person-year) at each age, from age 15 through age 49. This, it will be recalled, is likewise the principle of the life table — namely, a schedule of age-specific rates, combined successively by age (see 4:11).

The result is a hypothetical fertility history, based on birth rates instead of mortality rates. The total fertility rate represents all the births of an assumed cohort of women, starting at age 15, and undergoing this hypothetical fertility experience until the end of their childbearing period. The gross reproduction rate represents virtually the same experience, confined to *female* births only. (Note that it is simpler to combine birth rates than mortality rates. Birth rates do not reduce the numbers of the hypothetical cohort, which remains at its initial size. This size is usually set at $k = 1$, as mentioned in 2:18, and so the measurements refer to the hypothetical number of children born per woman.)

The major gain of information, as stated earlier, is secured by means of age-specific rates. These rates form a very useful pattern, with a wide basis of comparison. They reveal the distribution of the risks of childbirth during a year among different age groups of women;

---

[15] In particular, the general fertility rate utilizes no new information about these births not already provided by the crude birth rate. The same may be said of the child-woman ratio, though it does not represent any actual number of births.

or, they may be used to compare the experience at some age, at different times or places. They are only a *partial* record, representing just a portion of the full experience of each group of women. This portion is a similar stage in the reproductive life of women in most countries, though not necessarily the same stage. For example, in India, with an early pattern of childbearing, a birth rate for women aged 20-24 represents a somewhat earlier stage than the corresponding birth rate for women in England & Wales, where the onset of childbearing is later.

### 6:6 Actual Reproductive Histories

The other method of measuring fertility is to count the number of children born to some actual group of women. This is a simple and straightforward approach, and scarcely seems to warrant a separate explanation. However, there are some practical difficulties, again due to the nature of the available data.

By adding together the numbers of births to some group of women, from the beginning to the end of their childbearing period, we can assemble their complete reproductive history as a group. This contrasts with the previous approach: rather than the sum of the births of different women in the same year, it is the sum of the births of the same group of women. Naturally, these do not fall within the same year, but extend over a considerable period (from age 15 to age 50, or 35 years). The final figure is expressed as an average, the "mean number of children ever born." This is also called the "total completed family size" or "average size of family."[16] This measurement does not require the construction of an artificial or hypothetical cohort; it simply records the experience of an actual cohort, generally a cohort of women.

Where is this information found? There are three kinds of source material:

a. Conventional age-specific birth rates, calculated on the basis of yearly performance at successive dates. These can be computed from an ordinary registration (and census) system, if the birth rates are obtainable for a minimum period of 30 to 35 years. The birth rates must be shifted to a different order. Starting with the women whose births at ages 15-19 occurred between 1920 and 1925, for example, approximately the same cohort of women would be repre-

---

[16]In writings on the fertility of women, the term "size of family" always refers to the total number of children ever born per woman.

sented at ages 20-24 between 1925 and 1930, and so on.[17] When these age-specific birth rates are re-arranged five years apart, they represent successive periods in the experience of one cohort. This source can rarely be used, however, because few countries maintain such data over a sufficient number of years in comparable form.

b. Birth records of individual women, registered at the time when each birth occurred. With 35 years of unbroken records of this kind, a reproductive history can be compiled for each surviving woman who can be identified at the time of survey. This technique is instructive, but has little application, for such data are likewise very rare. The example in Table 6:2 is almost unique.

c. Retrospective reports. Nearly always, reproductive histories are based on reports by individual adults at the time of a census or special survey. These are given in response to direct questions about the past number of children ever born to each woman. If the date of each birth (or the mother's age) is also given, and tabulated, it is possible to construct a complete age-specific reproductive history for a cohort of the women. With more information, of course, various other aspects of the distribution of births can be studied.

The first difficulty of the reproductive history is already evident. Except in source "a," special tables are required, designed exclusively for this purpose. In addition, several other problems should be mentioned. Regardless of the source of data, a complete reproductive history requires a long and continuous record. It cannot be "complete" except for older women, with reference to their past experience. When derived from individual registration or retrospective reports (sources "b" and "c" above), the record is thus confined to the women who have survived to age 50 or beyond at the date of survey. This means that parts of the original cohorts are missing: women who died before the time of the census or survey are not included, and of course their fertility record is lacking. If these women differed in fertility from the women who were included, the reproductive history will be slightly biased. In this sense it is not "complete"; if drawn from data of source "a" above, however, this defect is absent.

Retrospective data may also be somewhat inaccurate. Remote events are often given the wrong dates, and one should assume that

[17] These birth rates may refer to one year in five (1920, 1925, 1930, etc.) or may be averages of five annual rates (1920-1924, 1925-1930, etc.). There is a discrepancy in adapting current registration data to this use (see footnote to Table 6:2), but it can safely be ignored.

there is some deliberately fictitious reporting of past experience.[18] On the other hand, there is no doubt about the matching of the births and the population: these two universes may be considered exactly the same.[19] This is an important advantage of retrospective data as a means of measuring the fertility of different groups in a population.

Age-specific birth rates may be derived from a reproductive history. They represent births per person-year lived by an actual group of women of completed childbearing – in other words, the average schedule of accumulation of children for the entire cohort. The sum of these rates represents the total size of completed family, or average "family size." It resembles the total fertility rate, but its meaning is different. The average size of family is the total number of children born to one group of women over a period of many years, whereas the total fertility rate is a total of partial experience of many groups, based on their performance during one year.

It is interesting to compare the two methods, applied to the same population (see 6:7). By convention, we commence with women age 50 and over (or perhaps 45 and over). It is advisable to separate these into several cohorts (women of ages 50-59, 60-69, 70-79, or similar groups), so that each group may be fairly homogeneous. Thus, if the oldest women tend to give reports that are less accurate, the errors are isolated from the younger cohorts; the separate groups may also reveal a trend of fertility, by showing a change in the experience of the different cohorts.

The reproductive history opens up some important and rewarding avenues of study, depending on the kinds of additional detail included in the statistics. For example, it is useful to have a table of women (of completed childbearing), classified by the total number of children ever born (see Table 6:4). With this material, we can calculate the proportions of the women at each stage who went on to have

---

[18] Obviously, these mistakes are more likely to happen among older informants (whose early births are more distant), people whose reports are given by someone else, or people whose culture does not attach importance to the exact dates of events. Furthermore, illiteracy will prevent people from aiding their recollection by reference to personal records. In some instances there may be motives for misrepresenting the facts. Seldom is there any opportunity to check the accuracy of these reports, and so there is always some reason to doubt their reliability.

[19] Except, of course, that some births may be distributed in the wrong age intervals (of mothers) because of inaccurate reporting of the date of birth. Then the age-specific birth rates would be distorted, even though the figure for completed family size might still be correct.

at least one additional child.[20]  It is still more useful to have a
table classifying the women by the order of each birth and the period
elapsed since the preceding birth.  With this material, we can calculate the proportions of women who had a birth of a given order within
a year after a birth of the previous order; these are the type of birth
rate most closely resembling the probabilities of a life table.[21]

Data of this kind sometimes represent the history of an entire
cohort of women, or sometimes the history of a group of *married*
women (whose experience is calculated from the date of marriage).
In some respects one or the other of these forms is advantageous,
though the principle of analyzing this experience is basically the
same.  However, these data are still very rare; and they raise special
problems — of a rather particular nature — that are too detailed to describe here.

The gain of precision by measuring fertility in this way appears
to be enormous.  At the same time, there is an awkward gain in the
amount of information that must be treated.  This unwelcome feature
arises because the increased precision is achieved through applying
a simple method (the basic notion of a proportion, explained in Chapter 2) to a more detailed classification of events, not by developing a
more complex method.  There is not yet a large body of experience
with the use of these procedures.  Undoubtedly their characteristics

---

[20]The calculation is exactly the same as that of any other proportion:
a number of women who had births of some order, $n$, divided by the universe
of women who were able to have these births (all women who had had $n-1$
births).  This form of measurement is discussed in L. Henry, *Fécondité des
Mariages: Nouvelle Méthode de Mesure* (Paris, 1952), (where it is called
"probabilité d'aggrandissement"), and "Fertility according to Size of Family," in *Population Bulletin of the United Nations*, No. 4 (New York, December 1954), where it is called "probability of increase [of family size]"; and
in N. B. Ryder, "Fertility," a chapter in P.M. Hauser and O.D. Duncan
(eds.), *The Study of Population: An Inventory and Appraisal* (forthcoming).

[21]This is the only type of birth rate that distinguishes rigorously between women who are exposed to the risk of childbirth and women who are
not.  For this reason, it is not limited to use with a reproductive history; it
can also be adapted to calendar-year data.  Birth rates for each order of
birth ("parity-specific birth rates") express the distribution of a year's
births among women grouped by the stage of family size that they have
reached.  This adaptation requires some special devices, involving arbitrary
approximations where these aspects of the distribution of births are unknown.  See L. Henry, "Fertility according to Size of Family," *Population
Bulletin of the United Nations*, No. 4 (New York, December 1954).  For an
example of adapting calendar-year data to fit a reproductive history, see
D.V. Glass and E. Grebenik, *The Trend and Pattern of Fertility in Great
Britain* (Part I: Report), Appendix 1 to Chapter 7 (London, 1954).

will be better known as the necessary data become available for additional countries. Now, however, the reader can only consult the technical writings as they appear.[22]

## 6:7 Comparison of the Two Principal Types of Approach

Which of these two methods is superior? In reality, this is not a genuine issue, for each represents a different aspect of fertility in a population. They are not expressions of the same facts. It is essential to distinguish carefully between the two forms and the information that each provides.

The distinction is very clear in Table 6:2, where both types of measurement can be drawn from the same body of data. Table 6:2 contains birth rates by age (births per person-year) for a sample of rural women surveyed in 1952.[23] The rates are arranged by cohort in each column: for the history of any cohort, simply read down a column. The rates of the same period therefore must be found in different columns: for the approximate yearly performance of women during a base period, read the figures along one of the diagonal lines.

The total number of children per woman in a cohort is assembled by adding the rates of that column, allowing for the fact that each rate of Table 6:2 represents five person-years. For example, the cohort born 1898-1902 (aged 50-54 in 1952) had an average of $(.10 + .31 + .33 + .32 + .27 + .11 + .01) \times 5$, or 7.25 births. The total fertility rate for the decade 1933-1942 (approximately) is found by adding diagonally in Table 6:2, $(.09 + .35 + .34 + .30 + .27 + .12 + .01) \times 5$, or 7.40[24] The first example refers to events among the

---

[22] See, in particular, the exploratory studies of Henry, Ryder, Glass and Grebenik, cited above. It seems obvious that this approach will have its major application to data of a single year or base period, for lack of a long series of data needed for an actual cohort measurement.

[23] These figures come from a survey of 3% of the households in Yunlin District, Taiwan, taken by C. H. Tuan. In this table, the women were grouped by cohort, according to their ages at time of survey (women of ages 50-54 in December, 1952 were born in 1898-1902, and so on). The reproductive histories were compiled in 5-year intervals for each cohort. By calculating the mean number of births per interval, then dividing by 5 (the number of years lived in each interval), the number of births per person-year was computed for that interval. Each birth rate of Table 6:2 consists of such a number of births per person-year.

[24] A moment's reflection is needed to appreciate what calendar period is represented (see the Note to Table 6:2). The cohort of women born 1918-1922 (aged 30-34 at the end of 1952) passed through ages 15-19 between

## TABLE 6:2

## AGE-SPECIFIC BIRTH RATES FOR WOMEN IN TAIWAN, 1952

for calculation of total fertility rates and reproductive histories

(data from sample survey, December, 1952)[a]

| Age at Birth of Children | Groups of Women by Date of Birth (Ages in 1952) | | | | | | | | | |
|---|---|---|---|---|---|---|---|---|---|---|
| | 1888-92 (60-64) | 1893-97 (55-59) | 1898-02 (50-54) | 1903-07 (45-49) | 1908-12 (40-44) | 1913-17 (35-39) | 1918-22 (30-34) | 1923-27 (25-29) | 1928-32 (20-24) | 1933-37 (15-19) |
| 15-19 | .09 | .10 | .10 | .11 | .12 | .10 | .09 | .07 | .05 | *.01* |
| 20-24 | .28 | .31 | .31 | .35 | .33 | .35 | .33 | .30 | *.14* | |
| 25-29 | .33 | .30 | .33 | .35 | .34 | .32 | .31 | *.16* | | |
| 30-34 | .29 | .29 | .32 | .30 | .28 | .27 | *.16* | | | |
| 35-39 | .25 | .25 | .27 | .25 | .21 | *.12* | | | | |
| 40-44 | .13 | .12 | .11 | .10 | *.06* | | | | | |
| 45-49 | .01 | .01 | .01 | *.01* | | | | | | |

fertility rate: 7.40, 6.85, 6.25

| | 6.90 | 6.90 | 7.25 | 7.35 | ← Children ever born |

(Number of Women in Sample)

| 106 | 145 | 231 | 291 | 436 | 438 | 486 | 630 | 777 |

Source: C. H. Tuan, "Reproductive Histories of Chinese Women in Rural Taiwan," *Population Studies*, Vol. 12, July, 1958, p. 43.

[a] Three per cent sample of rural households in Yunlin District.

*Note:* As explained in the text, the experience of cohorts is arranged in columns. Therefore the rates of the same calendar period must be found in different columns; they are indicated by the diagonal lines in the table. However, a 5-year age interval does not coincide with a 5-year calendar period. The cohort of women born 1928-1932 spent their first five years of life during the ten years from 1928 to 1937 (before the last of them reached age five). They passed through ages 15-19 during the ten years 1943-1952; most of this experience was concentrated near the middle of the period. During the same period, the cohort born 1923-27 passed through ages 20-24, the cohort born 1918-22 passed through ages 25-29, and so on.

For this reason, the rates beneath the lowest diagonal line are incomplete. For example, some of the 1928-32 cohort had not yet passed completely through the ages 20-24; some of the 1923-28 cohort had not passed through ages 25-29, etc. By the end of 1952, many of these women had not yet completed five person-years in these intervals. Hence the rates are not correct and are printed in italics. The rates would be approximately correct if they were computed by means of the actual number of person-years lived.

same group of women; the second refers to events of the same calendar period. Only a reproductive history, the first type, can represent the experience of a single cohort of women; but, being a record that extends over many years, it cannot refer to any particular base point within that period.

In this example, the numerical results are very close in both cases. The reproductive history of the cohort indicates a total of 7.25 births,[25] while the total fertility rate representing the period 1933-1942 is 7.40. This is because there has been very little change of fertility among these women.

The question of change, however, is more complex. Altogether three total fertility rates can be calculated from Table 6:2, as follows:

| Calendar Period | Total Fertility Rate |
|---|---|
| 1933-1942 | 7.40 |
| 1938-1947 | 6.85 |
| 1943-1952 | 6.25 |

The periods overlap somewhat, because different groups of women were passing through the same 5-year age interval at the same time.[26] These calendar-period rates give the appearance of *falling* fertility. We can also calculate three reproductive histories (or four if we disregard the small uncompleted portion of the 1903-07 cohort):

| Cohort of Women (by date of birth) | Average Children Ever Born |
|---|---|
| 1888-92 | 6.90 |
| 1893-97 | 6.90 |
| 1898-02 | 7.25 |
| 1903-07 | 7.35 |

---

1933 and 1942. This was also the period when the cohort born 1913-1917 was passing through ages 20-24, and the cohort of 1908-1912 was passing through ages 25-29, and so on at the other ages.

[25] This figure of 7.25 contains a chance error due to rounding of the separate age-specific rates. The actual average number of births per woman in this cohort was 7.17.

[26] Because of the peculiar form of the data, these total fertility rates give most weight to the births at the middle portion of each 10-year calendar period. See the Note to Table 6:2.

These cohort indices give an appearance of *rising* fertility. It is to be expected that the two types of measurement disagree when some change has occurred, because they are not based on the experience of the same groups of women.

(Actually, the falling total fertility rates of Table 6:2 represent chiefly a brief fluctuation, due to wartime conditions of the decade between 1940 and 1950. By examining the successive birth rates for a particular interval of age, along any horizontal line of figures in the table, the reader can verify that these age-specific rates were lower. A total fertility rate calculated for women of this district in the year 1951 is 7.94, the result of a fluctuation in the other direction. The average of several postwar rates is approximately the same as before the war.)

From the standpoint of accuracy, both types of measurement have certain advantages and weaknesses. These have already been considered in previous sections (6:4 and 6:5), and it is necessary only to mention them very briefly again. Annual birth rates can be computed from material that is widely available, permitting some measurement of fertility on the basis of more limited records. Reproductive histories, though less convenient, offer greater assurance that the universe of births matches the enumerated population of women. In either case, there are only very limited opportunities to detect the presence of errors.

From the standpoint of their meaning, as already pointed out, these two types of measurement refer to different aspects of fertility. Thus neither is the only "correct" way to measure the frequency of births in a population. For this reason they have been the source of much confusion in early writings on the subject. While a statistical view of childbearing patterns seems increasingly to refer to a cohort's experience — to imply the notion of "family size" — the actual measurement must be carried out in terms of calendar-year performance. In other words, the notion of fertility tends to be formulated according to one approach, but measured by the other. Through failure to recognize this distinction, the evidence of a base period is sometimes mistakenly followed to conclusions that might legitimately be reached only on the basis of reproductive histories.

## 6:8  Topics of Fertility Study

The subject of computing fertility indices cannot be properly covered by itself, even if it occupied the remainder of this chapter. It must also be considered in relation to their uses in studying fertility — particularly the level, changes and variations within a population, which are the topics of the next few sections.

In addition, a fertility investigation sometimes proceeds in special directions, due to the complex nature of the distribution of births. One of these is to analyze more closely the level of fertility, examining the pattern of steps toward the size of family that is finally reached, or the schedule of spacing successive births on the part of a group of women.[27] Another is to study the association between differences of fertility and individual sentiments toward family and related matters. These two topics occupy a substantial portion of current research, and they will receive further mention somewhat later in the chapter. But they require special sources of information (survey data or census tabulations) that are not yet generally available, and the methods employed are still haphazard. We cannot refer to a definite body of procedures for this type of investigation, since none yet exists. Hence the remaining sections are devoted principally to ways of treating the more standard types of data.

### 6:9  Determining the Level of Fertility

The level of fertility can be found by means of any of the indices discussed above, with somewhat varying results. In order to give these measurements any definite significance, some comparative standards are implied (see 5:6). Hence a conventional and familiar type of rate is often preferable. The crude birth rate is especially useful, like the crude death rate in measuring mortality, for it affords the widest possible basis for comparison with data of other populations.

Among calendar-year measurements, the other rates described in 6:4 provide a more reliable basis for comparisons. The general fertility ratio excludes most of the persons to whom births should not be attributed. The total fertility rate takes into account the distribution of a year's births among women by age. As pointed out in 6:5, however, all of these indices differ only slightly as measurements for national totals, unless there has been some disturbance of age and sex composition of the population by large-scale migration or other special events.

Judging from Table 6:3, a crude birth rate of 43 is an example of "high" fertility. It corresponds to a general fertility rate of approximately 180, and a total fertility rate of about 5.7. Similarly, "low" fertility by present world standards is illustrated by a crude birth rate of 10 to 15, and a total fertility rate of about 2.0. For the total population of a country, different types of rates usually corre-

---

[27] This rests principally on the evidence of reproductive histories (see 6:6, especially footnote 20).

spond fairly well; this may not hold true when rates are calculated for smaller groups within a population, or for a period following some rapid change. Standards of "high" or "low" fertility are those of a particular era, reflecting contemporary points of view. Formerly a crude birth rate of 40 or above was regarded as a normal occurrence, though now it attracts remark and often concern. The lower recorded crude birth rates, between 10-20 per thousand, may continue to be regarded as very "low," though they are no longer greeted with surprise or alarm.

The results obtained from reproductive histories (average completed family size) have already been illustrated in the examples of 6:7. It is expected that the average completed family size should fail to correspond perfectly to rates based on yearly performance. As we have seen in Table 6:2, with a stable level of fertility the two types of measurement applied in the same population will yield the same result, even though they do not refer to the same groups of people. A high figure according to one approach is usually found together with a high figure according to the other: they always *tend* to agree, because they are computed in the same way. It is a *change* in the level of fertility—particularly an abrupt fluctuation—that causes the two types of measurement to diverge. Hence the disagreement of these two approaches emerges most clearly in the analysis of shifting lev-

## TABLE 6:3

## COMPARISON OF FERTILITY INDICES

Based on Births of a Single Year or Short Period

| Country and Date | Crude Birth Rate | General Fertility Rate | Total Fertility Rate | Gross Reproduction Rate | Child-Woman Ratio |
|---|---|---|---|---|---|
| Venezuela, 1950-51 | 43.4 | 183 | 5.66 | 2.78 | 711 |
| Chile, 1951-53[a] | 34.2 | 141 | 4.20 | 2.06 | 517 |
| Japan, 1949-51 | 29.0 | 113 | 3.75 | 1.83 | 525 |
| 1952 | 23.7 | 91.7 | 3.00 | 1.46 | 507 |
| England & Wales, 1950-52 | 13.6 | 61.5 | 2.16 | 1.05 | 335 |

[a] From O. Cabello, "The Demography of Chile," *Population Studies*, Vol. 9, p. 244, March, 1956.

Sources: Vital statistics and census data, each country.

els of fertility (see 6:7).

A change of fertility is measured in the same manner as a change of mortality, by a series of observations at successive dates. Various indices may be used to describe a trend. However, most of them summarize the frequency of births in a single figure. In following this simplified course, studies of trend become committed to tracing changes in the general level of fertility, rather than changes in its pattern of distribution. This course is often unavoidable; but in consequence it is sometimes impossible to reach any definite conclusion on the basis of such evidence.

Though no new techniques are involved, some new problems are encountered in interpreting this evidence:

a. First, of course, the data themselves may be in error. It is not merely the defects of one period's birth statistics that are important. In comparing successive observations, the data of the other period must be equally good. Because of this, it may be worse to have one correct and one biased figure than to have two biased figures, if the inaccuracy is of a similar nature in both cases. Yet the separate observations must be tested separately. After doing this, there are no special criteria for judging a recorded trend (or lack of trend) of fertility, except to ask whether it appears plausible. This leads to a rather subjective decision, but it can benefit from a considerable weight of experience with these facts in a great many countries.[28]

Any "unexpected" pattern of change should be brought under careful scrutiny, to judge whether it is due to defects of the data. While annual birth rates normally fluctuate from year to year, a steady *rise* over a period of several years is unusual. In view of a widespread *downward* trend of fertility in recent decades, a rise of birth rates is often suspect unless preceded by a period of exceptionally low rates. For example, a rise of birth rates may be due to administrative improvements which extend the scope of birth registration (or to a deterioration in the scope of census administration).

What sorts of evidence can make such a trend appear plausible? A series of only two observations is an unsure indication of a trend. With a larger number of observations, independent of each other, any type of evidence is more persuasive.[29] Recent shifts in the composi-

[28]For a summary of these facts, see United Nations, Department of Social Affairs, Population Division, *The Determinants and Consequences of Population Trends*, Chapter 5.

[29]Some yearly fluctuations are offset by the practice of computing vital rates as the average of data of adjacent years. See 2:9.

tion of the population may have favored higher birth rates. Immigration of adults, or an increased number of marriages, may lead to larger annual numbers of births. In postwar Japan, the return of many people from abroad changed the sex ratio of marriageable adults and restored some separated families, and this was followed by a pronounced — but temporary — rise in the level of yearly birth rates. In several countries sudden progress in the control of malaria has removed a particular hazard to health and full-term delivery by pregnant women. Birth rates have risen abruptly, the connection being so close and consistent as to furnish grounds for belief.[30] Even in the absence of specific association of this kind, it appears that extended longevity of husbands and wives may increase the number of children borne by women, and also produce higher yearly birth rates, by protecting the women against the risk of interrupting their childbearing careers through widowhood.[31]

Where possible, the birth rates should be checked against some independent source — for example, a comparable series of child-woman ratios.[32] If census data by age are considered reliable, they may provide an approximate reconstruction of the annual numbers of births in preceding years, with the help of an appropriate life table (see 3:9). Data from sample surveys may corroborate or challenge an observed trend of rates. Even isolated medical reports or descriptions of health conditions may help to decide whether to reject the registered data. Unusual numbers of maternal or infant diseases, for example, lead to an expectation of unusual numbers of births or infant deaths. Internal inconsistencies in the registered data are some-

---

[30] See R. Raja Indra, "Fertility Trends in Ceylon," and M.K.H. Khan and M. Zia-ud-Din, "Effect of Malaria on the Birth Rate in the Punjab Province," United Nations, World Population Conference, 1954, Meeting No. 8 (Papers, Vol. 1, New York, 1955). See also the earlier study by C.A. Gill, "The Influence of Malaria on Natality," *Journal of the Malaria Institute of India* Vol. 3, pp. 201-252 (1940).

[31] A change in the customs of divorce, or shift of sentiment toward remarriage of divorced or widowed women, may achieve the same effect.

[32] However, these are of limited usefulness, since they also may reflect changes of mortality. A fall of infant mortality permits more babies to survive; counted in a later census, these will give higher values to child-woman ratios, giving a false appearance of rising birth rates. This is especially confusing. Just where the birth data are most in doubt, the statistics of infant deaths are also untrustworthy, and the "true" course of infant mortality may also be open to doubt. The child-woman ratio is further limited as an "independent" source, because it presumably depends on some of the same census data used in computing birth rates.

times obvious, and some types of bias can be detected by close study of the regulations for vital registration (particularly changes in these rules).[33]

b. Even if the data are reliable, what conclusions can be drawn from a movement of birth rates? Does it indicate a long-term change in the average size of completed families, or is it merely a fluctuation of yearly rates? In response to exceptional conditions, couples sometimes advance or delay their bearing of children. This may cause sharp movements of yearly rates, with little or no effect on the total size of family that they eventually attain. In other words, a change of annual rates may not be permanent; it may just reflect a shift in the scheduling of births.

This question is more difficult to answer. It concerns the method of observation, not defects in the statistical data. Usually the data are insufficient to compare the evidence of calendar-year rates and reproductive histories. But even without this handicap they would not provide a definite solution, for they do not refer to quite the same periods of time (see 6:7, above).

Consequently, the meaning of observed change of annual birth rates is often a matter of doubt. For example, a sudden increase of annual births since 1945, sometimes called the postwar "baby boom," was partly of a temporary nature (being the early output of very recent marriages), and partly a discernible trend toward larger families in many countries where fertility had formerly been rather "low." In a country of relatively high fertility, there is less opportunity for permanent *increase* of family size; here, when people have sought to control their fertility, it has typically been in the direction of limiting, not expanding it. The exercise of this control has produced the steadiest changes of fertility, and these changes have been predominantly downward.[34]

---

[33] Birth registration is known to lag behind the actual occurrence of births in many countries. In Costa Rica, for example, there was a sudden jump in the number of registered births in 1947, with the inclusion of many that had occurred (without registration) 20 years or more previously. (See R. Jiménez Jiménez, *Exactitud del Registro de Nacimientos y Algunos Análisis Demográficos de Costa Rica* [San José, 1957], p. 12).

[34] It is never safe to assume, however, that birth rates cannot go higher. Yearly rates have risen in many countries of already "high" fertility during the period of the recent "baby boom." Whether or not this is a temporary fluctuation is unclear and may perhaps never be ascertained, for in the future these same people may change their minds about the size of their families.

The evidence normally available is a series of calendar-year birth rates of some kind. Hence the nature of a trend, or even its existence, often is open to question. (For the same reason, the existence of a trend introduces some bias into the single observations of the level of fertility discussed in 6:4.) We can better assess an observed change if there is some information about the distribution of the calendar-year births. Particularly, comparison of age-specific birth rates reveals whether the change has been general or confined to certain age groups of women. Among women 15-24, for example, there may be a simple explanation if it coincides with a shift in marriage patterns. (If these women spent more person-years in marriage, the age-specific birth rates would be higher even though the fertility of married women remained exactly the same.) Thus, age-specific birth rates may suggest where to look for an explanation.

## 6:10 Differences of Fertility within a Population

This topic has assumed increasing importance in recent years. It permits a more detailed analysis of the *level* and observable *changes* of fertility, by raising two questions: (a) what are the separate contributions of various groups in the population to the national average of fertility at some particular time, and (b) which groups have contributed most to a change of birth rates in the total population? The latter question is also pursued for clues for the prediction of future changes.

It appears that fertility varies rather widely among the adults of every population. This is a consistent finding in all studies of the subject. The clearest indication is given by the distribution of women age 45 and over, who have virtually completed their childbearing, according to the number of children ever born. For example, it is obvious that the task of childbearing is spread very unevenly among women in the countries of Table 6:4, in spite of the fact that these countries do not represent the same level of average family size.

The task of analyzing these differences often appears needlessly complicated. In plainest terms, it is first necessary to find whether these unequal contributions can be traced to distinct groups in the population.[35] If fertility varies among these groups, we may ask what factors are associated with the pattern of differences. On the one hand, there are factors of motive and personal preference. On the other hand, if the variation of fertility seems unrelated to groupings suggesting the presence of such factors — if it is distribu-

---

[35]These differences are often referred to as "differential fertility."

ted in a more "random" pattern — then it may be due primarily to involuntary factors.

Both factors are always present in some degree. There is no clear line dividing the two; it is never safe to insist that one is the "correct" explanation because there is no evidence of the other. However, the widespread trend toward *decline* of fertility is attributed to deliberate action by the people themselves, limiting the size of their families.[36] The major observed variations have been traced to this decline, spread among different groups in the population. Hence, factors of personal preference in family size receive the greater emphasis, and will be discussed in the next sections.

To find these patterns, we simply compute fertility indices for some distinct groups in the population. Because childbearing varies by age, comparable age groups must be selected. It must also be decided whether to compare the fertility of men or of women; the following examples are based chiefly on the fertility of women.

Such indices are not easily obtained, for the data of births and of population must be divided into exactly corresponding groups. Typically these are categories of ethnic background, socio-economic status (indicated by "occupation" or a similar classification), place of residence, or perhaps educational level. We generally use any material of this kind that is available, if it appears to be adequate.

## 6:11 Comparison of Ethnic Groups

Consider, for example, the two principal population groups in Malaya, where people of Malay and Chinese extraction were nearly equal in numbers in 1947. There are many cultural differences between the two groups, and so it is of considerable interest to know whether or not they have developed similar patterns of fertility. Gross reproduction rates, estimated after a painstaking examination of the census and registration data, have indicated a higher level of fertility among Chinese (2.67 for all Malaysians, 3.25-3.37 for Chinese), both figures today being considered rather "high."

---

[36] There are innumerable ways of interfering with births that would otherwise occur. The subject is too large to be discussed here; we must confine ourselves, without digression, to the patterns of fertility. It is enough to add merely that: (a) one can interfere with the processes of reproduction at several stages—conception, gestation, or after birth (when final adjustments in the size of the living family can still be made); and (b) such action does not always have this purpose directly in mind—for example, infant feeding practices, when they prolong lactation, may hinder subsequent conception. Occasionally, all these devices are referred to as "birth control."

The estimating procedures illustrate some of the problems that are often encountered. First, the boundaries which separate ethnic groups are difficult to define in precise terms. But it is necessary to be precise, for there are two systems of classification, one for registered births and one for census data, and to some extent they are independent. If births and census population are not classified by exactly the same criteria, of course, they will fail to match. The administrative reports of Malaya are reassuring on this point, for the Malaysians and Chinese form groups that are easily distinguished.[37]

## TABLE 6:4

## DISTRIBUTION OF WOMEN AGED 50-59, BY NUMBER OF CHILDREN EVER BORN

Selected Countries (Census Data)

| Number of Children | Per Cents[a] | | | | |
| | Brazil 1940 | Mexico 1950 (ages 45-49) | Ceylon 1946 | Japan[b] 1950 | United States[b] 1950 |
|---|---|---|---|---|---|
| 0 | 15.8 | 21.4 | 18.5 | 10.5[b] | 18.1[b] |
| 1 | 5.5 | 6.5 | 6.0 | 8.5 | 17.5 |
| 2 | 5.8 | 6.9 | 7.4 | 7.9 | 20.3 |
| 3 | 6.0 | 7.1 | 8.0 | 9.1 | 14.4 |
| 4 | 6.5 | 7.1 | 8.8 | 10.2 | 9.9 |
| 5 | 6.8 | 7.5 | 9.4 | 11.2 | 6.2 |
| 6 | 7.1 | 7.5 | 9.3 | 11.1 | 4.3 |
| 7 | 6.7 | 6.6 | 9.1 | 10.1 | 2.9 |
| 8 | 7.4 | 6.5 | 7.9 | 8.8 | 3.5 |
| 9 | 6.6 | 5.8 | 6.4 | 5.9 | |
| 10 and over | 25.8 | 17.2 | 9.1 | 6.9 | 3.0 |
| Births per woman | 6.2 | 5.1 | 4.7 | 4.8 | 2.8 |

[a] The figures represent just those women who reported this information. Some of the columns do not add to exactly 100, due to rounding of numbers.

[b] These data refer only to women who have been married. Hence some childless women are not included.

---

[37] "Malaysians" include "Malays" and "Other Malaysians" as classified in the census. These two groups cannot be clearly distinguished, and so there is no other course but to combine them.

Besides custom and religion, they are set apart by their characteristic livelihood, community organization and a reluctance to intermarry, and to a large extent also live apart.

Second, we must ask whether the data give a comparable measurement of fertility in both groups. If not, obviously a comparison cannot be worth very much. In these data, different kinds of bias were found among Malaysians and among Chinese, with the result that different estimating procedures had to be devised for the two groups.[38]

Lacking the needed birth statistics, census data can sometimes be utilized. "Size of family" is a valid basis of comparison, though it refers to past rather than current performance (see 6:6). It may be possible only to use the simpler child-woman ratios (if the classification by ethnic group is comparable for adults and for children).

## 6:12  Fertility by Socio-Economic Groups

Such groupings present a more difficult problem of classification, which usually rests on a set of occupational classes of fathers or mothers. These groups vary widely in age composition, and so age-specific rates of some kind are essential.

Yearly rates may be computed in the usual manner; the difficulties all stem from the nature of the classification. Not only are the categories themselves troublesome; they do not pertain directly to births, which must be classified by the occupation of someone else — a parent — and by a different set of records. Hence there are excep-

---

[38]This of course introduces the possibility that the estimating procedures may bias the comparison. For Malaysians, the gross reproduction rate was computed by estimating age-specific birth rates from the census data of children ever born, by age of mother; these rates were augmented on the assumption that all children who died in infancy (also estimated) were unreported as births; the revised age-specific rates were taken to represent the calendar-year performance of Malaysian women.

For Chinese, two alternative gross reproduction rates were estimated. Age-specific birth rates were computed for all women in Singapore (where Chinese preponderated), and used in an "indirect" procedure like that of 6:4. Multiplied by the census population of women by age, these rates gave a number of "expected" births. The "expected" births were adjusted to agree, *first*, with the number of Chinese births actually registered; and, *second*, with a revised figure of Chinese births (revised on the assumptions that male babies were completely registered, that some female babies were unregistered, and that the true ratio between male and female births was 1.06 to 1. These assumptions lead to an estimate of under-registered births, and thence to revision of the registered number of births). From these estimates came the two reproduction rates cited in the text, 3.25 and 3.37. See T.E. Smith, *Population Growth in Malaya* (London, 1952), pp. 37-47 and 72-78.

tional opportunities for discrepancy between the universes of registered births and census population. It is always appropriate to keep an attitude of skepticism toward these birth rates, for there is no check on their accuracy.

Reproductive histories avoid the errors of matching between two sets of figures. However, they present some new difficulties, and some new aspects of problems already treated in 6:2. First, reproductive histories usually pertain to women, but most people who report some occupation are men. And men, who are more frequently the heads of households, constitute a better basis for classifying families according to their social or economic circumstances. In practice, we classify women by the occupations of husbands (or household heads), if these data exist, or measure the family size of men, if *this* information is provided.

Second, there is a problem of selecting an appropriate age group. In order to deal with "completed" families, parents under 50 years of age must be excluded; the age limits perhaps should be higher for men. However, at advanced ages many people have changed their livelihood, and no longer follow the same occupations as they did while most of their children were being born.[39] Obviously some compromise is necessary. Table 6:5, for example, presents the average family size of men by the principal types of industries[40] in which they worked in Brazil, according to the census of 1940. The material has been prepared for the age groups 40-49, 50-59, and 60-69.

It should be remembered that these groups represent slightly different stages of family size, and different stages in the occupational careers of the men. They also represent *different cohorts of men*, and hence the three columns could not possibly present exactly the same picture of fertility variation by industry group. But the pattern is remarkably similar in all three age groups. In the second portion ("B") of Table 6:5, each figure is expressed as a percentage of the figure for the total age group of men, for ease of comparison. By a wide margin, the group of men employed in agriculture had the largest families. Next came those working in extractive and manufacturing industries, transportation, and public administration. The smallest average family size was reported in the liberal professions.[41]

---

[39] This problem is present regardless of the manner of measuring fertility, because there is constant movement of people between occupations.

[40] For a discussion of this classification by economic activity, see Chapter 9.

[41] These data should not be interpreted without taking note of the dis-

It is difficult to draw conclusions from such data. Do they present recent patterns of fertility differences, or one established long ago when most of the births occurred? Have some occupational groups reported their births more completely in replying to the census question? Would the measurement of differences be improved by including data for younger men, or would this merely be a further complication?[42] There seem to be no general answers to these questions. In this instance, the statistics have already been subjected to very thorough study,[43] and there is reason to believe that the evidence of Table 6:5 is correct. Elsewhere, these questions must be faced with each set of similar material, and such confidence may not be justified.

### 6:13 Local Variations of Fertility

Birth rates by region or district are of interest by themselves, as an item of description of local conditions. They also show indirectly the influence of other factors, in the absence of more direct evidence (like the differences of mortality, discussed in 5:15).

The peculiar characteristics of a district may be associated with its fertility — a tendency to early or late marriage, the influence of an ethnic strain in the local population, a distinctive style of agricultural livelihood, the presence of recent migrants, a traditional or a changing view of family life, or perhaps the existence of alternative activities among women which might compete with childbearing.

Particularly, it is interesting to compare the fertility of city or town dwellers and rural residents, for they represent certain extremes

---

tribution of men by industry in Brazil. First, agriculture predominates; this is the reason why family size is so large in the entire population, for other industry groups have little numerical weight. Second, the distribution by industry is different for men aged 40-49, 50-59 and 60-69, chiefly by virtue of the gradual retirement from work with advancing age. The category, "without occupation" (which also includes cases of unknown occupation), contained 3 per cent of men 40-49, and over 11 per cent of men aged 60-69. Such information is essential in drawing conclusions from a table of this sort.          For a detailed discussion of this pattern, see G. Mortara, "Male Fertility in Relation to Economic Activity and Professional Status," Part 5, Chapter 9 in F. Lorimer et al., *Culture and Human Fertility* (Paris, 1954); *Pesquisas sôbre a Natalidade no Brasil*, Estudos de Estatística Teórica e Aplicada: Estatística Demográfica, Volume 10 (Rio de Janeiro, 1950).

[42] Data for younger men would include many uncompleted families, and reflect the differing age composition of occupational groups. If possible, it is advisable to deal with the younger and older men in separate groups.

[43] See G. Mortara, *op. cit.* (1950).

of living conditions, social environment and economic activity within a country. An urban environment often is favorable to lower birth rates, and may reveal the earliest signs of a trend toward smaller families.

But it is sometimes meaningless to base a comparison of behavior on the categories of "rural" and "urban" as they are defined in a census, for they are inherently vague, and marked by large inconsistencies from country to country. Where possible, it is preferable to separate cities and towns into size groups, for presumably the larger cities are the more "urban" in characteristics.

Of course, birth rates also reflect local peculiarities of administration. Many cities have persistent under-registration of births. For this reason, the comparisons are often made on the basis of child-woman ratios, which depend on census data alone. But most

## TABLE 6:5

## SIZE OF FAMILY OF MEN IN BRAZIL, BY TYPE OF EMPLOYMENT

(Men Aged 40-49, 50-59 and 60-69 in 1940, Classified by Industry)

| Age of Men / Industry | A. Average Number of Children Ever Born | | | B. Index Numbers (family size for all men = 100) | | |
|---|---|---|---|---|---|---|
| | 40-49 | 50-59 | 60-69 | 40-49 | 50-59 | 60-69 |
| Agriculture, etc. | 6.23 | 7.49 | 7.89 | 114 | 112 | 110 |
| Extractive Industries | 4.44 | 5.54 | 5.94 | 81 | 83 | 82 |
| Manufacturing | 4.55 | 5.65 | 6.35 | 83 | 85 | 88 |
| Transport & Communications | 4.35 | 5.28 | 5.80 | 80 | 79 | 81 |
| Public Administration | 4.26 | 5.45 | 6.30 | 78 | 82 | 87 |
| Commerce (merchants) | 4.17 | 5.21 | 5.96 | 76 | 78 | 83 |
| Real Estate and Finance | 3.06 | 4.24 | 5.40 | 56 | 63 | 75 |
| Services | 4.01 | 5.00 | 5.61 | 73 | 75 | 78 |
| Defense, Police | 3.62 | 4.71 | 5.43 | 66 | 71 | 75 |
| Liberal Professions | 2.95 | 3.81 | 4.16 | 54 | 57 | 58 |
| Domestic Service | 3.66 | 4.43 | 5.01 | 67 | 66 | 70 |
| All Men with Occupation | 5.54 | 6.79 | 7.39 | 101 | 102 | 103 |
| Men without Occupation | 3.19 | 4.58 | 5.68 | 58 | 69 | 79 |
| Total | 5.47 | 6.68 | 7.20 | 100 | 100 | 100 |

Source: Brazil. *Recenseamento Geral do Brasil*. Serie National. *Censo Demográfico, População e Hibitação*, Volume II, Table 46.

census data do not really meet the requirements. Due to inconsistencies in counting and in reporting of ages, and due to local variations of infant mortality, child-woman ratios usually cannot be relied upon for more than a tentative suggestion of fertility differences.

If conventional birth rates are used to measure local variations of fertility, there is the familiar problem of matching, between the universe of registered births and the universe of people enumerated in a census (see 3:10). A migration across local boundaries by the people represented in the denominator of the rate is scarcely ever exactly matched in the numerator. This obviously affects the value of the rates.[44] The effect is greater if there has been migration directly related to fertility, like the travel of expectant mothers to a neighboring hospital or to a former residence for delivery of their births. The child-woman ratio, on the other hand, in many instances may provide better matching (if young and dependent children migrate together with their mothers).

All these effects on fertility measurements are likely to be larger, the smaller the size of districts.

## 6:14  Explaining Differences of Fertility

So far we have considered only whether observed variations of fertility are affected by bias. At some point it becomes necessary to go beyond these matters, and seek to explain why the observed patterns exist. This implies a change to a new basis of discussion. While few new technical problems are introduced, there are many questions requiring considerable skill and judgment.

The principal question is, what are the motives that have led to different patterns in the building of families? Perhaps there is no longer a need to argue that personal motives are involved, though until recently it has been regarded as a controversial point. It is now

---

[44] Such movement has a distorting effect on local birth rates because the parents are counted in one locality, and the births are recorded in another. There are some mitigating factors. Those births which occur at the same time as the census are unaffected, but they are a small proportion of all births during the year. To some extent, there may be reason to assume that the effect of migration in one direction is offset by the effect of migration in the other. A "de jure" census (enumerating people at the place of usual, rather than actual, residence) may avoid some of this distortion. In some instances it may be possible to re-allocate births according to the parents' usual place of residence, if these special data have been provided (see 3:10 and 5:15). None of these factors offer complete freedom from bias of birth rates; some of them contain new sources of error. It is clear that this effect cannot be eliminated except by the use of reproductive histories.

accepted that people shift to a pattern of smaller families principally because they prefer smaller families, and proceed to exercise their choice by interfering with conception and childbirth.

However, as a subject of study, this situation is complicated by two facts: it is exceedingly hard to determine what are the "real" motives governing actual family size, and a large amount of variation in fertility still remains unexplained by these factors of personal preference. It might seem that the simplest course is to ask people directly why they have large or small families; and, indeed, this is sometimes done. But this course has some severe limitations. The information cannot be gathered from ordinary sources of data, and requires a special survey to ask people about their motives or intentions.

The responses to these questions do not agree very closely with actual behavior. Such opinions are subject to constant change, and may not be arrived at by conscious deliberation. Moreover, at the time of a survey, many people have not completed their childbearing, and may not have reached a final decision about ultimate size of family. It is therefore unrealistic to suppose that childbearing is fixed in advance by definite plans. To a large extent, the idea of "family planning" is an element introduced into the situation by the investigator.

Some of these difficulties can be met with specially designed questionnaires and other precautionary procedures. But often another (and less direct) type of procedure is used. When groups of different levels of fertility are observed in a population, we ask how they differ in other respects. This is found from the nature of their composition. For example, in Table 6:5, when men of Brazil are arranged by broad categories of livelihood, it is clear that the groups of highest fertility were those engaged in farming and related activities, rather than other types of work. Those groups in contact with the modern commercial and industrial life of the cities had families of smaller average size.[45]

Sometimes no variation is evident, and among the groups observed the level of fertility is nearly the same. This does not imply that there are no differences, nor that everyone desires families of the same size. It just means that the variation is distributed according to some other pattern, one that is not represented by the categories selected.

[45]Further study of data from the 1940 census of Brazil has shown that, for every livelihood category outside agriculture, families were smaller in Rio de Janeiro ("Distrito Federal") than in the country as a whole. See Instituto Brasileiro de Geografía e Estatística, *Estudos sôbre a Natalidade em Algunas Grandes Cidades do Brasil* (Rio de Janeiro, 1952).

What do these patterns signify, when they are observed? Smaller families are typically found among portions of a population that have been exposed to new influences. This is not surprising, since the shift toward a small size of family is of recent origin in most of the world. In countries of relatively "high" fertility, a widespread preference for smaller families is related to factors of change. (Where the prevailing level of fertility is relatively low, the explanation is more complicated, for smaller families are no longer an innovation.)

From this evidence of change, we can better appreciate the character of social trends, and discover where they have occurred and where they have lagged. In Brazil, it is evident that some of the differences among the groups of Table 6:5 were not large. We may conclude that the practice of family limitation, associated with the factors which these categories represent, was not yet very common.

# CHAPTER 7

# GROWTH OF POPULATION

Change in the size of a population, whether increase or decrease, is called "growth." Positive or negative, growth of population comes from only three sources — births, deaths and migration (see 1:1). It is not a separate aspect of a people's existence, but the outcome of these distinct factors.

Population growth attracts wide notice, because people often feel that it is related to their national "survival." There are several ambitious theories which treat it in relation to social and economic development. From the standpoint of measurement, however, we are concerned with a more modest set of objectives. This chapter outlines a few general characteristics of population growth, some conventional types of measurement, some of the basic relations with the structure of a population, and finally a very common practical application of such study, the projection of population trends into the future.

## 7:1 Some Characteristics of Population Growth

A few observations about the nature of population growth are helpful. First, it is the particular state of balance among the factors of birth, death and migration. It is not determined by any one of them alone. In a given instance, a great many different combinations of these factors are possible, and the balance is rather changeable from time to time. The course of human numbers has apparently fluctuated between increase and decrease throughout most of history.

In modern times, the almost universal trend has been an *increase*. This has become so widespread as to be accepted as a normal condition; stability or decline in numbers is commonly regarded as abnormal. In fact, this modern phase is of relatively recent origin. The growth since 1600, perhaps five-fold, has been a sudden spurt, quite unprecedented in any comparable earlier period. The general nature of growth is therefore not in accord with the popular conception about it.

Such an era of growth is not only unprecedented; it is inherently a transitory thing. Obviously nothing in the world can increase forever, for the amount of inhabitable space is limited. More important, growth tends to follow the pattern of compound interest, because increased people contribute to further increase during their lifetimes. A constant rate of growth would lead to ever greater increments of people. Even a small rate implies a tremendous yearly increase if it is continued for a long period. One of the chief advantages of a mathematical curve of population growth is a very clear demonstration of this point. This limitation applies to the current era of increase of the last three centuries, as well as to any period of growth.

The source of this recent rise of world population has been a large and sustained excess of births over deaths. It was made possible by an advancing control over the risks of death, during a period of very gradual declines of birth rates. Now it has also become possible to achieve natural increase by the route of higher birth rates. Of course, natural increase is the ultimate source of growth in the world as a whole, and perhaps also in certain regions of substantial size. But in a particular country, *migration* is likely to be of considerable weight, and is sometimes the dominant factor; it is responsible for some of the most rapid cases of growth in the past, and improved forms of communication now make it capable of still greater effect.

### 7:2 The Cyclical Pattern of Growth

Since growth is transitory, there must be a starting point, a period of some continuance, and an end. That is to say, the pattern is fundamentally a cycle. This is an essential point to remember in examining any given case of growth: we should recognize that it did not always exist, and that it will not last forever. In a very much idealized form, the cyclical nature of growth is illustrated in Chart 7:1. This is a curve based on a particular mathematical formula.[1] Actual cases are rarely regular or symmetrical like this one; nor is their duration so predictable (the current cycle of growth in world population, for example, does not yet show any sign of slackening). This cyclical aspect often is not evident during a short period of observation, and so it deserves special emphasis.

### 7:3 Migration and Population Growth

Migration is the most potent source of change in the size of a

---

[1] This particular curve is known as the "logistic" pattern of growth. See also the note in 7:13.

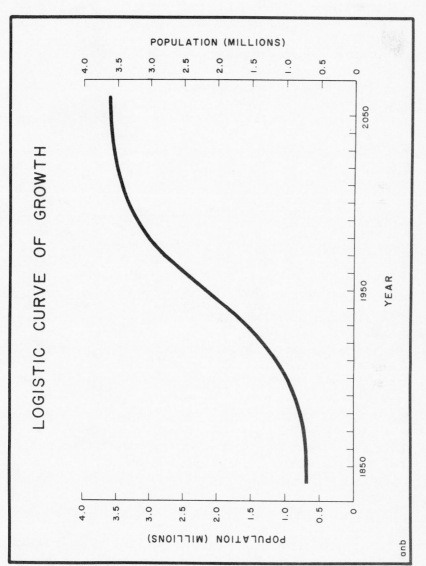

LOGISTIC CURVE OF GROWTH

POPULATION (MILLIONS)

YEAR

POPULATION (MILLIONS)

anb

Chart 7:1 Logistic curve of growth (fitted to partial data of Puerto Rico. See J. Janer, "Population Growth in Puerto Rico and Its Relation to Time Changes in Vital Statistics," *Human Biology*, Vol. 17, December 1945).

population. This is because the flow of migrants is subject to the widest fluctuations. It responds quickly to influences (like government policy, or opportunities for employment) that are themselves very changeable. As explained in Chapter 8, migrants usually differ in their composition from the general population, both at the place of origin and place of destination. The movement of people has been involved in some of the largest international differences in rates of growth, and it is the principal source of differences in growth within countries. It is always important to ask whether migration makes a contribution to observed instances of growth, apart from the contribution of natural increase. Unfortunately, as we shall see, there is often no satisfactory way of analyzing its effect.

## 7:4  Types of Measurement

The growth of population is measured in three ways: (a) as an observed change in the total number of people, (b) as a current process of replacement, or (c) as a change in the size of some sections of the population, such as age groups or livelihood classes.

The first of these, which is admirably simple and straightforward, is a comparison of two successive figures for the total population. These must be figures that are judged to be of comparable standard (of scope, completeness and geographical area). Usually they are the totals of census enumerations. The difference between the two figures $(P_2 - P_1)$ represents the amount of growth; the ratio

between the two figures $\left(\dfrac{P_2}{P_1}\right)$ measures their relative size. If preferred, this ratio may be computed as a percentage number, $\left(\dfrac{P_2}{P_1} - 1\right)$

$\times 100$. For example, censuses of 1931 and 1946 indicate that the population of Cyprus increased from 347,959 to 450,114, the ratio being 1.29358, or a growth of 29%, in about 15 years.[2]

---

[2] Comparable total figures are not assured by the use of census data. Cyprus is a small island, and one would expect rather few changes of census administration. But elsewhere it is very common to find that the scope of the figures varies from one census to the next. This is especially true if the censuses are separated by a long period, or if the government administration or the boundaries have been revised. The data can sometimes be reconciled by re-allocating in one set of figures the portions of the population that have been treated differently, or by subtracting them and measuring the growth of the remainder. But many discrepancies are not of an obvious kind, and escape attention (see 3:6). Almost any amount of trouble in finding

A ratio of growth gives a comparable measurement for different regions or local divisions within a country (if the enumerations were equally good in all sections).  It is also adequate for comparing the growth of different populations or different periods, provided that the time interval between censuses is the same.  When these intervals are not the same, the ratios must be put on a comparable basis.  This is done by converting them into annual *rates* of growth, somehow distributing the observed growth through the intercensal period.  We make the assumption that the rate of growth has remained constant, and ask what rate would have produced this change in the elapsed number of years.  In Cyprus, if the ratio of 1.29358 resulted from a constant rate of growth *(r)* each year, it would be equal to $(1 + r)^n$, where *n* is the number of years between the two censuses (see 2:8). (The 1931 census was dated April 28, and the 1946 census November 10, leaving an interval of 186 months between them, or 15½ years, to the nearest whole month.)  The value of *r* is found by reference to a table of logarithms:  $\log 1.29358 = n \log (1 + r)$, or $\dfrac{.11180}{n} = \log$ $(1 + r)$.  This means that $\log (1 + r) = .00721$, and $(1 + r) = 1.0167$, and $r = .0167$ or 16.7 per thousand.[3]  For comparison, the growth in the 10 years between the censuses of 1921 and 1931 (both taken in April) was $\dfrac{347,959}{310,715} = 1.11986$, which implies an annual rate of .0114 by this same formula.

There are sometimes reasons which prevent the use of this first approach.  It may be too crude, for it combines the effects of changes from all sources.  The data are not always adequate:  they may be insufficient (if the two census figures are not comparable, or if only one is available), or they may be too far apart (the longer the

---

these errors is worth while, for a measurement of growth is meaningless if it reflects only changes of administration.

[3]See 2:8.  This formula represents the effect of a yearly rate of growth calculated once a year.  If the rate of growth is assumed to operate continuously, it can be expressed as $\dfrac{P_2}{P_1} = e^{rn}$.  The calculation is quicker and more convenient by this second formula, requiring a different set of logarithm tables (see 1:7).  It is also a somewhat more realistic way of representing the effect of *r*.

intervening period, the less realistic the assumption of a constant rate of growth).[4]

The second approach is concerned with the process of replacement in the population, observed from the registration of vital events. Natural increase, the change due to the net effect of fertility and mortality, is measured directly from these records. It is the number of births minus the number of deaths, year by year. The *rate* of natural increase is this amount divided by the mid-year population. It is also equal to the crude birth rate minus the crude death rate, and this is usually a more convenient method of computation (see 2:9).

The rate of natural increase should not be confused with a rate of growth as described above. It is restricted to births and deaths, and cannot include the net gain or loss of migrants.[5] It very simply balances the effects of births and deaths each year, summarizing their current contribution to population growth. But the amount of natural increase fluctuates from year to year. It is subject to the influence of the population's composition on the crude birth rate and the crude death rate. If they are both biased in the same direction, there may be little or no effect on the rate of increase; if one is biased upward and the other downward, the effect is intensified. Hence the nature of such influence is very uncertain, and natural increase may not be a very reliable indication of growth, especially when based on the events of a single year.

In the absence of migration, the rate of natural increase and the rate of growth both represent the same thing.[6] A population without any migration is known as a "closed population," and this type of case has greatly aided the study of growth, especially in relation to structure (see 7:8). In modern times, however, no population has

---

[4]These standards of accuracy are less severe, however, than those of other measurements, and are more easily met. Only total figures are used, and not the detailed census data. But this does not mean that inaccurate total figures can furnish an accurate measurement of growth.

[5]The rate of natural increase may include some *indirect* effects of migration. If migrants have higher or lower fertility and mortality than the remainder of the population, their movement will have some influence on the annual birth and death rates.

[6]Although the two rates then represent the same thing, they are not identical. They are calculated differently, and one is based on the mid-year population while the other is based on the population at the beginning of the year. However, the discrepancy is too small to be a matter of much practical concern.

been completely closed against migration. There has been so much movement of people that the two measurements usually diverge – the actual change in a country cannot all be attributed to natural increase, and natural increase gives an incomplete account of total growth.

Besides growth of an entire population, particular categories also change in size. When these portions of the population grow unevenly, as they generally do, they alter its structure. They can be studied without any special procedures. A ratio of the numbers of people found in some category at two different dates indicates the "growth" of this section – for example, the trend of the population of "working ages" (15-64), or women of reproductive ages (15-49). (It may be sufficient, however, to compare the percentage-distributions of the population at the two dates.)

Some of those changes are directly related to the actual processes of growth, like shifts of the age and sex structure. Others, which involve some movement of people at will between categories, are only indirectly related to growth, according to the particular circumstances that may exist. A changing distribution of people by marital status or occupation, for example, or unequal development of city and rural populations, may be related to growth, but not very predictably. These two kinds of change should be distinguished, for they cannot have the same significance in relation to population growth.

### 7:5 Some Observed Rates of Growth

We have become accustomed to a good deal of variation in rates of growth. Table 7:1 shows some of this variation, with rates computed for different countries and periods. Most of these rates are based on census data.

Most values in Table 7:1 range between 0.66 per cent (France) and 3 per cent (Venezuela), illustrating a few combinations of natural increase and net migration that are found on a national scale. More extreme cases can also be found, owing chiefly to unusual patterns of migration (an average rate of 12 per cent for Israel between 1948-1955, or –0.3 per cent for Ireland between 1951 and 1955). Most of these rates refer to rather short periods, too short to reveal their full implications. A constant rate of only .005, or half of one per cent, would have been sufficient to produce the entire increase of the world's population between 1650 and 1950, from an estimated 550 million to about 2.5 billion people. Rates six times as large as this, now within reach of many countries, are obviously a very recent development.

Most countries depend on natural increase for growth. Here, too, there is considerable variation. A few specimens of these rates can be seen in Table 7:2. It is evident that birth rates and death rates are not linked so that they must rise or fall together, and so the rate of natural increase is not necessarily bound to either the one or the other. A low rate of increase may be found where the birth rate is high, and a fairly high rate of increase may occur when both birth and death rates are low. (Of course, the rate of increase is more likely to be large when the birth rate is high and the death rate is low.) With the spread of lower mortality, still higher rates of increase are possible. However, few countries have actually experienced them, because of the spreading decline of fertility.

### TABLE 7:1

### ANNUAL RATES OF GROWTH IN SELECTED COUNTRIES

(Computed from census data)

| Country | Period between Censuses (to nearest month) | Ratio of Census Figures[a] | Annual Rate of Growth (Per Cent)[b] |
|---------|--------------------------------------------|----------------------------|-------------------------------------|
| Venezuela | 1941-1950 ( 9.08 years) | 1.30747 | 2.95 |
| Ceylon | 1946-1953 ( 7.0 years) | 1.21650 | 2.80 |
| Canada | 1941-1951 (10.0 years) | 1.18606 | 1.71 |
| Brazil | 1940-1950 ( 9.83 years) | 1.26180 | 2.37 |
| Philippines | 1939-1948 ( 9.75 years) | 1.20213 | 1.89 |
| Switzerland | 1941-1950 ( 9.0 years) | 1.10368 | 1.10 |
| United States | 1940-1950 (10.0 years) | 1.14453 | 1.35 |
| France | 1946-1954 ( 8.17 years) | 1.05503 | 0.66 |
| Israel[c] | 1948-1955 ( 6.67 years) | 2.16693 | 11.59 |
| Ireland | 1951-1956 ( 5.0 years) | 0.97784 | -0.45 |

[a] The ratio is $P_2/P_1$, where $P_1$ is the population at the first census, and $P_2$ the population at the second census.

[b] The rate $r = \dfrac{\log_e(P_2/P_1)}{n} \times 100$, where $n$ is the number of years between censuses.

[c] Jewish population only. Latter figure is an estimate.

These measurements are crude, in the sense that the results are always dependent on the structure of a population. There is a further set of devices, based on certain hypothetical assumptions, designed to avoid this problem. They are described in the next two sections.

## 7:6 Hypothetical Models of Population Growth

Even when the influence of migration can be removed, the levels of fertility and mortality are rather changeable. They seldom become stabilized long enough to reveal just how they affect the process of replacement. And so a hypothetical example has been devised — called the "stable population" — which can be constructed from a

## TABLE 7:2

## VITAL RATES IN SELECTED COUNTRIES[a]

| Country and Dates | | Birth Rate | Death Rate | Rate of Natural Increase |
|---|---|---|---|---|
| Venezuela[b] | 1950-1954 | 44.7 | 10.6 | 34.1 |
| Taiwan[c] | 1906-1910 | 41.7 | 33.4 | 8.3 |
| | 1935-1939 | 45.7 | 20.7 | 25.0 |
| Japan[d] | 1920-1924 | 34.0 | 19.8 | 14.2 |
| | 1950-1954 | 23.8 | 9.4 | 14.4 |
| Canada | 1920-1924 | 28.2 | 12.3 | 15.9 |
| | 1950-1954 | 27.9 | 8.7 | 19.2 |
| England & Wales | 1920-1924 | 20.5 | 14.6 | 5.9 |
| | 1950-1954 | 21.4 | 12.6 | 8.8 |
| France | 1925-1929 | 18.5 | 17.3 | 1.2 |
| | 1950-1954 | 19.4 | 12.7 | 6.7 |

[a] Rates per 1,000 mid-year population. In most cases, estimates of mid-year population are taken from United Nations, *Demographic Yearbook*. Rates were computed by adding the data for population and births of the years indicated, and dividing. They represent the area at the dates indicated.

[b] Excluding population in certain areas not registered or enumerated.

[c] Taiwanese only.

[d] Japanese nationals only.

set of assumed conditions of fertility and mortality (see 5:5). By
fixing these conditions in advance, we can deduce some of their implications without the presence of disturbing factors.

Three such examples are commonly encountered:

(a) Net Reproduction Rate. This consists of a hypothetical
cohort of women, their deaths and all their female births during the
childbearing period. The net reproduction rate indicates the number
of daughters ever born to the cohort, according to a fixed schedule
of birth rates and death rates; in other words, the extent to which the
cohort of women eventually replaces itself under these assumed conditions. It is similar to the *gross* reproduction rate (see 6:5), which
represents fertility only, being the number of daughters expected if
no women in the cohort ever died (see 2:18 and Table 7:3, below).
The *net* reproduction rate uses the same age-specific birth rates;
however, it is based on the survivors of a cohort rather than on a cohort without mortality. (The cohort is taken directly from a life table.
The number of person-years at each age is therefore shown by the $L_x$
or $_nL_x$ column for females. The number of person-years *per person*
in the original cohort is $\dfrac{_nL_x}{l_0}$, as in Table 7:3.)[7] The calculation is

illustrated as follows:

Both rates refer to "synthetic" cohorts of women — cohorts
formed by piecing together the events of one short base period as if
they continued for 50 years.[8] The women of Chile did not actually

---

[7]To be more exact, the net reproduction rate is defined as $\underset{15}{\overset{49}{S}} b_x \left( \dfrac{L_x}{l_0} \right)$,

where $b_x$ represents the rate of female births per person-year at each age *(x)*,

and $\dfrac{L_x}{l_0}$ is the number of person-years lived at each age $(L_x)$, per woman born

into the original cohort $(l_0)$. This expression means "the sum of the daughters per woman in the cohort, beginning at age 15, up to the end of age 49."

The term "rate" is sometimes confusing here. Though the net reproduction rate is derived from the data of a base period, it is not the same as
a vital-statistics rate of births or deaths "per year." It covers the whole
reproductive period of the hypothetical cohort, and might be regarded as a
rate "per cohort" or "per generation" of these women.

[8]This is the same principle used in constructing a life table, as explained in 4:11. A net reproduction rate may also be computed for males
(using the same procedures), but not for both sexes together.

reproduce themselves at the rate of 1.375 per woman, or 1,375 per 1,000. Both fertility and mortality have been changing, and no actual group of women could have experienced this same set of rates at successive stages of life. The net reproduction rate rests on assumptions that do not represent any actual population. The result is significant in relation to the stable population. But it does not indicate the current level of reproduction in Chile in 1940, nor is it a measurement of fertility in Chile. The net reproduction rate may be very misleading if used for such a purpose; for this reason, it has fallen from favor as a type of measurement.

(b) Stable Population. By extension, the notion of a hypothetical cohort, with its own pre-determined schedule of birth and

## TABLE 7:3

## CALCULATION OF GROSS AND NET REPRODUCTION RATES FOR CHILE, 1939-1941

| (1) | (2) | (3) | (4) | (5) | (6) | (7) |
|---|---|---|---|---|---|---|
| | | | Gross Reproduction Rate | | Net Reproduction Rate | |
| Ages | Birth rates | Birth rates (daughters only) $(2) \times .49166^{a}$ | Person-years per woman in hypothetical cohort (with no mortality) | Expected female births per woman $(3) \times (4)$ | Person-years per woman in hypothetical cohort (mortality according to life table)[b] | Expected female births per woman $(3) \times (6)$ |
| 15-19 | .06498 | .03195 | 5 | .15975 | 3.46678 | .11076 |
| 20-24 | .17329 | .08520 | 5 | .42600 | 3.33145 | .28384 |
| 25-29 | .20728 | .10191 | 5 | .50955 | 3.18138 | .32421 |
| 30-34 | .19949 | .09808 | 5 | .49040 | 3.03389 | .29756 |
| 35-39 | .15315 | .07530 | 5 | .37650 | 2.88604 | .21732 |
| 40-44 | .07835 | .03852 | 5 | .19260 | 2.73298 | .10527 |
| 45-49 | .02872 | .01413 | 5 | .07065 | 2.57311 | .03636 |
| | | | Net Reproduction Rate = 2.23545 | | Net Reproduction Rate = 1.37532 | |

[a] .49166 is the proportion of all births that were female. Births have been adjusted for under-registration.

[b] These figures are ratios of $\dfrac{{}_5L_x}{l_0}$ , from the life table for Chile, 1940. See Table 4:1-a.

death rates, leads to a more significant type of model. An unbroken· series of these cohorts, one each year, would form a hypothetical population, determined by the operation of these same rates of fertility and mortality at each age. It is similar to the stationary, or life-table, population (discussed in 5:5). But in the stationary population, every cohort begins with the same number of "births" (100,000, or $l_0$ in the life table). In the stable population, new cohorts need not be of a fixed size, for they are determined by the birth rates together with the numbers of people in reproductive ages. Therefore, though the assumptions remain fixed, the size of the population may change.[9] The stable population has its own age structure, which is dependent on the combined effect of the schedules of birth rates and death rates, and on nothing else. Thus it reveals exactly what growth and age structure are implied by these specified conditions. Like the net reproduction rate, the stable population does not refer to any actual population. However, being a model, it shows very clearly the implications of any combination of these conditions that we wish to specify. Many questions about the general relations of vital rates, unanswerable by means of actual data, are clarified by incorporating these conditions in a stable population. The construction of this model is explained in detail in 7:7.

(c) Replacement Index. The replacement index is an approximation of the net reproduction rate, based on less information. The net reproduction rate indicates the number of daughters produced per woman, according to the specified conditions of fertility and mortality. These are also the conditions which determine the age composition in the stable or the stationary population. The relation between vital rates and age structure is valid in either direction. The replacement index starts from the age structure (when this and an appropriate life table are available, but age-specific birth rates are lacking). A child-woman ratio (see 2:6) is first computed for the actual population. The corresponding child-woman ratio is computed for the stationary population. The replacement index is a comparison of the first ratio $(R_a)$ with the second $(R_s)$, by dividing them in this

way: $\dfrac{R_a}{R_s}$ .[10] For example, in Chile, the child-woman ratio in 1940

[9] When the size of new cohorts does remain constant, the stable population neither increases nor decreases. Its size and composition remain the same, and it is also a stationary population. See 5:5.

[10] The stationary child-woman ratio $(R_s)$ is calculated from the $L_x$

was .4970 (after an adjustment of census data for incomplete enumeration).  For the life table of 1939-1941, it was .3677 (after making an adjustment for the sex ratio of births).[11]  The replacement index is

$$\frac{.4970}{.3677},$$

or 1.35.

The life-table population represents the stable population without growth, since its annual numbers of births are always the same. Hence an index of 1.00 would signify the same ratio of children to women as that in the stationary population, corresponding to a net reproduction rate of 1.00.  Chile's replacement index is close to the net reproduction rate of 1.38 (computed in Table 7:3), indicating a substantial excess of children compared with the stationary population of 1940.  The index itself is cruder than the net reproduction rate.  Usually its values are not quite the same:  it tends to give high values that are too high, and low values that are too low.  As a substitute for the net reproduction rate, the replacement index is not fully satisfactory, for when the data are inadequate for one, they are likely to be inadequate for the other.[12]

---

columns of a life table (see 5:5).  The number of children is $_5L_0$ (both sexes), and the number of women aged 15-49 is $_{35}L_{15}$ (female column only). A slight adjustment must be made, however.  A life table has 100,000 male "births" and 100,000 female "births."  An actual population has about 1.05 male births for each female birth.  In order to compare the child-woman ratio calculated from the life table with the ratio calculated from the actual population, the numbers of boys and girls in the life table must be properly balanced.  This is done by increasing the value of $_5L_0$ for males by the observed sex ratio of births.  Lacking this information, 1.05 is a reasonable estimate.  The child-woman ratio of the life table is then

$$\frac{(1.05) \; _5L_0^{males} + \; _5L_0^{females}}{_{35}L_{15}^{females}}.$$

[11]Adjusted registration data indicate about 1.034 male births for each female birth at this period, and this figure was used.

[12]There is a systematic discussion of this index by A. J. Lotka, "The Geographic Distribution of Intrinsic Natural Increase in the United States, and an Examination of the Relation between Several Measures of Net Reproductivity," *Journal of the American Statistical Association*, Vol. 31, pp. 273-294 (June, 1936).

## 7:7 Growth in the Stable Population

In the stable population, everything depends on a set of age-specific birth rates and a set of age-specific death rates. These are the conditions which determine the rate of growth, and they must also determine the age and sex composition. The best place to illustrate all these connections is in the stable population, where the disturbing effects of extraneous factors are absent.

A stationary population is the simplest case. It is drawn directly from a life table, where by definition there is neither increase or decrease. The numbers of males and of females by age are found in the separate columns of $L_x$.[13] The stationary population based on the life table of 1940 for Chile appears in Table 7:4 (Column 4 and Column 5). For males, the person-years are taken from the original source of this life table, and multiplied by the sex ratio of registered births in 1939-1941, or 1.03393. In this case, the total size of the population is $\overset{\infty}{\underset{0}{S}} L_x$, that is, the sum of the $L_x$ values in Table 7:4. The fertility of the stationary population always produces a number of births equal to $l_0$. The general birth rate is equal to the number of births (both sexes) divided by the total population. This is also equal to the death rate. When the rate of increase, $r$, is equal to zero, no further calculations are necessary.

If the population is not stationary, the determination of its structure is more complex. The effect of fertility must be taken into account separately. In this case, the stable population is constructed in two stages. First, we set down the age structure as it would be if the population were stationary (as just explained above, where $r = 0$). These are again the figures in Column 4 and Column 5 of Table 7:4. Then, these figures are revised to include the net effect of fertility and mortality as represented by $r$, the permanent rate of increase per person in the stable population. This is called the "intrinsic" rate of increase, to distinguish it from the crude rate of increase discussed in 2:9. Its value must be calculated separately

---

[13]This use of the life table was described in 5:5. If we assume that the life table represents a population in one particular year, instead of the life history of a cohort, then the numbers of person-years $(L_x)$ represent the average size of the population at each age. The same number of births (equal to $l_0$) occur each year, and this is equal to the number of deaths. The structure of the population remains the same indefinitely, with no change in the size of any age group.

(see below). The general birth and death rates in the stable population are calculated afterwards, since they depend on its age composition.

If we begin with a rate of increase of 10.73 per thousand, then

## TABLE 7:4

### STABLE POPULATION FOR CHILE, 1940[a]

| Age terval to x+5) (1) | Mid-point (x+2.5) (2) | $e^{-r(x+2.5)}$ (r = .01073) (3) | Stationary Population (Life table for Chile, 1940) | | Stable Population | | Total Population of 10,000[c] | |
|---|---|---|---|---|---|---|---|---|
| | | | Females $_5L_x$ (4) | Males $(1.03393)_5L_x$[b] (5) | Initial Calculation | | | |
| | | | | | Males (6) | Females (7) | Males (8) | Females (9) |
| 0-4 | 2.5 | .97353 | 387,006 | 392,634 | 382,241 | 376,762 | 622 | 613 |
| 5-9 | 7.5 | .92268 | 360,411 | 365,438 | 337,182 | 332,544 | 549 | 541 |
| 10-14 | 12.5 | .87448 | 355,480 | 360,510 | 315,259 | 310,860 | 513 | 506 |
| 15-19 | 17.5 | .82880 | 346,678 | 352,603 | 292,237 | 287,327 | 475 | 467 |
| 20-24 | 22.5 | .78551 | 333,145 | 339,474 | 266,660 | 261,689 | 434 | 426 |
| 25-29 | 27.5 | .74448 | 318,138 | 324,035 | 241,238 | 236,847 | 392 | 385 |
| 30-34 | 32.5 | .70559 | 303,389 | 308,737 | 217,842 | 214,068 | 354 | 348 |
| 35-39 | 37.5 | .66873 | 288,604 | 292,789 | 195,797 | 192,998 | 319 | 314 |
| 40-44 | 42.5 | .63380 | 273,298 | 275,103 | 174,360 | 173,216 | 284 | 282 |
| 45-49 | 47.5 | .60069 | 257,311 | 254,861 | 153,092 | 154,564 | 249 | 251 |
| 50-54 | 52.5 | .56931 | 239,545 | 230,942 | 131,478 | 136,375 | 214 | 222 |
| 55-59 | 57.5 | .53958 | 217,757 | 202,493 | 109,261 | 117,497 | 178 | 191 |
| 60-64 | 62.5 | .51139 | 191,379 | 170,287 | 87,083 | 97,869 | 142 | 159 |
| 65-69 | 67.5 | .48468 | 158,558 | 134,197 | 65,043 | 76,850 | 106 | 125 |
| 70-74 | 72.5 | .45936 | 120,293 | 95,654 | 43,940 | 55,258 | 71.5 | 89.9 |
| 75-79 | 77.5 | .43536 | 79,756 | 57,393 | 24,987 | 34,723 | 40.6 | 56.5 |
| 80-84 | 82.5 | .41262 | 45,195 | 29,495 | 12,170 | 18,648 | 19.8 | 30.3 |
| 85-89 | 87.5 | .39107 | 20,588 | 12,513 | 4,893 | 8,051 | 8.0 | 13.1 |
| 90-94 | 92.5 | .37064 | 7,262 | 4,049 | 1,501 | 2,692 | 2.4 | 4.4 |
| 95-99 | 97.5 | .35128 | 2,209 | 865 | 304 | 776 | 0.5 | 1.3 |
| 100-104 | 102.5 | .33293 | 444 | 95 | 32 | 148 | 0.05 | 0.2 |
| | | | | | 3,056,600 | 3,089,762 | 4974 | 5026 |

Based on life table for 1940, age-specific birth rates for 1939-1941.

1.03393 is the sex ratio of births in Chile, 1939-1941, after an adjustment for incomplete registration.

Based on the distribution of figures in Column 6 and Column 7, setting the total population (both sexes) equal to 10,000.

$r = .01073$. The effect of this rate of increase on each age interval of the stationary population is expressed as $e^{-ra}$, where:

$e^i$ is a number in the system of "natural" logarithms, depending on the particular value that we give to "$i$". This value consists of $-ra$, where

$r$ is the rate of increase in the stable population, remaining perpetually fixed

$a$ is the mid-point of each age interval (adopted as the approximate average age of the age group). The mid-point is $\left(x + \dfrac{n}{2}\right)$, that is, "age x plus one-half the number of years, $n$, included in the interval." With the normal 5-year intervals, this means $\left(x + \dfrac{5}{2}\right)$ or $x + 2.5$, the values used in Table 7:4 and Table 7:5.

The mid-point of each age interval is shown in Column 2 of Table 7:4. For each age interval, a value of $e^{-r(x+2.5)}$ is found by reference to the table of logarithms, and entered in Column 3.[14] The effect of this rate of growth is calculated by multiplying each age group in the stationary population by the corresponding value of $e^{-r(x+2.5)}$

These multiplications furnish an initial set of figures for the stable population at each age (Column 6 and Column 7). For the sake of convenience, they are always re-calculated as a distribution of some round number, giving the stable population a total size of 1,000 or 10,000 or 100,000. This re-calculation is done in the same manner as a percentage-distribution (see 2:12): for each age group,

---

[14] The tables of "the exponential function, $e^x$" are most convenient, as explained in 1:7. For example, the first value (for ages 0-4) in Table 7:4 is equal to $e^{-.01073(2.5)}$, or $e^{-.02682}$. In the table of logarithms, look for the value of $e^x$, where $x = -.02682$. This value is .97353, which is the first entry in Column 3. Note that there is a minus sign in the expression $-r(x+2.5)$; because of it, the values must be found in the portion of the logarithm table entitled "values of the descending exponential." When the expression is positive (as it is when $r$ itself is negative), the values should be found among the "values of the ascending exponential."

# CALCULATION OF INTRINSIC RATE OF INCREASE FOR CHILE, 1940

| (1) Age (x to x+5) | (2) Mid-point (x+2.5) | (3) Births per person-year (daughters only) | (4) Person-years lived per woman in hypothetical cohort $\left(\frac{_5L_x}{l_0}\right)$ | (5) Expected female births (3) × (4) | (6) Calculation of $\bar{a}'$ (2) × (5) | (7) $-r'(x+2.5)$ ($r' = .01062$) | (8) $e^{-r'(x+2.5)}$ | (9) $e^{-r'(x+2.5)}b_{x+2.5}\left(\frac{_5L_x}{l_0}\right)$ (5) × (8) |
|---|---|---|---|---|---|---|---|---|
| 15-19 | 17.5 | .03195 | 3.46678 | .11076 | 1.93830 | -.18587 | .83039 | .091974 |
| 20-24 | 22.5 | .08520 | 3.33145 | .28384 | 6.38640 | -.23897 | .78744 | .223507 |
| 25-29 | 27.5 | .10191 | 3.18138 | .32421 | 8.91578 | -.29208 | .74671 | .242091 |
| 30-34 | 32.5 | .09808 | 3.03389 | .29756 | 9.67070 | -.34518 | .70809 | .210699 |
| 35-39 | 37.5 | .07530 | 2.88604 | .21732 | 8.14950 | -.39829 | .67147 | .145924 |
| 40-44 | 42.5 | .03852 | 2.73298 | .10527 | 4.47398 | -.45139 | .63674 | .067030 |
| 45-49 | 47.5 | .01413 | 2.57311 | .03636 | 1.71710 | -.50450 | .60381 | .021955 |
| Total | | | | 1.37532 | 41.26176 | | | 1.003180 |

$$\bar{a}' = \frac{41.26176}{1.37532} = 30.00157$$

$$r' = \frac{1}{\bar{a}'}\log_e 1.37532 = \frac{1}{30.00157} \times .31865 = .010621$$

$$1 + E = 1.003180$$

$$E = +.003180$$

$$r \cong r' + \frac{E}{\bar{a}' + \frac{E}{r'}} = .010621 + \frac{.003180}{30.00157 + .29941} = .01073$$

219

$P_i$, the final figure is $\dfrac{P_i}{\text{Total of Col.6 \& Col. 7, or } 6{,}151{,}520}\, k.$

How is the rate of increase found? It must be known before ascertaining the age structure. This rate is related to the net reproduction rate, which is also a ratio of growth. The net reproduction rate represents a ratio of $\dfrac{F_2}{F_1}$ , the total number of daughters ever born per woman in a cohort of the stable population (or, the size of the second generation of females, divided by the initial size of the first generation). Hence the familiar formula for growth (see 7:4 and 2:8) applies: $\dfrac{F_2}{F_1} = e^{r\bar{a}}$ , where $\bar{a}$ is the average interval of years between mothers' and daughters' ages, called the "mean length of generation."

In Table 7:5, the net reproduction rate $\left(\dfrac{F_2}{F_1}\right)$ is calculated at 1.37524.

However, in order to find the rate of increase from this ratio, we must first find the value of $\bar{a}$. This presents the most difficult problem, for there is no simple way of calculating $\bar{a}$ precisely. Instead, we can first make an approximation of $\bar{a}$, and later estimate and correct the error involved. We begin in Table 7:5 by calculating the average age of mothers *in one cohort* of the stable population at the time of birth of their daughters,[15] or $\bar{a}'$. This is done by adding together the ages of all mothers when their daughters were born (the mid-point of each age group times the number of births, and summed), and dividing by the total number of births. In Table 7:5, $\bar{a}'$ is computed by multiplying the numbers in Column 2 and Column 5, summing the products; and dividing this sum by the total of Column 5, as follows: $\bar{a}' = \dfrac{41.26176}{1.37532} = 30.00157$ years. This is the first approximation of $\bar{a}$.

---

[15] This is the average interval between mothers' and daughters' ages in that cohort. Usually it is not quite the same as the corresponding average interval in the entire stable population, because the population may contain several cohorts of different sizes, reflecting any recent increase or decrease. The two intervals will be the same only when the population is stationary, where $r = 0$.

With this value of $\bar{a}'$, we can calculate $r'$, an approximate

value of $r$. If we assume that $\dfrac{F_2}{F_1} = e^{r'\bar{a}'}$, then $e^{r'\bar{a}'} = 1.37532$ and

$$r' = \frac{1}{\bar{a}'}\log_e\left(\frac{F_2}{F_1}\right), \text{ or } r' = \frac{1}{30.00157}\log_e 1.37532 = \frac{.31865}{30.00157} = .010621.$$

Now we can test how close the approximation, $r'$, is to the true value $r$. The rate of increase, $r$, is also related to the age-specific birth rates of a cohort of women in the stable population. This relation is summarized in a very important formula, $\overset{49}{\underset{15}{S}}\ e^{-r(x+0.5)}\ b_x\ L_x = 1$,

where $b_x$ is the age-specific birth rate at each age (daughters only). That is to say, when these items are multiplied, the sum of their products should be exactly 1.0.[16]

It is easy to perform this computation with the material of Table 7:5. Using the approximate value of $r' = .01062$, merely look up the value of $e^{-r'(x+2.5)}$ for each value of $-r'(x + 2.5)$ in Column 7 and Column 8, multiply by the items of Column 3, and sum the products in Column 9. (With a calculating machine these products can be cumulated without writing them down, and Column 9 becomes unnecessary.)

The result is 1.003180, which deviates slightly from the desired 1.0. It deviates by an amount of error, which may be called $E$. That is, $E = +.003180$. The error is present because the approximate value $r' = .01062$ was used instead of the true value of $r$, which is still unknown. There is an unknown discrepancy $(r - r')$ between these two values; it can be estimated very closely by assuming that

---

[16] As usual we use 5-year intervals of age instead of one-year intervals: multiply $e^{-r(x+2.5)}$ for each interval by $b_{x+2.5}$ $(_5L_x)$, as in Table 7:5. This is a slight modification of the original formula $e^{-ra}b_a l_a\ da$, which is based on the notion of infinitesimal intervals of age. (See L. Dublin and A. J. Lotka, "On the True Rate of Natural Increase," *Journal of the American Statistical Association*, Vol. 20, pp. 305-339 (September, 1925). When 5-year intervals are used, it thereby becomes somewhat less precise. We have arbitrarily limited the childbearing period to the interval between age 15 and age 50, to conform to customary usage.

$$r - r' = \dfrac{E}{\overline{a}' + \dfrac{E}{r'}}.$$ For the stable population of Chile, we can then cal-

culate $r = r' + \dfrac{E}{\overline{a}' + \dfrac{E}{r'}}$, or $r = .010621 + \dfrac{.003180}{30.00157 + .29941} = .01073.$[17]

After the stable population is constructed, as in Table 7:4, it is a simple matter to compute the intrinsic birth rate and death rate. The total number of female person-years is the total of Column 7, or 3,092,404. There are 100,000 female births, and so the female birth rate is $\dfrac{100,000}{3,092,404} = .03234.$ The number of male births is 100,000 × 1.03393, and the male birth rate must be $\dfrac{103,393}{3,059,116} = .03380.$ The birth rate for the entire stable population (both sexes), which is the figure usually wanted, is $\dfrac{203,393}{6,151,520} = .03306,$ or 33.06 per thousand.

The intrinsic death rate equals this birth rate minus the intrinsic rate of increase, or $(.03306 - .01073) = .02233,$ or 22.33 per thousand.

## 7:8  Growth and Age Structure

An actual population is more complex. Its vital rates do not remain fixed, and therefore give a less definite pattern to its structure. Its age composition is related to the past history of growth, however, and helps to determine the future capacity for growth.

This is most evident in the size of reproductive age groups in proportion to the total population. Having a large proportion of people at these ages is favorable to natural increase — with a given level of

---

[17] This scheme was developed by A. J. Coale, "A New Method for Calculating Lotka's $r$ —the Intrinsic Rate of Growth in a Stable Population," in *Population Studies*, Vol. 11 (July, 1957), pp. 92-94.

Another method has been in more common use (see Dublin & Lotka, [1925], and the exceptionally clear presentation in D. V. Glass, *Population Policies and Movements*, pp. 405-415). Compared with the earlier method, the procedure described here has the advantages of being shorter, simpler, burdened with fewer extraneous operations, and more accurate. For a still shorter, though less accurate method, see A. J. Coale, "The Calculation of Approximate Intrinsic Rates," *Population Index*, Vol. 22 (April, 1955), pp. 94-97.

fertility and mortality, they produce more births (and fewer deaths) than there would be with smaller groups of potential parents.

The size of these age groups is limited by the past numbers of children. This limitation will also exist in the future. A small proportion of children in the population is eventually unfavorable to a high rate of natural increase, for they contain relatively few potential parents. Therefore, observed rates of growth are sometimes misleading, because they may give an unreliable indication of future capacity for increase.

The age structure is illustrated graphically as a *population pyramid*. Age groups are arranged in strata, youth at the bottom, old age at the top.[18] The typical shape of such a pyramid is shown in Chart 7:2, with two contrasting cases of India and Sweden. It is broad at the base, tapering upward according to the past numbers of births and deaths that have formed it. The pyramid for India, for example, is broader at its base, because a large supply of children has been added to the population each year. The Swedish population is much less concentrated in its younger age groups. In fact, in 1930 the youngest group (0-4) was actually smaller than the one directly above it; the same group, aged 20-24 in 1950, is still considerably smaller than the adjacent strata in Chart 7:2.

We refer to a population as "old" or "young," according to the relative weight of old and young age groups in the total. A young population is not necessarily one tending to increase, though growth and youth have generally been found together. The pattern of age composition is formed by a long accumulation of births and deaths, and so it is a rather persistent feature, not changed in just a few

---

[18]For the sake of comparison, population pyramids are drawn in a standard manner. Each age stratum is represented by a horizontal bar, extending outward from the center (males to the left, females to the right). The bars are based on the percentage distribution of the entire population by age and sex, like the data of the stable population in Table 7:4 (Columns 8 and 9, treating their total as 100.0 instead of 1000). The distribution must include both sexes, in order to show their proper proportion to the total. If different pyramids are to be compared, they should have the same scale (or at least the same ratio between the units on the vertical scale and the units on the horizontal scale. Even the same population looks very different if this relation is altered.

A pyramid conveys at a glance the entire shape of the age structure. It also shows any gross irregularities due to special past events (such as a war, epidemic or age-selective migration), fluctuations of fertility, inaccurate reporting of age, or to widespread omission of people of some age group by the census enumeration. It is the most widely used of all graphic devices in population studies.

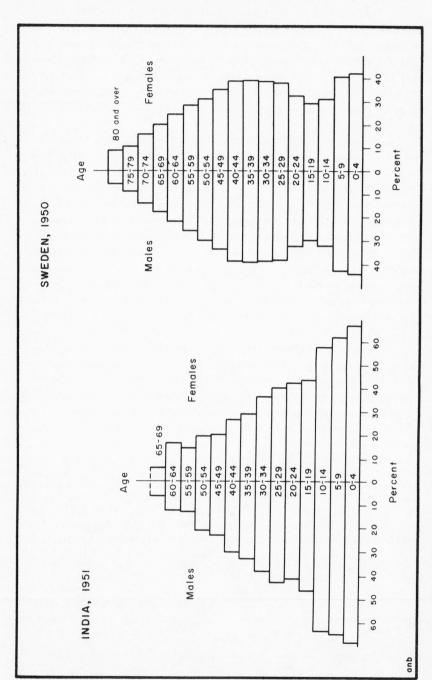

Chart 7·2 Population pyramids for India and Sweden. (Beyond age 70, data are unavailable in 5-year age intervals for

years.  Irregularities, like age or sex groups of exceptional size, reflect unusual numbers of births and deaths in some particular cohort
at some time in the past.  An irregular pattern of age composition indicates some fluctuations in the sequence of past events.  One of
these can be matched against the other, because their effect always
remains in the same cohort or cohorts.  An abnormally small cohort
can be traced by age through the data of successive censuses, and
perhaps traced to an original deficit of births or an extraordinary
period of infant mortality.

The same information would be conveyed in a percentage-distribution of population.  For some purposes such detail is unnecessary.  A broad outline of age structure is provided by the use of larger intervals of age, as in Table 7:6, allowing several cases to be
compared briefly.  For example, among the countries of Table 7:6, it
is useful to distinguish the proportions of children under 15 years of
age.  In three cases a recent census indicates that 35 per cent or
more of the population were less than 15 years old; over half were
under age 20.  In a few, a later census reveals a decline in this percentage as compared with some earlier date, and there are signs that
these populations are becoming less "youthful."  In those countries
with a long history of low vital rates, children are far less plentiful
(as low as 22 per cent in Sweden in 1930).

At the highest ages the situation is approximately reversed.
With high proportions in the young age groups, it would be almost impossible for the percentages age 65 and over to be very large (see
Table 7:6).  Furthermore, where the youthful pattern is found, it is
usually consistent throughout all ages.  This is evident even within
the intermediate age groups, 15-64.  The people of a "young" population are generally concentrated in the lower half of this interval (e.g.,
Brazil and India), and are divided more evenly between the upper and
lower portions where an "older" pattern prevails (as in Sweden and
France).

Where there have been recent gains or losses of migrants, they
are often visible as an excess or shortage of young adults, inconsistent with the composition of the population in other ages.  (This is especially true when data of men and women are tabulated separately.)

Being widely available, age statistics offer material that is
valuable for many purposes, not just for analyzing growth and reproduction.  Aspects of age structure have some significance for nearly
every type of population study, from the general state of health and
mortality, to marriage patterns and questions of manpower and dependency.

## 7:9  Age Structure and the Past History of Vital Events

In an actual population, the age structure has an uneven pattern of origin in past events.  Though it cannot be formulated precisely, as in a stable population, the relation between them is fundamentally the same.  Without migration, each year's births and deaths are the only way of changing the size of a population, and also the only way of changing the size of the several age groups.  Every addition or subtraction, by a birth or a death, becomes a part of some age group.

As illustrated in Chart 7:2, the age structure of a population consists of these groups, or strata, one added each year.  The size

## TABLE 7:6

## POPULATION DISTRIBUTED BY AGE, SELECTED COUNTRIES

### (Census data)

| Country | Year | Per Cent of Total Population[a] | | | | |
|---------|------|------|-------|-------|---------------|--------|
|         |      | 0-14 | 15-39 | 40-64 | 65 and over | Total[b] |
| Philippines | 1948 | 44.2 | 39.4 | 13.3 | 3.2 | 100.1 |
| Venezuela[c] | 1950 | 42.0 | 39.8 | 15.6 | 2.7 | 100.1 |
| Mexico | 1950 | 41.8 | 38.6 | 16.3 | 3.4 | 100.1 |
| Egypt[c] | 1947 | 38.1 | 39.0 | 19.8 | 3.1 | 100.0 |
|  | 1937 | 39.2 | 38.4 | 18.8 | 3.7 | 100.1 |
| India | 1951 | 38.3 | 39.1 | 19.3 | 3.3 | 100.0 |
| Ceylon | 1946 | 37.2 | 42.3 | 17.0 | 3.4 | 99.9 |
|  | 1911 | 40.9 | 41.2 | 15.6 | 2.3 | 100.0 |
| Hong Kong | 1931 | 25.2 | 53.5 | 19.4 | 1.9 | 100.0 |
| France | 1954 | 23.3 | 33.0 | 31.5 | 12.1 | 99.9 |
| United States | 1950 | 26.9 | 37.9 | 27.1 | 8.1 | 100.0 |
|  | 1910 | 32.1 | 43.2 | 20.4 | 4.3 | 100.0 |
| Sweden | 1950 | 29.4 | 29.5 | 30.9 | 10.2 | 100.0 |
|  | 1930 | 22.1 | 41.7 | 27.0 | 9.2 | 100.0 |

[a] Distribution is based on those persons classified by age in the census.

[b] Because these percentages are rounded, some will not add to exactly 100.0.

[c] Excluding certain known categories of people not fully included in the census.

of each group in later years is determined by its original number of births, minus its accumulated number of deaths thereafter.  The percentage of the population in each group — its size relative to the total — therefore must be determined in some way by the numbers of births and deaths relative to the population, the birth and death rates.

This relation appears less simple, however, when it is considered in detail.  It is subject to several complications that have already been mentioned:  changing birth rates, especially short fluctuations (see 3:8); various patterns of mortality by age and sex; and of course migration, which alters the age composition produced by vital rates alone.  (Migrants might also be treated as additions or subtractions in specific age groups, but they do not follow a very definite or constant schedule according to age, and their influence on age structure is unpredictable.)  Most important of all, the population of different ages has been formed, not by a single set of birth and death rates, but by the rates of a long period, as long as the age of the oldest members of the population.  This fact aggravates the task of coping with all the other difficulties above.

## 7:10  Determination of Age Structure in a Stable Population

Today there are very few actual populations that are closed against migration, and their past fertility and mortality are not very comparable.  For a good illustration we must turn to a stable population, where all these conditions are known in advance, migration being excluded entirely.

Let us begin with the stable population calculated from the vital rates of Chile, 1940.  The data come from Table 7:4, combining both sexes (Column 8 plus Column 9).  Its age structure is plotted with a solid line (A-I and B-I) in Chart 7:3-A and 7:3-B.  For comparison, two other stable populations have been constructed, one based on the relatively low death rates of Japan and the other based on the relatively high death rates of India; both populations have Chile's age-specific birth rates.[19]  These two examples are also plotted in Chart 7:3-A, with dotted line (A-II) and broken line (A-III).  The three populations of Chart 7:3-A represent a considerable range of mortality conditions.  They have crude ("intrinsic") death rates of 10, 23, and 31.  All have about the same intrinsic birth rate of 32-34.

---

[19]These populations are constructed on the basis of life tables of the two countries at the dates indicated.  They represent general levels of mortality higher and lower than Chile's.  The male expectation of life at birth was 61 years for Japan and 32 for India, which may be compared with 41 years for Chile.

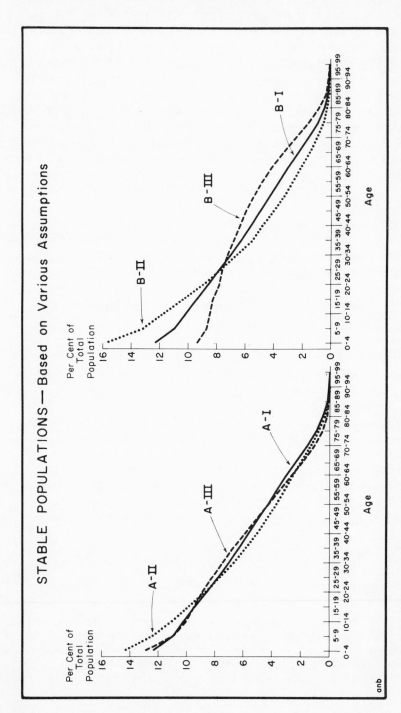

Chart 7:3    Stable populations, by age, based on various assumptions.    Part A: based on same age-specific birth rates, different mortality rates;    Part B: based on same mortality rates, different birth rates.    (See discussion in text,

Together these three cases introduce different sets of death rates, while the birth rates remain the same. The result is that they are nearly indistinguishable in their age composition. (For the sake of simplicity, we have ignored differences of sex composition, which are rather minor.)

In the second portion of the graph, Chart 7:3-B, there are stable populations based on three different levels of fertility, all with the same level of mortality. They all follow the mortality schedule of Chile (according to the life table of 1940). Combined with this, one example (B-I, again indicated by a solid line) has the age-specific birth rates of Chile (1939-1941), with an intrinsic birth rate of 34 per thousand. Another has an intrinsic birth rate of 43, and its age structure is shown by the dotted line (B-II). The third (shown by the broken line B-III) has an intrinsic birth rate of 24. [20]

The result here is striking. In Chart 7:3-B, the populations are very different. The example with higher fertility (B-II) is much younger in its age composition, and the one with the lower fertility (B-III) is markedly older. After comparing Chart 7:3-A and Chart 7:3-B, the conclusion is obvious: varying the assumed levels of fertility has profoundly affected the age composition, and varying the assumed levels of mortality has not. [21]

### 7:11 Effects of Changes in Vital Rates on Age Structure

A stable population represents fixed, not changing, conditions.

---

[20] These three populations (B-I, B-II, B-III) all have the same age-specific death rates; but, since their age structure is different, their intrinsic death rates are not quite the same (see 5:6). They are calculated from the life table of Table 7:4, as explained in 7:7, by arbitrarily selecting the different values of $r$ shown below. The "intrinsic" rates of these examples are as follows:

|  | Chart 3-A | | | | Chart 3-B | | |
|---|---|---|---|---|---|---|---|
|  | Birth rate | Death rate | Increase |  | Birth rate | Death rate | Increase |
| A-I | .034 | .023 | .011 | B-I | .034 | .023 | .011 |
| A-II | .032 | .010 | .022 | B-II | .043 | .022 | .021 |
| A-III | .034 | .031 | .003 | B-III | .024 | .024 | .001 |

(For the different schedules of mortality in Chart 5:2-A, life tables of India and Japan must be consulted.)

[21] An example similar to this can also be found in F. Lorimer, "Dynamics of Age Structure in a Population with Initially Higher Fertility and Mortality," in [United Nations] *Population Bulletin*, No. 1 (December, 1951), pp. 31-41.

Even as a rather special case, it provides the clearest possible illustration, for the influence of fertility on age structure is unlike that of mortality, whether they are constant or changing.

Why are their effects so distinct? The reason lies in the different incidence of births and deaths by age. The effects of fertility and mortality do not enter the age structure at the same place. Births of any particular year add to the number of *infants*, and to no other age group. A higher birth rate in that year, unless accompanied by a rise of the death rate for infants, results in a larger percentage of infants in the population than before. A lower birth rate leads in the opposite direction – toward a smaller percentage of infants.

The effects of mortality, on the other hand, are spread through all ages. Everyone is the same age at the time of birth, but afterwards people may die at any time of life. If the general level of mortality rises or falls, the age structure is not altered unless the mortality is affected in greater degree at some ages than at others. A change of mortality must itself be unequally distributed by age if it is to have an uneven effect on the age composition of the population.[22]

As a matter of fact, changes in mortality actually *are* unequal by age. But the ordinary pattern of death rates by age is so strong that it still prevails over the kinds of change so far observed. Even in countries of relatively low mortality, where there is a greater degree of control over the major causes of death, death rates by age still follow the shape of the familiar U-shaped curve (see 4:2). Death rates among infants have remained many times higher than death rates in, let us say, later childhood; and the high mortality in older age groups, though steadily reduced by modern medicine, has little effect on age structure, because few people survive to be affected.

Hence the effects of fertility changes are directly transmitted to the age structure of the population, whereas the typical changes of mortality have a very limited influence. The consequences of migration are especially hard to discern, for people of all ages may migrate, but rates of migration by age are rather unpredictable.

---

[22]Strictly speaking, this argument applies only to changes of mortality which correspond to a uniform proportional shift in age-specific rates of *surviving* (not the rates of dying). In Chapter 4 it was explained that these two rates are very closely related (that is, $p_x = 1 - q_x$). See A. J. Coale, "The Effects of Changes in Mortality and Fertility on Age Composition," in *Milbank Memorial Fund Quarterly*, Vol. 34 (January, 1956), pp. 79-114.

However, for most purposes it is sufficient to be aware of the general tendency, and not the full details, of determination of age structure in the stable population. Actual populations do not correspond closely enough to the model to permit very detailed analogies between the two.

## 7:12  Effects of Changes in Age Structure on Vital Rates

There is another side to the subject: given some change in age structure, what is the influence on vital rates?

Of course, age-specific rates are not directly affected. They are computed separately for each age group, and are independent of the size of any other age group. Crude birth and death rates, on the other hand, always depend in some degree on the age and sex composition of the population.[23]  The crude birth rate is more sensitive to certain specific changes, because fewer age groups are involved. If the proportion of women in the reproductive ages (15-49) is increased or reduced (age-specific birth rates remaining the same), the crude birth rate must also rise or fall. Within this group, younger women contribute most of the births, and so changes in the proportions of women at these ages have the most bearing on the crude birth rate. The ages of greatest fertility are also ages of low mortality. Therefore, the rate of growth may be doubly influenced by the age and sex composition of the population.

When are such effects encountered? Naturally, some difference of age structure is likely to be present in any comparison between two or more populations. But the cause of most large peculiarities or rapid shifts of age composition is migration, and hence this type of influence on vital rates is generally associated with some movement of people on a substantial scale.

Large numbers of people often migrate in unaccustomed directions, forming special groups that are withdrawn from one population and introduced into another. Since migrants are predominantly young adults, their departure tends to raise the general death rate in the place of origin, and their arrival tends to reduce the death rate at their destination. The same movement has opposite effects on crude birth rates, if the migrants include women of child-bearing ages. In many cases these factors are negligible, depending on whether or not the migration alters the age composition noticeably in either place. When it is appreciable, migration has a significance in the future pattern of age structure beyond the immediate fact of presence or absence of the migrants themselves.

## 7:13  Population Projections

The study of population growth has one specific practical ap-

---

[23]This is also true of the "intrinsic" rates presented in 7:10, which cannot be computed except by reference to the age composition of the stable population. With different age structure, the identical schedule of age-specific death rates yielded different intrinsic rates (see footnote 20).

plication, which is to calculate population trends of the future. These calculations are called by various names – future population, forecasts, extrapolations, estimates, or projections. They consist merely of extending some plausible pattern of growth from the past into the future.[24] Hence they must outline an unknown course of vital events by means of assumptions. As we shall see, these assumptions really are exceedingly simple and exceedingly arbitrary.

Any calculations of future population are by their nature hypothetical. As actual predictions, they usually turn out rather poorly. In order to make a reliable estimate of the future, we should have to predict the future conditions affecting all the vital processes in a population. At present this is not possible, except by accident.

> Calculations bearing upon future population generally involve, however, considerable uncertainty. Our knowledge of the forces underlying changes in mortality, fertility, marriage and migration is very incomplete, and precise effects of suspected causes cannot at present be ascertained. Even if our understanding of the past were more complete, the future would inevitably be uncertain. It is not and may never be possible, therefore, to predict the course of these elements in the future with any great confidence. That is why any word such as "estimate" or "forecast" should be avoided in this connexion, in order not to give an impression that what lies ahead can be seen more clearly than it actually can. "Projection" is a term intended to imply no more than an illustrative calculation based upon certain given assumptions.[25]

Starting from some data of a population, we make a projection by introducing an assumed course of vital events, moving either forward or backward in time. There are three principal ways to proceed: (a) projecting the total amount of growth of a given period, (b) projecting an observed rate of growth, and (c) projecting the size of age and sex groups of the population independently. The first two types are relatively crude; projections of the third type, "c," begin by calculating the assumed numbers of births and deaths of age and sex groups of the census population, which determine the size of the estimated population. Obviously, the nature of the assumptions is very

---

[24] Population projections are also extended into the past. This is especially useful in reconstructing probable trends of an undocumented past period and in testing the consistency of different censuses, as described in 3:9. The procedures are virtually identical.

[25] P. R. Cox, *Demography* (Cambridge, England, 1950), pp. 232-233.

important, and they must be definitely stated.[26]

(a) A population figure can be projected for a limited period beyond the date of a census by means of vital statistics. This estimate cannot extend into the future, for it is based on vital events already registered. It follows the outline presented in 1:1. With the effect of births $(B)$, deaths $(D)$ and net migration $(M)$, the population at a later date $(P_2)$ must be the initial population $(P_1)$ with the additions or subtractions of these vital events during the intervening period: $P_2 = P_1 + B - D + M$. This procedure is especially convenient in making estimates for small subdivisions of a country, where the vital rates differ but do not warrant a separate study. It is also useful when a short period of one or a few years is involved. However, in addition to the census or other figure for this initial population, the vital statistics must be complete, and this is usually not the case. Without scrutiny these data should not be accepted as unbiased. Vital statistics are ordinarily compiled by calendar year, and must be reconciled with the date of the census. This can be done by addition and subtraction if there are tables of vital statistics by month of occurrence; otherwise the vital events between the census date and the beginning or end of the year must be estimated by interpolation (see 5:4, footnote 7).[27]

Lacking the necessary vital statistics, it is sometimes safe to project the population for a short period (a few years) on the basis of the amount of growth in some previous period. The observed amount of change is calculated and added to (or subtracted from) the census population, without the need to differentiate between natural increase and net migration. But it may not be reasonable to assume that this observed amount of change will recur. If the change is obtained from two figures several years apart, some yearly average of growth is

---

[26]Projections are not the same as informal estimates of population, which may be arrived at on the basis of fragmentary or non-statistical information, or by mere guesswork. Such conjectural estimates have a legitimate place; indeed, they may be preferable to the usual forms of projection if the data are poor. However, this section is concerned with standard procedures applied to data that are presumed to be accurate. Conjectural estimates do not fit in this category, and cannot be appraised against the results of similar operations elsewhere.

[27]This procedure can also be applied separately to age groups, but it is usually too laborious. Also, it is possible to incorporate some corrections for known errors of the data. See United Nations, Population Branch, *Methods for Population Projections by Sex and Age* (Population Studies, No. 25, New York, 1956), Chapters 2 and 4.

probably needed, and in this case the next procedure is preferable.

(b) The annual rate of growth (see 7:4) observed in some past period can be projected. If the periods (observed and estimated) are equally long, the ratio of observed growth $(P_2/P_1$, as defined in 2:8$)$ is sufficient; it is simply multiplied by the census population, and the result is an estimated figure $(\overline{P}_3)$. The date of this estimate follows $P_2$ by the same number of years that separate $P_2$ and $P_1$.

For a period of some other length, this ratio must be converted to an annual rate of growth, as explained in 7:4. (Alternatively, assuming no net effect of migration, the crude rate of natural increase may be used.) With a value of $r$, the arithmetical operations consist of substituting this value in one of the growth formulas (see 2:8) and calculating the estimated population.[28] The second formula is more convenient, written in the form $\overline{P}_3 = P_2\, e^{rn}$. Indeed, it is so convenient that it deserves a few words of caution. It lends itself to careless use, because a population can be projected for 100 years as easily as for one month. The actual rate of growth is dependent on many variable factors, and does not have an independent existence. It does not really remain constant; to hold it constant for an extended period is a very unrealistic assumption.

(c) The third type of projection is based on separate assumptions about the course of mortality and fertility, letting the growth be determined by them. Births and deaths are calculated in relation to each age and sex group of the enumerated population. Each of these groups is exposed to the assumed rate of mortality for, let us say, five years. This reduces their numbers, and makes them all five years older. Each age group of women is exposed to an assumed birth rate, year by year, the result being annual estimated num-

---

[28] With these same formulas, the same rate of growth $(r)$ also can be used to interpolate between census observations, or to make estimates for prior dates, reconstructing some of the earlier growth of the population before the first reliable census. The assumption of a constant rate of growth always becomes a weakness if it is maintained for more than a few years.

By means of a more elaborate type of assumption, the rate can be allowed to vary during the course of growth. The usual form is called the "logistic" pattern of growth: beginning at zero, the rate rises to an assumed maximum level, and returns again to zero, describing a complete cycle of growth. This pattern is of rather casual interest. It is no less arbitrary than the assumption of a constant rate, for the logistic rate of growth follows a path determined by a few observations, without any analysis of the underlying factors. Projections by means of a logistic curve are not necessarily superior to those of any other procedure.

bers of births (which become subject to the effect of mortality along with the rest of the population). Thus fertility and mortality follow a definite schedule, by age, and the population is modified as if with the passage of time.

The computation is briefly illustrated in Table 7:7 and Table 7:8, projecting the enumerated population of Chile from 1940 to 1945. The assumed pattern of death rates is taken directly from the life table of 1940. Births each year are calculated by the general fertility rate (average figure for 1939-1941) applied to the estimated female population of childbearing age.[29] The assumptions are sometimes more refined: (a) they may be made more specific, by applying specific birth rates to married women only or to separate order-of-birth groups of women, or (b) they may be made more complex, by modify-

---

[29]The effect of five years' mortality is expressed by the survival

ratio, $\dfrac{_5L_{x+5}}{_5L_x}$, for each age group. These ratios are shown in Table 7:8;

they were computed from the life table of 1940. To illustrate, the female

population ages 20-24 in 1940, times the survival ratio $\dfrac{_5L_{25}}{_5L_{20}}$, yields an es-

timate of the age group of women 25-29 in 1945.

The female population of ages 25-29 each year must be estimated by interpolation. A straight-line method is usually advisable (see 1:7). The census enumerated 1,316,140 women 15-49 in 1940; our estimate for 1945 is 1,428,236, with a change of 112,096 in five years. To interpolate, merely

add $\dfrac{1}{5}$ of this figure, or 22,419, to the census figure for each year after 1940.

Every age group of women from 15 to 49 may be treated in this way. However, in Table 7:8 the entire group 15-49 was estimated together.

These yearly estimates of the age group 15-49 are multiplied by the general fertility rate (.1386), producing yearly estimates of births (Table 7:8, Column 4). The births were separated by sex, 51.2 per cent male and 48.8 per cent female (based on the arbitrary sex ratio of 105). The births of

1941, times the survival ratio $\dfrac{L_4}{l_0}$, provide the estimate of children age 4 in

1945; for children age 3, births of 1942 and the ratio $\dfrac{L_3}{l_0}$; and so on (Column

7). The sum of these figures (for male births) is the estimate of boys age 0-4 in 1945. The number of girls is estimated in the same manner (see Table 7:8).

# TABLE 7:7

## PROJECTION OF 1940 ENUMERATED POPULATION OF CHILE TO 1945

### According to Age-Specific Mortality in the Life Table of 1940 and Projected Numbers of Births, 1940-1945

| Ages | Males | | | Females | | |
|---|---|---|---|---|---|---|
| | Census Population Nov. 1940 | Survival Ratio[a] | Projected Population Nov. 1945 (thousands)[b] | Census Population Nov. 1940 | Survival Ratio[a] | Projected Population Nov. 1945 (thousands)[b] |
| 0-4 | 313,667 | .93073 | 370[c] | 308,336 | .93128 | 360[c] |
| 5-9 | 321,952 | .98651 | 292 | 312,905 | .98632 | 287 |
| 10-14 | 306,807 | .97807 | 318 | 302,490 | .97524 | 309 |
| 15-19 | 256,321 | .96277 | 300 | 256,482 | .96096 | 295 |
| 20-24 | 218,871 | .95452 | 247 | 238,059 | .95495 | 246 |
| 25-29 | 204,395 | .95279 | 209 | 222,506 | .95364 | 227 |
| 30-34 | 177,431 | .94834 | 195 | 174,974 | .95127 | 212 |
| 35-39 | 155,405 | .93959 | 168 | 165,587 | .94697 | 166 |
| 40-44 | 136,983 | .92642 | 146 | 131,692 | .94150 | 157 |
| 45-49 | 109,145 | .90615 | 127 | 106,840 | .93096 | 124 |
| 50-54 | 86,081 | .87681 | 98.9 | 87,940 | .90904 | 99.4 |
| 55-59 | 68,181 | .84095 | 75.5 | 66,408 | .87886 | 79.9 |
| 60-64 | 55,443 | .78806 | 57.3 | 62,780 | .82850 | 58.4 |
| 65-69 | 32,586 | .71279 | 43.7 | 33,784 | .75887 | 52.0 |
| 70-74 | 22,562 | .60001 | 23.2 | 28,537 | .66301 | 25.6 |
| 75-79 | 11,799 | .59391 | 13.5 | 14,166 | .56667 | 18.9 |
| 80-84 | 6,958 | .42424 | 7.01 | 11,109 | .45554 | 8.03 |
| 85-89 | 2,703 | .32358 | 2.95 | 4,138 | .35273 | 5.06 |
| 90 and above | 2,636 | .21363[d] | 0.875 0.563 | 4,880 | .30419[d] | 1.46 1.48 |
| Total | 2,489,926 | | 2,695 | 2,533,613 | | 2,733 |

[a] Ratios of $_5L_{x+5}/_5L_x$ from the life table of 1940. See 5:4.

[b] Each age group is advanced 5 years in age between 1940 and 1945. These figures are rounded; if they were to be used in further calculation, they should not be rounded.

[c] This is the figure estimated in Table 7:8, Column 7.

[d] Here it is assumed that the survival ratio of the group "90-94" applies to the entire age group "90 and above".

*Note:* Signs of incomplete enumeration have been discovered in the 1940 census of Chile (see the source for the life table, Table 4:1). For the sake of illustration these defects are ignored here. But they should serve as a warning that poor census data may produce poor projections, regardless of the assumptions about fertility and mortality.

Sources: *Census of 1940;* Life Table for 1940 (see Table 4:1); results of Table 7:8.

ing the birth or death rates at the beginning of each new five-year period. There is an obvious need for these refinements if a realistic estimate for more than a few years is attempted.[30] But their efficacy is questionable, unless they are manipulated with considerable talent and skill.

This method of Table 7:7 emphasizes an important point about growth of population. The survivors of the population of 1940 are determined by the level of mortality and the number of people already present; fertility affects only the numbers born afterwards. This type of projection treats each of these factors separately. For a few years after the census date, the major elements of projection are the base population (by age) and the proportions at each age that survive. The population by age is fixed at the time of the census, and the rates of survival are subject to rather little change at most ages.[31] Hence, the estimates may be very near reality until the effect of fertility begins to occupy a larger place in the projected population, which happens as the projection goes farther away from the base population.[32]

Cumbersome as it is, does this procedure offer any advantage? The chief gain is that it simulates the actual effect of births and deaths in the population. They are distributed among the people already present, according to the actual age and sex structure. It also shows the effects of the assumed vital rates on age and sex structure, and includes these structural changes in the future estimates of births and deaths. Compared with the other types of projection, this procedure relies less on the nature of its assumptions, and more on the actual composition of the population.[33] As a by-product, it also

---

[30] Frequently accurate prediction is not the goal. Many projections have the purpose of illustrating the result of a fixed course of vital rates in the population, without regard to the likelihood of realizing these conditions. See, for example, the projections and discussion in F.W. Notestein and others, *The Future Population of Europe and the Soviet Union, 1940-1970* (Geneva, 1944).

[31] Even with a substantial change of mortality rates, the rates of *survival* are relatively stable, because they are the larger: at most ages, the majority of people manage to survive. Moreover, the typical pattern of mortality by age (see Chart 4:1-B) still persists, which means that a general change of mortality is spread over many ages.

[32] Then the nature of the fertility assumption may become the predominant element, and this has been the weakest point in existing estimates.

[33] The procedure has often given rather poor estimates of future population. This has happened because the assumptions were inappropriate, not

provides estimates of the future composition by age and sex as well as a total figure.

Using five-year age groups, this third method furnishes figures exactly five years from the date of the base population, or at some interval that is a multiple of five years.[34] This is illustrated in Table 7:7. Longer projections are usually made in successive 5-year steps, moving the people to the next higher age group with each step. By additional steps, the total period of projection can be extended indefinitely. The limit lies in the usefulness of the results. They soon cease to have any value as predictions of future numbers of people. Even with the introduction of changing age-specific rates, attempts to make long-range predictions (longer than, say, 10 years) have been singularly unsuccessful. It is now being recognized that, while these more complex assumptions provide more flexibility, they are no less arbitrary.

Introducing migration into such projections is the most difficult aspect, and the most arbitrary of all. Assumptions about future migration by age and sex have almost no merit as predictions. They serve only the purpose of hypothetical illustration. There is no guide, like a life table or schedule of birth rates, to suggest a reasonable age-specific pattern. Migration that is already recorded, however, can be included in a projection and may add information of great value.[35] Sometimes it is preferable to prepare a projection ex-

---

the method. It has been suggested that projection of this kind can be improved, retaining very simple assumptions about the course of vital rates, by taking into account more aspects of the composition (especially marital status and order of birth of the women). See J. Hajnal, "The Prospects for Population Forecasts," *Journal of the American Statistical Association*, Vol. 50, (June, 1955), pp. 309-322.

[34] Otherwise the conventional 5-year age groupings cannot be preserved, except by special interpolation techniques not discussed here. Of course, after these 5-year steps are made, interpolated estimates for the growth of intervening years can be made by the straight-line device explained above (footnote 29).

[35] Migrants present a special problem: should their births and deaths be estimated during the 5-year period in which they have moved? They could spend only part — an unknown part — of this time as members of the projected population. The simplest solution, satisfactory for most purposes, is to assume that all migrants have moved on the final day of the period; which means that the births and deaths of immigrants during this period all belong to some other population, and the births and deaths of emigrants during this period all belong to the projected population. Thereafter all immigrants are treated as part of the projected population, and all emigrants are ignored.

cepting migrants completely, in order to illustrate the effects of the assumed birth and death rates alone.

Population projections should be made only after extensive study of the patterns and trends of the past. In many cases they are inadvisable. But frequently the demand for estimates of future popu-

## TABLE 7:8

## PROJECTION OF BIRTHS IN CHILE, 1940 TO 1945, AND THE SURVIVORS ON NOVEMBER 28, 1945

Assuming General Fertility Rate Remains Constant at .1386
(Calculated for 1939-1941)

| (1) | (2) | (3) | (4) | (5) | (6) | (7) | (8) |
|---|---|---|---|---|---|---|---|
| Years | Women[b] Ages 15-49 on Nov. 28 | Estimated[c] Mid-Year Population of Women 15-49 | Projected Numbers of Births — Both Sexes (3) x .1386 | Males[d] (4) x .5122 | Survival[e] Ratio | Male Survivors, Nov. 28, 1945 (5) x (6) | (Age in 1945) |
| 1940 | 1,316,140 | | | | | | |
| 1941 | $1,338,559$ | 1,327,350 | 183,971 | 94,230 | $L_4/l_0 = .71715$ | 67,577 | 4 |
| 1942 | $1,360,978$ | 1,349,768 | 187,078 | 95,821 | $L_3/l_0 = .72412$ | 69,386 | 3 |
| 1943 | $1,383,397$ | 1,372,188 | 190,185 | 97,413 | $L_2/l_0 = .73769$ | 71,861 | 2 |
| 1944 | $1,405,816$ | 1,394,606 | 193,292 | 99,004 | $L_1/l_0 = .76994$ | 76,227 | 1 |
| 1945 | 1,428,236 | 1,417,026 | 196,400 | 100,596 | $L_0/l_0 = .84859$ | 85,365 | 0 |
| Total | | | | | | 370,400[f] (rounded) | |

[a] This is the ratio of registered births (yearly average) 1939-1941 to the census population of women ages 15-49, after registration figures were increased by 10.5 per cent to allow for births omitted. See O. Cabello et al., *Tablas de Vida para Chile, 1920-1930-1940*, p. 52.

[b] Interpolated between the census figure for 1940 and the projected number of women for 1945 (see Table 7:7), by adding 1/5 of the difference each year. The interpolated numbers are italicized.

[c] Interpolated between adjoining numbers of Column 2 (see 1:7).

[d] Assuming a constant ratio of 1.05 male births per female birth.

[e] Taken from life table for Chile, 1940 (see Source of Table 4:1).

[f] Survivors of female births are estimated in the same manner. They are equal to the projected numbers of births (Column 4 minus Column 5) times the female survival ratios which can be taken from Table 4:1. This number (rounded) is 359,000.

Source: Table 7:7; birth registration; life table for 1940.

lation is such that they must be made. The basic forms of computation, described above, are elementary. Aside from these, the results are determined by the assumptions that we adopt; and the choice of assumptions must be governed, not by any general rule, but by particular conditions of each case. It is usually desirable to select a procedure that seems best to fit the purpose; to keep the assumptions as simple as possible and consider their probable biases; to employ vital rates that are contemporary with the census data, if they seem appropriate; and to restrict projections of future population to short periods. If intended as predictions to guide administrative decisions, completed projections should be revised frequently in the light of new factual evidence. Finally, a great deal of misunderstanding in the use of projected estimates may be avoided if the assumptions are fully explained, with stress on the hypothetical character of the figures.

# CHAPTER 8

# MIGRATION AND THE

# DISTRIBUTION OF POPULATION[1]

Most of the vital processes analyzed in demography move rather slowly, and take a considerable amount of time in working out their consequences. They are delayed by the periods required for people to grow to maturity and reproduce new generations. Migration usually disrupts the "normal" course of these processes. It can be very rapid in its effects, transferring millions of persons in a matter of months, and altering significantly the distribution of people and their activities.

With these potentialities, migration is associated with large and rather sudden changes. For this reason it is often unpredictable, and difficult to study. It is closely connected with economic fluctuations and important national events, and probably occupies more attention than any other topic in demography.

## 8:1 Migration and Demographic Analysis

Migration is one of the vital processes which alter the size of a population. Excepting natural increase, it is the only source of change in the population of a particular territory.

But the records of migration do not lend themselves so well to study as those of births and deaths. It is impossible to register every trip made by every person. The statistics comprise only certain kinds of movement, chiefly movement of a more or less permanent character, though not entirely so. Their meaning depends partly on the type of the area or territorial subdivision (see 8:2). Thus the sum of the

---

[1]Many of the following remarks on migration statistics were prepared as a working paper for the United Nations Seminar on Population in Asia and the Far East, held in Indonesia, November, 1955.

numbers of migrants of local areas is not necessarily the correct national total that is desired.  A person who moves from one town to
another in the same province is a migrant within this area, but is not
a migrant between provinces or between countries.  A study of migration begins with a selection of some category of migration; and the
nature of the category determines the type of migration that is measured.

Except for its contribution to population growth, migration is
treated as a separate topic in demography.  This is due largely to
some problems of statistical definition and measurement, and to pre-
occupation with one result of migration — the place of migrants in
the composition of the population at their destination — rather than
with the process of change.

## 8:2 Statistical Definitions of Migration

Analysis of migration presents some peculiar problems.  The
records of migration are probably the least satisfactory of all population data.  This is partly because their collection is poorly organized, and partly because migration is inherently difficult to standardize in units for counting.

One finds migration data collected by various agencies.  They
are seldom kept together with ordinary vital registration; as a minor
by-product of administration they cannot be spared enough attention
to maintain a high standard of quality.  Governments interest themselves primarily in recording the migrants from other countries, and
do little to keep data on movement from place to place within the
same country.  Consequently much is written on international migration, and rather little about internal migration.  Even international migrants are a neglected group:  the information recorded is inaccurate,
some whole categories are often excluded, and the enforcement is
slipshod.[2]  Comparisons of migration data from different countries
reveal inaccuracies, inconsistencies, gaps and sometimes overlap-
ping, without parallel in regular vital statistics.

Yet the fault is partly that migration is a vague statistical con-
cept, with few uniform criteria to distinguish who is a migrant and

---

[2] Some governments do not even take full responsibility for the collection of these data.  Some accept reports from private sources, combine reports from official and private agencies, or allow the duties of record-keeping to overlap between different official agencies. See United Nations, Department of Social Affairs, *Problems of Migration Statistics* (New York,
1949), Chapter II.  This publication also proposes standards for the improvement of migration data.

who is not.  First, of course, a migrant is a person who travels.  This is the only unambiguous element in the entire subject.  "Migrants" are obviously some smaller category of travellers, but the difficulty is encountered whenever the limits of that category are to be defined. Various criteria have been proposed — for example, to include all travellers who are not merely visitors or transients, to restrict the category to those whose travel is connected with a change of occupation, or to require that their journey should have at least some minimum duration (say, one year).  On slight reflection it is obvious that these, or any others, are arbitrary.  Any particular definition is beyond the control of the research worker.  Its consequences have to be accepted and anticipated when we use the figures to measure the amount of migration.

Although many agencies keep information about migrants, they collect only two kinds of statistical data.  One is a record of the persons who pass some check point, border station or port of entry — *transit statistics*.  The other is a record of persons, present at some particular time, who previously were not — this information is provided most reliably by *census statistics by place of birth*.  Place-of-birth statistics separate the population into persons born in the area of enumeration and persons born elsewhere (who must have migrated into the area at some time).[3]  Let us see how migrants are defined in these two kinds of data:

a.  *Territorial scope*.  In any set of statistics, a traveller must cross a boundary of some sort before he can be counted as a migrant.  It may be the border of a country, or of a city or town, or merely the gate of a railway station. Migration, therefore, must always have specific reference to some territory.  The *size of the territorial district* of counting becomes part of the statistical definition of what a migrant is.  Where the distances are small, "international" migration may be very casual compared to the internal movement in a larger country.[4]  In analyzing statistics of internal migration, the choice of the territorial unit is equivalent to selecting the kind of migrants to be studied:  movement of people between the largest provinces of a

---

[3]Similar information is sometimes obtained by census statistics by place of *previous residence* (say, 1, 3 or 5 years ago).  Such data share most of the same problems as place-of-birth statistics.

[4]For example, people make daily business trips between Hong Kong and China, whereas some of the largest mass movements in history have taken place *within* the borders of China.  See also United Nations, Population Division, *Sex and Age of International Migrants* (Population Studies No. 11, New York, 1953), p. 4.

country may be very different in pattern from movement among its minor civil divisions. For this reason, it is hazardous to compare figures on internal migration in different countries, or figures on external migration between countries of grossly unequal size. This difficulty applies almost equally to the two types of data mentioned above.

b. *Gross or net numbers of migrants.* Transit data always have specific reference to a period of time. They indicate how many people were recorded entering an area during that period, and how many people were recorded leaving. Either of these figures may be of interest for some purpose, but usually the *net* amount of movement is needed — the number who entered minus the number who left. If immigrants died during this period, it will appear according to the transit data that they were still resident in the area. Census data refer to a particular moment (the day or week of the actual enumeration), but the people classified as born elsewhere may have entered the area at any time since birth. The *migration* indicated by census data therefore does not refer to any particular period, except when special tabulations are provided to show this. Census figures of migrants *always* represent a net balance,[5] but cover an indefinite period of time that varies among different individuals. The effects of mortality are always deducted in advance: the migrants recorded by the census are people who both entered the area and survived to the census date.

c. *Permanence or duration of stay.* Transit data ordinarily do not indicate how long individuals remain in the area. However, the net balance of arrivals and departures makes it possible to eliminate most persons whose visit was very brief, provided the period is short (say, one year or less). Thus, a net balance of immigration during a year suggests that some of the arrivals are more than just transient visitors, though this may be misleading. A net balance of immigration for several successive years is a stronger indication that some of the migrants have become permanent residents (though some allowance may have to be made for deaths among the immigrants). Census data give no indication of the duration of stay, unless special tabulations are provided to show the length of residence in the area by each person (usually since the most recent date of entry). Among immigrants, the chance of being enumerated on a census day is less

---

[5] This is the net balance of *in*-migrants from other areas. It may not be the full net balance, for it does not take into account people who were born in the area and who moved away (unless they can be found in statistics at their destinations).

for those whose stay is brief, greater for those whose stay is long; hence census data give emphasis to the more permanent parts of the immigrant community.

     d. *Single moves and migration by stages.* Migration sometimes does not happen all at once, by a single move from the place of origin to the ultimate destination. A migrant often passes through an area where transit statistics are kept, or stays there for a short time before moving on. Migrant mine and plantation workers have often settled for a year or more at their first place of work, and then moved elsewhere to follow another occupation. Depending on the purpose of an investigation, it may be desirable to take notice of intermediate moves, or to ignore them and trace migrants to a more permanent destination. Transit data count each *move* separately, and record the number of moves, not the number of migrants. Census data count each *migrant* as one, and exclude any separate consideration of the number of moves; with census data, there is still no way to determine whether a person's place of residence is intermediate in a series of moves or more or less permanent.

     e. *Seasonal fluctuations and the time of observation.* Migration is often irregular in its flow, rising or diminishing rapidly. Depending on the purpose of investigation, either the fluctuations or more gradual trends may be of interest. Transit data, if compiled successively for short periods, reveal fluctuations from period to period; if these data are combined into longer periods, they can be made to show more gradual trends. There is a tendency for census data to smooth out a good deal of brief fluctuation, representing the cumulated effect of moves over a longer interval of time. However, if the date of a census coincides with an extreme high or low point in a year's migration (for example, in the movement of labor to and from seasonal work), then census data cease to provide this stabilized sort of index of migration and may become very misleading.

## 8:3 "Internal" and "International" Migration

     It has been customary to draw a sharp line between "internal" and "international" movement, particularly in the earlier writings on the subject. The distinction has been chiefly a matter of convenience. It comes from a unique era of population movements, in which some of the relatively empty areas of the world were settled by migrants from other countries. Until this century the statistics of migration (such as they were) pertained to only international migrants. With scarcely any records of other movements, international migration was studied, and internal migration neglected.

     Today the movement of people across national boundaries is

severely restricted and regulated, though it has by no means stopped. At the same time, movement *within* national boundaries has greatly increased, accompanying accelerated economic and social changes. The differences of language, custom or occupation encountered by migrants within a large country are sometimes greater than those of moving to another country.[6] We may wish to distinguish types of migration or reasons for moving, but they do not fit into these two categories. It is now more common to study migration as migration, without regard to the political status of the boundaries that people happen to cross.

## 8:4 Measuring the Volume of Migration

Given some set of statistics, there is a problem of choosing a basis for measuring the volume of migration. This may be approached: (a) from the standpoint of the effects on the sending area, (b) from the standpoint of the effects on the receiving area, or (c) from the standpoint of the migrants as a separate group. Which basis is selected, of course, depends on the purpose of the investigation.

The migrant group itself is not exactly the same from these three different standpoints.[7] More important, however, a distinct standard of measurement is called for in each instance: (a) the ratio of the number of migrants to the population of the sending area, (b) the ratio of migrants to the population of the receiving area, or (c) the absolute number of migrants, or perhaps some ratio to the number of migrants in some other period. The transfer of over one million people from China to the Malayan peninsula, for example, has been a minor quantity in relation to a Chinese population of more than 500

---

[6] Furthermore, movement of people between countries may be "internal" migration from the standpoint of the particular region. We now pay more attention to the factors prompting people to move than to the types of boundaries that are crossed. See D. Kirk, *Europe's Population in the Interwar Years* (Geneva, 1946), Chapters 2,9.

[7] At the moment of migration the migrant group is not quite the same as it would be at any later date, in either the place of origin or the place of destination. Its size changes by deaths during and after migration. Its composition changes (due to aging, marriages, occupational shifts, and the like). These changes naturally increase with the passage of time; in short periods they are likely to be small. The emigrants who leave a sending area are not exactly the same as the immigrants who arrive at a receiving area: some of the former go to different destinations, and some of the latter come from different origins.

million; but it supplied more than half the present population of
Malaya and Singapore.[8]

## 8:5  The Volume of Migration:  Transit Statistics

We shall first consider statistics showing migrants as a separate group.  These come from a register of events as they occur, the
numbers of people entering and leaving an area in a given period.  As
the record of the migrants themselves, this material might seem to be
the best source of migration data.  Actually, however, it has very limited uses, and now has a rather secondary position.

It does have certain advantages.  For example, the flow of migrants to and from a country can be traced year by year, including the
fluctuations in response to business or wartime conditions (see Table
8:1).  Only current transit records provide this current information.
They are the sole direct statistics of emigrants, for most census data
pertain to immigrants (see 8:3).  Furthermore, they reveal movement
in both directions, which is not shown by census data (except as
mentioned in 8:7).  They furnish the only statistical description of
the composition of the migrants at the time of migration.[9]

But most of the characteristics of the migrant groups change;
people constantly shift their occupations, marital status, religion and
educational attainment.[10]  Transit records are not very faithfully
kept, except at international borders.  Even there they are very incomplete.  Some countries include, and some exclude their own nationals from their statistics of external migration.  Naturally, clandes-
tine migration is not included in transit records, which are associated
with border controls.  (There is a better chance of getting this information from the indirect measures discussed below.)

Owing to these shortcomings, transit data are not always dependable, and scarcely ever embrace the migration within a country.
For this reason we generally turn to indirect sources to measure the
amount of internal migration.

---

[8]A considerable part of this group consists of people of Chinese de-
scent born in Malaya — i.e., the natural increase of the original migrants.
This case is another illustration of the discrepancies encountered between
different figures.

[9]See United Nations, Population Division, *Sex and Age of International Migrants* (New York, 1953).

[10]Only the place of birth and date of birth, and sex, remain the same.
For this reason census statistics are the most useful migration data where
immigrants are concerned, if they contain this information.

## 8:6   The Volume of Migration:   Census Statistics by Place of Birth

Increasingly, censuses ask the place of birth of each person. Many countries now include tables of population by place of birth in their census publications.  If the tabulations are so arranged, they can be used to study both internal and international migration.

An example of such a table is shown in Table 8:2, very much abridged.  The population of Mexico in the census of 1950 was classified by place of birth ("born in Mexico," "born outside Mexico," "born in same subdivision," "born in another subdivision").  At a glance one can see how many people alive in 1950 were immigrants, how many were staying in another state or territory (a subdivision other than the one of birth).[11]  The past net migration into each State or Territory is also apparent from the complete table of original data (subject to limitations mentioned below).  Many currents of past migration can be measured by percentages calculated from this material:

Per cent of Mexico's population born abroad

Per cent of residents in the Federal District born abroad

Per cent of foreign-born residing in the Federal District (or any subdivision)

Per cent of residents in the Federal District (or any subdivision) born in another subdivision (i.e., "internal migrants")

Per cent of the Federal District's in-migrants who were born in the State of Yucatán (or any other subdivision)

If the table also shows in detail the place of birth for each place of residence, we can calculate the place of residence of the past *out*-migrants from any State (i.e., the distribution of internal migrants by destination).  A very comprehensive picture of past migration, by place of ultimate origin and place of destination (in Mexico) at the census date, emerges from these figures.

It is easy to see that the inclusion of a few characteristics in the census tabulations (even no more than sex and age) increases their effectiveness enormously, by permitting all measurements to be made separately for each category.  No special procedures are involved; only a patient rearrangement of the census tables (which sometimes is rather laborious if the distributions by place of origin

---

[11]The subdivisions of Mexico in 1950 were States (of which there were 28), Territories (of which there were 3), and one Federal District. In other words, these are relatively large territorial units.  Tables by larger or smaller units would show a somewhat different migrant population.

have not already been combined in a single table).[12]

Without doubt such tables are the most dependable source of statistics about migration, for their accuracy in general can be tested together with the rest of the census.[13] Their limitations are of another sort. Place-of-birth data indicate only the difference between place of birth and place of residence (in some territorial units, already mentioned in 8:2, which need not concern us here).  This is not

## TABLE 8:1

### MIGRATION TO AND FROM MALAYA AND SINGAPORE
### 1929 - 1939

| Year | Arrivals | Departures | Net Migration ("-" indicates a net loss of migrants) |
|---|---|---|---|
| 1929[a] | 407,419 | 76,649 | 330,770[a] |
| 1930 | 507,708 | 522,218 | - 14,510 |
| 1931 | 330,146 | 517,675 | -187,529 |
| 1932 | 246,738 | 427,716 | -180,978 |
| 1933 | 250,126 | 288,575 | - 38,449 |
| 1934 | 494,753 | 352,664 | 142,089 |
| 1935 | 548,339 | 423,133 | 125,206 |
| 1936 | 525,621 | 442,812 | 82,809 |
| 1937 | 760,453 | 493,247 | 267,206 |
| 1938 | 465,564 | 434,526 | 31,038 |
| 1939 | 383,738 | 386,450 | - 2,712 |

[a] Before 1930, data pertained to "Straits Settlements" only, and departures included only Indians.

Source:  United Nations, Population Division, *Sex and Age of International Migrants: Statistics for 1918-1947* (New York, 1953), Table 62. See also United Nations, Population Division, "International Migrations in the Far East during Recent Times," *Population Bulletin*, No. 1 (December 1951) and No. 2 (October 1952).

--------

[12]See I. B. Taeuber, *Population of Japan* (Princeton, 1958), Chapter 7.

[13]That is to say, we can ascertain the general adequacy of the census, the accuracy of its age reporting, and perhaps certain of its idiosyncrasies (see 3:9).  It is not practicable to test the place-of-birth statistics directly.  If the census data are judged otherwise satisfactory, the place-of-birth information probably may be accepted without serious reservation.

a direct measurement of migration, since they do not indicate the number who moved during a given period. Hence they do not provide a "rate" of migration.[14] A considerable (but unknown) period may have elapsed between the migration and the census date; this period can be no longer than the age of a particular cohort of people, which means that cross-classification by age is very helpful extra information. Used as statistics of net migration, place-of-birth data have two principal "leaks": there is no record of multiple moves by the same persons (whether known migrants had moved more than once, or whether some who once moved are not detected because they returned to the place of birth).

These limitations are not always serious if they are recognized and taken into account in drawing conclusions about migration. Used with caution, place-of-birth statistics of a census have potentially the greatest wealth of information about migration that has ever been available.

### TABLE 8:2

### MIGRATION BETWEEN CIVIL DIVISIONS,[a]
### ACCORDING TO PLACE-OF-BIRTH STATISTICS IN MEXICO
(Census of 1950)

| Place of Residence | Place of Birth | | | |
|---|---|---|---|---|
| | Same Subdivision[a] | Other Subdivision[a] | Total Born in Mexico | Born in Foreign Countries |
| Entire Country | 22,293,679 | 3,314,631 | 25,608,310 | 182,707 |
| Federal District | 1,600,218 | 1,385,037 | 2,985,255 | 65,187 |
| Yucatán | 507,491 | 7,992 | 515,483 | 1,416 |

[a] Here the term "subdivision" refers to States (28), Territories (3), and one Federal District of Mexico in 1950. See text, 8:6.

Source: Mexico, Population Census of 1950, *Resumen General*, Table 5 (Mexico City, 1953).

---

[14] Though by very laborious rearrangement and estimations, they may offer useful approximations. See E. S. Lee *et al.*, *Population Redistribution and Economic Growth, United States, 1870-1950*, Volume 1: Part 1, *Migration Estimates*, (Philadelphia, 1957).

Where place-of-birth statistics are lacking, similar conclusions can sometimes be reached from census data classified by nationality or ethnic groups. Whereas statistics by place of birth indicate migrants only indirectly (by means of the *survivors* of migrant groups), statistics by ethnic origin are not migration data at all. However, they do refer to groups that may be composed predominantly of migrants — "Japanese" in Brazil, "Koreans" in Japan, "Indians" in Malaya — wherever these groups have remained distinct in the populations to which they have migrated. Ethnic-origin tables give a poorer record of migration when they include the descendants of immigrants (born in the place of residence) classified together with the original migrants. Furthermore, by this classification immigrant groups tend to lose some members who merge in the general population.

"Ethnic origin" or "national origin" is an indefinite census category, while the category of "foreign-born" is always definite. Both provide valuable information about the effects of immigration (see 8:10), though it is not the same information in both cases.

## 8:7 The Volume of Migration:  Indirect Measurement (Census and Vital Statistics)

Even without transit or place-of-birth statistics, we can get an approximate view of migration from ordinary census and vital statistics if these meet certain requirements. There must be two censuses not too many years apart, and all the data must be comparable in scope, accuracy and territorial divisions. Under favorable circumstances the approximation may be very close, so close as to be as good as actual statistics of migrants. These indirect procedures are best suited to analysis of *internal* movement. For the sake of simplicity we shall explain them on the assumption that there is no external migration; migrants to or from a country can be taken into account with some additional trouble.

The various measurements of this kind are all fundamentally the same. The gain or loss of population between two censuses is first calculated for each subdivision of the country (see 2:8). The portion due to births or to mortality is removed, by adding and subtracting the registered births and deaths (or an estimate thereof). The remaining change is attributed to migration in each subdivision. It is the migration of a definite period (the period between censuses); but it represents only the *net* migration, and not both the origins and destinations of any group of migrants.

A crude approximation is secured very simply. By assuming that the rate of natural increase is nearly the same in the major parts of the country, we may attribute the observed inequalities of growth wholly to migration. This yields a quick and convenient indication of the *relative* gain or loss of migrants by each subdivision. If the rates of natural increase differ, this procedure may give a distorted picture of migration. But it is often sufficient as a rough index, especially at a preliminary stage of inquiry.

A much closer approximation is secured by adding and subtracting the numbers of registered births and deaths to remove the effect of natural increase. The gain or loss that remains is an estimate of net migration between the censuses. However, some attention must be given to the accuracy of the birth and death statistics. Any omission or bias in these registration figures is transmitted directly to the estimates of migration. These estimates may be no more accurate than the crude estimates above.

Finally, if the period between censuses is 5 years or some multiple of 5 years, the net intercensal migrants of each subdivision can be estimated at each age and sex. This is a large gain of information and worth the extra work involved. A cohort is identified by means of 5-year or 10-year age groups in the two census populations. For example, the group between ages 15-19 in 1940 was 25-29 in 1950. By removing the estimated deaths of this cohort in the intervening period, we can attribute a discrepancy between its expected size and its actual size in 1950 to the net effect of migration. In this manner we obtain estimates of the (net) numbers of migrants between 1940 and 1950, by their ages in 1950 and by sex.[15] Note that births may be ignored in dealing with the population over 10 years of age in 1950; they do not enter into cohorts that were already born. Given adequate census data by age and sex (which must be assumed[16]), the accuracy of these estimates depends on the accuracy of the estimated effect of *mortality* on each cohort.

It is seldom practicable to use the statistics of registered deaths for this purpose. Either of two simple estimating procedures is available, both based on the assumption of equal age-specific mortality in all sections of the country.

---

[15] It is scarcely worth while to go to such trouble unless males and females are treated separately.

[16] As illustrated below (Table 8:3), this calculation is identical with the test for accuracy described in 3:9. In other words, the same result may be attributed either to defects of data or to migration. In either case, the choice is a matter of assumption. Obviously this is an inappropriate test of accuracy when there has been migration, and a poor way to estimate migration where defects are suspected. An appraisal of census data by age and by subdivision, and a general knowledge of migratory currents of the country help in formulating assumptions that are reasonable.

a. The loss of people from each cohort in a province or district can be estimated from the loss from the corresponding cohort in the total population. This is expressed as a ratio of cohort size in two censuses, for example, $\dfrac{\text{a cohort in 1950}}{\text{the same cohort in 1940}}$ (see also 3:9).

If there was no external migration (or very little) during this period, by 1950 the group of ages 15-19 in a subdivision of the 1950 population should be reduced by nearly the same degree as the group of ages 15-19 in the entire country. In Table 8:3, the ratios of cohort size in Brazil are shown for each 10-year age group in 1950 (Column 4; data by 5-year groups would be preferable if available). Then, to calculate the gain or loss of migrants in the Federal District, these ratios are applied to the 1940 population of the District (each age

TABLE 8:3

ESTIMATION OF NET MIGRANTS TO THE FEDERAL DISTRICT IN BRAZIL, 1940 - 1950, BY AGE IN 1950 (MALES ONLY)

(Based on census data)[a]

| (1) | (2) | (3) | (4) | (5) | (6) | (7) | (8) |
|---|---|---|---|---|---|---|---|
| | Total Country | | | Federal District | | | |
| Age in 1950 | Census Population 1940[b] | Census Population 1950 | Ratios of Cohort Size (3)/(2) | Census Population 1940 | "Expected" Population 1950 (5)×(4) | Census Population 1950 | Estimated Net Migration 1940 to 1950 (7)-(6) (thousands) |
| 10-19 | 6,179,477 | 5,809,235 | .94009 | 179,800 | 169,028 | 216,242 | 47.2 |
| 20-29 | 4,839,884 | 4,414,772 | .91216 | 170,206 | 155,255 | 248,659 | 93.4 |
| 30-39 | 3,485,153 | 3,145,715 | .90260 | 179,670 | 162,170 | 183,872 | 21.7 |
| 40-49 | 2,466,499 | 2,246,107 | .91065 | 150,175 | 136,757 | 137,903 | 1.1 |
| 50-59 | 1,789,582 | 1,360,580 | .76028 | 101,877 | 77,455 | 83,104 | 5.6 |
| 60-69 | 1,053,453 | 728,802 | .69182 | 59,836 | 41,396 | 41,597 | 0.2 |
| 70-79 | 524,655 | 247,755 | .47222 | 24,561 | 11,598 | 11,902 | 0.3 |

[a] Neglecting the effect of some migration from abroad during this decade, and a difference in the date of the two censuses (the 1940 census was dated September 1, the 1950 census July 1). People who did not state their ages are omitted.

[b] Advanced 10 years of age.

Sources: Censo Demográfico (1950), Distrito Federal (Rio de Janeiro, 1951); Instituto Brasileiro de Geografia e Estatística, Análises Críticas de Resultados dos Censos Demográficos (1956), p. 88.

group), yielding an "expected" population over age 10 in 1950 (Column 6; see also 3:9). The discrepancy between the "expected" population and the census population is assumed to represent migration, in or out (Column 8). The result is an estimate of net migration between census dates, by age and sex of migrants, between ages 10 and 80. These are the ages of most migration. They are also the ages at which an erroneous assumption about mortality is least likely to distort the results. Unless a total estimate of migration is desired, migrants below age 10 and above age 80 usually may be ignored.[17]

b. The effect of mortality on each cohort can also be estimated by means of a life table. This procedure is just as simple, merely the application of survival ratios[18] corresponding to the ages through which each cohort passes between the censuses. A set of these survival ratios would yield an "expected" population by age and sex in 1950 in the absence of migration. As before, the discrepancies between the expected population and the observed population serve as estimates of migration by age and sex. A life table that does not fit the facts, of course, will not give an accurate estimate (see 3:9).

The numbers of migrants may also be estimated by going backward in time from the census of 1950 (see Table 3:2). Actually, neither procedure is completely rigorous, for both of them allocate incorrectly the effect of mortality among the people who migrated. The flaw is slightly different in the two cases. Where the net balance of

---

[17] Table 8:3 provides no estimate of migrants below 10 years of age, for they were born after 1940. If desired, these figures can be calculated by treating registered births in the same manner of Table 3:3. But at these ages it may be advisable to make some allowance for different levels of mortality in different sections of the country.

Table 8:3 also provides no estimate of migrants in the highest age group (age 80 and above in 1950). Hence this procedure does not yield a *total* number of migrants, except by special assumptions at the highest and lowest ages. (It may be assumed that people over age 80 in the Federal District, for example, were distributed by age according to the pattern of the total population, or the population of some other country.) But nearly all migration falls in the middle range of ages, and this information *is* provided by Table 8:3.

[18] A survival ratio represents the proportion of survivors in a cohort from one age to another according to the mortality of the life table. It is multiplied by the number of people in the cohort at the earlier date; the product is the "expected" number surviving at the later date. Generally speaking, the survival ratio is $L_{x+10}/L_x$. For the age group 15-19 in 1940, it might be calculated $L_{27}/L_{17}$. See 5:5.

migration (in either direction) is small, the error from this source is likely to be small.[19]

After these estimates of migration are complete, it is not clear just how "rates" of migration by age and sex should be computed. Since the estimates pertain to the separate cohorts (from which they were derived), they might be expressed as ratios at the beginning or the end of the period — that is, ratios to the population by age and sex at the first census, or at the second. (The migrants attributed to the cohort of ages 15-19 in 1940, of course, should be attributed to the age group 25-29 in 1950, owing to the advance in this cohort's ages.) Strictly speaking, in order to be consistent with the notion of a vital-statistics rate, we should compute a "rate of migration" with a denominator representing the number of person-years lived by the cohort during the period (see 2:14). This number of person-years is customarily calculated from the mid-point between the numbers of people present at the beginning and at the end of the period.[20]

In practice, however, it matters very little how the ratios are computed, since they are usually intended for comparisons among themselves, not with data of other countries. For this purpose it is not even necessary to compute a vital-statistics rate of "migration per person-year"; a simple ratio of net migrants to the appropriate age groups is sufficient.

Errors in the numerator — the estimated numbers of migrants — are a greater problem. These numbers are secured by comparing data of two separate censuses, perhaps together with some mortality data. All of these figures contain some inaccuracies; and all inconsistencies are concentrated on the estimates of migration. Even if no large defects are apparent from an inspection of these data, there may be unsuspected errors in the resulting estimates for subdivisions of a country.[21] If gross defects have been found in the census data, these

---

[19] For detailed discussion of these problems, see D. S. Thomas, *Research Memorandum on Migration Differentials* (New York, 1938), Appendices.

[20] For example, the number of person-years lived by the age group 15-19 from 1940 to 1950 would be approximately half the combined size of this group in 1940 and the 25-29 group in 1950, times 10, the number of years intervening.

[21] For example, censuses which allocate the population by usual place of residence ("de jure population") may give results that are very different from those of a census based strictly on place of enumeration ("de facto population"). Migration estimates derived from one "de jure" census and one "de facto" census may be definitely spurious. It is obvious that conclusions about migration are more secure if the census enumerations were consistent in allocating people to places within the country.

indirect estimates are inappropriate for those age groups or sections of a country that are affected.

## 8:8 Special Surveys

In many social surveys it has been possible to inquire about past migration of the people surveyed. On a sample basis more detailed information can be secured; the questions may touch on the duration of stay in the place of present residence, and perhaps on intermediate moves before arrival there. Such data are basically the same as place-of-birth statistics, with the advantage that more information about each person can be gathered from a sample survey. With adequate planning these data can be made to give a comprehensive picture of past movement of the sample population. The smaller scale and expense of a sample survey permits more detail in the cross-tabulations of migrants by personal characteristics.[22]

## 8:9 The Redistribution of Population

The principal effect of migration follows directly from the nature of the process. Since a net migration is a transfer of people from one place to another, it redistributes the population of any territory. In many instances the changing distribution of population is of greater interest than the migration itself, for it adds to the problems of public policy. Viewed from the opposite side, programs of economic development also tend to increase the movement of persons from place to place, contributing to the volume of migration.

The distribution of people among the subdivisions of a country is indicated by almost any census or register of the population. For administrative reasons these sub-totals are the first statistics to be tabulated. The distribution may also be described in terms of ratios of the "density" of people to the total land area, housing facilities, capacity of public transportation, cultivated land, or any other peculiarly local feature of importance for human activities (see 2:7).

To describe a change in this distribution requires at least two different points of observation, at different times (see 7:4). A changing allocation of people is also a redistribution of their activities, and so it is associated with many sorts of economic and social change. Hence we often wish to compare the statistics of migration with the indices of social, economic and technical change.

---

[22]Survey data may provide useful statistics of migration even where no census data have been available for many years. See H. J. Heeren (ed.), "The Urbanization of Djakarta," *Ekonomi dan keuangan Indonesia*, November, 1955 [Reprint, in English], pp. 1-43.

In addition, two aspects of a changing distribution of population receive special attention:  the worldwide trend of urban growth, and changes of the composition of the population.

## 8:10  Migration and Changing Composition of the Population

Migration is selective.  It does not transfer entire populations (except on very rare occasions), but favors only certain categories of people.  Since these represent elements removed from the sending population and added to the receiving population, the redistribution by migration is also a change in the composition of population at both places.

These effects can be described in either the place of origin or the place of destination; or (to a limited extent) in actual transit statistics.  In order to find what contribution is made by migration, it is necessary to identify the migrants in the statistics and ascertain their composition separately; many changes are attributable to events within an area and are not directly related to migration.  Data about the composition of migrant groups in a population are rare.  The indirect estimations of net migration by age and sex (8:7) are peculiarly valuable because they furnish this much detail when no other information is at hand.

A great deal of statistical evidence about the characteristics of migrant and non-migrant populations must be adapted from data which pertain to ethnic or national communities — that is, to groups of earlier migrants (and their descendants) who have remained distinct at their destination.  This material is very commonly found in census tables.  It does not, however, separate very accurately the migrant and non-migrant groups.  Not all migrants do remain apart, and the categories become somewhat blurred by intermarriage; the age structure is soon altered completely if descendants are classified together with their parents.  But such figures, more often than place-of-birth tables, have the cross-tabulations needed to describe the composition of migrant groups.

Though ethnic or national communities in a population are not quite the same as migrant groups, they reveal many effects of migration.  The use of these materials is purely descriptive.  The available figures are assembled so as to compare the composition of migrant groups with the composition of the rest of the population.  In livelihood, language, levels of literacy and age structure[23] they sometimes keep their special characteristics for a considerable time.

---

[23]This information becomes less useful as the groups replenish themselves by natural increase.

There is always an element of doubt about the actual meaning of such census classifications; but census data furnish the most comparable source of information, item by item, about these population groups.[24]

It is when a comparison goes beyond the use of census data that it encounters most difficulties.  Birth rates and death rates for different ethnic communities, for example, are subject to unpredictable errors, owing to lack of precise agreement in the classification of vital registration and the census.  Comparisons of data from more than one census, like ratios of growth for ethnic or nationality groups, are easily distorted by inconsistent census practice.  All comparisons of this sort are affected by differences of sex and age composition; therefore they should be conducted separately by age and sex.[25]

### 8:11  Migration and the Growth of Cities

The most consistent pattern in migratory currents today is a rural-urban drift of population.  That share of a country's migration that does not open new areas to agriculture now goes to towns and cities.  Cities have broader fields of employment and a newer way of life than rural areas.  And these attractions often coincide with rural distress, which helps to induce people to move.

These factors are closely related to the location of modern industry.  There is more gain from commerce and manufacturing in urban areas, and little room for farming, and so cities have become predominantly sites of non-agricultural activities.  Consequently cityward migration is a normal accompaniment of industrial development.  In industrializing countries the growth of city populations is commonly the

---

[24]Naturally the boundaries of these groups are indistinct.  The classification of people will therefore vary according to the criteria adopted in the planning of a census, and according to habits of thought among the census takers who do the classifying.  Ethnic groups are often classified differently in successive censuses; consequently their composition is inconsistently reported.  Since the categories themselves are indefinite, there is no remedy for these defects, though the worst can be avoided by a cautious and skeptical attitude toward these data.

[25]For some purposes it is sufficient to apply the percentage-distributions (by occupation, marital status, etc.) at each age to a "standard" population (see 5:16), in order to present the results more easily by reducing the detail of the material.  Standardized percentages have a doubtful advantage in most cases, and incur a definite loss of information.  They are inadvisable until one is thoroughly familiar with the implications of the procedure and the peculiarities of the data under study.

most conspicuous of all population movements.[26]

Removal to cities is migration, as is the transfer of people elsewhere. The growth of a city is measured in the same manner as the growth of population in any other place. The study of urban migration would present no new problems were it not for a few matters of definition. First there is the question, what is a city? The categories of "urban" and "rural" are fundamentally vague. They sometimes refer to any political unit larger than some arbitrary figure (say, 2,500) in population, and sometimes just to subdivisions having a certain type of municipal administration. The criteria not only vary by country; they may be inconsistent at different times in the same country.[27] Some cities, moreover, are more "urban" than others. The only solution is to adopt some reasonable standard — for example, "cities of 50,000 people or more" or "cities of municipal rank, comprising. . ." — and to state clearly what it is, recognizing that the nature of the standard will be an arbitrary influence in the results. It is meaningless just to separate places into the groups "urban" and "rural."

Unfortunately some of these inconsistencies are nearly always present. They cannot be overlooked in comparisons of city populations at different dates. One must make some effort to put such materials into comparable form. Since population statistics are usually tabulated according to the *current* political status of each place, the different tables must be reconciled by reference to subdivisions of the cities themselves, consolidating or removing the data necessary to permit an accurate comparison. No special procedures are required, though it is sometimes necessary to estimate the age and sex

---

[26] A good deal of international migration is also a form of rural-urban movement of people. The drawing power of large cities does not stop at national boundaries.

[27] There are frequent shifts in the boundaries and administrative organization of cities, especially during rapid growth. Hence a place listed as the same city may be (in reality) two different entities at different times, not properly comparable in statistical indices. The growth of a city's population is often exaggerated because an investigator has not taken the trouble to find that its area has been enlarged. Census data published for the "urban" category of population are seldom comparable at different dates, because new places have been classified as "cities." Even the criterion of city *size* is not always satisfactory, because the growth of population will eventually raise a city from one category to the next larger one. It is necessary to ascertain *which* places are represented in the urban population. Inconsistencies can then be reconciled in some fashion, as explained in the text.

composition of very small subdivisions.

After this is accomplished, the study of urban migration resolves itself into a few familiar topics — the contribution of migration to city growth, the origins and destinations of migrants, and the effects on the composition of city populations. The rest of the task is chiefly a matter of preparing the available statistical tables and describing their contents. In view of the typical circumstances of urban migration, however, there are some points which receive special emphasis.

Cities are capable of extremely rapid growth of population. Natural increase may contribute to this, but the greater part of rapid urban expansion consists of migrants. A trend toward an "urbanized" way of life depends on a rather large flow of migration, which has repercussions throughout a society. Hence it is important to weigh the various aspects of the case. Urban migration of course can be measured against the size of the city — expressed as a "rate" of migration or similar figure (or a series of age-specific rates). But rapid growth of a small urban population in a large rural region may be insignificant from the standpoint of migration in the rural area. Therefore we also compare the movement with changes outside the cities. One can calculate the proportional share of the observed net migration between subdivisions of a country that has gone to certain cities. The population in rural areas may be growing at the same time. Urban migration offsets some of the natural increase in rural areas; with the help of (reliable) vital statistics, we can calculate approximately how much of rural growth has been absorbed by cities. For the cities themselves (if their vital statistics are reliable) it is also of interest to calculate the proportion of their growth in a given period that is due to net migration.[28]

Urban migration tends to be the most selective. People usually go to cities for rather specific purposes. Especially in an industrializing agricultural region, the city offers a set of inducements that is peculiar to the urban environment. This is revealed in the distinctive occupational composition of city populations, and perhaps in the age and sex composition of the migration. Very often men in the younger working ages are preponderant in the early stages of urban growth. Where the population is already highly urban in its distribution, the

---

[28] It should be noted that the last three of these suggested indices refer to a specific period of time; the migration estimate must also refer to the same period. The proportional share of the observed migration that has gone to a particular destination can be calculated on any basis, provided that it is the same in the numerator as in the denominator (see 2:4).

migrations become more diverse in character. A great many moves are from city to city; in an urban culture, migration does not remain typically a rural-to-urban shift of population.

Finally, the drawing power of cities is also selective according to the place of origin, as shown by a distribution of urban migrants by place of birth. However, not all migrants to cities become permanent residents. There is a constant return movement of some people to rural areas or a further movement to other towns and cities, which most statistics of migration fail to reveal.

# CHAPTER 9

# MANPOWER AND WORKING ACTIVITIES[1]

Nearly every country needs some facts about the distribution of working activities among its people. Statistics of the size and composition of the working population reflect the social and economic conditions of livelihood. Economic programs contain, at least implicitly, some allocations of manpower in various pursuits, and these plans require an inventory of the country's manpower resources.

Getting good statistics of economic activity is a large task; it is, perhaps, the most troublesome aspect of a modern census. Analyzing these data is wholly descriptive. It involves no special questions of technique, but consists of separating the numbers into the categories that are given, and comparing them. In other words, it depends on the *classification* of working activities, and this is the source of the major problems of analysis. Hence the study of manpower patterns is concerned chiefly with the procedures followed in collecting the information. These are beyond the control of the analyst, and vary from case to case; here we can only summarize some of the general features and the topics of research to which they are related.

## 9:1 Sources of Data

A country's resources of manpower are found, of course, among its people. The term "manpower" refers to the number of actual or potential workers in a population. It is measured in units of persons, not units of work. Because there are continual changes in people's working activities, it is necessary to count them all at some particular time, as nearly as possible at the same moment or short period. For this reason census data are generally preferable, since this is

---

[1]Some of this material was previously published as the paper, "Demographic Aspects of Manpower in the Far East," in *Population Bulletin of the United Nations* No. 5, pp. 28-33 (New York, 1956).

262

the sort of information that a census provides.[2] Virtually the same data are sometimes secured by a sample survey, when its design is similar to that of a census.

A census contributes in two ways to the analysis of manpower. It classifies people according to economic activity, and provides a total population figure against which to measure the size of the economically active portion. It is essential that everyone in the population should be brought into the classification, and this is another reason why census-type data are so appropriate.[3]

Classification of economic activity in most census statistics has two stages: determining whether a person works (is "economically active") or not, and showing what sort of work (or non-working activity) he does. These facts can be secured by a few questions on the census schedule — as few as one or two, depending on what definition of economic activity is adopted. The mere recording of this valuable information is very easy. The principal task is the preparation of standards and instruction of enumerators (a complicated and delicate matter), and cross-tabulating these data with other characteristics of the enumerated persons (a very expensive process).[4]

## 9:2 Definitions of Economic Activity

It is not easy, however, to set up a scheme for determining which people are "economically active" and which people are not. This implies a standard for judging what activities constitute "productive work," and some consistent criteria to judge what degree of performance is sufficient to class a person as "active."

It is probably true that most people fall clearly into one category or the other. But in every country there are many who do not fit

---

[2]See 1:4. Other sources are useful for more limited purposes. Factory and trade union statistics, records of employment offices or unemployment insurance, all contain information about *parts* of the working population. They represent specially selected parts, however, and are less comprehensive than a census.

[3]Even census data on manpower are distorted if very many people are omitted. Exclusion of substantial groups like military forces, labor camps or plantation workers may reduce or nullify the value of certain conclusions from these data.

[4]The publication of census statistics of economic activity is so expensive that it is sometimes curtailed for the sake of economy. Without cross-tabulations with other personal characteristics, however, they lose most of their usefulness.

easily into either. Those working in family enterprises, especially if their efforts are part-time and unpaid, are among the most difficult to classify. The application of the scheme to every member of a population involves endless problems of detail, which have to be solved by rules that are equally detailed. No set of rules is really satisfactory for all cases. Through long experience in census-taking, certain definitions have been found to give good results.[5]

There have been two main types of standard to define what is and what is not economic activity. The first is to ask each person what is his usual occupation, or "gainful work," without inquiring exactly when the work was done. According to this approach, the economically active are simply those who report some usual occupation in the census (sometimes referred to as the "gainfully occupied"). As a precaution against careless or inconsistent reporting, specific rules may apply to borderline cases, especially defining typical cases to be classed as "not occupied" (for example, persons "living on income," inmates of special institutions, students, etc.). With this same information, each economically active person also can be classified according to the nature of his occupation.

The other type of standard defines the economically active population as the "labor force." This represents the number of people actually at work (or seeking work) during some particular short period. It is, of course, more complex to administer. Like the standard of the "gainfully occupied," the measurement of the labor force requires rules of classification to determine who should be considered economically active and who should not, but the stated time period supplies a more definite criterion. More than one question is required on the census schedule, the actual number depending on the nature of the subsidiary information desired.[6] An extra category is sometimes distinguished: the numbers of "unemployed," or people not actively

---

[5]In addition to the census standards of economic activity developed by individual countries, the subject has come under review by international agencies. See, for example, United Nations, *Application of International Standards to Census Data on the Economically Active Population*, Population Studies No. 9, New York, 1951. See also R. Luna-Vegas, "Notes Regarding the Improvement of Census Standards on the Economically Active Population," *Proceedings of the World Population Conference, 1954*, Volume 4, pp. 729-738 (New York, 1955); and R. García-Frías and O. A. de Moraes, "Determinación de la Población Economicamente Activa, con Fines de Comparabilidad Internacional," Estadística,Vol. 46 (June 1955), pp. 211-219.

[6]See United Nations, *Application of International Standards . . . ,* *Population Studies* No. 9, New York, 1951, pp. 14-17.

working at the stated date, but "seeking work." (The "unemployed" are tabulated separately, but usually treated as a sub-class of the economically active because they are only temporarily out of work.)

Thus, although the information is collected at approximately the same time for everyone in the population, it refers to work performed at some other time. For the "labor force" the date of employment must be exactly specified, but for the "gainfully occupied" the basis of classification is the usual or customary role of each person during some indefinite period. This is the clearest distinction between the two standards.[7]

Both types of definition are found throughout the world. The standard of the "labor force" has been developed fairly recently. It would be inaccurate to say positively that one or the other is "better." Where an individual's occupation is a fairly steady status and changes are not frequent, the real situation may be more accurately reflected by the notion of the "gainfully occupied"; with the more definite standard of the "labor force," there is some doubt about the reliability of replies — in particular, "unemployment" as defined above is a rather indistinct category in most countries. Obviously, a census question about the usual or customary occupation is easier to administer, requiring less supervision.

Where wage labor is common, where changes of occupation are frequent and the periods of employment are fairly definite, the "labor force" is a more sensitive measure of fluctuations in the *volume* of employment, enabling us to separate the people who are temporarily not working. The numbers of "gainfully occupied" provide a poor gauge of the volume of employment during times of rapid change, because people report an occupation once held when they no longer engage in it. Hence the notion of the "labor force" is most useful in relatively industrial countries.

The two standards reflect different conceptions of the nature of economic activity. They both describe the same situation somewhat differently, though this depends also on other factors besides the type of definition (on the quality of administrative organization for a census, for example). All statistics of the economically active population therefore contain many arbitrary elements. It is imperative to find out what these elements are — how the census was planned, and what criteria were adopted. However, it should not be overlooked in discussing their relative merits that these two standards often

---

[7]However, an actual census may be intermediate between the two. See United Nations, *op. cit.*, p. 5.

give very similar results in the way they classify the economically active.[8]

Both standards are based on the notion of an "economically active" population as the group to be counted and classified. There is of course an advantage in following a fairly uniform practice, in order to be able to compare the evidence in one country with that of another. However, other classifications of economic activities have been devised. The censuses of India follow a different scheme; in 1951, for example, the population was separated into "self-supporting persons," "earning dependents," and "non-earning dependents." It is an interesting experiment and has considerable merit; but the results are not comparable with data on the economically active population elsewhere, and therefore cannot readily be appraised in relation to other evidence.

### 9:3 Factors Determining Labor Supply

The portion of the population that is "economically active" is very similar in most countries. Full-time work is concentrated in early and middle adulthood. The very young and very old do not follow regular occupations (except to a minor extent), but are dependent on the support of others. Hence the people between these two extremes are the group from which the supply of labor is drawn.

It is conventional to treat the number of people from 15 to 64 years of age as the group supplying the bulk of the economically active, calling it the "population of working ages."[9] (This age interval actually includes most — but not all — people who report an occupation.) Using this convention we can make crude comparisons of manpower resources, including cases which lack statistics on economic activities, or countries whose occupational statistics are not comparable. The size of this group in relation to the rest of the population shows some of the conditions which age structure imposes on the livelihood of a population (see the first column of percentages in Table 9:1).

In countries of relatively high fertility, which gain large numbers of younger people each year, the age structure is weighted with

---

[8]This is very fortunate, because such a classification is inherently arbitrary (regardless of the particular standard adopted). There is no hypothetically "correct" line separating the economically active from the rest of the population. The distinction itself is an artificial element introduced by the census.

[9]This corresponds to the usage of "women of childbearing ages," discussed in 2:17.

a large proportion of children too young to work (and of course with some people who are too old). In the first four countries of Table 9:1, the people aged 15-64 range from 53 to 59 per cent of the total population.[10] By contrast, in lower-fertility countries (represented by France and the United States in Table 9:1), a much greater majority of the population is found in these ages of most productive work, and the age structure places a smaller burden of dependency on those who are working. This is also expressed somewhat differently by the ratios in the next column of Table 9:1 (persons of "dependent" ages per 100 persons of working ages), calculated from the same data. In the United States, for example, where in 1950 there were 55 persons in the "dependent" ages per 100 aged 15-64, it is evident that age structure is more favorable to effective use of people in productive activities.

These illustrations show just the effect of age structure on the degree of dependency. The burden in every country is heavy; the

## TABLE 9:1

## POPULATION OF "WORKING AGES" (15-64)

### (Census Data)[a]

| Country and Year | Per Cent 15-64 to Total Population | Ratios: Persons of "Dependent" Ages per 100 Persons of "Working Ages" | Distribution of People 15-64 | |
|---|---|---|---|---|
| | | | Per Cent 39 and Below | Per Cent 40 and Above |
| Philippines, 1948 | 52.7 | 90 | 75 | 25 |
| Mexico, 1950 | 54.9 | 82 | 70 | 30 |
| India, 1951 | 58.4 | 71 | 67 | 33 |
| Egypt, 1947 | 58.8 | 70 | 66 | 34 |
| Canada, 1951 | 61.9 | 62 | 61 | 39 |
| France, 1954 | 64.6 | 55 | 51 | 49 |
| United States, 1950 | 65.0 | 55 | 58 | 42 |

[a] Based only on those persons classified by age.

[10] Of the people of "dependent ages," those age 65 and over are a small share of the total population — between 3 and 5 per cent in the same countries. They are exceeded by many times by the younger group, under age 15, which is responsible for the main burden of dependency.

variation is chiefly a result of the past history of birth and death rates in each case (see 7:9). Though the size of these age groups sets a maximum limit to the number of workers available at any moment,[11] other factors help to determine the number who are actually working. To appreciate the actual resources of a country's potential manpower, it is necessary to examine other aspects of its composition which affect the utilization of the total. These fall under two main headings: the age and sex composition of the "population of working ages," and the extent of working activities among the men and the women at each age.

### 9:4 Differences by Sex

In most of the world livelihood is considered to be primarily a male responsibility. This division of labor gives predominantly to men the duties and the title of providing support for their families. It does not mean that men are the only ones who work; however, they do most of the work classed as "economic activity" in any census, especially when such activity is carried on outside the household.

The work of women is normally conducted on a different basis. It is also regarded differently, and is less often reported as gainful employment in census or survey returns. Though increasing, wage labor by women is still not very common in most countries, especially in the rural sections. During much of their adulthood women are fully engaged in duties of housekeeping and nurture of children, which may require a large output of effort but do not enter the occupational statistics. Census data are very difficult to interpret on this point, and are often misleading if taken at face value.

Table 9:2 shows some returns of the economically active in several countries, and is sufficient to indicate that such data are inadequate to measure the activity of men and women in the same terms. The reporting for women, moreover, is variable from country to country, and from place to place within a country. For this reason statistics of the economically active population are usually studied for males alone. Occupation data for women should generally be excluded before comparing the distribution of working activities in different places or population groups; if desired, they can be analyzed with profit as a separate topic.

---

[11] For further comparisons of manpower resources in relation to age structure of various countries, see J. D. Durand, "Population Structure as a Factor in Manpower and Dependency Problems of Under-Developed Countries," in United Nations, *Population Bulletin of the United Nations, No. 3*, New York, October 1953.

Besides the different standards of economic activity for men and for women, countries do not all assign the same lower age limit to the working population. Some recognize any occupation that is reported; others instruct their enumerators to disregard the reported occupation of anyone under age 14, 11, 10 or other age.[12] Therefore the figure for the total working population, even separated by sex as in Table 9:2, often refers to an arbitrarily limited group which varies between countries. This inconsistency can be avoided by using data by age groups.

## 9:5 Employment and Age

The extent of some pursuit of livelihood follows a typical pattern by age. This is shown by the percentages of economically active[13] in Table 9:3. Between about 25 and 50 years of age nearly all

### TABLE 9:2

## ECONOMICALLY ACTIVE POPULATION
### Per Cent of Total Population, by Sex (All Ages)

(Census Data)

| Country and Year | Males | Females | Standard of Economic Activity | Lower Age Limit |
|---|---|---|---|---|
| Philippines, 1948[a] | 46.0 | 13.9 | (labor force) | 10 |
| Mexico, 1950 | 56.8 | 8.7 | (usual occupation) | 12 |
| Ceylon, 1946 | 57.8 | 18.2 | ( ''        '' ) | 10 |
| Egypt, 1947 | 66.7 | 9.1 | ( ''        '' ) | 5 |
| Japan, 1950 | 54.7 | 33.0 | (labor force) | 14 |
| Canada, 1951 | 58.4 | 16.9 | ( ''      '' ) | 14 |
| Ireland, 1951 | 62.9 | 22.3 | ( ''      '' ) | 14 |

[a] 1,638,624 "housewives," added by the census authorities to the total of economically active women, have been removed.

[12] See United Nations, Population Division and Statistical Office, *Population Census Methods* (Lake Success, N.Y., 1949), p. 110.

[13] These proportions of participation in economic activity by age are often called "labor force participation rates." They do not, however, represent a number of events happening in a given period. Since they are no more

men report some regular occupation. Such statistics yield very similar percentages for almost all countries, notwithstanding wide variations that exist in economic life. In a few cases the percentages are exceptionally high or exceptionally low (for example, in Costa Rica and the United States in Table 9:3). Here it is advisable to look for inconsistencies of census practice.

The principal differences in the proportion of men working for a living are found, first, among the young who are commencing work, and among the old who are in the course of retirement. The proportion of males at ages 15 to 24 engaged in some occupation varies rather widely; the difference becomes very striking when the groups aged 10-14 are compared. In predominantly agricultural countries, the pressure of necessity forces young men to go to work more often at an early age, while in industrial regions the entry into an occupation has gradually been delayed.

At older ages, it is usually the case that people retire from work earlier in industrial countries (see Table 9:3). These differences, too, may be due partly to varying statistical definitions of economic activity.[14] Largely, however, the pattern reflects the nature of the work, which permits older people to linger on in agriculture and related occupations after their period of maximum productivity is over. In small-scale farming, for example, there are many tasks that can be performed adequately, perhaps not efficiently, by older workers, delaying their full retirement.

The age pattern of participation in economic activity should be viewed in relation to the age structure of these populations. It is the countries at the greatest disadvantage in age structure that develop the pattern of early employment shown in Table 9:3. In other words, this is one way of offsetting part of the burden of dependency which they carry. Because large proportions of people are in the young age groups, a fairly small increase of the percentage employed between, say, ages 10 and 14 produces a *large* increase in actual number employed. (By the same argument, variation in percentages economically active at higher ages has rather little effect in the total number of people working.)

---

than proportions or percentage figures, there seems to be no need to call them anything but proportions or percentages. It is generally confusing to introduce a new term for such a purpose.

[14] There is a tendency for census data based on "usual occupations" to indicate larger proportions of workers at older ages than the "labor force" (see 9:2), because many people continue to report an occupation when they no longer are very active in it.

The influence of the age composition within the "working ages" is suggested by the last two columns of Table 9:1. Again the same countries are contrasted. In the "older" populations (illustrated by France and the United States), the people of working ages are older too. The economically active population would be young in the "younger" populations even if boys were not put to work at so early an age, for a large part of the group aged 15-64 is concentrated in the lower half of the interval.

By their large reservoirs of young workers and their practices of early employment, these countries achieve a balance between the numbers of economically active and dependents that compares favorably with many of the highly industrialized countries.[15] This numerical balance is achieved by mass employment of people without spe-

## TABLE 9:3

## PER CENT OF MALES ECONOMICALLY ACTIVE
### By Age, in Selected Countries

(Census Data)

| Age Group | Philippines 1948 | Ceylon 1946 | Costa Rica 1950 | United States 1950 | Turkey 1945 |
|---|---|---|---|---|---|
| 10-14 | 27.3 | 14.1 | 30.4[b] | 2.5[c] | 48.7[d] |
| 15-19 | 68.8 | 59.2 | 91.1 | 44.6 | 79.9 |
| 20-24 | 90.1 | 83.3 | 96.7 | 81.9 | 90.0 |
| 25-34 | 97.4 | 96.9 | 98.4 | 92.1 | 93.0 |
| 35-44 | 97.3 | 98.6 | 98.6 | 94.5 | 93.6 |
| 45-54 | 96.0 | 93.9[a] | 97.6 | 92.0 | 93.1 |
| 55-64 | 88.1 | 88.5[a] | 94.8 | 83.4 | 88.9 |
| 65 and over | 60.4 | 70.9[a] | 74.0 | 41.5 | 79.0 |

[a] Age groups are 45-59, 60-69, 70 and over.

[b] Census did not recognize economic activity of persons under age 12.

[c] Census did not recognize economic activity of persons under age 14.

[d] This percentage probably includes some boys under age 10 reported as economically active, but not tabulated separately.

[15] See J. D. Durand, "Population Structure as a Factor...," in United Nations, *Population Bulletin of the United Nations* No. 3, New York, October 1953, pp. 7-8.

cial skills, and inflicts its own cost in terms of low output per person. Successive groups of people entering the ages of economic activity are increasing each year, in a situation characterized by shortage of jobs rather than shortage of workers.

## 9:6  The Unoccupied Population

In studying the distribution of working activities, we must also go into the activities of the people of working ages who report no occupation. Unfortunately the statistics are neither complete nor reliable in most instances. Nevertheless it is helpful to consider the principal factors associated with non-work — education, infirmities, leisure and marital status — using whatever data may be available.

a. *Education.* There is one obvious reason for the early employment of males in predominantly agricultural regions and the later pattern in many industrial countries. Some of the years corresponding to those spent in early work in a rural region are spent elsewhere in education. Schooling is foremost among the activities keeping boys, and to a lesser extent girls, out of regular work. This is partly because it has become a customary expectation, but also because it is considered essential to the maintenance of an industrial economy based on high levels of specialized skill.

Whereas most agricultural countries probably could well afford, on a national scale, to withdraw a large part of their youth from work which is low in productivity, they can ill afford to provide similar training to age groups so large in proportion to the entire populations. With so many children, the cost of extending general education for even one year is very high, and it has appeared cheaper to provide employment than schooling. In a longer view of things, however, there is an increasing tendency to balance the cost of providing such training against the cost of not providing it, and the emphasis on public education in subjects of practical application may be expected to increase. This implies some shift in the pattern of early employment, and eventually a higher level of skill throughout the economically active population. The younger age groups are a very efficient route for introducing new skills into a young population.

b. *Infirmities.* In every population there are people afflicted with infirmities which prevent or curtail their working activities. Blindness, deafness, or protracted illness may make it impossible to follow a regular occupation; or, as some scattered census data on this subject suggest, may restrict them to agricultural work, where partial unemployment is more easily absorbed. Especially during past periods of less adequate medical services, infirmities have withdrawn some people of all working age groups from economic activity, and reduced the vigor and efficiency of others. Some ailments have a greater incidence with advancing age, and contribute to the pattern of retirement from work shown in Table 9:3. The available statistical material on the subject is scarce and not very reliable; special studies are probably necessary before the effects of infirmity can be fully appreciated.

c. *Leisure.* There are also people of working age whose wealth or social position enables them to abstain from work, through choice rather than necessity. Breakdowns of the economically inactive population in census data show some of them in the category of "living on income or rents." Such groups are fairly small in relation to the entire population. They should not be neglected on this account, for their influence in the economy may be disproportionately large owing to the resources that they control.

d. *Marital Status.* Marriage and family responsibilities are associated in various ways with participation in economic activity. Eventual marriage is almost universal in all countries. Among men, as we have seen, so is some form of occupation: the same social and economic pressures encourage both.

Women, on the other hand, often must choose between one and the other, for household duties and motherhood are incompatible with many occupations. As mentioned earlier, this does not prevent women from participating in the essential work of the economy, but it does interfere with their taking up work outside the home, particularly full-time wage labor. This conflict is often expressed in popular sentiments against wage employment of women away from the family, or in the feeling that certain occupations are simply not women's work.

In spite of this widespread prejudice against it, some employment of women is actually found in every country. There are various solutions to this conflict. In those places where women in considerable numbers have gone into regular factory, commercial or professional jobs, many have delayed marriage beyond the usual ages. Women also help on a part-time basis in producing articles made in household or "cottage" enterprises, or in agriculture, where their work can be added to other household duties. As their childbearing period ends, older women become more available for other work. Prejudice does not always prevent the hiring of women when their wages are lower than those of men. Even the family responsibilities of women, where they have begun to enter occupations outside the home, have become lighter, as attested by the lower birth rates of industrial areas. But where these responsibilities are still relatively heavy, they are a strong barrier to the greater use of women's efforts in productive pursuits.

## 9:7 Types of Economic Activity

Together with the distinction between the economically active and inactive, a census generally asks the type of occupation of each working person. Indeed, the expense of getting one sort of information is scarcely worth while unless the other is secured. The apparatus for getting this information ranges from a single item on a census schedule to a series of several closely related questions designed to provide more accurate classifications of people.[16]

This material has many uses. It describes something about the work of each individual, and these facts are valuable from a great many points of view. However, the arbitrary element in classifying the different types of economic activities is even larger than that in separating the economically active from the inactive. The categories are likewise artificial, since they do not correspond to distinct groups in the population. They are more numerous, and consequently involve more decisions in assigning each person to a class. There is no reliable way of judging the adequacy of these statistics when they have been tabulated.[17]

## 9:8 The Working Population by Type of Activity

Whether the economically active population is defined as persons reporting an occupation or as the labor force, its distribution by type of activity is closely related to the economic organization of a

---

[16] This subject has been given long and careful study. The discretionary judgments are usually centralized in the hands of the census office, where they can be kept more uniform than the opinions and guesses of field enumerators. It would be impossible to summarize briefly the large body of methods developed for this purpose. See United Nations, Population Division and Statistical Office, *Application of International Standards...*, Chapters 3-6.

[17] That is to say, there is no satisfactory standard of comparison for these figures. In taking a census, the most difficult decisions tend to be resolved by declaring an occupation to be unclassifiable (or just reported as "unknown"). Experience has shown that the category "other occupations" or "other industries" tends to receive a large share of all occupations. The advance planning of a census has the task of preventing this residual class from becoming a catch-all for all doubtful cases. Probably it should contain less than, say, 10 per cent of the total economically active population. If its share is larger, it is reasonable to assume that this part of the census has received poor supervision.

country. There are two ways of distinguishing the type of activity: the *occupation* of each individual (the actual type of work performed — farmer, bricklayer, lathe operator, or typist), or the *industry* where the person is employed (agriculture, building construction, machine shop, or banking institution).

The two kinds of classification are not the same. Some occupations can be performed in several industries. The industrial classification of workers does not always indicate what work they do. (Some highly organized building construction firms or farming enterprises, for example, employ large numbers of clerical and other workers.) This distinction should not be overlooked; ignoring it has very often led to confusion. Unfortunately, some censuses have not consistently used one kind or the other, but have adopted a mixture of the two; this also leads to confusion.

Naturally it is safest to compare the occupational structure of population groups (territorial subdivisions, or ethnic or nationality groups) recorded by the *same* census. A comparison for the same population at different dates is extremely valuable, for it indicates changes in the utilization of manpower. But it gives an accurate indication of these changes only if the census procedures have remained similar. The actual sets of categories, and sometimes the whole basis of classification, may be modified in successive censuses.[18]

The classifications vary widely among countries. Though comparisons between different countries are sometimes practicable, they must be confined to rather broad categories, and the data demand a minute search for inconsistencies.[19] Statistics from special surveys may occasionally be used in this way, but they are not likely to correspond very closely to any other set of figures.

A shifting distribution of manpower among very broad categories reveals only broad sorts of change. A stable pattern of distribution does not necessarily denote a lack of change. In Japan, where census data are available during the period of rapid development from

---

[18] At considerable cost, some countries prepare comparable tables showing what the results in one census would have been according to the criteria of the other. See Table 9:4.

[19] Even the broad categories of economic activity in different countries may not be comparable in their contents. It is not enough that they appear to be similar. International summaries — even the very useful collection in the *United Nations Demographic Yearbook* for 1956 (Tables 12 and 13) — are apt to be misleading because they lack the essential details to show what is contained in the broad categories.

1920 to 1950, the effect on the distribution of workers among the principal groups of industries has been less than one might expect (see Table 9:4).  Among economically active men, these major groupings reflect a decline in the proportion who were agricultural workers (44 per cent to 36 per cent), and varying degrees of increase in the share of workers in other fields.  (Whether a change is "large" or "small" depends to some extent on how it is viewed; the increased share of construction workers, from 4.2 per cent to 6.5 per cent, is small in relation to the total working population, but is 50 per cent greater than the proportional share before.  The increase in the actual *number* of male construction workers was 100 per cent, from 7 million in 1920 to over 14 million in 1950.)

Among women, the proportions reveal a much wider distribution of those employed outside agriculture in 1950; but those who reported an occupation were nearly as much concentrated in agriculture as before.  The number of women reported as engaged in construction work (for example) increased by 15 times by 1950.

However, the largest social and economic changes in Japan during this period took forms which are not apparent in the broad categories of Table 9:4.[20]  The situation in 1920 was already greatly different from that of one or two decades earlier.  As revealed in Table 9:4, the entire economically active population grew from 27 million to 35.6 million, and this is a change of large dimensions.

In the larger perspective of world affairs, what do such studies signify?  The occupational composition of the working population describes one of its solutions to the problems of livelihood.  Therefore a set of these figures indicates roughly one country's position in relation to the experience of other regions.[21]  Over half the regions of

---

[20]In this instance it is also possible to make a closer comparison, for Japan's Bureau of Statistics published an adjusted table for 1920 corresponding in greater detail to the classes of 1950 (see *Census of 1950*, Volume 8, Table 50).  For a very thorough analysis of manpower changes in Japan during this period, in its many aspects, see I. B. Taeuber, *Population of Japan* (Princeton, 1958) Chapter 5.

[21]See the series of articles by the International Labour Office, "The World's Working Population": "Some Demographic Aspects," *International Labour Review*, Vol. 73 (February, 1956), pp. 152-176; "Its Industrial Distribution," *International Labour Review*, Vol. 73 (May, 1956), pp. 501-521; "Its Distribution by Status and Occupation," *International Labour Review*, Vol. 74 (August, 1956), pp. 174-192.  See also United Nations, Economic and Social Council, "Progress Report on the Manpower Survey in Latin America" (New York, 1955, 39 pp.).

# TABLE 9:4

## DISTRIBUTION OF ECONOMICALLY ACTIVE POPULATION BY INDUSTRY

Japan, 1920 and 1950[a]

| Industry | Males | | Females | |
|---|---|---|---|---|
| | 1920 | 1950 | 1920 | 1950 |
| *A. Actual Numbers (thousands)* | | | | |
| Agriculture & Forestry | 7626 | 8171 | 6290 | 8356 |
| Fisheries | 490 | 615 | 37 | 66 |
| Mining | 324 | 525 | 96 | 66 |
| Construction | 710 | 1426 | 7 | 106 |
| Manufacturing | 2892 | 4042 | 1547 | 1648 |
| Commerce (wholesale & retail) | 1831 | 2406 | 819 | 1557 |
| Banking, Insurance, Real Estate | 118 | 241 | 13 | 122 |
| Transportation & Communication | 1068 | 1610 | 65 | 201 |
| Services | 864 | 1655 | 1068 | 1402 |
| Government | 564 | 1154 | 16 | 222 |
| Not Classifiable | 334 | 26 | 190 | 11 |
| Total, Economically Active | 16820 | 21870 | 10146 | 13755 |
| *B. Percentage Distribution* | | | | |
| Agriculture & Forestry | 45.3 | 37.4 | 62.0 | 60.7 |
| Fisheries | 2.9 | 2.8 | 0.4 | 0.5 |
| Mining | 1.9 | 2.4 | 1.0 | 0.5 |
| Construction | 4.2 | 6.5 | 0.1 | 0.8 |
| Manufacturing | 17.2 | 18.5 | 15.2 | 12.0 |
| Commerce (wholesale & retail) | 10.9 | 11.0 | 8.1 | 11.3 |
| Banking, Insurance, Real Estate | 0.7 | 1.1 | 0.1 | 0.9 |
| Transportation & Communication | 6.4 | 7.4 | 0.6 | 1.5 |
| Services | 5.1 | 7.6 | 10.5 | 10.2 |
| Government | 3.4 | 5.3 | 0.2 | 1.6 |
| Not Classifiable | 2.0 | 0.1 | 1.9 | 0.1 |
| Total, Economically Active | 100.0 | 100.1 | 100.1 | 100.1 |

a Being rounded, numbers will not always add to the totals shown.

*Note:* The original figures of 1920 were thoroughly rearranged by the Bureau of Statistics, at the most detailed stage of classification, so as to correspond to the industry categories of the 1950 census.

In 1920, workers were classified by usual occupation, including those at any age who reported an occupation; many ''unemployed'' persons are included. In 1950, the census used a *labor-force* standard. These figures represent the people (age 14 and over) classed as "employed" at the time of the census; ''unemployed'' persons are excluded. For a more exact comparison, the ''unemployed'' may be added to the data of 1950. (The census report contains a table for this purpose, showing unemployed persons who had worked before, according to their former type of employment.)

Source: Census of 1950, *Volume 8, Final Report,* Table 50.

the world are heavily dependent on agriculture, for example, and this is reflected in high proportions of the economically active reporting their type of work as farming.

A shift in the distribution of manpower away from this dependence on agriculture is rather easy to discern. Other changes, especially the development of nonagricultural types of work, are matters of greater detail, and they must be investigated in greater detail.[22]

A concentration of people working in agriculture has been associated with a low amount of product per worker. This situation is commonly found together with young age structure, and therefore high ratios of dependents to economically active, favorable to early employment of the young. Conducted on a small scale, agriculture also depends on traditional techniques which do not require formal education. It offers a way of caring for the aged and the infirm, giving them an opportunity to contribute slightly to their own support. Hence it has been known as a field where a large population can be maintained even though many of them are only partially employed – a field of "hidden unemployment." Permanently increased levels of living in agricultural countries require a shift of activities, away from farming and towards a larger share of more productive pursuits. In this regard, studies of changing occupational structure have a direct bearing on "economic development."

### 9:9  Distribution of Workers by "Status"

It is well recognized that in any particular industry there are different ways of engaging in economic activity. Some people have supervisory positions, some subordinate; some are employers of others, some employees. Some operate their own enterprises, neither supervisors nor supervised (farmers being conspicuous in this last group). In order to distinguish some of these roles, many censuses collect and tabulate information about the "status" of each economically active person.

The attempt has not been very successful. The status classes cut across all the ordinary industry categories; but the actual differences of status are not consistent in the various lines of activity. The result is a classification that is vague, without the same significance in different populations or portions of the same population. Often the data are useful for some limited purpose, if it is possible

---

[22]See, for example, A. J. Jaffe and R. O. Carleton, *Occupational Mobility in the United States 1930-1960* (New York, 1954), I. B. Taeuber, *Population of Japan* (Princeton, 1958), Chapters 4 and 7.

to ascertain what criteria were observed in attributing working status to individuals.[23]

## 9:10  Migration and Type of Work

In most cases migrants are composed predominantly of people of working ages, and often predominantly of men. This is not just fortuitous; few people can decide to migrate without reference to their livelihood. Migrants ordinarily contain a high proportion of workers, and a low proportion of dependents. Hence to some extent migration is economically an advantage to a receiving area, and a drain on the sending area. In particular, young adults migrating to cities leave rural sections with a more burdensome age structure than before. By migration cities gain the services of young and vigorous workers, and do so at the expense of rural communities.

This explanation, though valid, is insufficient. Certain other factors should be considered. For example, without emigration, the working population in sending areas might not be fully utilized. Where there is "hidden unemployment," the removal of some manpower is not always a serious loss. The value of the services of workers who have migrated is likely to be higher at their destinations: this is one of the reasons for moving. The same statement applies to movement between countries. "So far as the exporting and receiving countries are concerned, the migration from one to the other tends to improve the balance of labor in relation to economic opportunity."[24] Whether the *net* effect of migration has been a gain or a loss in a given instance is difficult, if not impossible, to decide.

Migration also redistributes manpower among various types of activity (see 8:10). This is especially true of the movement from farming to other kinds of work. The patterns of manpower utilization in agricultural regions are, of course, patterns established in a rural environment. It is large cities of rapid growth and frequent change that have been most congenial to economic development. As mentioned before, the spread of industry has been primarily an urban phenomenon.

In cities which have reached a substantial size, the distribution of the working population by type of activity ceases to resemble

---

[23]See United Nations, Population Division and Statistical Office, *Application of International Standards* ... , Chapter 6.

[24]A. J. Jaffe and C. D. Stewart, *Manpower Resources and Utilitization* (New York, 1951), p. 321.

that of rural districts. The contrast is greatest where traditional forms of agriculture persist; modern mechanized farming methods are sometimes indistinguishable from industrial enterprise. Employment of children, the discouragement of female wage labor, low levels of technical skill, and the disadvantages of age structure are all more characteristic of the rural than of the urban setting. Therefore, changing utilization of manpower in most of the modern world is first discerned through the growth and changing composition of employment in cities.[25]

[25]See also 8:11.

# CHAPTER 10

# CONCLUSION

The preceding chapters have covered the principal topics studied by means of census and registration data. Fortunately, nearly all the essential background can be covered at this introductory level.

Naturally there are other techniques beyond the selected group that has been presented. For the most part they consist of the same operations, applied to different population characteristics or different categories. Most of the literature now lies within reach of the reader who has come this far.

The next step is to find out how the foregoing procedures are applied. There are few formal textbooks, and these are rather specialized, dealing chiefly with actuarial subjects. On the other hand, scattered through journals and occasional publications there are many examples of the wider uses of population data. They illustrate the variety of problems to be investigated, and suggest various types of questions that may be asked. A brief guide to some of this literature will be helpful.

First, the study of mortality is especially important from a methodological point of view. The effects of mortality lend themselves to representation by the simple and effective means of the life table. The life table describes age-specific mortality, affords convenient comparisons, and is instrumental in making population estimates, as already discussed in Chapters 4 and 5.[1] An *Appendix* is provided (pp. 286-305), explaining the construction of abridged life tables from registration and census data.

Up to a point, this *Appendix* will serve. But one should become more thoroughly conversant with the life table, for it is the basis of hypothetical models which describe other vital processes. Summaries

---

[1] See also United Nations, Population Branch, *Age and Sex Patterns of Mortality; Model Life-Tables for Under-developed Countries* (New York, 1955).

of these other applications are given in H. H. Wolfenden, *Population Statistics and Their Compilation* (revised edition, Chicago, 1954); in L. I. Dublin, A. J. Lotka and M. Spiegelman, *Length of Life* (revised edition, New York, 1949); in M. Spiegelman, *Introduction to Demography* (Chicago, 1955); and in P. Cox, *Demography* (Cambridge, England, 1950). In particular, the principle of the life table is sometimes adopted for representing the effect of marriage in the single population, and the effect of working activities in the population without gainful occupation.[2]

Because the population by age is the same as the survivors of yearly cohorts of births, it reflects the effect of mortality on the initial cohorts. Hence, where registration of deaths is defective or lacking, life tables can sometimes be calculated by approximate methods from census data. These procedures presuppose a knowledge of conventional life-table methods; they are too detailed for discussion within the scope of this book. They are explained in G. J. Stolnitz, *Life Tables from Limited Data: A Demographic Approach* (Princeton, 1956); and G. Mortara, *Methods of Using Census Statistics for the Calculation of Life Tables and Other Demographic Measures*, [United Nations] *Population Studies*, No. 7 (New York, 1949).

The investigation of other topics is at a simpler stage of technique. It is therefore essential to become familiar with the typical patterns of distribution of population characteristics and the typical defects of population data. A large amount of weight must be given to such factors. These "typical" patterns, however, are subject to considerable variation—greater than supposed in many earlier writings. For practical guidance in many specific problems, two works should be helpful: A. J. Jaffe, *A Handbook of Statistical Methods for Demographers* (Washington, D.C., 1949), and D. J. Bogue and E. M. Kitagawa, *Techniques of Demographic Research: A Laboratory Manual* (forthcoming).

The study of fertility presents somewhat more formidable problems. As explained in Chapter 6, it is handicapped by the difficulty of defining what is being measured. Certain proposed improvements are still rather tentative; some have been mentioned in Chapter 6.

---

[2]See J. Hajnal, "Aspects of Recent Trends in Marriage in England and Wales," *Population Studies*, Vol. 1 (June, 1947); see also New Zealand, Department of Statistics, "New Zealand Tables of Working Life, 1951," (supplement to *Monthly Abstract of Statistics*, February, 1956), and S. Wolfbein, "The Length of Working Life," *Population Studies*, Vol. 3 (December, 1949). The working-life table has a specific practical application in planning retirement and pension programs.

One improvement is to examine any pattern of fertility together with the pattern of marriage, since the two are very closely related. If the proportions married (among adults of marriageable ages) vary, a considerable variation of birth rates is possible with little or no change in the fertility of married people. The conclusions to be drawn after comparing different birth rates may depend largely on the distribution of marriage in the population. A summary of these relations is to be found in the Chapter by N.B. Ryder, "Fertility," in P.M. Hauser and O.D. Duncan, *The Study of Demography: An Inventory and Appraisal* (forthcoming).

Owing to limitations of space, the rather detailed question of marriage patterns could not be taken up as a separate topic in this book. See, however, J. Hajnal, "Age at Marriage and Proportions Marrying," *Population Studies*, Vol. 7 (November, 1953), and "The Marriage Boom," *Population Index*, Vol. 19 (April, 1953); also K. Davis, "Statistical Perspective on Marriage and Divorce," *Annals of the American Academy of Political and Social Science*, Vol. 272 (November, 1950).

A large and exceptionally careful study of fertility, worthy of special note, is in D. V. Glass and E. Grebenik, *The Trend and Pattern of Fertility in Great Britain, A Report on the Family Census of 1946* (published in two parts, as Volume 6 of a series of *Papers* by the Royal Commission on Population, in London, 1954).[3] The most detailed study of fertility yet available for the United States is P. K. Whelpton, *Cohort Fertility* (Princeton, 1956). A more general treatment, presented at a more advanced level, is L. Henry, *Fécondité des Mariages: Nouvelle Méthode de Mesure* (Paris, 1952).[4] An unusually wide selection of illustrative material is examined in F. Lorimer, et al., *Culture and Human Fertility* (Paris, 1954).

Regarding models of population growth, there are several commentaries on aspects of the stable population. They reveal some limitations of such a model, particularly in analogies with an actual population. Eventually, one or more of the following should be examined: G. J. Stolnitz and N. B. Ryder, "Recent Discussion of the Net Reproduction Rate," *Population Index*, Vol. 15 (April, 1949); P. H. Karmel, "The Relations between Male and Female Nuptiality in a Stable Popu-

---

[3] See also Volume 2 of this series, titled *Reports and Selected Papers of the Statistics Committee.*

[4] See also L. Henry, *Anciennes Familles Genevoises. Etude démographique: XVIe-XXe Siécle* (Paris, 1956), and "Analysis and Calculation of the Fertility of Population of Under-developed Countries," *(Population Bulletin of the United Nations*, No. 5, July 1956).

lation," *Population Studies,* Vol. 1 (March, 1948); J. Hajnal, "Some Comments on Mr. Karmel's Paper, 'The Relations ...'," *Population Studies,* Vol. 2 (December, 1948).

More generally, several works furnish a descriptive background about population growth and development. The most comprehensive is the study published by the United Nations, Population Division, *Determinants and Consequences of Population Trends (Population Studies,* No. 17, New York, 1953). A survey of population growth in relation to economic conditions is given in PEP (Political and Economic Planning), *World Population and Resources* (London, 1955). A historical survey of the growth and expansion of European populations is found in A. M. Carr-Saunders, *World Population* (Oxford, 1936). Another standard work of this nature is W. S. Thompson, *Population Problems* (several editions). A very large compendium of information and opinions, contributed by scholars and interested parties from every part of the world, is contained in the *Proceedings of the World Population Conference,* held in Rome, 1954 (six volumes of Papers, published in New York, 1955). These papers cover a wide variety of topics; a few have already been cited earlier in this book.

Two books of readings, primarily from American sources, are available, edited by J. J. Spengler and O. D. Duncan, *Demographic Analysis: Selected Readings* (Glencoe, Ill., 1956); and *Population Theory and Policy: Selected Readings* (Glencoe, Ill., 1956). These contain reprints of many papers and articles which are difficult to procure in their original form.

There is an extremely large list of special studies for particular areas, far too voluminous to be summarized here. Most countries with population statistics also have their own literature on the subject. A list of these sources would be too encyclopedic to attempt here. A great many references appear in the text, linked to the topics under discussion.

There are systematic bibliographies of this material. Foremost is the *Population Index,* published quarterly at Princeton, N.J. since 1935. Entries are annotated, and there are also brief articles on special subjects. A more selective guide to recent works, chiefly in the United States, is provided by H. T. Eldridge, *The Materials of Demography: A Selected and Annotated Bibliography* (forthcoming); the remarks on individual works are more detailed. These American sources can be supplemented by the regular annotations in the journal, *Population* (published in Paris), a quarterly periodical which is also one of the principal sources of regular articles of research about populations.

*Population Studies* is an English journal devoted exclusively to this field, published (in London) three times yearly. Several periodicals have occasional papers about population, notably *Estadística* (Washington, D.C.), *Journal of the American Statistical Association* (Washington, D.C.), *Milbank Memorial Fund Quarterly* (New York), *Journal of the Royal Statistical Society* (London).

The *Population Bulletin of the United Nations* is published irregularly, interspersed with more substantial monographs in a series titled *Population Studies;* these are compiled and in large degree written—anonymously—by members of the staff of the United Nations Population Branch (Department of Social Affairs). References in the text have cited these United Nations publications rather liberally, for they are wide in scope and are generally obtainable. In addition, as mentioned in Chapter 1, the Statistical Office of the United Nations has published, at approximately yearly intervals, the *Demographic Year Book*, which provides the largest collection of comparable population statistics available in one source. A textual section, varying in different issues, describes the nature of the data, and some possible criteria of adequacy.

# APPENDIX TO CHAPTER 4

# CONSTRUCTION OF ABRIDGED LIFE TABLES

Chapter 4 describes the structure of a life table in sufficient detail for most purposes. It is expected that published life tables will usually be available where required.

However, occasionally there is a need for a life table where none exists, or for a period not covered by existing tables. For this reason, and in order to develop closer acquaintance with the problems involved, this *Appendix* explains how to construct abridged life tables. The methods chosen are not the most elegant or the most refined, but they are very practical examples. As shown in Table 4:6, they may yield results that are very close to those of a "complete" life table from the same date.

## 4:14 Construction of Abridged Life Table from Death Registration and Census Data

We shall discuss in detail three common procedures—one in this section, and two in 4:15 and 4:16. In reality, all three use the same basic method, the approximation of $_nq_x$ by means of an age-specific death rate $(_nM_x)$ calculated from census and death registration data; they merely represent three ways of doing this. If circumstances require, two or more may be combined in preparation of the same table—for example, one may be substituted for another at some age if the data are unreliable or inconveniently tabulated. It is important to specify what scheme has been followed, and to describe with special care any unusual steps of this kind.

The first procedure is to compute values of $_nq_x$ by an extension of the formula for single-year values, as explained in 4:10. The abridged life table can be constructed in the following steps:

a. Between ages 5 and the highest interval (see step "e"), compute death rates for each five-year group: $_5M_x = \dfrac{_5D_x}{_5P_x} k$, where $_5P_x$ is an estimate of the mid-year population between ages $x$ and $x+5$, $_5D_x$ is the number of deaths in the same age interval during the year (or a yearly average for some other base period), and $k$ is equal to 1. The base period should be cited as the date of the life table. If the data include a few ten-year rather than five-year age groups, compute $_{10}M_x$ at these intervals (by substituting

"10" for "5" in the formula above).

b. At ages 1-4, compute $_4M_1 = \dfrac{_4D_1}{_4P_1}\cdot k$. This age interval deserves

careful attention, for the data (both census results and registered deaths) are often deficient at these ages and because errors here have a large influence at later ages in the hypothetical cohort.

c. Convert $_nM_x$ to $_nq_x$ by the formula $\dfrac{2n\,_nM_x}{2+n\,_nM_x}$, being careful to

use the correct size of interval $(n)$ in each case. For a five-year interval,

the formula is $\dfrac{10\,_2M_x}{2+5\,_5M_x}$; for a four-year interval, $\dfrac{8\,_4M_x}{2+4\,_4M_x}$. A somewhat

more accurate formula is available, which makes an allowance for the gradual shift of single-year values of $q_x$ within a larger interval.[1]

d. At age 0, the infant mortality rate $(q_0)$ might be calculated as

the proportion of deaths among a cohort of births. But the usual classification of the data prevents this (see 5:8). The infant death rate is used instead (as an estimate), computed as the ratio of infant deaths to the number

of births during the same year $\dfrac{D_0}{B}k$, where $k$ is equal to 1). This estimate

will nearly always be improved if the base period is lengthened to three

years $\left(\dfrac{D_0^1 + D_0^2 + D_0^3}{B_0^1 + B_0^2 + B_0^3}\right)$, because some of the discrepancies will then be

cancelled out. If the data of births or deaths are to be revised (to compensate for errors that are known to exist), this should be done before computing the infant death rate. The number of person-years lived during infancy $(L_0)$ must be estimated arbitrarily. After $q_0$ is calculated, $l_1$ can be determined; then, a reasonable approximation of $L_0$ is $.3\,l_0 + .7\,l_1$.

e. The highest interval of age needs slightly different treatment. It includes everyone at "age $x$ and above," and hence does not contain the same number of years as the other intervals. It is often set by the nature of

---

[1] This refinement is $_nq_x = \dfrac{_nM_x}{\dfrac{1}{n} + \,_nM_x\left[\dfrac{1}{2} + \dfrac{n}{12}\left(_nM_x - .09\right)\right]}$. See T. N. E. Greville,

"Short Methods of Constructing Abridged Life Tables," *The Record of the American Institute of Actuaries*, Vol. 32, Part 1 (June, 1943), p. 37. The value of .09 is arbitrary, but adequate to fit a wide variety of situations.

the data (the final age category in the source tables may be "70 and above," or "80 and above"). If not, it is advisable to consolidate the data for elderly people into one group, "70 and above" or "75 and above," and terminate the life table with this group. Beyond these ages, the records are likely to be unreliable in their details.[2] When the final group is "70 and above," compute the death rate $_\infty M_{70}$, using the population and the deaths registered

at all those ages $\left( \dfrac{_\infty D_{70}}{_\infty P_{70}} \right)$. The mortality rate from age 70 to the end of

life $(_\infty q_{70})$ is always 1.0, since everyone in the life-table cohort must die during this interval. This means that $_\infty d_{70} = l_{70}$ : there will be as many deaths in the hypothetical cohort after age 70 as there are people left to die.

The value of $_n L_x$ is estimated at $\dfrac{l_x}{_n M_x}$, and so $_\infty L_{70} = \dfrac{l_{70}}{_\infty M_{70}}$. This is also

equal to $T_{70}$.

Alternatively, one of the schemes in 4:15 or 4:16 may be followed, utilizing additional data to secure values over age 70.

f. The column, $_n P_x$, is not needed, but can be computed if desired from values of $_n q_x$ or $l_x$ (see 4:8). Alternatively, $_n P_x$ may be calculated and $_n d_x$ may be omitted, since it is possible to calculate values of $l_x$ from $_n P_x$.

g. The other columns are determined very simply after $_n q_x$ is complete: $_n d_x = {_n q_x} \cdot l_x$; $l_{x+n} = l_x - {_n d_x}$, or $l_{x+n} = l_x \cdot {_n P_x}$; $_n L_x = \dfrac{n}{2} (l_x + l_{x+n})$; $T_x = T_{x+n} + {_n L_x}$; $e_x = \dfrac{T_x}{l_x}$. (See 4:5 and 4:8.)

To illustrate, let us apply this procedure to the data of the Federation of Malaya, 1947. In this year a census was taken (on September 23), and statistics of registered deaths and births are available for 1946, 1947 and 1948. Death statistics were published in five-year intervals of age up to "age 55 and over." Below, these data are made into a life table for "Malaysians," who form a separate and roughly comparable group. The census figures are taken as the estimate of the mid-year population; a closer estimate might be attempted, but in view of the quality of the data this would probably be a superfluous refinement. The Federation of Malaya did not include Singapore, but did contain four-fifths of the total Malaysian population of all Malaya.

We find this appraisal of the statistics:

"There is little doubt that death registration is considerably more

---

[2] Even in a "complete" life table, the upper values are extrapolated from the rates at younger ages. However, actual data are often used up to age 90, or even above.

complete than birth registration of Malaysians. Burial is accompanied
by the standard Muslim ritual, and deaths cannot pass unnoticed by
the local community, with the possible exception of infant deaths . . . .
    "The published statistics of death registration in Malaya divide
deaths by race, sex and age . . . . Most of the various age-reporting
errors noted in discussing the census age tables [exaggerating the
ages of very young children, lower standards of accuracy among
women and where levels of literacy were low] are also apparent in the
death registration statistics. In fact there appears to be an even
greater tendency to report age as a round number for the purposes of
death registration than in answer to the census questionnaire."[3]

This same author also found signs of large omissions in the registration in
the State of Kelantan (where death rates seemed inexplicably low and births
seemed underreported). He therefore subtracted the deaths and the population recorded in Kelantan before making his final computations, and we follow his example here. During 1946-1948 there were 16,420 male infant
deaths registered among Malaysians in this region, and 126,602 births; the
infant death rate was 16,420/126,602, or .1297, which we treat as the infant
mortality rate for males during this period.
    Above infancy, the numbers of deaths and of enumerated males by age
(assumed to be the mid-year population of 1947) are copied in Column 2 and
Column 4 of Table 4:4 (the State of Kelantan having been removed). In Column 3, the population figures are multiplied by 3, preparatory to computing
age-specific death rates; this has the same effect as dividing the numbers
of deaths by 3 (for a yearly average), but is slightly more accurate. In Column 5 are the values of $_nM_x$, and in Column 8 these are converted into mor-

tality rates by assuming that, above age one, $_nq_x = \dfrac{2n \, _nM_x}{2 + n \, _nM_x}$ ; Columns 6

and 7 are intermediate, and merely help in evaluating the formula for $_nq_x$.

    The other columns can be completed with very little difficulty. The
reader is invited to compute the remainder of this abridged life table, according to the steps set forth above. There are two arbitrary decisions to
be taken regarding the column, $_nL_x$: it may be assumed that $_1L_0 = .3 \, l_0$

$+ .7 \, l_1$, and that $_\infty L_{55} = \dfrac{l_{55}}{_\infty M_{55}}$ . (Alternatively, the procedures of 4:15 or

4:16 may be substituted, provided that the substitution is fully explained.)

## 4:15 Construction of Abridged Life Table by Reference to a "Standard" Table[4]

The work of constructing an abridged table can be somewhat simpli-

---

[3] T. E. Smith, *Population Growth in Malaya* (London, 1952), p. 56.

[4] This method is taken from T. N. E. Greville, "United States Abridged Life
Tables, 1945," in *Vital Statistics—Special Reports*, Vol. 23, No. 11, Washington,
D.C. (1947).

## COMPUTATION OF "ABRIDGED" LIFE TABLE
### FOR MALAYSIANS, 1946-1948
Based on Census Population and Registered Deaths
(Federation of Malaya, excluding State of Kelantan)

| (1) | (2) | (3) | (4) | (5) | (6) | (7) | (8) |
|---|---|---|---|---|---|---|---|
| Ages | Census Population (Malaysians) $\underline{a}/$ | Col. (2) × 3 | Deaths during the period 1946 to 1948 (3 years) | $_nM_x$ (Col. 4 ÷ Col. 3) | Intermediate Computations $n \cdot {_nM_x}$ | $2n \cdot {_nM_x}$ | $_nq_x$ (Col. 7 ÷ Col. 6) $\underline{b}/$ |

| | | | Males | | | | |
|---|---|---|---|---|---|---|---|
| 0-1 | 23,497 | 70,491 | 16,420 | .23294 | .23294 | .46588 | .12970 $\underline{c}/$ |
| 1-4 | 84,059 | 252,177 | 11,259 | .04465 | .17860 | .35720 | .16396 |
| 5-9 | 111,025 | 333,075 | 5,150 | .01546 | .07730 | .15460 | .07442 |
| 10-14 | 90,610 | 271,830 | 2,205 | .00811 | .04055 | .08110 | .03974 |
| 15-19 | 64,109 | 192,327 | 1,634 | .00850 | .04250 | .08500 | .04162 |
| 20-24 | 56,341 | 170,523 | 1,965 | .01152 | .05760 | .11520 | .05599 |
| 25-29 | 55,568 | 166,704 | 2,248 | .01348 | .06740 | .13480 | .06520 |
| 30-34 | 47,339 | 142,017 | 2,693 | .01896 | .09480 | .18960 | .09051 |
| 35-39 | 42,751 | 128,253 | 2,715 | .02117 | .10585 | .21170 | .10053 |
| 40-44 | 36,228 | 108,684 | 3,537 | .03254 | .16270 | .32540 | .15046 |
| 45-49 | 27,178 | 81,534 | 3,068 | .03763 | .18815 | .37630 | .17197 |
| 50-54 | 21,873 | 65,619 | 4,125 | .06286 | .31430 | .62860 | .27162 |
| 55+ | 42,395 | 127,185 | 16,587 | .13042 | .65210 | | |

| | | | Females | | | | |
|---|---|---|---|---|---|---|---|
| 0-1 | 23,006 | 69,018 | 13,349 | .19341 | .19341 | .38682 | .11189 $\underline{c}/$ |
| 1-4 | 84,155 | 252,465 | 11,183 | .04430 | .17720 | .35440 | .16278 |
| 5-9 | 112,356 | 337,068 | 5,068 | .01504 | .07520 | .15040 | .07247 |
| 10-14 | 91,951 | 275,853 | 2,086 | .00756 | .03780 | .07560 | .03710 |
| 15-19 | 69,936 | 209,808 | 1,848 | .00881 | .04405 | .08810 | .04310 |
| 20-24 | 69,928 | 209,784 | 2,507 | .01195 | .05975 | .11950 | .05802 |
| 25-29 | 67,802 | 203,406 | 2,971 | .01461 | .07305 | .14610 | .07048 |
| 30-34 | 51,619 | 154,857 | 2,842 | .01835 | .09175 | .18350 | .08773 |
| 35-39 | 44,522 | 133,566 | 2,762 | .02068 | .10340 | .20680 | .09832 |
| 40-44 | 38,245 | 114,735 | 2,988 | .02604 | .13020 | .26040 | .12224 |
| 45-49 | 25,971 | 77,913 | 2,165 | .02779 | .13895 | .27790 | .12992 |
| 50-54 | 23,814 | 71,442 | 3,419 | .04786 | .23930 | .47860 | .21373 |
| 55+ | 50,804 | 152,412 | 15,212 | .09981 | .49905 | | |

[a] Census was taken September 23, 1947. These data are assumed to represent the mid-point of the 3-year interval 1946-1948. The few people whose ages were not reported (1,128 males and 985 females) have been omitted. Alternatively, they might have been distributed as suggested in 3:12.

[b] Values of $_nM_x$ are converted to $_nq_x$ by the approximate formula $_nq_x = \dfrac{2n \cdot {_nM_x}}{2 + n \cdot {_nM_x}}$

[c] These values are infant death rates, male and female, as described in the text.

Sources: *A Report on the 1947 Census of Population* (London, 1949), Tables 12 and 13. Malayan Union and Federation of Malaya, *Report on the Registration of Births and Deaths, 1946, 1947, 1948.*

fied, by referring to a life table already in existence. This method utilizes calculations originally carried out for another table, and is therefore subject to some hidden limitations. It should not be used unless the mortality rates being measured are very similar to those measured in the "standard" life table. If the mortality rates are not similar, or if the two populations are very different in their age composition, the method can lead to considerable errors. It is best suited to preparing a second life table, in a different year, for the same population represented by the published table, or preparing a series of tables for sub-divisions of a country when an accurate life table is available for the total country.

There are not many openings in a life table for such a short cut; most of the relations between the terms are already clear and concise, and only a few involve approximations of some sort. The most important approximation is the conversion of an age-specific death rate $\left(_n M_x\right)$ to a mortality rate $\left(_n q_x\right)$. We adopt the relation $\left(\dfrac{_n q_x}{_n M_x}\right)$ between these two terms in the "standard" life table, and transfer it to the new data in order to calculate the mortality rate $\left(_n q_x\right)$ for the new life table.[5] Values of $_n L_x$ and the final values of $e_x$ may also be found by reference to the "standard" table, or just as explained in 4:14.

The steps of computation are outlined as follows (using the symbols $q'_x$, $M'_x$, $l'_x$, and $e'_x$ to distinguish values drawn from the "standard" life table):

a. Between age 5 and the final age interval, compute age-specific death rates from the new data, as in 4:14: $_5 M_x = \dfrac{_5 D_x}{_5 P_x}$.

b. At ages 1-4, compute $_4 M_x = \dfrac{_4 D_1}{_4 P_1}$.

c. In the life table chosen as standard, compute the ratio $\dfrac{_n q'_x}{_n M'_x}$ for each corresponding interval of age. Then, convert $_n M_x$ into $_n q_x$, multiplying it by the ratio just computed: $_n q_x = _n M_x \left(\dfrac{_n q'_x}{_n M'_x}\right)$. If the intervals of

___

[5]Both terms, of course, must appear in the published table that is taken as a "standard." This imposes another limitation in the use of the method, for the column of age-specific death rates is not always published together with the rest of the table. In this book these death rates are called "$M_x$," in order to avoid the confusion between this and another term, $m_x$, in the life table itself. (See 4:10.) The death rates will be given other symbols by other authors; very often both are called "$m_x$."

age in the standard life table do not correspond to those required in the life table under construction, the "standard" values of $_nM_x'$ and $_nq_x'$ must first be re-calculated in the proper intervals. It may be necessary to re-arrange the original data (mid-year population and registered deaths) and re-calculate those that must be changed; mortality rates $(_nq_x')$ are easily re-calculated in any interval $\left( _nq_x' = \dfrac{l_{x+n}'}{l_x'} \right)$.

    d. At age 0, it is probably best to make an estimate of $q_0$ as illustrated in 2:15. The "standard" life table may be of no help, unless it suggests a procedure that seems practical and appropriate to be applied to the new data. The value of $L_0$ may be computed as $L_0 = l_0 - \left( \dfrac{l_0' - L_0'}{d_0'} \right) \times d_0$; or as suggested in 4:14.

    e. At the highest interval of age we may draw more heavily from the "standard" life table. Here any method is very arbitrary; moreover, most actual data are least reliable at the highest ages, and whatever course is followed is of little consequence to the rest of the life table. Let us assume that the life table being constructed ends with the upper interval "age 70 and above." The value of $_\infty q_{70}$ of course is 1.0; the value of $l_{70}$ is determined by the series of $_nq_x$ at all lower ages (see 4:3). The next step is to find a value for the expectation of life at age 70, $(e_{70})$, which may be done in either of two ways:

    (1) Compute the death rate among persons age 70 and above $\left( _\infty M_{70} = \dfrac{_\infty D_{70}}{_\infty P_{70}} \right)$, and compute the ratio $\dfrac{l_{70}'}{T_{70}'}$ in the "standard" life table.

Then, estimate the expectation of life by assuming $e_{70} = \dfrac{\dfrac{l_{70}'}{T_{70}'}}{_\infty M_{70}}$. Afterwards, calculate the number of years lived by the life-table cohort after age $\cdot 70$ $(T_{70} - l_{70} \times e_{70})$. This is also the value of $_\infty L_{70}$.

    (2) Alternatively, simply adopt the value of $e_{70}'$ in the "standard" table as the estimate, assuming $e_{70} = e_{70}'$. (This may be a superior estimate, because it does not involve the unreliable death rates at these ages.) Afterwards, calculate $T_{70}$ as indicated above.

    f. There is no need for the column, $p_x$.

    g. Values of $l_x$ and $_nd_x$ are prepared as before. The "standard" table permits a different approximation of $_nL_x$ on the basis of $l_x$ and $_nd_x$:

$$_nL_x = n \times l_x - \left( \frac{n \times l_x' - _nL_x'}{_nd_x'} \right)_nd_x, \text{ where } n \text{ is the number of years in the}$$

interval of age.[6] It requires one or more extra intermediate columns for computation, depending on whether a calculating machine is available. Alternatively, $_nL_x$ may be found by the approximations of 4:14; this will be preferable when the column, $_nL_x'$, does not appear in the "standard" table. The column, $T_x$, is assembled from these values of $_nL_x$, calculating the highest value as indicated above.

As cautioned above, this method is not always appropriate; it should be restricted to measuring conditions of mortality very similar to those of the life table adopted as the "standard." Its chief virtue is a saving of labor. But the saving is not substantial unless the same "standard" life table is applied to the construction of several new tables.

Also, there is a possibility that this method may be more accurate than other techniques for constructing abridged life tables. It retains some advantages of more elaborate procedures—(the detail, the effects of careful smoothing and of certain adjustments of the data).[7] These advantages are greatest for the mortality of young children and old persons (ages 1-4 and the final or highest interval of age), and so the method may sometimes be expedient for use at these ages even if other means are employed at the other ages.

For the sake of illustration, a life table is computed by this means for males in the Federal District of Venezuela, using the published life table of 1941-1942 as the "standard" (see Table 4:5). The values of $_nM_x'$ are computed from the registered deaths of 1941 and 1942 and the census of December, 1941, the mid-point of the two-year period (Column 2). The values of $_nq_x'$ (Column 3) are taken from the published life table. The ratio of these two values at each age ( $_nq_x' / _nM_x'$ ) is shown in Column 4. This is an "estimating ratio," for later use.

With these preparations completed, we must compute the values of $_nM_x$ from the registered deaths (1941-1942) and census population (1941) of the Federal District (Column 5). The same intervals of age are followed. Finally, the values of $_nq_x$ for the Federal District can be calculated by multiplying each death rate ( $_nM_x$ ) by the estimating ratio at that age interval (see Column 6). Thereafter, the other columns of the life table may be calculated by any appropriate means. (In Table 4:5, however, there is no value for $q_0$; hence the subsequent columns would not be comparable with those of other life tables.)

(Note that the intervals of age in this life table are rather large, 10

---

[6] This approximation was suggested by M. Spiegelman, *Introduction to Demography* (Chicago, 1955), p. 91.

[7] On the other hand, these factors may make the method *less* accurate, and there are no definite criteria for discovering whether it is advantageous or not.

## TABLE 4:5

## COMPUTATION OF "ABRIDGED" LIFE TABLE FOR FEDERAL DISTRICT OF VENEZUELA

By Reference to Published Life Table for Entire Country, 1941-1942
(Males only)

| (1) | (2)[b/] | (3)[c/] | (4) | (5)[d/] | (6) |
|---|---|---|---|---|---|
| | Entire Country | | | Federal District | |
| Ages | $_nM'_x$ | $_nq'_x$ | Ratio: $(_nq'_x) \div (_nM'_x)$ | $_nM_x$ | $_nq_x$ (Col.5)×(Col.4) |
| 0 | a/ | | | | |
| 1-4 | .02191 | .08481 | 3.8708 | .01457 | .05640 |
| 5-9 | .00532 | .02612 | 4.9098 | .00242 | .01188 |
| 10-19 | .00392 | .03906 | 9.9643 | .00281 | .02800 |
| 20-29 | .00793 | .07682 | 9.6873 | .00578 | .05599 |
| 30-39 | .01150 | .10994 | 9.5600 | .01171 | .11195 |
| 40-49 | .01630 | .15130 | 9.2822 | .01801 | .16717 |
| 50-59 | .02336 | .21468 | 9.1901 | .03113 | .28609 |
| 60-69 | .04282 | .35885 | 8.3804 | .05541 | .46436 |
| 70 and over[e/] | | 1.00000 | | | 1.00000 |

[a] Data at this age were considered unreliable, and were not used.

[b] Computed from registered deaths (1941 and 1942) and census data (1941), entire country.

[c] From published life table for Venezuela (see *Estadística*, March, 1951).

[d] Computed from registered deaths (1941 and 1942) and census data (1941), Federal District.

[e] No value of $_nM_x$ is needed here, for $_nq_x$ is necessarily equal to 1.0.

Sources: *Seventh Population Census of Venezuela*, Volume 1, Tables 1, 2; Volume 8, Tables 1, 2.
*Anuario Estadístico de Venezuela, 1942*, Tables 104, 105 (Caracas, 1943).

years each above age 10. This is unavoidable, owing to the limitations of statistics available for subdivisions of the country. Consequently, the life table may perhaps be less accurate than it would be if based on more detailed data. It will definitely be less useful, for these are inconvenient intervals for most applications of a life table. Therefore the construction of such a table may not be worth while; mortality can be compared in the Federal District and the entire country by means of age-specific death rates, $_nM_x$. No rate of infant mortality has been computed in Table 4:5. Venezuela's statistics of deaths among infants are regarded as very questionable.[8] They are not comparable in accuracy with death statistics at other ages, and it would be misleading to include them in the life table without some separate study and appraisal. Fortunately most applications of the life table do not depend on having this one value.)

## 4:16  The Reed-Merrell Method of Constructing Abridged Life Table

Another method of converting $_nM_x$ to $_nq_x$ has been devised by Reed and Merrell. It goes farther in standardizing the separate decisions about procedure, and in reducing the labor of computation. These two authors found a set of constant values relating $_nM_x$ and $_nq_x$ through a wide range of observations, based on many early life tables for the United States (instead of upon just one "standard" table).[9] They have prepared special tables summarizing these relations, where values of $_nq_x$ can be read from the entries opposite given values of $_nM_x$. Thus some of the most laborious computations are performed in advance.

Obviously, this method is most dependable when applied to data like those on which it is based. It fits mortality data of the United States very well; corresponding constants calculated for other countries might be slightly different, especially among infants. Caution should be observed in applying it to data of other countries—especially at the very young and very old ages, where arbitrary judgments and adjustments of data are often required. But very likely this method will be satisfactory at most ages, and will not lead to serious error even at the ages of greatest doubt. Compared with the prodigious errors from other sources (from the use of the death rate, $_nM_x$, and from the basic data themselves), the errors due to this particular procedure cannot be very large.

The steps may be described as follows:

    a.  Compute values of $_5M_x$ for each five-year age group between age 5 and the highest interval to be shown in the life table, as illustrated in Table 4:6.

---

[8]See E. Míchalup, "Las declaraciones de edad," *Proceedings of the World Population Conference, 1954* (New York, 1955), Volume 4, pp. 191-199.

[9]L. J. Reed and M. Merrell, "A Short Method for Constructing an Abridged Life Table," *The American Journal of Hygiene*, Vol. 30, No. 2, pp. 33-62, September, 1939. It is impossible in this short space to give an account of the technique by which these relations were determined. A clear description is furnished by the authors in their article.

b. At ages 1-4, compute $_4M_1$. Or, if the data permit, compute a death rate at age 1 and another death rate at ages 2-4 ($_1M_1$ and $_3M_2$).

c. Convert these death rates to $_nq_x$. With the Reed-Merrell method, merely find the computed value of $_nM_x$ in the appropriate table (one of Table 4:7, prepared for this purpose), and read off the corresponding tabulated value of $_nq_x$. The procedure is the same at all ages; there is one table giving values for $_4M_1$, one for $_5M_x$, and two short ones for $_1M_1$ and $_3M_2$. These tables are abridged to save space, and represent $_nM_x$ in only three decimal places. Since death rates are usually computed to four or five decimal places, they contain more detail than the values shown in Table 4:7. In order to make use of this extra information, one must interpolate between values given in the table. A special column (marked "$\Delta$") is provided for the sake of convenience; it indicates the difference between each value of $_nq_x$ and the next higher value. For example, if $_5M_x$ is .03442, the nearest reading in Table 4:7 for $_5q_x$ is the value corresponding to $_5M_x = .034$, or .157310. The difference between this and the next entry (corresponding to $_5M_x = .035$) is .004261. The difference between .034 and the actual death rate is .00042. To interpolate between these two values of $_5q_x$, first locate the actual death rate between two tabulated values of $_5M_x$:$\left(\dfrac{.00042}{.035 - .034}\right) = .42$;

multiply this by "$\Delta$": (.42 $\cdot$ .004261 = .001789); and add this product to the first value of $_5q_x$,(.157310 + .001789 = .15910, rounding off the last digit).

This last figure, .15910, is the interpolated value of $_5q_x$. These steps may be followed in the example for Chile, in Table 4:6. Comparison shows these to be very close to the values of Table 4:1-a.

d. At age 0, probably the best course is to compute an infant death rate as in 4:14. The authors provide a table for converting $M_0$ to $q_0$, but it is not appropriate for data unlike those of the United States, and is not reproduced here.[10]

e. The authors also present a scheme for computing the column of $_nL_x$ values. Though practical, it is cumbersome and offers no special advantage for countries outside the United States, not being related to the procedure for converting $_nM_x$ into $_nq_x$. The column, $_nL_x$, may be calculated according to the steps outlined in 4:14 or 4:15, or by reference to the original source of the Reed-Merrell method.[11]

---

[10] In particular, the conversion table at age 0 makes an adjustment for infants omitted during the census enumeration, according to the estimated under-enumeration by State in the United States in 1910, 1920 and 1930. It would be unwarranted to apply these adjustments to the data of other countries. Moreover, the census enumeration of infants is often notoriously poor, and may be an unreliable basis for calculating an infant death rate.

[11] Reed and Merrell, *op. cit.*, pp. 43-50.

# TABLE 4:6

## COMPUTATION OF "ABRIDGED" LIFE TABLE
## FOR CHILE, 1939-1941

### By Method of Reed and Merrell
### (Females only)

| (1)<br>Ages | (2)<br>Census<br>Population,<br>1940<br>a/ | (3)<br>Average<br>Yearly<br>Deaths,<br>1939-1941<br>a/ | (4)<br>$_nM_x$<br>(Col. 3 ÷<br>Col. 2) | (5)<br>$_nq_x$<br>b/ | (6)<br>($_nq_x$ from<br>published<br>life table)<br>c/ |
|---|---|---|---|---|---|
| 0 | | | | .18933 | (.18848) |
| 1-4 | 248,750 | 7,061 | .02838 | .09939 | (.10277) |
| 5-9 | 314,841 | 1,199 | .00381 | .01883 | (.01689) |
| 10-14 | 310,478 | 1,156 | .00372 | .01834 | (.01621) |
| 15-19 | 263,255 | 1,825 | .00693 | .03396 | (.03309) |
| 20-24 | 244,345 | 2,206 | .00903 | .04408 | (.04347) |
| 25-29 | 228,382 | 2,120 | .00928 | .04552 | (.04591) |
| 30-34 | 179,492 | 1,731 | .00964 | .04695 | (.04715) |
| 35-39 | 169,959 | 1,762 | .01037 | .05077 | (.05067) |
| 40-44 | 135,170 | 1,560 | .01154 | .05600 | (.05551) |
| 45-49 | 109,661 | 1,398 | .01275 | .06215 | (.06216) |
| 50-54 | 90,262 | 1,452 | .01609 | .07758 | (.07833) |
| 55-59 | 68,162 | 1,537 | .02255 | .10730 | (.10482) |
| 60-64 | 64,438 | 1,900 | .02949 | .13789 | (.14192) |
| 65-69 | 34,676 | 1,634 | .04712 | .21157 | (.20567) |
| 70-74 | 29,290 | 1,871 | .06388 | .27645 | (.2857) |
| 75 and over | | | | 1.00000 d/ | |

[a] Based on adjusted data given in O. Cabello, J. Vildósola, and M. Latorre, *Tablas de Vida para Chile, 1920-1930-1940* (Santiago, 1953), Tables 24 and 15.

[b] Read from the appropriate part of Reference Table 4:7 (reproduced from article by Reed & Merrell), after interpolating between tabulated values of "$_nM_x$" as described in the text. Value of $q_0$ was assumed to be the same as the infant death rate for 1939-41, based on adjusted data of births and infant deaths shown in O. Cabello, *et al.* (cited above).

[c] Taken from Table 4:1-a, in Chapter 4, for the sake of comparison.

[d] Value is 1.0, by assumption.

## TABLE 4:7

## REFERENCE TABLE: VALUES FOR CONVERTING $_nM_x$ TO $_nq_x$

## PART A

Values of $q_1$ associated with $m_1$ by the equation:

$$q_1 = 1 - e^{-m_1 (.9510 - 1.921 \, m_1)}$$

| $m_1$ | $q_1$ | $\Delta$ | $m_1$ | $q_1$ | $\Delta$ |
|---|---|---|---|---|---|
| | | .000 | | | .000 |
| .000 | .000 000 | 949 | .050 | .041 847 | 725 |
| .001 | .000 949 | 944 | .051 | .042 572 | 721 |
| .002 | .001 893 | 939 | .052 | .043 293 | 717 |
| .003 | .002 832 | 934 | .053 | .044 010 | 712 |
| .004 | .003 766 | 930 | .054 | .044 722 | 708 |
| .005 | .004 696 | 925 | .055 | .045 430 | 704 |
| .006 | .005 621 | 920 | .056 | .046 134 | 699 |
| .007 | .006 541 | 916 | .057 | .046 833 | 696 |
| .008 | .007 457 | 911 | .058 | .047 529 | 692 |
| .009 | .008 368 | 907 | .059 | .048 221 | 687 |
| .010 | .009 275 | 902 | .060 | .048 908 | 683 |
| .011 | .010 177 | 897 | .061 | .049 591 | 679 |
| .012 | .011 074 | 893 | .062 | .050 270 | 675 |
| .013 | .011 967 | 887 | .063 | .050 945 | 671 |
| .014 | .012 854 | 884 | .064 | .051 616 | 666 |
| .015 | .013 738 | 878 | .065 | .052 282 | 663 |
| .016 | .014 616 | 875 | .066 | .052 945 | 659 |
| .017 | .015 491 | 869 | .067 | .053 604 | 654 |
| .018 | .016 360 | 866 | .068 | .054 258 | 650 |
| .019 | .017 226 | 860 | .069 | .054 908 | 647 |
| .020 | .018 086 | 856 | .070 | .055 555 | 641 |
| .021 | .018 942 | 852 | .071 | .056 196 | 639 |
| .022 | .019 794 | 847 | .072 | .056 835 | 634 |
| .023 | .020 641 | 842 | .073 | .057 469 | 630 |
| .024 | .021 483 | 838 | .074 | .058 099 | 626 |
| .025 | .022 321 | 834 | .075 | .058 725 | 622 |
| .026 | .023 155 | 829 | .076 | .059 347 | 617 |
| .027 | .023 984 | 825 | .077 | .059 964 | 614 |
| .028 | .024 809 | 820 | .078 | .060 578 | 610 |
| .029 | .025 629 | 816 | .079 | .061 188 | 606 |
| .030 | .026 445 | 812 | .080 | .061 794 | 602 |
| .031 | .027 257 | 807 | .081 | .062 396 | 598 |
| .032 | .028 064 | 802 | .082 | .062 994 | 594 |
| .033 | .028 866 | 799 | .083 | .063 588 | 590 |
| .034 | .029 665 | 793 | .084 | .064 178 | 585 |
| .035 | .030 458 | 790 | .085 | .064 763 | 583 |
| .036 | .031 248 | 785 | .086 | .065 346 | 578 |
| .037 | .032 033 | 781 | .087 | .065 924 | 574 |
| .038 | .032 814 | 776 | .088 | .066 498 | 570 |
| .039 | .033 590 | 772 | .089 | .067 068 | 566 |
| .040 | .034 362 | 768 | .090 | .067 634 | 562 |
| .041 | .035 130 | 763 | .091 | .068 196 | 559 |
| .042 | .035 893 | 760 | .092 | .068 755 | 554 |
| .043 | .036 653 | 755 | .093 | .069 309 | 551 |
| .044 | .037 408 | 750 | .094 | .069 860 | 547 |
| .045 | .038 158 | 746 | .095 | .070 407 | 542 |
| .046 | .038 904 | 742 | .096 | .070 949 | 540 |
| .047 | .039 646 | 738 | .097 | .071 489 | 534 |
| .048 | .040 384 | 733 | .098 | .072 023 | 532 |
| .049 | .041 117 | 730 | .099 | .072 555 | 527 |
| .050 | .041 847 | 725 | .100 | .073 082 | |

## PART B

Values of $_3q_2$ associated with $_3m_2$ by the equation:

$$_3q_2 = 1 - e^{-3 \, _3m_2 - 008(3)^3 \, _3m_2^2}$$

| $_3m_2$ | $_3q_2$ | $\Delta$ | $_3m_2$ | $_3q_2$ | $\Delta$ |
|---|---|---|---|---|---|
| | | .00 | | | .00 |
| .000 | .000 000 | 2 996 | .010 | .029 576 | 2 911 |
| .001 | .002 996 | 2 987 | .011 | .032 487 | 2 903 |
| .002 | .005 983 | 2 979 | .012 | .035 390 | 2 895 |
| .003 | .008 962 | 2 970 | .013 | .038 285 | 2 886 |
| .004 | .011 932 | 2 962 | .014 | .041 171 | 2 878 |
| .005 | .014 894 | 2 953 | .015 | .044 049 | 2 870 |
| .006 | .017 847 | 2 945 | .016 | .046 919 | 2 862 |
| .007 | .020 792 | 2 936 | .017 | .049 781 | 2 854 |
| .008 | .023 728 | 2 928 | .018 | .052 635 | 2 845 |
| .009 | .026 656 | 2 920 | .019 | .055 480 | 2 837 |
| .010 | .029 576 | 2 911 | .020 | .058 317 | |

## PART C

Values of $_4q_1$ associated with $_4m_1$ by the equation:

$$_4q_1 = 1 - e^{-4 \, _4m_1 (.9806 - 2.079 \, _4m_1)}$$

| $_4m_1$ | $_4q_1$ | $\Delta$ | $_4m_1$ | $_4q_1$ | $\Delta$ |
|---|---|---|---|---|---|
| | | .00 | | | .00 |
| .000 | .000 000 | 3 906 | .020 | .072 370 | 3 316 |
| .001 | .003 906 | 3 875 | .021 | .075 686 | 3 289 |
| .002 | .007 781 | 3 843 | .022 | .078 975 | 3 262 |
| .003 | .011 624 | 3 812 | .023 | .082 237 | 3 235 |
| .004 | .015 436 | 3 781 | .024 | .085 472 | 3 209 |
| .005 | .019 217 | 3 750 | .025 | .088 681 | 3 183 |
| .006 | .022 967 | 3 720 | .026 | .091 864 | 3 156 |
| .007 | .026 687 | 3 689 | .027 | .095 020 | 3 131 |
| .008 | .030 376 | 3 659 | .028 | .098 151 | 3 104 |
| .009 | .034 035 | 3 630 | .029 | .101 255 | 3 079 |
| .010 | .037 665 | 3 600 | .030 | .104 334 | 3 054 |
| .011 | .041 265 | 3 570 | .031 | .107 388 | 3 028 |
| .012 | .044 835 | 3 542 | .032 | .110 416 | 3 003 |
| .013 | .048 377 | 3 512 | .033 | .113 419 | 2 979 |
| .014 | .051 889 | 3 484 | .034 | .116 398 | 2 954 |
| .015 | .055 373 | 3 455 | .035 | .119 352 | 2 929 |
| .016 | .058 828 | 3 427 | .036 | .122 281 | 2 905 |
| .017 | .062 255 | 3 399 | .037 | .125 186 | 2 882 |
| .018 | .065 654 | 3 372 | .038 | .128 068 | 2 856 |
| .019 | .069 026 | 3 344 | .039 | .130 924 | 2 834 |
| .020 | .072 370 | 3 316 | .040 | .133 758 | |

## PART D

Values of ${}_5q_x$ associated with ${}_5m_x$ by the equation:

$${}_5q_x = 1 - e^{-5\,{}_5m_x - .008\,(5)^3\,{}_5m_x^2}$$

| ${}_5m_x$ | ${}_5q_x$ | Δ | ${}_5m_x$ | ${}_5q_x$ | Δ | ${}_5m_x$ | ${}_5q_x$ | Δ |
|---|---|---|---|---|---|---|---|---|
| | | .00 | | | .00 | | | .00 |
| .000 | .000 000 | 4 989 | .050 | .223 144 | 3 952 | .100 | .399 504 | 3 116 |
| .001 | .004 989 | 4 965 | .051 | .227 096 | 3 935 | .101 | .402 620 | 3 100 |
| .002 | .009 954 | 4 943 | .052 | .231 031 | 3 915 | .102 | .405 720 | 3 085 |
| .003 | .014 897 | 4 920 | .053 | .234 946 | 3 897 | .103 | .408 805 | 3 070 |
| .004 | .019 817 | 4 897 | .054 | .238 843 | 3 879 | .104 | .411 875 | 3 056 |
| .005 | .024 714 | 4 876 | .055 | .242 722 | 3 861 | .105 | .414 931 | 3 041 |
| .006 | .029 590 | 4 852 | .056 | .246 583 | 3 842 | .106 | .417 972 | 3 026 |
| .007 | .034 442 | 4 830 | .057 | .250 425 | 3 824 | .107 | .420 998 | 3 011 |
| .008 | .039 272 | 4 808 | .058 | .254 249 | 3 807 | .108 | .424 009 | 2 998 |
| .009 | .044 080 | 4 786 | .059 | .258 056 | 3 788 | .109 | .427 007 | 2 982 |
| .010 | .048 866 | 4 763 | .060 | .261 844 | 3 770 | .110 | .429 989 | 2 969 |
| .011 | .053 629 | 4 742 | .061 | .265 614 | 3 753 | .111 | .432 958 | 2 953 |
| .012 | .058 371 | 4 720 | .062 | .269 367 | 3 735 | .112 | .435 911 | 2 940 |
| .013 | .063 091 | 4 698 | .063 | .273 102 | 3 717 | .113 | .438 851 | 2 926 |
| .014 | .067 789 | 4 676 | .064 | .276 819 | 3 700 | .114 | .441 777 | 2 91. |
| .015 | .072 465 | 4 655 | .065 | .280 519 | 3 682 | .115 | .444 688 | 2 897 |
| .016 | .077 120 | 4 633 | .066 | .284 201 | 3 665 | .116 | .447 585 | 2 883 |
| .017 | .081 753 | 4 612 | .067 | .287 866 | 3 647 | .117 | .450 468 | 2 870 |
| .018 | .086 365 | 4 590 | .068 | .291 513 | 3 630 | .118 | .453 338 | 2 855 |
| .019 | .090 955 | 4 570 | .069 | .295 143 | 3 613 | .119 | .456 193 | 2 842 |
| .020 | .095 525 | 4 547 | .070 | .298 756 | 3 596 | .120 | .459 035 | 2 827 |
| .021 | .100 072 | 4 527 | .071 | .302 352 | 3 579 | .121 | .461 862 | 2 815 |
| .022 | .104 599 | 4 506 | .072 | .305 931 | 3 562 | .122 | .464 677 | 2 800 |
| .023 | .109 105 | 4 485 | .073 | .309 493 | 3 545 | .123 | .467 477 | 2 787 |
| .024 | .113 590 | 4 464 | .074 | .313 038 | 3 528 | .124 | .470 264 | 2 773 |
| .025 | .118 054 | 4 444 | .075 | .316 566 | 3 511 | .125 | .473 037 | 2 760 |
| .026 | .122 498 | 4 423 | .076 | .320 077 | 3 495 | .126 | .475 797 | 2 746 |
| .027 | .126 921 | 4 402 | .077 | .323 572 | 3 478 | .127 | .478 543 | 2 733 |
| .028 | .131 323 | 4 382 | .078 | .327 050 | 3 461 | .128 | .481 276 | 2 720 |
| .029 | .135 705 | 4 361 | .079 | .330 511 | 3 445 | .129 | .483 996 | 2 707 |
| .030 | .140 066 | 4 341 | .080 | .333 956 | 3 429 | .130 | .486 703 | 2 693 |
| .031 | .144 407 | 4 321 | .081 | .337 385 | 3 412 | .131 | .489 396 | 2 680 |
| .032 | .148 728 | 4 301 | .082 | .340 797 | 3 396 | .132 | .492 076 | 2 667 |
| .033 | .153 029 | 4 281 | .083 | .344 193 | 3 380 | .133 | .494 743 | 2 655 |
| .034 | .157 310 | 4 261 | .084 | .347 573 | 3 364 | .134 | .497 398 | 2 641 |
| .035 | .161 571 | 4 241 | .085 | .350 937 | 3 347 | .135 | .500 039 | 2 628 |
| .036 | .165 812 | 4 221 | .086 | .354 284 | 3 332 | .136 | .502 667 | 2 616 |
| .037 | .170 033 | 4 201 | .087 | .357 616 | 3 316 | .137 | .505 283 | 2 603 |
| .038 | .174 234 | 4 182 | .088 | .360 932 | 3 300 | .138 | .507 886 | 2 590 |
| .039 | .178 416 | 4 162 | .089 | .364 232 | 3 284 | .139 | .510 476 | 2 577 |
| .040 | .182 578 | 4 143 | .090 | .367 516 | 3 268 | .140 | .513 053 | 2 565 |
| .041 | .186 721 | 4 123 | .091 | .370 784 | 3 253 | .141 | .515 618 | 2 552 |
| .042 | .190 844 | 4 104 | .092 | .374 037 | 3 237 | .142 | .518 170 | 2 540 |
| .043 | .194 948 | 4 085 | .093 | .377 274 | 3 222 | .143 | .520 710 | 2 527 |
| .044 | .199 033 | 4 066 | .094 | .380 496 | 3 206 | .144 | .523 237 | 2 515 |
| .045 | .203 099 | 4 047 | .095 | .383 702 | 3 191 | .145 | .525 752 | 2 503 |
| .046 | .207 146 | 4 028 | .096 | .386 893 | 3 176 | .146 | .528 255 | 2 490 |
| .047 | .211 174 | 4 008 | .097 | .390 069 | 3 160 | .147 | .530 745 | 2 478 |
| .048 | .215 182 | 3 990 | .098 | .393 229 | 3 145 | .148 | .533 223 | 2 466 |
| .049 | .219 172 | 3 972 | .099 | .396 374 | 3 130 | .149 | .535 689 | 2 454 |
| .050 | .223 144 | 3 952 | .100 | .399 504 | 3 116 | .150 | .538 143 | 2 442 |

## PART D (Continued)

Values of $_5q_x$ associated with $_5m_x$ by the equation:

$$_5q_x = 1 - e^{-5\,_5m_x - .008\,(5)^3\,_5m_x^2}$$

| $_5m_x$ | $_5q_x$ | $\Delta$ | $_5m_x$ | $_5q_x$ | $\Delta$ | $_5m_x$ | $_5q_x$ | $\Delta$ |
|---|---|---|---|---|---|---|---|---|
| | | .00 | | | .00 | | | .00 |
| .150 | .538 143 | 2 442 | .200 | .646 545 | 1 904 | .250 | .730 854 | 1 476 |
| .151 | .540 585 | 2 430 | .201 | .648 449 | 1 894 | .251 | .732 330 | 1 469 |
| .152 | .543 015 | 2 418 | .202 | .650 343 | 1 885 | .252 | .733 799 | 1 462 |
| .153 | .545 433 | 2 406 | .203 | .652 228 | 1 876 | .253 | .735 261 | 1 453 |
| .154 | .547 839 | 2 394 | .204 | .654 104 | 1 866 | .254 | .736 714 | 1 447 |
| .155 | .550 233 | 2 382 | .205 | .655 970 | 1 856 | .255 | .738 161 | 1 439 |
| .156 | .552 615 | 2 371 | .206 | .657 826 | 1 847 | .256 | .739 600 | 1 432 |
| .157 | .554 986 | 2 359 | .207 | .659 673 | 1 838 | .257 | .741 032 | 1 424 |
| .158 | .557 345 | 2 347 | .208 | .661 511 | 1 829 | .258 | .742 456 | 1 417 |
| .159 | .559 692 | 2 336 | .209 | .663 340 | 1 819 | .259 | .743 873 | 1 409 |
| .160 | .562 028 | 2 324 | .210 | .665 159 | 1 810 | .260 | .745 282 | 1 403 |
| .161 | .564 352 | 2 313 | .211 | .666 969 | 1 802 | .261 | .746 685 | 1 395 |
| .162 | .566 665 | 2 301 | .212 | .668 771 | 1 792 | .262 | .748 080 | 1 388 |
| .163 | .568 966 | 2 290 | .213 | .670 563 | 1 783 | .263 | .749 468 | 1 381 |
| .164 | .571 256 | 2 279 | .214 | .672 346 | 1 774 | .264 | .750 849 | 1 374 |
| .165 | .573 535 | 2 267 | .215 | .674 120 | 1 765 | .265 | .752 223 | 1 366 |
| .166 | .575 802 | 2 257 | .216 | .675 885 | 1 756 | .266 | .753 589 | 1 360 |
| .167 | .578 059 | 2 245 | .217 | .677 641 | 1 747 | .267 | .754 949 | 1 353 |
| .168 | .580 304 | 2 234 | .218 | .679 388 | 1 739 | .268 | .756 302 | 1 345 |
| .169 | .582 538 | 2 223 | .219 | .681 127 | 1 729 | .269 | .757 647 | 1 339 |
| .170 | .584 761 | 2 211 | .220 | .682 856 | 1 721 | .270 | .758 986 | 1 332 |
| .171 | .586 972 | 2 201 | .221 | .684 577 | 1 712 | .271 | .760 318 | 1 325 |
| .172 | .589 173 | 2 190 | .222 | .686 289 | 1 704 | .272 | .761 643 | 1 318 |
| .173 | .591 363 | 2 180 | .223 | .687 993 | 1 695 | .273 | .762 961 | 1 311 |
| .174 | .593 543 | 2 168 | .224 | .689 688 | 1 686 | .274 | .764 272 | 1 304 |
| .175 | .595 711 | 2 157 | .225 | .691 374 | 1 678 | .275 | .765 576 | 1 298 |
| .176 | .597 868 | 2 147 | .226 | .693 052 | 1 669 | .276 | .766 874 | 1 291 |
| .177 | .600 015 | 2 137 | .227 | .694 721 | 1 661 | .277 | .768 165 | 1 284 |
| .178 | .602 152 | 2 125 | .228 | .696 382 | 1 652 | .278 | .769 449 | 1 278 |
| .179 | .604 277 | 2 115 | .229 | .698 034 | 1 644 | .279 | .770 727 | 1 271 |
| .180 | .606 392 | 2 105 | .230 | .699 678 | 1 636 | .280 | .771 998 | 1 264 |
| .181 | .608 497 | 2 094 | .231 | .701 314 | 1 627 | .281 | .773 262 | 1 258 |
| .182 | .610 591 | 2 083 | .232 | .702 941 | 1 619 | .282 | .774 520 | 1 251 |
| .183 | .612 674 | 2 073 | .233 | .704 560 | 1 611 | .283 | .775 771 | 1 245 |
| .184 | .614 747 | 2 063 | .234 | .706 171 | 1 602 | .284 | .777 016 | 1 239 |
| .185 | .616 810 | 2 053 | .235 | .707 773 | 1 595 | .285 | .778 255 | 1 231 |
| .186 | .618 863 | 2 042 | .236 | .709 368 | 1 586 | .286 | .779 486 | 1 226 |
| .187 | .620 905 | 2 032 | .237 | .710 954 | 1 578 | .287 | .780 712 | 1 219 |
| .188 | .622 937 | 2 022 | .238 | .712 532 | 1 570 | .288 | .781 931 | 1 213 |
| .189 | .624 959 | 2 012 | .239 | .714 102 | 1 562 | .289 | .783 144 | 1 206 |
| .190 | .626 971 | 2 002 | .240 | .715 664 | 1 555 | .290 | .784 350 | 1 201 |
| .191 | .628 973 | 1 992 | .241 | .717 219 | 1 546 | .291 | .785 551 | 1 193 |
| .192 | .630 965 | 1 982 | .242 | .718 765 | 1 538 | .292 | .786 744 | 1 188 |
| .193 | .632 947 | 1 972 | .243 | .720 303 | 1 531 | .293 | .787 932 | 1 182 |
| .194 | .634 919 | 1 962 | .244 | .721 834 | 1 522 | .294 | .789 114 | 1 175 |
| .195 | .636 881 | 1 952 | .245 | .723 356 | 1 515 | .295 | .790 289 | 1 169 |
| .196 | .638 833 | 1 943 | .246 | .724 871 | 1 507 | .296 | .791 458 | 1 163 |
| .197 | .640 776 | 1 933 | .247 | .726 378 | 1 500 | .297 | .792 621 | 1 157 |
| .198 | .642 709 | 1 923 | .248 | .727 878 | 1 492 | .298 | .793 778 | 1 151 |
| .199 | .644 632 | 1 913 | .249 | .729 370 | 1 484 | .299 | .794 929 | 1 145 |
| .200 | .646 545 | 1 904 | .250 | .730 854 | 1 476 | .300 | .796 074 | 1 139 |

## PART D (Continued)

Values of $_5q_x$ associated with $_5m_x$ by the equation:

$$_5q_x = 1 - e^{-5\,_5m_x - .008(5)^3\,_5m_x^2}$$

| $_5m_x$ | $_5q_x$ | Δ | $_5m_x$ | $_5q_x$ | Δ | $_5m_x$ | $_5q_x$ | Δ |
|---|---|---|---|---|---|---|---|---|
| | | .00 | | | .000 | | | .000 |
| .300 | .796 074 | 1 139 | .350 | .846 261 | 874 | .400 | .884 675 | 667 |
| .301 | .797 213 | 1 133 | .351 | .847 135 | 869 | .401 | .885 342 | 663 |
| .302 | .798 346 | 1 128 | .352 | .848 004 | 865 | .402 | .886 005 | 660 |
| .303 | .799 474 | 1 121 | .353 | .848 869 | 860 | .403 | .886 665 | 656 |
| .304 | .800 595 | 1 115 | .354 | .849 729 | 856 | .404 | .887 321 | 653 |
| .305 | .801 710 | 1 110 | .355 | .850 585 | 850 | .405 | .887 974 | 649 |
| .306 | .802 820 | 1 103 | .356 | .851 435 | 847 | .406 | .888 623 | 646 |
| .307 | .803 923 | 1 098 | .357 | .852 282 | 842 | .407 | .889 269 | 642 |
| .308 | .805 021 | 1 092 | .358 | .853 124 | 837 | .408 | .889 911 | 638 |
| .309 | .806 113 | 1 087 | .359 | .853 961 | 833 | .409 | .890 549 | 635 |
| .310 | .807 200 | 1 080 | .360 | .854 794 | 828 | .410 | .891 184 | 632 |
| .311 | .808 280 | 1 075 | .361 | .855 622 | 824 | .411 | .891 816 | 628 |
| .312 | .809 355 | 1 070 | .362 | .856 446 | 819 | .412 | .892 444 | 625 |
| .313 | .810 425 | 1 063 | .363 | .857 265 | 816 | .413 | .893 069 | 621 |
| .314 | .811 488 | 1 059 | .364 | .858 081 | 810 | .414 | .893 690 | 618 |
| .315 | .812 547 | 1 052 | .365 | .858 891 | 807 | .415 | .894 308 | 614 |
| .316 | .813 599 | 1 047 | .366 | .859 698 | 802 | .416 | .894 922 | 612 |
| .317 | .814 646 | 1 042 | .367 | .860 500 | 798 | .417 | .895 534 | 607 |
| .318 | .815 688 | 1 036 | .368 | .861 298 | 793 | .418 | .896 141 | 605 |
| .319 | .816 724 | 1 030 | .369 | .862 091 | 789 | .419 | .896 746 | 601 |
| .320 | .817 754 | 1 026 | .370 | .862 880 | 785 | .420 | .897 347 | 598 |
| .321 | .818 780 | 1 019 | .371 | .863 665 | 781 | .421 | .897 945 | 594 |
| .322 | .819 799 | 1 015 | .372 | .864 446 | 776 | .422 | .898 539 | 592 |
| .323 | .820 814 | 1 009 | .373 | .865 222 | 773 | .423 | .899 131 | 588 |
| .324 | .821 823 | 1 003 | .374 | .865 995 | 768 | .424 | .899 719 | 585 |
| .325 | .822 826 | 0 999 | .375 | .866 763 | 764 | .425 | .900 304 | 581 |
| .326 | .823 825 | 0 993 | .376 | .867 527 | 760 | .426 | .900 885 | 579 |
| .327 | .824 818 | 0 988 | .377 | .868 287 | 756 | .427 | .901 464 | 575 |
| .328 | .825 806 | 0 982 | .378 | .869 043 | 751 | .428 | .902 039 | 572 |
| .329 | .826 788 | 0 978 | .379 | .869 794 | 749 | .429 | .902 611 | 569 |
| .330 | .827 766 | 0 972 | .380 | .870 542 | 744 | .430 | .903 180 | 566 |
| .331 | .828 738 | 0 967 | .381 | .871 286 | 739 | .431 | .903 746 | 562 |
| .332 | .829 705 | 0 962 | .382 | .872 025 | 736 | .432 | .904 308 | 560 |
| .333 | .830 667 | 0 957 | .383 | .872 761 | 732 | .433 | .904 868 | 556 |
| .334 | .831 624 | 0 952 | .384 | .873 493 | 728 | .434 | .905 424 | 554 |
| .335 | .832 576 | 0 947 | .385 | .874 221 | 723 | .435 | .905 978 | 550 |
| .336 | .833 523 | 0 941 | .386 | .874 944 | 720 | .436 | .906 528 | 548 |
| .337 | .834 464 | 0 937 | .387 | .875 664 | 716 | .437 | .907 076 | 544 |
| .338 | .835 401 | 0 932 | .388 | .876 380 | 712 | .438 | .907 620 | 541 |
| .339 | .836 333 | 0 927 | .389 | .877 092 | 708 | .439 | .908 161 | 539 |
| .340 | .837 260 | 0 922 | .390 | .877 800 | 705 | .440 | .908 700 | 535 |
| .341 | .838 182 | 0 917 | .391 | .878 505 | 700 | .441 | .909 235 | 532 |
| .342 | .839 099 | 0 912 | .392 | .879 205 | 697 | .442 | .909 767 | 530 |
| .343 | .840 011 | 0 907 | .393 | .879 902 | 693 | .443 | .910 297 | 526 |
| .344 | .840 918 | 0 903 | .394 | .880 595 | 689 | .444 | .910 823 | 524 |
| .345 | .841 821 | 0 897 | .395 | .881 284 | 686 | .445 | .911 347 | 521 |
| .346 | .842 718 | 0 893 | .396 | .881 970 | 682 | .446 | .911 868 | 518 |
| .347 | .843 611 | 0 888 | .397 | .882 652 | 678 | .447 | .912 386 | 514 |
| .348 | .844 499 | 0 884 | .398 | .883 330 | 674 | .448 | .912 900 | 513 |
| .349 | .845 383 | 0 878 | .399 | .884 004 | 671 | .449 | .913 413 | 509 |
| .350 | .846 261 | 0 874 | .400 | .884 675 | 667 | .450 | .913 922 | |

# PART E

Values of $_{10}q_x$ associated with $_{10}m_x$ by the equation:

$$_{10}q_x = 1 - e^{-10\,_{10}m_x - .008(10)^3\,_{10}m_x^2}$$

| $_{10}m_x$ | $_{10}q_x$ | Δ |
|---|---|---|
| | | .00 |
| .000 | .000 000 | 9 959 |
| .001 | .009 959 | 9 874 |
| .002 | .019 833 | 9 792 |
| .003 | .029 625 | 9 709 |
| .004 | .039 334 | 9 627 |
| .005 | .048 961 | 9 546 |
| .006 | .058 507 | 9 465 |
| .007 | .067 972 | 9 384 |
| .008 | .077 356 | 9 305 |
| .009 | .086 661 | 9 225 |
| .010 | .095 886 | 9 147 |
| .011 | .105 033 | 9 068 |
| .012 | .114 101 | 8 990 |
| .013 | .123 091 | 8 913 |
| .014 | .132 004 | 8 836 |
| .015 | .140 840 | 8 760 |
| .016 | .149 600 | 8 684 |
| .017 | .158 284 | 8 608 |
| .018 | .166 892 | 8 534 |
| .019 | .175 426 | 8 459 |
| .020 | .183 885 | 8 386 |
| .021 | .192 271 | 8 312 |
| .022 | .200 583 | 8 239 |
| .023 | .208 822 | 8 167 |
| .024 | .216 989 | 8 095 |
| .025 | .225 084 | 8 023 |
| .026 | .233 107 | 7 953 |
| .027 | .241 060 | 7 882 |
| .028 | .248 942 | 7 812 |
| .029 | .256 754 | 7 743 |
| .030 | .264 497 | 7 673 |
| .031 | .272 170 | 7 606 |
| .032 | .279 776 | 7 536 |
| .033 | .287 312 | 7 470 |
| .034 | .294 782 | 7 402 |
| .035 | .302 184 | 7 336 |
| .036 | .309 520 | 7 269 |
| .037 | .316 789 | 7 204 |
| .038 | .323 993 | 7 139 |
| .039 | .331 132 | 7 073 |
| .040 | .338 205 | 7 010 |
| .041 | .345 215 | 6 946 |
| .042 | .352 161 | 6 881 |
| .043 | .359 042 | 6 820 |
| .044 | .365 862 | 6 756 |
| .045 | .372 618 | 6 695 |
| .046 | .379 313 | 6 633 |
| .047 | .385 946 | 6 572 |
| .048 | .392 518 | 6 511 |
| .049 | .399 029 | 6 450 |
| .050 | .405 479 | 6 391 |

| $_{10}m_x$ | $_{10}q_x$ | Δ |
|---|---|---|
| | | .00 |
| .050 | .405 479 | 6 391 |
| .051 | .411 870 | 6 332 |
| .052 | .418 202 | 6 273 |
| .053 | .424 475 | 6 214 |
| .054 | .430 689 | 6 156 |
| .055 | .436 845 | 6 098 |
| .056 | .442 943 | 6 041 |
| .057 | .448 984 | 5 985 |
| .058 | .454 969 | 5 928 |
| .059 | .460 897 | 5 872 |
| .060 | .466 769 | 5 816 |
| .061 | .472 585 | 5 762 |
| .062 | .478 347 | 5 706 |
| .063 | .484 053 | 5 653 |
| .064 | .489 706 | 5 598 |
| .065 | .495 304 | 5 546 |
| .066 | .500 850 | 5 492 |
| .067 | .506 342 | 5 439 |
| .068 | .511 781 | 5 388 |
| .069 | .517 169 | 5 335 |
| .070 | .522 504 | 5 284 |
| .071 | .527 788 | 5 234 |
| .072 | .533 022 | 5 182 |
| .073 | .538 204 | 5 132 |
| .074 | .543 336 | 5 083 |
| .075 | .548 419 | 5 033 |
| .076 | .553 452 | 4 984 |
| .077 | .558 436 | 4 935 |
| .078 | .563 371 | 4 887 |
| .079 | .568 258 | 4 840 |
| .080 | .573 098 | 4 791 |
| .081 | .577 889 | 4 745 |
| .082 | .582 634 | 4 698 |
| .083 | .587 332 | 4 652 |
| .084 | .591 984 | 4 605 |
| .085 | .596 589 | 4 560 |
| .086 | .601 149 | 4 515 |
| .087 | .605 664 | 4 470 |
| .088 | .610 134 | 4 425 |
| .089 | .614 559 | 4 382 |
| .090 | .618 941 | 4 337 |
| .091 | .623 278 | 4 294 |
| .092 | .627 572 | 4 251 |
| .093 | .631 823 | 4 209 |
| .094 | .636 032 | 4 166 |
| .095 | .640 198 | 4 123 |
| .096 | .644 321 | 4 083 |
| .097 | .648 404 | 4 041 |
| .098 | .652 445 | 4 000 |
| .099 | .656 445 | 3 959 |
| .100 | .660 404 | 3 920 |

| $_{10}m_x$ | $_{10}q_x$ | Δ |
|---|---|---|
| | | .00 |
| .100 | .660 404 | 3 920 |
| .101 | .664 324 | 3 879 |
| .102 | .668 203 | 3 840 |
| .103 | .672 043 | 3 800 |
| .104 | .675 843 | 3 762 |
| .105 | .679 605 | 3 723 |
| .106 | .683 328 | 3 685 |
| .107 | .687 013 | 3 646 |
| .108 | .690 659 | 3 610 |
| .109 | .694 269 | 3 571 |
| .110 | .697 840 | 3 535 |
| .111 | .701 375 | 3 499 |
| .112 | .704 874 | 3 462 |
| .113 | .708 336 | 3 426 |
| .114 | .711 762 | 3 390 |
| .115 | .715 152 | 3 355 |
| .116 | .718 507 | 3 320 |
| .117 | .721 827 | 3 285 |
| .118 | .725 112 | 3 251 |
| .119 | .728 363 | 3 216 |
| .120 | .731 579 | 3 183 |
| .121 | .734 762 | 3 149 |
| .122 | .737 911 | 3 116 |
| .123 | .741 027 | 3 083 |
| .124 | .744 110 | 3 050 |
| .125 | .747 160 | 3 018 |
| .126 | .750 178 | 2 986 |
| .127 | .753 164 | 2 954 |
| .128 | .756 118 | 2 923 |
| .129 | .759 041 | 2 891 |
| .130 | .761 932 | 2 861 |
| .131 | .764 793 | 2 830 |
| .132 | .767 623 | 2 799 |
| .133 | .770 422 | 2 769 |
| .134 | .773 191 | 2 740 |
| .135 | .775 931 | 2 710 |
| .136 | .778 641 | 2 680 |
| .137 | .781 321 | 2 652 |
| .138 | .783 973 | 2 623 |
| .139 | .786 596 | 2 594 |
| .140 | .789 190 | 2 567 |
| .141 | .791 757 | 2 538 |
| .142 | .794 295 | 2 511 |
| .143 | .796 806 | 2 483 |
| .144 | .799 289 | 2 456 |
| .145 | .801 745 | 2 429 |
| .146 | .804 174 | 2 402 |
| .147 | .806 576 | 2 376 |
| .148 | .808 952 | 2 350 |
| .149 | .811 302 | 2 324 |
| .150 | .813 626 | 2 298 |

## PART E (Continued)

Values of $_{10}q_x$ associated with $_{10}m_x$ by the equation:

$$_{10}q_x = 1 - e^{-10\,_{10}m_x - .008(10)^3\,_{10}m_x^2}$$

| $_{10}m_x$ | $_{10}q_x$ | Δ | $_{10}m_x$ | $_{10}q_x$ | Δ | $_{10}m_x$ | $_{10}q_x$ | Δ |
|---|---|---|---|---|---|---|---|---|
| | | .00 | | | .00 | | | .000 |
| .150 | .813 626 | 2 298 | .200 | .901 726 | 1 290 | .250 | .950 213 | 693 |
| .151 | .815 924 | 2 273 | .201 | .903 016 | 1 274 | .251 | .950 906 | 683 |
| .152 | .818 197 | 2 248 | .202 | .904 290 | 1 259 | .252 | .951 589 | 675 |
| .153 | .820 445 | 2 222 | .203 | .905 549 | 1 244 | .253 | .952 264 | 666 |
| .154 | .822 667 | 2 198 | .204 | .906 793 | 1 228 | .254 | .952 930 | 658 |
| .155 | .824 865 | 2 174 | .205 | .908 021 | 1 215 | .255 | .953 588 | 649 |
| .156 | .827 039 | 2 149 | .206 | .909 236 | 1 199 | .256 | .954 237 | 641 |
| .157 | .829 188 | 2 125 | .207 | .910 435 | 1 185 | .257 | .954 878 | 633 |
| .158 | .831 313 | 2 102 | .208 | .911 620 | 1 171 | .258 | .955 511 | 624 |
| .159 | .833 415 | 2 078 | .209 | .912 791 | 1 157 | .259 | .956 135 | 617 |
| .160 | .835 493 | 2 054 | .210 | .913 948 | 1 142 | .260 | .956 752 | 608 |
| .161 | .837 547 | 2 032 | .211 | .915 090 | 1 129 | .261 | .957 360 | 601 |
| .162 | .839 579 | 2 008 | .212 | .916 219 | 1 115 | .262 | .957 961 | 593 |
| .163 | .841 587 | 1 986 | .213 | .917 334 | 1 102 | .263 | .958 554 | 585 |
| .164 | .843 573 | 1 964 | .214 | .918 436 | 1 088 | .264 | .959 139 | 577 |
| .165 | .845 537 | 1 941 | .215 | .919 524 | 1 075 | .265 | .959 716 | 570 |
| .166 | .847 478 | 1 920 | .216 | .920 599 | 1 062 | .266 | .960 286 | 562 |
| .167 | .849 398 | 1 897 | .217 | .921 661 | 1 049 | .267 | .960 848 | 555 |
| .168 | .851 295 | 1 876 | .218 | .922 710 | 1 036 | .268 | .961 403 | 548 |
| .169 | .853 171 | 1 855 | .219 | .923 746 | 1 024 | .269 | .961 951 | 541 |
| .170 | .855 026 | 1 833 | .220 | .924 770 | 1 011 | .270 | .962 492 | 534 |
| .171 | .856 859 | 1 813 | .221 | .925 781 | 0 998 | .271 | .963 026 | 526 |
| .172 | .858 672 | 1 792 | .222 | .926 779 | 0 986 | .272 | .963 552 | 520 |
| .173 | .860 464 | 1 771 | .223 | .927 765 | 0 974 | .273 | .964 072 | 513 |
| .174 | .862 235 | 1 751 | .224 | .928 739 | 0 962 | .274 | .964 585 | 506 |
| .175 | .863 986 | 1 731 | .225 | .929 701 | 0 950 | .275 | .965 091 | 499 |
| .176 | .865 717 | 1 711 | .226 | .930 651 | 0 939 | .276 | .965 590 | 493 |
| .177 | .867 428 | 1 692 | .227 | .931 590 | 0 926 | .277 | .966 083 | 486 |
| .178 | .869 120 | 1 672 | .228 | .932 516 | 0 916 | .278 | .966 569 | 480 |
| .179 | .870 792 | 1 652 | .229 | .933 432 | 0 904 | .279 | .967 049 | 473 |
| .180 | .872 444 | 1 633 | .230 | .934 336 | 0 892 | .280 | .967 522 | 467 |
| .181 | .874 077 | 1 615 | .231 | .935 228 | 0 882 | .281 | .967 989 | 461 |
| .182 | .875 692 | 1 596 | .232 | .936 110 | 0 871 | .282 | .968 450 | 455 |
| .183 | .877 288 | 1 577 | .233 | .936 981 | 0 859 | .283 | .968 905 | 449 |
| .184 | .878 865 | 1 559 | .234 | .937 840 | 0 849 | .284 | .969 354 | 443 |
| .185 | .880 424 | 1 540 | .235 | .938 689 | 0 839 | .285 | .969 797 | 436 |
| .186 | .881 964 | 1 523 | .236 | .939 528 | 0 827 | .286 | .970 233 | 431 |
| .187 | .883 487 | 1 505 | .237 | .940 355 | 0 818 | .287 | .970 664 | 426 |
| .188 | .884 992 | 1 487 | .238 | .941 173 | 0 807 | .288 | .971 090 | 419 |
| .189 | .886 479 | 1 470 | .239 | .941 980 | 0 797 | .289 | .971 509 | 414 |
| .190 | .887 949 | 1 452 | .240 | .942 777 | 0 787 | .290 | .971 923 | 408 |
| .191 | .889 401 | 1 436 | .241 | .943 564 | 0 777 | .291 | .972 331 | 403 |
| .192 | .890 837 | 1 418 | .242 | .944 341 | 0 767 | .292 | .972 734 | 397 |
| .193 | .892 255 | 1 402 | .243 | .945 108 | 0 758 | .293 | .973 131 | 392 |
| .194 | .893 657 | 1 386 | .244 | .945 866 | 0 748 | .294 | .973 523 | 387 |
| .195 | .895 043 | 1 368 | .245 | .946 614 | 0 738 | .295 | .973 910 | 381 |
| .196 | .896 411 | 1 353 | .246 | .947 352 | 0 729 | .296 | .974 291 | 377 |
| .197 | .897 764 | 1 337 | .247 | .948 081 | 0 720 | .297 | .974 668 | 371 |
| .198 | .899 101 | 1 320 | .248 | .948 801 | 0 710 | .298 | .975 039 | 366 |
| .199 | .900 421 | 1 305 | .249 | .949 511 | 0 702 | .299 | .975 405 | 361 |
| .200 | .901 726 | 1 290 | .250 | .950 213 | 0 693 | .300 | .975 766 | 356 |

## PART E (Continued)

Values of $_{10}q_x$ associated with $_{10}m_x$ by the equation:

$$_{10}q_x = 1 - e^{-10\ _{10}m_x - .008\,(10)^3\ _{10}m_x^2}$$

| $_{10}m_x$ | $_{10}q_x$ | $\Delta$ | $_{10}m_x$ | $_{10}q_x$ | $\Delta$ | $_{10}m_x$ | $_{10}q_x$ | $\Delta$ |
|---|---|---|---|---|---|---|---|---|
| | | .000 | | | .000 | | | .0000 |
| .300 | .975 766 | 356 | .350 | .988 667 | 175 | .400 | .994 908 | 82 |
| .301 | .976 122 | 352 | .351 | .988 842 | 173 | .401 | .994 990 | 82 |
| .302 | .976 474 | 346 | .352 | .989 015 | 171 | .402 | .995 072 | 80 |
| .303 | .976 820 | 342 | .353 | .989 186 | 168 | .403 | .995 152 | 80 |
| .304 | .977 162 | 337 | .354 | .989 354 | 165 | .404 | .995 232 | 77 |
| .305 | .977 499 | 333 | .355 | .989 519 | 163 | .405 | .995 309 | 77 |
| .306 | .977 832 | 328 | .356 | .989 682 | 161 | .406 | .995 386 | 76 |
| .307 | .978 160 | 323 | .357 | .989 843 | 158 | .407 | .995 462 | 74 |
| .308 | .978 483 | 319 | .358 | .990 001 | 157 | .408 | .995 536 | 73 |
| .309 | .978 802 | 315 | .359 | .990 158 | 153 | .409 | .995 609 | 72 |
| .310 | .979 117 | 310 | .360 | .990 311 | 152 | .410 | .995 681 | 71 |
| .311 | .979 427 | 306 | .361 | .990 463 | 149 | .411 | .995 752 | 70 |
| .312 | .979 733 | 302 | .362 | .990 612 | 147 | .412 | .995 822 | 69 |
| .313 | .980 035 | 297 | .363 | .990 759 | 145 | .413 | .995 891 | 68 |
| .314 | .980 332 | 294 | .364 | .990 904 | 143 | .414 | .995 959 | 66 |
| .315 | .980 626 | 289 | .365 | .991 047 | 141 | .415 | .996 025 | 66 |
| .316 | .980 915 | 285 | .366 | .991 188 | 139 | .416 | .996 091 | 64 |
| .317 | .981 200 | 282 | .367 | .991 327 | 136 | .417 | .996 155 | 64 |
| .318 | .981 482 | 277 | .368 | .991 463 | 135 | .418 | .996 219 | 63 |
| .319 | .981 759 | 274 | .369 | .991 598 | 133 | .419 | .996 282 | 61 |
| .320 | .982 033 | 269 | .370 | .991 731 | 130 | .420 | .996 343 | 61 |
| .321 | .982 302 | 266 | .371 | .991 861 | 129 | .421 | .996 404 | 60 |
| .322 | .982 568 | 263 | .372 | .991 990 | 127 | .422 | .996 464 | 58 |
| .323 | .982 831 | 258 | .373 | .992 117 | 125 | .423 | .996 522 | 58 |
| .324 | .983 089 | 255 | .374 | .992 242 | 123 | .424 | .996 580 | 57 |
| .325 | .983 344 | 252 | .375 | .992 365 | 121 | .425 | .996 637 | 56 |
| .326 | .983 596 | 248 | .376 | .992 486 | 120 | .426 | .996 693 | 56 |
| .327 | .983 844 | 244 | .377 | .992 606 | 117 | .427 | .996 749 | 54 |
| .328 | .984 088 | 241 | .378 | .992 723 | 116 | .428 | .996 803 | 53 |
| .329 | .984 329 | 237 | .379 | .992 839 | 114 | .429 | .996 856 | 53 |
| .330 | .984 566 | 234 | .380 | .992 953 | 113 | .430 | .996 909 | 52 |
| .331 | .984 800 | 231 | .381 | .993 066 | 111 | .431 | .996 961 | 50 |
| .332 | .985 031 | 228 | .382 | .993 177 | 109 | .432 | .997 011 | 51 |
| .333 | .985 259 | 224 | .383 | .993 286 | 107 | .433 | .997 062 | 49 |
| .334 | .985 483 | 221 | .384 | .993 393 | 106 | .434 | .997 111 | 49 |
| .335 | .985 704 | 218 | .385 | .993 499 | 104 | .435 | .997 160 | 47 |
| .336 | .985 922 | 215 | .386 | .993 603 | 103 | .436 | .997 207 | 47 |
| .337 | .986 137 | 212 | .387 | .993 706 | 101 | .437 | .997 254 | 47 |
| .338 | .986 349 | 209 | .388 | .993 807 | 100 | .438 | .997 301 | 45 |
| .339 | .986 558 | 206 | .389 | .993 907 | 098 | .439 | .997 346 | 45 |
| .340 | .986 764 | 203 | .390 | .994 005 | 096 | .440 | .997 391 | 44 |
| .341 | .986 967 | 200 | .391 | .994 101 | 096 | .441 | .997 435 | 43 |
| .342 | .987 167 | 197 | .392 | .994 197 | 093 | .442 | .997 478 | 43 |
| .343 | .987 364 | 194 | .393 | .994 290 | 093 | .443 | .997 521 | 42 |
| .344 | .987 558 | 192 | .394 | .994 383 | 090 | .444 | .997 563 | 42 |
| .345 | .987 750 | 188 | .395 | .994 473 | 090 | .445 | .997 605 | 40 |
| .346 | .987 938 | 186 | .396 | .994 563 | 088 | .446 | .997 645 | 40 |
| .347 | .988 124 | 184 | .397 | .994 651 | 087 | .447 | .997 685 | 40 |
| .348 | .988 308 | 180 | .398 | .994 738 | 085 | .448 | .997 725 | 38 |
| .349 | .988 488 | 179 | .399 | .994 823 | 085 | .449 | .997 763 | 39 |
| .350 | .988 667 | 175 | .400 | .994 908 | 082 | .450 | .997 802 | |

(Reproduced, with permission, from *The American Journal of Hygiene*, September, 1939.)

# INDEX

Abridged life table, 107 ff.
  construction, 286 ff.
  notation, 108
  person-years lived, 109
Absolute numbers, 16, 17, 148
Accuracy, 23, 57, 88, 146, 154, 181
  in reporting, 9, 68
Actual cohort, basis of measure-
    ment, 116
Actuarial notion of risk, 50
Adjustments of data
  estimating ratio, 46, 49-50, 87,
    140, 163, 164, 175
  methods available, 49, 50 n., 87
Age
  and tests of data, 82
  and vital rates, 65, 132n., 178,
    217, 229ff.
  childbearing, 24, 50, 51
  composition of population, 8, 17,
    60, 132, 135n., 225, 267
  defects of data, 65ff., 88-89
  errors of reporting, 6, 66, 146
  exact, 95, 115
  importance of, 6
  interval, 95
  life table, 95
  reckoning, 6, 66n.
  stable population, 216ff., 222, 227
  working ages, 266, 270
Age-specific vital rates, 42-47,
    48-50, 65, 89, 126, 136, 212,
    234ff.
Aliens, 257
Annual basis of vital rates, 3, 19,
    29, 42, 50, 207, 234
Attitudes
  about fertility, 170

about mortality, 138
about work, 272
Average figures
  effect of averaging, 43, 121, 135n.
  number of children born, 180,
    193-195
  vital rates, 35-36, 43-44, 49-50,
    53, 121

Balance of births and deaths (See
    Natural increase)
Base period, of vital rates, 35-36,
    141
Benjamin, B., 83
Bibliographies of source material,
    5n., 284
Birth
  control, 194n.
  live birth, 9, 35, 80
  plural births, 170
  rates, 33-37, 48-50, 81, 88-89,
    171ff., 213, 216
  sex ratio, 23, 64, 132n., 216
  year of birth, 66n.
  See also Fertility
Birthday
  date, 6
  and age, 6, 66n.
Birth statistics
  adjustments, 49, 129n.
  compulsory registration, 9, 82
  defects, 9, 35, 50, 64, 76ff.,
    80-82, 177n., 190
  delayed reporting, 81, 192n.
  failure to report, 82, 87-88
  place of occurrence, 81
  special problems, 168ff.
  tests, 77ff.

306